MICROECONOMICS: Theory and Applications

MICROECONOMICS

THEORY AND APPLICATIONS

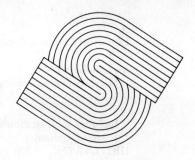

ROBERT Y. AWH

Professor of Economics
Mississippi State University

JOHN WILEY & SONS, INC.

New York · Chichester · Brisbane · Toronto

Library of Congress Cataloging in Publication Data

Awh, Robert Y
  Microeconomics: theory and applications.

  Includes bibliographical references.
  1. Microeconomics.   I. Title.
HB171.5.A87   330   75-38643

Printed in Singapore

10 9

To My Students

ABOUT THE AUTHOR

Robert Y. Awh (pronounced Oh) is professor of economics at Mississippi State University. He received his B.A. in commerce and M.A. in economics from Yonsei University, Korea, his Ph.D. in economics from the University of Florida, and was a post-doctoral fellow at Rice University. For more than fifteen years, he has taught undergraduate and graduate courses in economics at various schools. His published papers cover such areas as microeconomics, economic development, economic education, fiscal policy, and monetary economics. He is a member of the American Economic Association, the Royal Economic Society, the Korean Economic Association, the Southern Economic Association, and Omicron Delta Epsilon. He is the current (1975–76) president of the Midsouth Academy of Economists.

PREFACE

This book is written for students to help them learn intermediate microeconomics. I have attempted to combine a concise but rigorous presentation of microeconomic theory with real world applications of the theoretical tools developed in the text.

First of all, this is a textbook on intermediate micro theory. Thus, I have attempted to give an *accurate presentation of up-to-date microeconomic theory* appropriate for intermediate students. In discussing theory, I have tried to be concise and avoided lengthy verbiage. However, I have not hesitated to show the same analytical model from several different angles (verbal, graphical, and mathematical), when I felt that such repetition enhanced the reader's understanding. To avoid the pitfalls of many textbooks that introduce undefined technical terms, I strived to show all new terms in boldface, and defined them when they appeared for the first time. The book contains most of the standard topics in microeconomics. However, the selection of topics as well as the emphasis given to them was influenced by this simple query: Is the topic useful in explaining and predicting real world economic phenomena? Some standard fares in microeconomics that failed to meet the criterion, for example, classical oligopoly models and some aspects of monopolistic competition, were excluded from the text. On the other hand, topics such as intertemporal economic decisions, which are not usually incorporated in microeconomic texts, are included because they passed the usefulness or relevancy criterion with flying colors.

No mathematical knowledge is presupposed for this book. Only elementary plane geometry and the most rudimentary high school algebra are employed within the main body of the text. However, mathematical footnotes and appendixes are provided for those students who find this approach more convenient.

To show the relevance of abstract economic tools in explaining and predicting worldly economic phenomena, *practically every chapter contains some application sections*. These sections either apply the analytical tools developed in the chapter to answer some simple economic questions or present empirical data that demonstrate the relevance of the abstract concepts or tools introduced in the chapter. It is hoped that such applications give added motivation for the reader to master the analytical tools, which often seem too abstract and barren to the uninitiated.

Perhaps one of the best ways to learn economics is to solve exercise problems that test one's comprehension of the analytical tools. Accordingly, the reader is urged to work out the exercises given at the end of each chapter. For those instructors and students who share my conviction about the value of more exercises, this text has a companion volume, *Exercises in Microeconomics*, specifically designed to complement the main text. This exercise book contains many relatively simple problems that help the reader master and apply the concepts and tools introduced in the text. I have designed the *Exercises* to be a learning aid that enhances the student's understanding and that allows him to enjoy a sense of accomplishment. Thus, I have consciously avoided too difficult problems, which may frustrate and turn off the student.

Many people assisted me in writing this book. First of all, I thank my students who read various versions of the manuscript and offered valuable suggestions from the reader's point of view. Detailed comments by Professor Rodney D. Peterson of Simon Fraser University and Colorado State University were most useful, as were the criticisms and suggestions of Professors John W. Ashley of California State University at Hayward, L. Randolph McGee of the University of Kentucky, and Robert D. McMinn of Texas A and I University. I would also like to express my appreciation to my colleagues Robert Crosslin, J. Anderson Davis, Billy J. Eatherly, Pepper Holland, Robert Howell, and G. W. Parker for their assistance at various stages of my work. Three young ladies, Julie Karre, Margaret Simpson, and Debbie Withers, typed many versions of this manuscript. I thank each of them for performing the seemingly endless chore, always with a smile. I am indebted to Paul Lee and Ron Lewton of Wiley/Hamilton for their excellent editorial work. Finally, I thank my wife and my three sons for allowing me to work on this book for such a long period of time.

ROBERT Y. AWH
Mississippi State, Mississippi
April 1975

CONTENTS

Contents

Contents

CHAPTER SIX: MARKET DEMAND AND ELASTICITY OF DEMAND   117

CHAPTER SEVEN: THE THEORY OF PRODUCTION:

PHYSICAL ASPECTS 151

CHAPTER EIGHT: THE THEORY OF PRODUCTION:

PHYSICAL ASPECTS —

CONTINUED 169

CHAPTER NINE: PRODUCTION DECISIONS AND COSTS   193

CHAPTER TEN: SHORT-RUN AND LONG-RUN COSTS   213

CHAPTER ELEVEN: The Firm And Alternative
                Market Structures   235

Contents

CHAPTER FOURTEEN: PRICE AND OUTPUT UNDER PURE MONOPOLY 289

Contents

CHAPTER FIFTEEN: INDUSTRIAL CONCENTRATION AND OLIGOPOLY

CHAPTER SIXTEEN: FURTHER TOPICS IN OLIGOPOLY AND MONOPOLISTIC COMPETITION

Contents

CHAPTER NINETEEN: GENERAL EQUILIBRIUM AND WELFARE ECONOMICS   427

Contents

MICROECONOMICS: Theory and Applications

CHAPTER ONE

INTRODUCTION

The aim of this book is to help you learn microeconomics, the knowledge of which is indispensable in analyzing a myriad of worldly economic problems. Since microeconomics is a branch of economics, let us in this chapter see why economic problems arise, what economics is about, and what microeconomics in particular is about. Discussions of the main features of microeconomic analysis, the significance of the concept of economic efficiency, and the relevance of microeconomics in the real world conclude this introductory chapter.

1-1 THE ECONOMIC PROBLEMS

Human wants for goods and services are virtually unlimited, but it is not possible to produce everything for everyone because no society has the resources to do so. *Thus, every society faces the basic economic problems—the necessity of choosing what, how, and for whom to produce, and how to achieve economic growth.*[1]

Different societies solve their economic problems in different ways: by custom and tradition, by central direction, by the market mechanism, or by some combination of these.[2] *Tradition* is the primary force that arranges the production and distribution of

[1] For detailed discussion of the functions of an economic system, see Frank H. Knight, *The Economic Organization* (New York: Kelley and Millman, 1951).

[2] For three approaches to the solutions of the economic problems, see Robert L. Heilbroner, *The Making of Economic Society*, 3d ed. (Englewood Cliffs, N.J.: Prentice-Hall, 1970), Ch. 1.

goods in many primitive, agrarian societies. In a tradition-oriented economy, problems of what, how, and for whom are solved by long-established customs and tradition. Sons follow their fathers' occupations; tasks and skills are passed on from generation to generation. Distribution is also accomplished by following the age-old patterns, which are well understood by everyone.

Command or *central direction* is another important manner in which the problems of providing for the material well-being of society are solved. Totalitarian socialist societies such as the Soviet Union and mainland China are contemporary examples of economies that rely on central direction in solving their economic problems.

The market system is the third way of solving the economic problems. In this system of economic organization, individuals seeking their own interests interact voluntarily among themselves and solve the economic problems of production, distribution, and growth. The American economy is such a market-directed economy, in which private individuals seeking their own benefits play the central role in the solution of the economic problems.

Of course, societies need not (and, in fact, do not) solve their economic problems by relying on only one of the above three approaches. Some combination of the elements of tradition, command, and market will be found in practically all modern societies. The U.S. economy is said to be a market-centered one because of the central role played in it by the market mechanism. But the U.S. economy is also referred to as a mixed economy, since governments (the command element) also play rather important roles in production, distribution, and provision for economic growth.

In summary, there are many different ways in which a society can solve its economic problems. The salient fact, however, is that no society can escape its economic problems—the necessity of making choices about what, how, and for whom to produce, and selecting the means of providing for economic growth.

1-2 ECONOMICS, MACROECONOMICS, AND MICROECONOMICS

Every society must allocate its scarce resources among alternative uses to solve the economic problems of production, distribution, and growth. Traditionally, economists assumed (tacitly) the full employment of resources to be the normal state of affairs, and concentrated on the question of allocating scarce resources among competing ends. *Thus, economics has frequently been defined as the study of the allocation of scarce resources among competing ends.* In Western countries, most economists have been interested in examining the manner in which resources are allocated through the market.

Since the mid-1930s, it has become a well-established convention to divide the subject matter of economics into two subfields, macroeconomics and microeconomics. *Macroeconomics,* which is the child of the Great Depression of the 1930s, *is primarily concerned with the study of fluctuations in the levels of employment, aggregate income, and the general price level, and of the ways to prevent such fluctuations.*

Microeconomics, which is the heir to the traditional "principles" of economics, *deals primarily with the determination of relative prices and allocation of resources among competing ends under full-employment conditions.* Microeconomics deals with the study of the manner in which consumers allocate their limited income among various goods and services, the ways in which business firms seek desired prices and output rates, the procedures by which business firms hire their resources and provide income to various resource owners, and the way in which activities of consumers, producers, and resource owners fit together to solve the economic problems of a market-oriented economy.

In a sense, it is unfortunate that economics is somewhat arbitrarily subdivided into macro- and microeconomics.[3] After all, the student of economics must learn both branches of economics well, because it is not possible to understand many economic problems without the knowledge of both micro- and macroeconomics. For instance, to study the problems of economic growth or development, one must comprehend not only such macroeconomic issues as factors affecting aggregate levels of saving and investment, and fiscal and monetary policies, but such microeconomic issues as investment criteria and effects of subsidies and taxes. Similarly, one

---

[3]Economists do not all agree as to how micro- and macroeconomics should be distinguished. Among some of the criteria proposed by various economists for distinguishing the two branches are: (1) distinction according to how one looks at the economy—a microscopic versus telescopic view of the economy; (2) distinction according to whose actions are analyzed—individual components of the economy such as consumers and firms in microeconomics versus aggregate economic variables such as income and unemployment in macroeconomics; (3) distinction according to the role played by price—relative prices play an important role in microeconomics, but are usually left behind the scene in macroeconomics; (4) distinction according to the level of abstraction—microeconomics, which seeks general "principles," abstracts much more than macroeconomics, which examines problems and policies particular to a given time and place. For more details, see "Micro- and Macro-economics: Contested Boundaries and Claims of Superiority," in Fritz Machlup's *Essays in Economic Semantics* (New York: W. W. Norton, 1967), pp. 97–144.

cannot study the problems of inflation and unemployment—the twin evils that have plagued us in recent years—without examining such macro and micro issues as aggregate levels of expenditures, pricing practices of large corporations, and behavior of labor unions. The "energy crisis" of recent years not only affects different industries in different ways, but influences the aggregate levels of economic activities.

Clearly, micro- and macroeconomics complement each other, and frequently it is impossible to analyze economic issues without employing both tools. The economic profession is well aware of such complementarity between the two branches of economics. However, the current practice in economic education is to teach the tools of economic analysis in two separate doses of micro- and macroeconomics. And our subject matter is microeconomics. Let us begin by examining the rudiments of the methodology of microeconomic analysis.

1-3 THE METHODOLOGY OF MICROECONOMIC ANALYSIS

Microeconomics attempts to explain how scarce resources are allocated among competing ends through the market mechanism in the real world. However, the real world is composed of an immense, bewildering array of facts, which defy ready comprehension. To make some sense out of the complex economic world and to derive economic propositions that have explanatory and predictive power, the economist *abstracts* from the complex world and builds economic models. That is, he selects a few variables and relationships that appear to be important for the problem under examination, and focuses his attention on these alone. To abstract is not to ignore the complexity of the real world; rather, it is a necessary procedure in discovering reality, which otherwise remains too complex to be understood.

ECONOMIC MODELS

A model is merely a theoretical construct or analytical framework composed of a set of assumptions from which conclusions are derived. Let us get an overview of the nature of model building in microeconomics by referring to Figure 1-1. The *first* step is to abstract from the complex real world: the model builder must select the variables and relationships among them that seem most pertinent to the problem he attempts to analyze. This step produces the economic model, which contains a set of assumptions regarding the relevant variables and the relationships among them. The *second* step is to apply logical deductions to the model and derive a the-

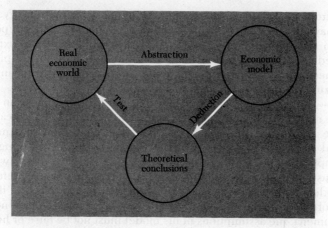

Figure 1-1   Economic model building

oretical or logical conclusion(s). The *third* step is to test the conclusion(s) against real world phenomena. If the conclusion(s) does not agree with the observed empirical data, a new model with more plausible assumptions is formulated. A new conclusion(s) is derived, and so on.

Typically, microeconomic analysis is confined to the first two steps above. Microeconomic theory is primarily concerned with deducing a set of conclusions from a set of assumptions. Thus, a microeconomic model is a deductive model, which offers "if-then" propositions. It states that if a set of assumptions or postulates is given then certain conclusions will follow. For example, consider the following model, in which the conclusion follows logically from the assumptions of the model.

If (1) the consumer attempts to maximize his utility,
(2) two goods, *A* and *B*, are substitutes, and (3) the
price of *A* decreases while the price of *B* remains the
same, *then* the consumer will purchase more *A* and less *B*.

USEFULNESS VERSUS REALISM OF ASSUMPTIONS

In order to understand economic phenomena in the complex real world, we must build economic models based on simplified assumptions. Frequently, the real world provides assistance in formulating the needed set of assumptions. However, the assumptions of an economic model may or may not be realistic. For instance, in the economic model of consumer behavior cited above, assumption 2 may be based on a real world observation, while assumption 3 may be purely hypothetical. Assumption 1 defies an actual observation and may only be a partial truth. Indeed, the value of a model depends not on the "realism" of its assumptions but on its ability to explain or predict real world events.[4] Economic models built on simplified (not necessarily realistic) assumptions serve as powerful means for analyzing relations between actual phenomena.

Most economists agree that the assumptions of an economic model need not directly meet the test of empirical verification. At the same time, they also agree that the conclusions of a model should be tested against empirical evidence, thus subjecting the assumptions of the model to an indirect test. A model or theory whose conclusion(s) agrees better with the observed phenomena is preferred to models with less explanatory or predictive power. Clearly, if one is to obtain a model that can explain or predict observed economic phenomena, the assumptions of his model must not be false or highly improbable on the basis of available empirical data: such a set of assumptions leads to conclusions that are contradicted by observed facts.[5]

In applying microeconomic propositions to the analysis of an actual problem, one must remember that microeconomic models, in their quest for generality, have to abstract from details of the real world. For instance, the conclusions of the microeconomic models of the firm provide only a bare skeleton of the behavior of any particular firm in the real world. To analyze a specific firm's behavior, many details particular to the firm must be introduced into a model specifically designed for the purpose.

COMPLEMENTARY ROLES OF INDUCTION AND DEDUCTION

We have seen that most microeconomic models are deductive in nature. However, the role played by *empirical investigation* or *induction* in the development of microeconomic models must also be appreciated.

The method of induction in developing a theoretical proposition is to gather data on various economic variables, perform statistical operations on them, and establish some systematic relationships among the variables involved. Economists who specialize in applying statistical techniques to empirical data in testing the conclusions of a model or in developing a theoretical proposition based on empirical data are called *econometricians.*

[4]Milton Friedman, "The Methodology of Positive Economics," in *Essays in Positive Economics* (Chicago: The University of Chicago Press, 1953), pp. 3–43.
[5]Ernest Nagel, "Assumptions in Economic Theory," *American Economic Review, Paper and Proceedings,* May 1963, pp. 211–219.

6

The development of deductive microeconomic models is influenced by inductive or empirical investigations in two important ways. First, a theory—unlike a mere speculation—is an empirically testable proposition.[6] If the conclusions of a model are contradicted by an empirical investigation, then the model must be modified or discarded. If a model is not contradicted by empirical tests, it is accepted until a model having better explanatory and predictive power is developed. (Note that empirical studies cannot prove the correctness of a model; they can merely reject or not reject the hypothesis.) Second, the task of selecting appropriate assumptions for a microeconomic model is greatly facilitated by the empirical evidence accumulated by inductive studies.

Empirical investigators, on the other hand, are importantly assisted by deductive economic propositions in formulating their statistical research plans.

THE MAXIMIZATION HYPOTHESIS

A fundamental behavioral assumption on which many microeconomic models rest is *the maximization hypothesis—the assumption that an economic agent attempts to maximize something.* For instance, consumers are assumed to seek maximum utilities or satisfactions; firms or producers are assumed to attempt to maximize their profits, sales receipts, or market shares; and resource owners are assumed to be after maximum wages, rentals, etc. The other side of the coin of the maximization hypothesis is the minimization of something undesirable. Thus, firms are assumed to seek minimum losses, and households are assumed to try to minimize their disutilities.

Obviously, the assumption of economic agents attempting to maximize their goals is an oversimplification of the real economic world. Yet, it has proved to be a highly useful assumption that has helped to produce many microeconomic models with explanatory and predictive power. There are several reasons for the popularity of the maximization hypothesis in economic model building. First, it is a rather simple and plausible assumption about the behavior of an economic agent. It is difficult to find another behavioral assumption that is as simple and as plausible. Second, the concept of a maximum is precise. One can readily ascertain whether the maximum for a certain thing has been reached, and how the economic agent involved will react given the assumption of maximization. Compare this with such other concepts as "satisficing" behavior, which is difficult to quantify precisely. Third, the mathematical techniques for solving maximization or minimization problems are well developed and relatively simple.

[6]Paul A. Samuelson, *Foundations of Economic Analysis* (Cambridge, Mass.: Harvard University Press, 1947), p. 4.

CETERIS PARIBUS ASSUMPTION

In attempting to establish the relationship between variables, physical scientists can conduct controlled experiments. For instance, an agronomist can isolate the relationship between the amount of a particular fertilizer and the growth of a crop by keeping temperature, moisture, and lighting constant. In economics, such controlled experiments are not practical. The technique economists use in their attempt to isolate the relationship between variables is *the ceteris paribus (or other things being equal) assumption.* For instance, to examine the effect of an increase in price on consumers' purchases, we assume that other variables such as income, expectations regarding further price changes, tastes, and prices of related goods will remain constant.

In applying economic models to specific situations, we must pay careful attention to the assumptions employed. For example, the conclusions suggested by a model in which a large number of small firms compete with each other must not be misapplied to a situation in which a single firm monopolizes the market. Similarly, the conclusions of a *ceteris paribus* model would not hold true if its assumption(s) is violated. For example, other things being equal, a reduction in the price of a good will increase its sale. But such an increase in sale might not materialize if consumers expected prices to go even lower.

The analytical technique used to study the effect of, say, a change in price on the quantity demanded and supplied of a good, while assuming other things to remain unchanged, is referred to as a partial equilibrium analysis. The major justification for such an approach comes from its simplicity and the absence of a significant interrelationship between one market and others. Thus, while partial equilibrium analysis might be appropriate for all florists in a single town, it might be inappropriate for the study of a major change in the prices of motor vehicles, which tends to cause many repercussions in the rest of the economy.

COMPARATIVE STATICS APPROACH

What will be the impact of an *excise tax—a per unit tax imposed on a commodity such as the tax on cigarettes—*on the price and sales of the taxed commodity? To answer such a question, the economist frequently compares the equilibrium position before the tax and the equilibrium position after the tax. *By equilibrium, the economist means a situation in which there is no further tendency to change.* For example, if the buyers are buying all they wish at the going price and sellers are selling all they care to sell at the same price, both parties are satisfied and there is no net tendency for the price to change; the equilibrium price is established. *Economic* *analysis that confines its attention to equilibrium positions is called statics.*[7] *An analysis that compares equilibrium positions corresponding to two or more sets of circumstances is referred to as comparative statics.* Microeconomics relies heavily on the comparative static analysis. For instance, in order to examine the effect of an excise tax on the price and output of a commodity, we can compare the equilibrium price and output before the tax with the equilibrium price and output that prevail after the imposition of the tax.

POSITIVE VERSUS NORMATIVE ECONOMICS

As the final note on methodology, we must note the distinction between positive and normative economics. *Positive (or scientific) economics studies the actual economic entities and relationships among them.* It strives to formulate economic models with explanatory and predictive value. At least in principle, it is devoid of value or ethical judgment; that is, it describes and relates observable facts without saying whether they are good or bad. For example, a model may hypothesize that the business firm wishes to maximize its profit because this hypothesis helps explain and predict the firm's behavior. The model draws no inferences as to the ethical implications of the hypothesis. Those economists who hold that economics should deal only with scientifically testable propositions and that it should have nothing to do with value judgments are called *logical positivists.*

Normative economics is explicitly concerned with economic goals and policies to achieve these goals. It is concerned with the question of what "ought to be" and not just what "is" as in the case of positive economics. Economic policies in the real world affect some people favorably, and others unfavorably. Thus, economic policies must be determined in view of both (1) the knowledge of economic conditions and the relationship among various economic variables involved and (2) the consideration of *equity* or *distribution,* which is basically the matter of values or ethics. Positivist economists stress that economists *qua* economists have no special competence in analyzing the issues of equity or distribution, and argue that economists should confine themselves to showing the methods of achieving alternative goals specified to them and the consequences of adopting alternative goals. On the other hand, there are economists who hold that economists *qua* citizens are as good judges of equity or values as anyone else in society, because there are no experts in equity. Furthermore, they argue, economists are in a better position to evaluate the relative importance of economic and equity issues involved,

[7]Study concerned with the time path of economic relationships is called *economic dynamics;* the cobweb model described in Appendix 2B is an example of a dynamic model.

and, therefore, economists have obligations to offer policy recommendations based on their economic analysis as well as their values.

Such controversy, however, does not affect us much in this book, because our primary concern is with positive economics. Even those readers whose ultimate concern is economic policies for the material betterment of society must first learn their lessons in positive economics. Positive economics is a prerequisite to normative economics.

1-4 ECONOMIC EFFICIENCY

Our main concern in this book is the study of scientific propositions in microeconomics. We are interested in understanding the relationship between economic variables and in acquiring some basic tools of analysis with which to investigate economic issues confronting us. In our study of microeconomics in the following pages, we shall frequently raise the question of economic efficiency. *A situation (state, or configuration) is said to be efficient (or Pareto optimal) if it is not possible to make anyone better off without making someone else worse off. Similarly, a situation is said to be inefficient if it is possible to make someone better off without making anyone else worse off.* It is the basic presumption of this book that, other things being equal, efficiency is desirable.

In the following pages, we shall find many occasions on which we apply the efficiency criterion in evaluating a particular economic arrangement. For instance, we ask what the consumer must do if he is to allocate his income efficiently among various goods and services. Similarly, we ask how the producer can attain efficiency in production. We query about the efficiencies of various market arrangements, such as perfect competition, monopoly, and oligopoly. Toward the end of the book in Chapter Nineteen, we shall examine the efficiency of a competitive economy in exchange, in production, and in choosing the composition of output.

The notion of economic efficiency is a rather abstract (or general) concept that has a great deal of applicability. When the economist talks of allocative efficiency, efficiency in production, etc., he is not introducing a new concept of efficiency. Rather, he is referring to the conditions required to attain efficiency (as defined above) in exchange, in production, etc.

1-5 RELEVANCE OF MICROECONOMICS

We have learned that microeconomics is mostly composed of deductive theories that rest on simplifying assumptions. We must now hasten to add that microeconomics is nevertheless a very relevant subject that has a great deal to say about important worldly affairs that confront us. The relevance of microeconomics in the real world is readily demonstrated by the following list of economic issues, for the solution of which the tools of microeconomics are indispensable.

Pollution control, draft versus volunteer army, equal pay for equal work, income versus excise tax, monopoly versus competition, controlled versus freely fluctuating prices, farm subsidies and acreage allotment, minimum wages, guaranteed annual income, negative income tax, public assistance, energy crisis, wage and price control, . . .

This list can be expanded almost endlessly. As a matter of fact, it is difficult to visualize any major economic, social, or political issue whose solution does not require some knowledge of microeconomics. In order to emphasize the relevance of microeconomic models in the real world, most of the following chapters will conclude with some applications of the microeconomic models developed in the chapter.

The world is indeed full of challenging problems for which we must find solutions. However, our concern with the relevant worldly issues and our desire to solve them must be preceded by a course of study that will help equip us for the tasks. The primary purpose of this book is to help equip the reader with some simple tools of microeconomics, with which he can analyze more intelligently the economic issues surrounding him.

EXERCISES 1

Introduction

1-1 "Economic principles based on many simplifying assumptions are fine in theory, but irrelevant for practical policy decisions. In order to make the theory more relevant, we must build it on the foundation of realistic assumptions." Comment.

1-2 *Equilibrium* is a value-neutral concept; it simply describes a situation in which there is no net tendency to change. Give an example of (1) a highly desirable equilibrium, and (2) a highly undesirable equilibrium.

1-3 Explain the meaning of the term *comparative statics* using the example of the effect of a hard freeze in Florida on the price of Florida oranges. (Make sure to spell out all assumptions. A simple supply and demand graph may be useful.)

1-4 Economics is concerned with choice among alternatives. Speculate as to how economics may be used to analyze the social choice between volunteer versus draft army. (Later compare your answer with that found in Chapter Nine of the text.)

1-5 Since resources are scarce relative to wants, it is important to be efficient in the solution of the economic problems. How would you define efficient production? (Later compare your answer with the definition offered in Chapter Seven of the text.)

1-6 A university president proclaims, "Our student body is the best. I will not trade it with any other in the nation." Is this statement a testable proposition? If not, how would you reword it to get a testable proposition out of it?

CHAPTER TWO

DEMAND, SUPPLY, AND MARKET PRICE

This is a warm-up chapter in which we shall review the concepts of demand and supply and the way they interact to establish price and output of a good. Toward the end of the chapter, we demonstrate the usefulness of the simple tool of demand and supply analysis in studying the impacts of such real world problems as price support and price controls, lax versus strict control of drugs, and an excise tax — tax per unit levied on a commodity. For those who would like to pursue somewhat more rigorous topics, the appendixes present discussions of the stability condition and cobweb models.

2-1 MARKET DEMAND: A GENERAL DEFINITION

In a market-oriented economy, the allocation of resources is accomplished through prices, which are established by the interaction of demand and supply in the marketplace. It is no wonder that all sorts of people talk about demand and supply: men on the street, financial columnists, politicians, as well as economists refer to them constantly. Someone once said that even a parrot could be made into an economist: all he must learn are the two words, *demand* and *supply*. Let us begin with the concept of market demand.

A market is the context in which voluntary exchanges take place between buyers and sellers. It may or may not refer to a specific location. For instance, the market for ready-mix concrete is usually localized. But the stock market is not a specific locality; rather, it is the context in which securities are exchanged.

The quantity of a good that would be purchased in a given market in a given period depends on many things: price of a good, prices of substitutes and complements, stocks of the good already possessed by consumers, wealth and its distribution, size of income and its distribution, tastes of the consumers, price expectation, advertisement, weather, and so on. *The term market demand describes the relationship between the quantities of an economic good that would be purchased by all consumers in a given market and the values of various independent variables affecting the purchase of the good.*[1] Thus, a general expression of a market demand function is given by

$$Q_d = f(x_1, x_2, \ldots, x_n)$$

where Q_d is the quantity that would be purchased in the market and x_i's are the values of variables affecting the quantity purchased.[2]

By specifying the form of the function and the values of the variables, we can obtain the market demand function of a specific good. For example, it may be given by

$$Q_d = 200 - 5x_1 + 3x_2 + 1.5x_3$$

where x_1, x_2, and x_3 show price of the good, price of a substitute, and consumers' income. Note that the quantity of the good demanded, Q_d, will change as any one or more of the variables included in the demand function changes.

The following are some important characteristics of a demand function. (1) A demand function is a *hypothetical construct* that shows various quantities that would be purchased at various possible values of the independent variables. Since the variables affecting the quantity demanded must assume some specific values at any given time, only one quantity demanded can be actually observed in the market. (2) The demand function shows the *maximum quantities* that would be purchased at various sets of the values of the variables. If the quantity available in the market is less than the quantity demanded, all available quantities will be purchased, but the consumers will refuse to buy any more than the quantity demanded even if more units are available in the market. (3) The

[1] In this chapter, we are concerned with the market demand, market supply, and market price. Frequently, for the sake of brevity, we shall omit the word market and speak simply of demand, supply, and price. However, there are other concepts of demand and supply. For instance, an *individual* demand describes the relationship between the quantity of a good purchased by a single consumer and the variables affecting his purchase. For more details, see section 6-2.

[2] For the sake of brevity, the expression, x_i's, is used to indicate $x_1, x_2, \ldots, x_n$.

quantity demanded is a *flow*; it refers to the quantity purchased per unit of time, such as a week, month, or year. Since the flow varies depending on the amount of time involved, a quantity without the unit of time specified has no economic meaning.

The reader has undoubtedly encountered many references to quantity in economic literature that did not specify the unit of time. This is because many economists assume that the unit of time is known to the reader from the context. For the sake of brevity, we shall also follow this widespread convention and refer to quantities as tons, bushels, etc., without specifying the unit of time involved. However, the reader should remember that a quantity is a flow and that whenever there is any ambiguity, the unit of time involved must be specified.

2-2 THE CONVENTIONAL NOTION OF MARKET DEMAND: DEMAND AS A PRICE-QUANTITY RELATION

In the previous section, market demand was defined as a multivariable relationship between quantities purchased and other relevant variables. While this definition is useful in showing that quantity purchased is determined by many factors, its usefulness in an intermediate microeconomics course is severely limited due to its complexity; the study of a multi-variable demand relation requires analytical tools that go beyond this text. To make demand a useful analytical tool at an elementary level, we employ the technique of the partial equilibrium analysis, in which all but one independent variable are assumed to remain constant. Depending on the purpose of the study or on the emphasis to be placed, we can single out a two-variable relationship such as a price-quantity, income-quantity, substitute price–quantity, or an advertising-quantity relationship, while assuming that all other variables are held constant. The price that must be paid in using the partial analysis is the details that must be sacrificed. But this sacrifice of details is amply compensated by a host of analytical insights that become attainable.

MARKET DEMAND: CONVENTIONAL DEFINITION

Since a two-variable relationship is a special case of the general concept of market demand, we may speak of a price-demand, income-demand, advertising-demand, etc. However, it has been a long-established *convention* in economics to use the terms *demand*, *demand schedule*, and *demand curve* to describe a two-variable price-quantity relationship. We succumb to this convention, and will use the word *demand* where the term *price-demand* may be more appropriate. *Thus, market demand, in the conventional sense, is the functional relationship between the quantities of a good that would be purchased by all consumers in a given market and prices of the good, ceteris paribus. A mathematical expression for a market demand equation can be written generally as*

$$Q_d = f(p)$$

where we use the more descriptive letter p (rather than x_1) for price of the commodity.[3] A specific equation of demand can be obtained if the form and parameters of the equation are specified. For example, it may take the following simple linear form:

$$Q_d = 110 - 10p$$

A graphic or schedular representation of a price-quantity relationship, ceteris paribus, produces a market demand curve or a market demand schedule. The market demand schedule and curve representing the above equation, $Q_d = 110 - 10p$, are shown in Table 2-1 and Figure 2-1, respectively.

Table 2-1 Market Demand Schedule

PRICE (p) PER UNIT	QUANTITY DEMANDED (Q_d) PER UNIT OF TIME
9	20
8	30
7	40
6	50
5	60

GENERAL VERSUS CONVENTIONAL
MARKET DEMAND: AN EXAMPLE

A hypothetical example may clarify the relationship between the general concept of a demand function and the demand curve as a price-quantity relationship alone. Suppose a general demand function for good x takes the following specific form.

$$Q_d = 100 - 2p_x + p_y + .1M$$

[3]A demand in this conventional sense can be written in terms of the general demand function as follows

$$Q_d = f(p, \bar{x}_2, \ldots, \bar{x}_n)$$

where p is price of the good and the bar over other symbols indicates that they are being held constant.

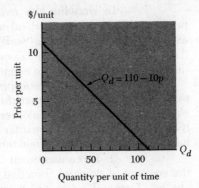

Figure 2-1 Demand curve

This demand function states that the quantity demanded of good x is related to its own price, the price of a substitute, y, and consumers' income, M. To get the (price-quantity) demand curve we must take p_y and M in the above equation as given. Let us assume $p_y = 5$ and $M = 100$. Then

$$Q_d = 100 - 2p_x + p_y + .1M$$
$$= 100 - 2p_x + 5 + .1(100)$$
$$= 115 - 2p_x$$

Therefore, the demand curve (which confines its attention to the price-quantity relationship, *ceteris paribus*) is

$$Q_d = 115 - 2p_x$$

CHARACTERISTICS OF CONVENTIONAL MARKET DEMAND

Several important characteristics of a market demand curve (equation, or schedule) as a price-quantity relationship must be noted.

The three characteristics of a general market demand function hold just as well for the conventional notion of demand. Thus, the demand curve is a *hypothetical* construct that indicates the *maximum* quantities that would be purchased at various prices, and the quantity demanded, Q_d, is a *flow*, that is, a quantity per unit of time.

There are additional characteristics of the market demand curve that are noteworthy. The market demand curve shows the price-quantity relationship under the *ceteris paribus*, or *other things being equal assumption*. It assumes that the circumstances of the market relating to income, taste, prices of related goods, advertising, etc., remain the same.

17

In drawing the market demand (and supply) curves, price is shown on the vertical axis and quantity on the horizontal axis. This practice has been well established in economics since the days of Alfred Marshall, the famous neoclassical economist who introduced graphic analysis into economics.

One of the basic propositions of demand theory states that *the lower the price, other things being equal, the greater will be the quantity purchased.*[4] In other words, a demand curve has a negative slope. Economists consider this proposition so basic that they have named it *the law of demand.*

It is conventional among economists to distinguish the concept of demand from that of quantity demanded, that is, purchased. *Demand refers to an entire schedule, graph, or equation; quantity demanded refers to the quantity purchased at a particular price.* In terms of our earlier examples, demand is the entire schedule (Table 2-1), the whole curve (Figure 2-1), or the equation (say, $Q_d = 110 - 10p$). Quantity demanded, on the other hand, refers to, say, 40 units per period purchased at the price of $7 per unit—a specific value obtained from the demand schedule, demand equation, or demand curve.

2-3 MOVEMENT ALONG VERSUS A SHIFT IN THE DEMAND CURVE

In most economic literature, the terms *movement along the demand curve* and *shift in the demand curve* are distinguished in the following manner. A *movement along a demand curve* refers to a change in quantity demanded due to a change in its own price. A *shift in the demand curve* occurs with a change in the value of a variable other than its own price in the general demand function. Note that this distinction is a graphic counterpart of the distinction between quantity demanded and demand referred to above.

Example: Consider a small college town in which the only two places where students can purchase prepared food are the college cafeteria and a nearby hamburger stand. Assume that the college cafeteria has raised its food prices by some 20 percent. As the result of this price increase, the cafeteria finds its sales lower, and the hamburger stand near the campus is happily surprised by increased sales. In this example, the quantity demanded (but not the demand itself) has changed for the cafeteria food, and the demand itself has changed for hamburgers at the hamburger stand. Referring to Figures 2-2 and 2-3, let us see why. As the price of cafeteria food is raised

[4]This proposition will be established later in Chapters Three and Four.

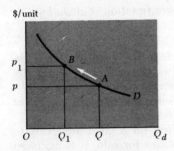

Figure 2-2 Change in quantity demanded (movement along a demand curve)

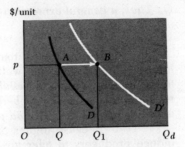

Figure 2-3 Change in demand (a shift in the demand curve)

from p to p_1 in Figure 2-2, the *quantity demanded* decreases from Q to Q_1 units per period. The movement involved is along the demand curve from point A to point B. There is no new demand curve involved: thus, there has not been any change in the demand (curve) for the cafeteria food.

Because cafeteria food is now more expensive relative to hamburgers at the stand, more students flock to the hamburger stand. The *increased demand* for hamburgers is represented by the rightward and upward *shift* of the demand curve from D to D' in Figure 2-3. Because the demand has increased, the hamburger stand is now selling QQ_1 more units of hamburgers even though its price remains unchanged at p dollars per unit. Note that an increase in demand is accompanied by an increase in quantity demanded but *not* vice versa.

Among the usually mentioned variables that shift a demand curve are the buyers' income, their taste, and prices and availabilities of related goods (substitutes or complements). The list can be readily expanded. For example, price expectations on the good itself or on the related goods, weather, newspaper and magazine articles, changing fashions, advertising, and general economic conditions tend to affect—either directly or indirectly—the demand for a good.

2-4 MARKET SUPPLY

Most of the things we have said with regard to demand apply to market supply or supply, with minor modifications. *Market supply is most generally defined as the relationship between quantities supplied by all sellers in a market Q_s and variables affecting*

Q_s. Thus, a general expression for a *supply function* is given by

$$Q_s = g(x_1, x_2, \ldots, x_n)$$

Having noted that supply is really a multivariable relationship, we follow the well-entrenched convention of using the terms, *supply, supply schedule, and supply curve to refer to the price-quantity relationship between various quantities of a good that would be offered for sale and prices of the good.*

Because higher prices offered for a good are likely to induce producers to offer greater quantities for sale, it is assumed that a supply curve has a *positive slope*. The location of a supply curve may be shifted by such factors as a change in production technology, input prices, weather, anti-pollution measures, and transportation facilities available.

The distinction between the concepts of *quantity supplied* and *supply* as well as between a *movement along* a supply curve and a *shift* of a supply curve is entirely analogous to that of the demand curve.

2-5 DEMAND, SUPPLY, AND MARKET PRICE

In order to see how the price and output of a good are determined in the market, we must bring the demand and supply curves together and study their interaction. We shall assume that prices are determined freely in the market and that there is no governmental or monopolistic interference. Price and output determination can be analyzed arithmetically (verbally), graphically, or algebraically. All three approaches are reviewed below, because each tends to enhance the others and some readers may find one easier than the others. In each case, we will assume that the market demand and supply equations are given by $Q_d = 110 - 10p$ and $Q_s = 20p - 100$, respectively.

ARITHMETIC (OR VERBAL) APPROACH

The demand schedule of Table 2-1 and the supply schedule derived from the supply equation $Q_s = 20p - 100$ are shown together in Table 2-2. Comparing the Q_d and Q_s columns, it is obvious that at any price higher than $7 per unit, the excess of the quantity supplied over the quantity demanded will exert a downward pressure on price. This tendency for the price to move down is indicated in the last column by the arrows that point downward. Similarly, if the price is lower than $7, the excess of the quantity demanded over the quantity supplied will tend to push the price upward. Now, at the price of $7, the quantities demanded and supplied are both equal to 40 units. What the buyers are willing to purchase at the

Table 2-2 Demand, Supply, and the Equilibrium Price and Output

PRICE (p) PER UNIT	QUANTITY DEMANDED (Q_d) PER UNIT OF TIME	QUANTITY SUPPLIED (Q_s) PER UNIT OF TIME	DIRECTION OF CHANGE IN PRICE
$9	20	80	↓
8	30	60	↓
7	40	40	Equilibrium
6	50	20	↑
5	60	0	↑

price is exactly matched by what the sellers are willing to offer at that price. Both parties are satisfied, and there is no net tendency for the price to change. *Thus, $7 is the equilibrium market price, from which there is no net or inherent tendency to change.*

In summary, the equilibrium market price and output are established when quantity demanded Q_d equals quantity supplied Q_s. If $Q_s > Q_d$, price tends to fall. If $Q_s < Q_d$, price tends to rise.

GRAPHIC APPROACH

The demand and supply curves are brought together in Figure 2-4. The horizontal axis is simply labeled Q since it represents both Q_d and Q_s. This graph shows vividly that the equilibrium price and output are established at the point of intersection of the demand and supply curves. If the price is higher than $7, $Q_s > Q_d$ and the price tends to fall. At any price lower than $7, similarly, the excess of Q_d over Q_s tends to raise the price. When the demand and supply curves intersect, $Q_s = Q_d$ and the equilibrium price and output ($7 and 40 units in this case) are established.

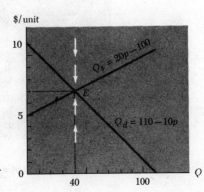

Figure 2-4 Determination of equilibrium price and output

21

ALGEBRAIC (MATHEMATICAL) APPROACH

The equilibrium price and output can also be determined by a simultaneous solution of the demand and supply equations. The demand and supply equations involved are

$$Q_d = 110 - 10p \text{ and}$$
$$Q_s = 20p - 100$$

We know that $Q_d = Q_s$ in equilibrium. In view of this equilibrium condition, it follows immediately that

$$110 - 10p = 20p - 100$$
$$30p = 210$$
$$p = 7$$

Substituting $p = 7$ to either the demand or supply equation, we know that the equilibrium quantity is 40 units.

2-6 SHIFTS IN DEMAND OR SUPPLY CURVE

The effect of a shift in the market demand or supply on the equilibrium market price and output can be readily analyzed. Let the curves labeled D and S in Figure 2-5 be the prevailing market demand and supply curves. Point E shows the current equilibrium market price and output. Suppose an increase in demand shifts the demand curve to the position shown by the white line. What happens to the equilibrium price and quantity in the market? The comparison of E' (the new point of intersection between D' and

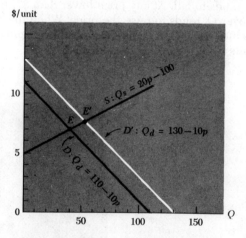

Figure 2-5   Effects of a shift in demand

S) and the old equilibrium point E makes it clear that price and output in the market will both increase.

Of course, the reader can solve the problem mathematically by solving the following set of equations

$$Q_d' = 130 - 10p$$
$$Q_s = 20p - 100$$
$$Q_d' = Q_s$$

and learn that the precise equilibrium market price and quantity are $7.67 and 53.3 units, respectively.

If the market demand and supply schedules are available, the solution can be identified arithmetically from the table. The analytical problem associated with a shift in the market supply curve is entirely analogous.

Note how the price mechanism has responded to an increase in demand: it has raised the price and induced more to be supplied to meet the increased demand for the good.

2-7 PRICE SUPPORT AND PRICE CEILINGS: An Application

We have seen that, in the absence of artificial interference by government or monopolistic forces, the interaction of demand and supply for a commodity tends to establish the equilibrium price, which clears the market without creating any shortage or surplus. Let us now apply the tool of demand-supply analysis to see why a surplus or shortage will develop if price is set higher or lower than the equilibrium price by such a device as a price support or control.

Consider the case of a *price support* program for an agricultural product. Suppose the market demand and supply data for cotton are as depicted by Figure 2-6. The government, considering the equilibrium price, P, to be too low for the farmers, establishes $F as *the support (or floor) price, at which the government guarantees to purchase all output offered to it.* At the price of $F per unit, the quantity demanded is FA while the quantity supplied is FB; thus, there is a *surplus* of AB units in the market.

The U.S. government, through its Commodity Credit Corporation (CCC), maintains a variety of price support programs for such farm products as cotton, wheat, corn, tobacco, rice, peanuts, dairy products, sugar beets, wool, and tung nuts. In order to maintain the support prices of various farm products, CCC essentially purchases the surpluses and stores them. From Figure 2-6, it is clear that the price support program benefits the cotton farmers as a group: they can not only produce more but sell their output at a higher price. But who pays for the program? First, consumers who have to pay higher prices for their cotton goods bear an important part of the cost of supporting the price of cotton. Second, the American people in general, who have to pay taxes to support various CCC programs, share the burden of the price support program. Third, according to Figure 2-6, it is clear that the price support program will reduce the quantity demanded from *PE* (the original equilibrium output) to *FA* units. Yet, the farmers are led to increase their output to *FB* units, which exceeds the original equilibrium output. Whether this is good or bad is a value judgment. But the fact is clear that farmers are encouraged to produce at a rate that the buyers are not willing to purchase.

Let us now consider the effect of imposing a *price ceiling above which the price of the controlled commodity is not allowed to rise.* Assume that the government, in its effort to curtail the rate of inflation, sets the price ceiling at $*C* per unit in Figure 2-6. At this price, the quantity demanded exceeds the quantity supplied, and there develops the *shortage* of *GH* units.

Those who are fortunate enough to find the good at the ceiling price benefit from the low price. Those who have to wait in a long line hoping to buy the good or those who must return empty-handed are hurt. Producers who must curtail their operations due to the low price ceiling are also hurt. When a legal price ceiling is established, many buyers who are willing to pay higher prices cannot find the good. *Thus, a price control program sooner or later breeds black markets, in which the good is sold illegally at prices higher than the legal ceiling.*

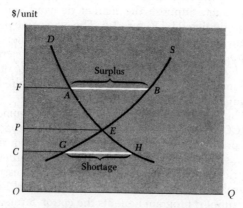

Figure 2-6 Surplus and shortage

Before we leave this discussion of price floors and ceilings, the reader should note that such terms as *surplus* and *shortage* are defined with reference to a specific price. For instance, in Figure 2-6 a surplus exists at the price of $F per unit; no surplus or shortage appears at the price of $P; and a shortage develops at any price lower than $P. Clearly, *surplus* and *shortage* are *relative* terms that become meaningful only with reference to the price involved. When one vaguely talks of a shortage or surplus of a certain good, he must mean shortage or surplus at the going price. Also note that a meaningful support (ceiling) price must be higher (lower) than the equilibrium market price.[5]

2-8 LAX VERSUS STRICT DRUG CONTROL: An Application

Let us now apply the tool of demand and supply analysis to study the effects of a more strict enforcement of laws against drugs (such as heroin and cocaine). The market demand for drugs may be considered as the sum of (1) the demand by drug addicts and (2) the demand by drug users who are not yet addicted. The market demand curve for drugs is represented by the solid black curve, *DAN*, in Figure 2-7.[6] Since drug addicts' purchases of drugs are not likely to be influenced significantly by drug prices, their demand curve is represented by the steep line segment, *DA*. Nonaddicts' demand curve for drugs, on the other hand, is represented by the flatter downward-sloping curve, *AN*, indicating that quantity demanded will increase significantly as price decreases. The supply for drugs is shown by the positively sloped white curve, *S*: the higher the price, the greater will be the willingness of the supplier to offer greater quantities for sale.

Suppose the demand curve, *DAN*, and supply curve, *S*, shown in Figure 2-7 describe the situation that prevails if the use or sale of drugs is controlled rather loosely. The interaction of demand and supply curves will establish the equilibrium price and quantity for drugs at *E*. Now what happens if the anti-drug laws are strengthened and more strictly enforced? Faced with an increased possibility of being arrested and prosecuted, the demand curve of nonaddict drug users will become much steeper. The addicts' demand for drugs may be assumed to remain the same because they are likely to consume the same quantities of drugs even in the face of an increased danger of arrest. Thus, the new demand curve is represented by *DAN'*. The dotted segment, *AN'*, represents the decreased demand

[5] Economists frequently employ such parenthetical expressions to avoid repeating similar statements.
[6] In section 6-1, we will examine the procedure by which individual demand curves are summed to obtain the market demand curve.

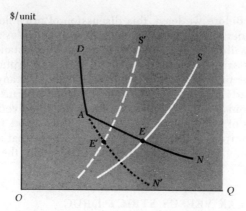

Figure 2-7   Effects of more strict drug control

by nonaddicts in the face of an increased danger. As for the supply curve, stricter enforcement of anti-drug laws will increase the suppliers' risks of being arrested and prosecuted. Thus, the supply curve shifts to the left and upward as shown by S'. The combined effect of the changes in demand and supply is to reduce the usage of drugs (as long as the demand or supply curve is not a vertical line). Whether the new market price will be higher or lower than the old one depends on the relative magnitudes of shifts in the demand and supply curves. For instance, E' in Figure 2-7 would have been higher (lower) than the indicated position if the supply curve had shifted more than (less than) the S' curve shown.

Once the supply curve hits the demand curve at its steep segment, DA, a more strict control can hardly reduce drug usage. It merely raises the price of drugs, reflecting the added cost of greater secrecy and the increased risk premiums wanted by the suppliers. A successful reduction in drug usage under these circumstances can be achieved only if medical treatment and educational programs reduce the number of addicts (and potential addicts).

2-9 THE SHIFTING AND INCIDENCE OF AN EXCISE TAX: An Application

The persons (or firms) who pay a tax do not necessarily bear or absorb all of the tax themselves. For example, tobacco companies that pay the excise tax on cigarettes definitely pass an important part of the tax burden to cigarette smokers. The knowledge of *the incidence—the final resting place(s)—of a tax*, therefore, is vital in determining the economic (and equity) aspects of the tax.

Let us now see why the simple tool of supply and demand analysis is indispensable in studying the incidence of *an excise tax—a per unit tax imposed on a specific good such as gasoline, cigarettes, and cameras.* Let the market demand and supply for the good involved be shown by *D* and *S* curves in Figure 2-8. The equilibrium price and output for the market are given by $P and *Q* units. Suppose that the government now imposes an excise tax. How would such a tax affect the market demand and supply curves? Since the consumers' willingness to buy the product is not in any way affected by the tax, the market demand curve remains the same. The effect of the excise tax on the market supply curve, however, is represented by its upward (or leftward) shift. For example, if the suppliers were willing to supply *Q'* units at the price of *Q'J* dollars per unit before the tax, they will be willing to supply the same quantity only if the price is now *Q'E'* dollars—the sum of the original price plus the excise tax they must turn over to the government. (We may say that the market supply curve has shifted *leftward* because at any given price the quantity that would be offered for sale will be less than before, reflecting the lower after-tax price received by the suppliers.)

The market supply curve that includes the excise tax is shown by the white line, *S'*. The new equilibrium is established at *E'*. Now the consumers must pay $C per unit, which is *PC* dollars higher than before. The price the suppliers can retain after paying the excise tax to the government is $B per unit, which is *BP* dollars lower than before. Thus, we note that a part of the excise tax is *shifted forward* to the consumers and a part is *absorbed* by (or *shifted*

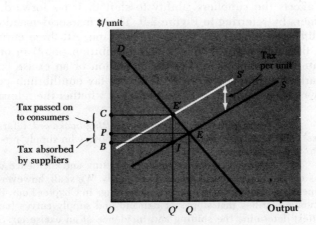

Figure 2-8   Effects of an excise tax

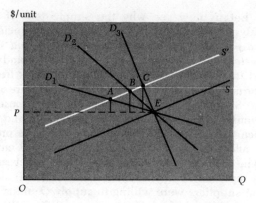

Figure 2-9 Slopes of the demand (and supply)
curves and shifting of an excise tax

backward to) the suppliers.[7] But this is not the whole story. Note
that the market output is reduced from Q to Q' units. Thus, the
owners of resources no longer needed to produce the taxed commodity also bear the burden of the excise tax. Furthermore, the buyers
who no longer purchase the good because of the higher price bear,
in an unspecified sense, some of the tax burden.

The vital question to be answered now is, What determines how much of the tax is shifted forward to the consumers and
how much is absorbed by the business firms? The answer is, the
slopes of the demand and supply curves.[8]

Let us examine how the steepness of the market demand
curve affects the suppliers' ability to shift their tax forward to the
consumers by referring to Figure 2-9. Three market demand curves
with different slopes are shown in the graph. All three curves are
drawn through point E (the pre-tax equilibrium point) in order to
facilitate the comparison. Let the imposition of an excise tax shift
the market supply curve to S'. The after-tax equilibrium position
is shown by point A, B, or C depending on whether the relevant de-

[7]More rigorously, the phrase, *shifting backward*, refers to the
business' ability to pass the tax backward to those who supply productive
inputs to this business.

[8]Many textbooks explain the shifting and incidence of a tax
in terms of the elasticities of demand and supply. We shall, however, stress
that slopes and elasticities are not the same things in Chapter Four. Richard
A. Musgrave clarifies that slopes of demand and supply curves (not their
elasticities) determine the shifting and incidence of an excise tax. See his
Theory of Public Finance (New York: McGraw-Hill, 1959), pp. 288–292.

mand curve is D_1, D_2, or D_3, respectively. The length of the vertical line segment from point *A*, *B*, or *C* to the dashed line *PE* shows the amount of increase in the consumer price that will occur, given the respective demand curve. Examining the relationship between the amount of the price increase and the slope of the demand curve, we note that as the demand curve becomes steeper, a greater amount of the excise tax is passed forward to the consumers. Therefore, we conclude that *the flatter the demand curve, the more difficult* it is *to shift* a tax forward to the consumers and the smaller is the increase in the price paid by the consumers.

      The reader should be able to show, in an analogous manner, that the flatter the supply curve, the easier it is to pass the tax forward to the consumer and the larger is the increase in the price paid by the consumers.

APPENDIX 2

A. The Condition
for Market Stability

In the preceding pages we have observed that the equality of demand and supply resulted in an equilibrium. When the price was higher than the equilibrium price, the excess of quantity supplied over quantity demanded tended to bring the price down. When the price was lower than the equilibrium price, on the other hand, the shortage tended to bid the price up toward the equilibrium level. If there were no such *negative feedback—a movement back to equilibrium whenever there is any divergence from the equilibrium—* the equilibrium price and quantity in the market would not have been attained. Indeed, there is *no guarantee* that a given set of market demand and supply curves would produce an equilibrium. First, there is no reason why the initial condition is one of an equilibrium. If it was not an equilibrium position, the adjustment process may or may not lead to an equilibrium. Second, even if the initial condition was one of equilibrium, this equilibrium may be displaced by changing demand and supply conditions. A given displacement may be followed by adjustments that tend to restore the equilibrium, or it may be followed by responses that tend to magnify the displacement.[9]

*An equilibrium is said to be **stable** if a displacement from the equilibrium is followed by a return to the equilibrium, and **unstable** if it is not.* A stable market model is shown in Figure 2-10. If price is higher than the equilibrium level, quantity supplied Q_s exceeds quantity demanded Q_d; and this excess of Q_s over Q_d tends to lower the price to the equilibrium level. Similarly, when price is lower than the equilibrium price, Q_s is smaller than Q_d, and this shortage tends to

[9]For details, see Figure 2-16 and accompanying explanations in Appendix 2B.

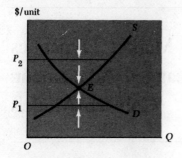
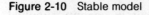

Figure 2-10   Stable model

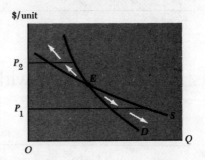

Figure 2-11   Unstable model

push the price up to the equilibrium level. In Figure 2-11, which shows an unstable model, things are quite different. When price is higher than the equilibrium price, there is a shortage ($Q_s < Q_d$); when price is lower than the equilibrium level, there is a surplus ($Q_s > Q_d$). Such a model is unstable; if the equilibrium is disturbed, the price will keep getting further and further away from the equilibrium level.

In conclusion, in order for the market model to be stable, a price above the equilibrium level must produce a surplus ($Q_s > Q_d$) and a price below the equilibrium level must be accompanied by a shortage ($Q_s < Q_d$).[10] Alternatively, this stability condition may be stated as follows: above the equilibrium price, the supply curve must lie to the right of the demand curve; and below the equilibrium price, the supply curve must lie to the left of the demand curve.

---

[10]In advanced literature, this is called the *Walrasian stability condition*. There are different definitions of stability, and our text statement violates the Marshallian stability condition if the supply curve is negatively sloped. The reader who is interested in details should consult James M. Henderson and Richard E. Quandt, *Microeconomic Theory: A Mathematical Approach*, 2d ed. (New York: McGraw-Hill, 1971), pp. 132–142.

B. Market Dynamics with Lagged Adjustment: Cobweb Models

Since production takes time, the adjustment in quantity supplied is likely to lag behind a price change. Agricultural commodities are good examples. A farmer may, in view of the current high price of wheat, wish to increase his supply of wheat, but it takes a full season to do so. Production of some commodities such as hogs, beef cattle, and oranges may require two or more seasons. Thus, the effect of price on quantity supplied cannot become visible in the marketplace until two or more time periods elapse.

THE ASSUMPTIONS OF A COBWEB MODEL

Let the commodity involved be wheat so that there is a lag of one period (season) in supply. The assumptions involved in a cobweb model are as follows:

1. There is nothing new in the market demand curve. As usual, the demand curve relates the quantity demanded in the current period to the price in the current period. That is,

    $$D_t = a - bp_t$$

    where a and b are constants and t denotes the time period. (In order to avoid a double subscripted symbol such as $Q_{d,t}$ we use D_t to denote the quantity demanded in the market in time period t.)
2. The *market supply curve*, however, *shows the lagged relationship* between the price in the previous period and the quantity supplied in the current period. That is,

    $$S_t = c + dp_{t-1}$$

    where c and d are constants.
    Farmers believe that the price in the previous period will prevail in the current period as well, and adjust their output accordingly. The possibility that such adjustments in current production may affect the market price in the current period seems never to occur to the suppliers in the cobweb model.

3. The farmers will *sell their output at whatever price* it will fetch in the market, assuring that quantities supplied and demanded are equal and no one goes with an unsatisfied demand or unsold stock. That is, we assume

$$D_t - S_t = 0$$

PRICE AND OUTPUT ADJUSTMENTS IN COBWEB MODELS

In Figure 2-12a, let the initial period price be given by p_1. Farmers, believing that this price will prevail in the next period, t_2, produce Q_2 and place it in the market at whatever price it can command. Given the demand curve, D, and the quantity supplied, Q_2, the price that clears that market in period t_2 is p_2. Believing this low price will prevail in period t_3, the farmers reduce the output in t_3 to Q_3. This limited supply in t_3, however, sells for p_3 and so on. Notice that a price that is higher than the equilibrium price initiates an adjustment process in both price and quantity supplied. But the price does not approach the equilibrium price gradually, rather it continuously overshoots the mark and oscillates above and below the equilibrium price. *The price, however, gets closer and closer to the equilibrium price as the adjustment process continues. Thus, this case is referred to as the model of damped oscillation, or simply as the convergent case.* The cobweblike appearance in Figure 2-12a explains the origin of the term *cobweb model*. Figure 2-12b plots the movement of price against time. This time series of price clearly

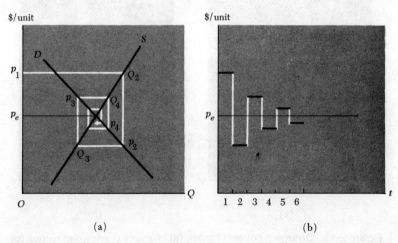

Figure 2-12 Convergent cobweb model; (a) changes in price and output, (b) time path of price

shows that the oscillation is damped and the market price converges to the equilibrium price with time.

Now examine Figure 2-13a. Let, again, the initial period price be p_1. Farmers, believing this price to prevail in the following period, produce Q_2 in period 2. This, however, can be sold only at the price of p_2. Disappointed, the farmers produce Q_3 for period 3 which sells at the price of p_3. Encouraged, the farmers now increase their production in period 4 to Q_4 only to find the disappointingly low market price of p_4. Notice that, *as this adjustment process goes on, the magnitudes of diversion around the equilibrium price get larger and larger. The model under examination is that of an explosive oscillation, or of a divergent case.* The time path depicted in Figure 2-13b clearly shows the explosive nature of the model. Note that such explosive models make economic sense only within some "normal" range; price, for instance, cannot go below zero.

Figures 2-14a and b show the cobweb model with the so-called *perpetual oscillations.* The initial price, p_1, evokes the period 2 output of Q_2 which sells only for the low price of p_2. Discouraged farmers reduce their output in period 3 to Q_3 which fetches the high price of p_1 in period 3. Happy farmers, believing this high price will prevail in the next period as well, increase the period 4 production to Q_2 — which can only be sold at the price of p_2, and so on. The process goes on and on and the *price oscillates perpetually around the equilibrium price.*

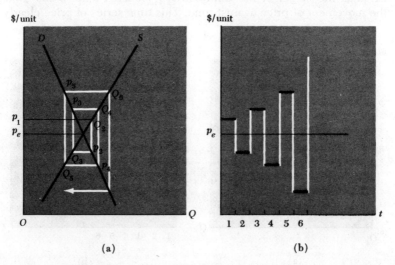

Figure 2-13 Divergent cobweb model; (a) changes in price and output, (b) time path of price

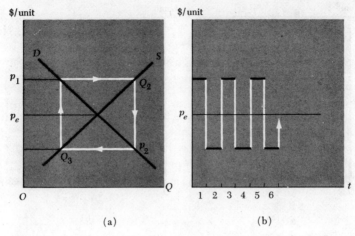

Figure 2-14 Perpetually oscillating cobweb model; (*a*) oscillations in price and output, (*b*) time path of price

To keep the exposition uncluttered, little has been said about the oscillation of the output above and below the equilibrium output. The reader who understands the oscillation of price, however, should have little difficulty in tracing out the time path of output for each of the three cases discussed. (The reader may wish to, using a dotted line, superimpose the time path of output over the time series of price on each of the above three graphs.)

STABILITY OF COBWEB MODELS

What determines the stability of a cobweb model? That is, what makes a cobweb model converge, diverge, or perpetually oscillate? The answer is provided by the relative sizes of the absolute slopes of the market demand and market supply curves. A cobweb model converges (diverges, oscillates perpetually) if the *absolute slope* of the demand curve is less than (greater than, equal to) the absolute slope of the supply curve. In Figure 2-12*a*, the absolute slope of the supply curve exceeds that of the demand curve, and the model is stable. In Figure 2-13*a*, the absolute slope of the supply curve is smaller than that of the demand curve and the model is divergent. The equality of the absolute slopes in Figure 2-14*a* makes the model oscillate perpetually.

The stability condition of the cobweb model holds true even in the unlikely case in which the supply curve has a negative slope. Examine Figures 2-15*a* and *b*. Though they do not resemble

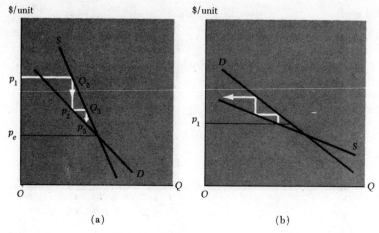

Figure 2-15 Uncobweblike cobweb models; (a) convergent case, (b) divergent case

cobwebs, the assumptions of the model involved are identical to those of the earlier cobweb models except for the slopes of the supply curves. Given the initial period price of p_1 in Figure 2-15a, the farmers in the second period produce Q_2 which sells for the price of p_2, and so on. The model converges to the equilibrium position without oscillation. The model is stable because the absolute slope of the supply curve is steeper than that of the demand curve. On the other hand, the model in Figure 2-15b is unstable because the absolute slope of the supply curve is less than that of the demand curve. The original price of p_1 which is higher than the equilibrium price initiates explosive increases in price away from the equilibrium.[11]

THE SIGNIFICANCE OF COBWEB MODELS

What is the significance of the cobweb model? First, it sheds important insights into the factors determining the stability or instability of a market model. The model makes it quite clear that the existence of a self-equilibrating market depends on (1) the negative feedbacks, (2) the magnitudes of the negative feedbacks and (3) the timing of the adjustments. In order to reach an equilibrium position, an excess of price over the equilibrium price must induce

[11]A hyperinflation in a disturbed economy or a stock market crash may be described by such an explosive model.

a decrease in price (*negative feedbacks*). If the *magnitude* of negative feedback is such that the extent by which the new price falls below the equilibrium price is smaller than the amount by which the old price exceeded it, the model converges. In Figure 2-16 if $AB > BC$, the model is stable. If $AB < BC$, the model is explosive; and the model oscillates perpetually if $AB = BC$. The oscillations in the cobweb model take place, for one thing, because of the inability of supply to adjust immediately (or continuously) to a change in price. Thus, the *timing* of adjustment is another factor affecting the stability of a market model.

　　　Second, another major virtue of the cobweb model is the dynamic nature of the model itself. *Most analyses in this book are of static nature, which concentrates on the direction of change (towards or away from equilibrium) and on comparisons of the equilibrium positions before and after the change (comparative statics). The theory of economic dynamics concerns itself with the time path of variables from some arbitrary initial conditions, and is interested in what happens over time in the adjustment process.* The cobweb model is a simple dynamic model that shows the effect of a lagged supply on the adjustment process involving prices and outputs at various periods of time. It is virtually the only dynamic model that will appear in this book.

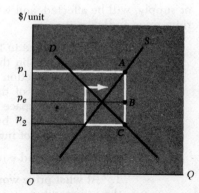

Figure 2-16 Magnitudes of negative feedbacks and stability of cobweb models

EXERCISES 2

Demand, Supply, and Market Price

2-1 "Prices guide the flow of resources in a market-centered economy like ours. Thus, if beef is in short supply, it is best to let its price rise. Notwithstanding consumers' loud protests, this is the best way to eliminate the shortage and bring the price down in the long run." Do you agree? Why?

2-2 The price of a good has increased from one year to the next. Graphically demonstrate that this increase in price could have been accompanied by an increase in demand, a decrease in demand, or an unchanging demand.

2-3 The equilibrium quantity of a good sold has increased from one year to the next. Graphically demonstrate that this phenomenon is consistent with an increase, a decrease, or an unchanging supply.

2-4 For each of the following, discuss which, demand or supply, will be affected, and what is the likely impact on equilibrium price and quantity.

1. A hard freeze in Florida damages citrus fruits
2. The impact on the domestic steel price of relaxing the export restriction on steel scraps
3. Curtailment of the U.S. space program on the salaries or jobs of space engineers
4. Curtailment of business plant and equipment outlays on the rate of interest

2-5 The demand equation is $Q = 90 - 3p$.

1. At what price would no one be willing to buy any of the commodity?

2.   If the commodity is given free, what is the quantity demanded?

3.   If the price is reduced by one unit (say, a dollar), by how much will the quantity demanded change?

2-6   The supply function is given by $Q = 5p + 50$.

1.   Sketch the supply curve and show what restrictions on output must be placed.

2.   Suppose a law should limit the maximum output to 200 units:

> (a)   Sketch the new supply curve in your graph for question 1.
> (b)   Show the equations that will describe the supply function under this limitation.

2-7   For the following pair of equations, determine algebraically the equilibrium price and output.

$$Q_d = 6 - p; \; Q_s = 3p - 2$$

2-8   Draw simple demand-supply diagrams, and discuss the impact on price and output of the following:

1.   An increase in demand, *ceteris paribus*
2.   An increase in supply, *ceteris paribus*
3.   Increases in both demand and supply

CHAPTER THREE

THEORY
OF CONSUMER BEHAVIOR

The consumers in the United States spent around 900 billion dollars in 1974. Their dollar votes influence importantly the level and composition of goods and services produced in the American economy. Thus, it should come as no surprise to the reader to learn that the theory of consumer behavior forms an important part of microeconomics. In this chapter, we shall explore the nature of consumer preferences, and develop a model of consumer choice.

Consumption decisions are made by individuals or household groups.[1] For instance, while an individual may choose his cafeteria lunch as he wishes, a new house or an automobile is likely to be purchased by a joint decision of the members of a household. For the sake of simplicity, we shall assume that households will behave in the same manner as individual consumers and present our analysis in terms of an individual consumer's decision making.

3-1 THE CONSUMER

Individual consumers can spend their money as they please. They may purchase goods and services after carefully examining the alternatives available, or they may buy impulsively or from sheer habit. They may even be eccentric like professors who wear out-of-style clothes and spend fortunes on books and journals, or spendthrifts who purchase dozens of expensive sport cars. But we

[1]Some consumption decisions are made by such other groups as schools, churches, and fraternal groups.

assume that all consumers behave in a *consistent* manner. This assumption of a consistent (or rational) behavior is necessary to develop a model of consumer behavior that can predict an individual consumer's response to a given set of circumstances.[2] *Thus, we assume that every consumer attempts to maximize utility — the want-satisfying quality of a good — and possesses a stable preference or taste that has the following properties:*

1. For every two bundles of commodities, the consumer knows whether he *prefers* A to B, or B to A, or whether he is *indifferent* between A and B.
2. If the consumer prefers A to B and B to C, then he prefers A to C. That is, the consumer's preference is consistent or *transitive.*[3]
3. A larger bundle of goods is always preferred to a smaller bundle. A bundle is larger than the other if it contains more of one good and at least as many of the other goods. This is the so-called *nonsatiety requirement.*

3-2 INDIFFERENCE CURVES: GRAPHIC REPRESENTATION OF PREFERENCES

Let us confine our attention to the simple case of the two-commodity world. Here, the consumer's preference function

[2] Much can still be said with regard to a *group* behavior because eccentric behaviors may be minor relative to the total group and deviate randomly around the more usual behaviors.

[3] Mathematically the preference or utility function may be written

$$U(q) = f(q_1, q_2, \ldots, q_n)$$

where q_i shows the quantity of commodity i.

Indifference relation **I** is reflexive, symmetric, and transitive. That is,

(a) A is indifferent to itself, AIA

(b) If AIB, then BIA, and

(c) If AIB and BIC, then AIC

Preference relation **P** is antireflexive, antisymmetric, and transitive. That is,

(a) A is not preferred to A, $A\not{P}A$

(b) If APB, then $B\not{P}A$, and

(c) If APB and BPC, then APC

For more details, see Cliff Lloyd's *Mircoeconomic Analysis.* (Homewood, Ill.: Irwin, 1967), Ch. 1, or S. Wu and J. Pontney, *An Introduction to Modern Demand Theory* (New York: Random House, 1967), pp. 56–59.

can be depicted by indifference curves. The consumer knows, for every combination of two goods, *x* and *y*, whether he prefers combination *A* to combination *B*, or *B* to *A*, or whether he is equally satisfied with either *A* or *B*. *An indifference curve is the locus of the combinations of two goods that are equally satisfactory to a consumer, or to which the consumer is indifferent. A schedular representation of an indifference curve is called an indifference schedule.* In Figure 3-1, the curve labeled I_0 is an indifference curve. Since it is an indifference curve, all combinations on it must be equally satisfactory to the consumer. Thus, combinations $A(1,6)$, $B(2,4)$, $C(4,2)$, and $D(7,1)$, just to name a few points on the curve, show various combinations of two goods *x* and *y* for which the consumer is indifferent.

Though it cannot be said that all economic quantities are intrinsically positive, we confine our attention to the positive economic quantities, and accordingly to the positive (northeast) quadrant of the two-dimensional Cartesian space. *This positive portion of the x-y plane is referred to as the commodity space.* Notice that the indifference curve, I_0, *partitions* the commodity space into two parts. The space to the right and above the curve contains combinations or bundles of goods *x* and *y* that are preferred to those on the indifference curve; all combinations on or to the left and below

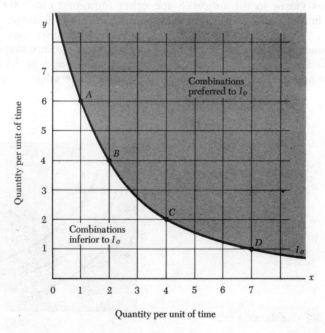

Quantity per unit of time

Figure 3-1   Indifference curve

I_0 contain collections of goods equal to or less preferred to those on I_0.

Three indifference curves are shown in Figure 3-2. Combination J on indifference curve I_2 must be preferred to combination K on I_1, since J contains more x and more y. Similarly, combination L on I_0 is less preferred to combination K. By definition, all combinations that are on the same indifference curve are equally preferred. Thus, it is clear that an indifference curve that lies further away along a ray from the origin is preferred to those that are closer to the origin.

A set of indifference curves such as those shown in Figure 3-2 is called an **indifference map**. An indifference map is a graphic device describing the taste of a certain individual consumer. It satisfies the postulated properties of consumer preference. The indifference map shows, for every two collections of goods, whether the consumer prefers one to the other, or is indifferent between them. Since combinations that lie on a higher indifference curve are always preferred to those that lie on a curve below it, the transitivity and nonsatiety requirements are also satisfied.

3-3 PROPERTIES OF INDIFFERENCE CURVES

We have already observed that an indifference curve that lies further away from the origin is always preferred to the one that lies closer to the origin. Some other important characteristics of indifference curves we must be familiar with are as follows.

There are an infinite number of indifference curves. In the commodity space there are an infinite number of points, and there is an indifference curve that passes through each point in the commodity space. Thus, between any two indifference curves, we can

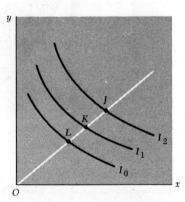

Figure 3-2 Indifference map

draw an infinite number of indifference curves. An indifference map, therefore, is merely a partial set of indifference curves shown for an expository purpose.

Indifference curves must have negative slopes. Because an indifference curve shows the locus of the combinations of two goods *x* and *y* that are equally preferable to a consumer, an increase in *x* must be offset by a decrease in *y* and vice versa. So long as each commodity yields a positive utility (a necessary consequence of the nonsatiety postulate), the consumer can stay on the same indifference curve only if an increase in *x* is compensated by a decrease in *y*. The curves that do not have negative slopes, such as those shown in Figure 3-3, cannot be indifference curves: in all three cases combination *B* is clearly preferable to combination *A*.

Indifference curves cannot intersect or be tangent. Suppose that two indifference curves intersect as shown in Figure 3-4. The combination *M* is clearly preferable to *N* since *M* contains more of both *x* and *y*. *M*, however, is indifferent to *L*, which lies on the same indifference curve; *N* is also indifferent to *L* for the same reason. Since both *M* and *N* are indifferent to *L*, by the transitivity of indifference relation, *M* and *N* must be indifferent to each other. This, however, contradicts the fact that *M* is preferred to *N*. Accordingly, indifference curves cannot intersect. The logical impossibility of two or more indifference curves being tangent to each other can be similarly proved.

Indifference curves must be convex to the origin. Consider in Figure 3-5 the movement along the indifference curve from *A* to *B* to *C*, etc. For notational simplicity, we shall use *x* and *y* (rather than q_x and q_y) to represent the quantities of two goods *x* and *y*. Each time the consumer adds a given quantity, Δx, of *x* to his commodity

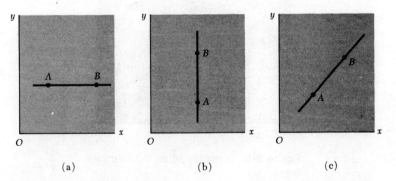

Figure 3-3 Impossible shapes of an indifference curve; (*a*) horizontal curve, (*b*) vertical curve, (*c*) positively sloped curve

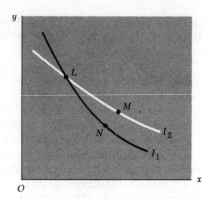

Figure 3-4 Nonintersection of indifference curves

bundle, the quantity of y he is willing to give up, Δy_i, for each additional unit of x becomes successively smaller.[4] The ratio at which the consumer is willing to exchange y for x, that is, the numerical or absolute slope of the indifference curve, $-\Delta y/\Delta x$, must decline. The reader may notice that we are so far merely assuming that an indifference curve is convex to the origin. The proof of this proposition, however, will be given in section 3-8.

The slope of an indifference curve, $\Delta y/\Delta x$, at any point on it shows the amount of y needed to compensate the consumer for

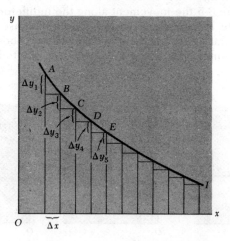

Figure 3-5 Convexity of an indifference curve

[4] We use Δy_i as the shorthand notation for $\Delta y_1, \Delta y_2, \ldots, \Delta y_n$.

the loss of one unit of x. *The negative of the slope of an indifference curve is called the marginal rate of substitution*, MRS. That is,

$$\text{MRS} = -\Delta y / \Delta x$$

Since the substitution involved is between x and y, some economists talk of the marginal rate of substitution of y for x, while others refer to that of x for y. It really is immaterial whether the verbal definition is in terms of substituting y for x or the other way around. The slope of an indifference curve at a point (or a given interval) is the same for movements in either direction.

The absolute slope of an indifference curve declines (increases) as we move along it to the right (to the left). Thus, we may speak of a principle of either decreasing or increasing marginal rate of substitution, and both terminolgoies have been used. "It is probably better," as Stigler suggests, "to avoid either terminology and simply to describe this normal situation as one of convex indifference curves."[5]

When two goods are completely interchangeable, they are perfect substitutes. For example, the consumer is always willing to exchange one ten-dollar bill for two five-dollar bills. The indifference curve for perfect substitutes is a straight line, along which the marginal rate of substitution is constant. The indifference map for perfect substitutes is composed of negatively sloped straight lines, as shown in Figure 3-6.

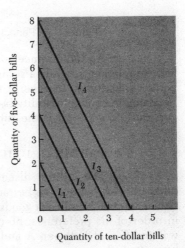

Figure 3-6 Perfect substitutes

[5]*The Theory of Price*, rev. ed. (New York: Macmillan Company, 1952), p. 73.

When two goods must be used together in a fixed proportion as in the case of right and left shoes, they are said to be perfect complements. As shown in Figure 3-7, an indifference curve for perfect complements is given by line segments having 90° angles in them. In order for the consumer to move from I_1 to I_2 in Figure 3-7, he must obtain one more left shoe and one more right shoe. If he were to receive two or more right shoes and no more left shoes, he would still remain on I_1. The 90° angles in the indifference curves indicate that an increase in only one of the perfect complements does not increase the consumer's utility.

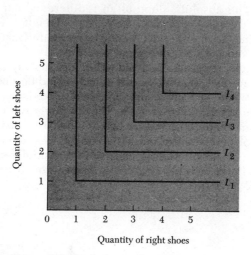

Figure 3-7   Perfect complements

An indifference curve with a 90° angle in it depicts perfect complements, while a straight line indifference curve represents perfect substitutes. In general, the curvature of an indifference curve indicates the substitutability between the two goods: the greater the curvature, the poorer is the substitutability between the two goods.

3-4 CARDINAL UTILITY: A DIGRESSION

The utilities discussed in the previous sections are ordinal utilities, which can be ranked such as first, second, and third. Given any two bundles of goods, the consumer was able to rank them in order of his preference: he either preferred A to B, or B to A, or was indifferent between A and B. It was not necessary to know by how much the consumer preferred one bundle to the other; nor was it necessary to find the quantitative measurement of the utility associated with any bundle of goods.

Nineteenth-century neoclassical economists (such as W. Stanley Jevons, Léon Walras, Alfred Marshall, and Francis Edgeworth) assumed that the consumer could assign a cardinal measure— which can be counted, such as 10, 15, and 20—of utility to each commodity bundle. Thus, the cardinal utility theorists talked of bundle A having 10 utils, bundle B having 25 utils, and so on. *(A util is the imaginary unit in which cardinal utility was measured.)* They further assumed that the total utility gained by the consumer was simply the sum of the utilities derived from individual commodities.[6] For example, if the consumer gained 50 utils from good x and 10 utils from good y, the total utility secured by him was said to be 60 utils.

An important tool of economic analysis introduced by cardinal utility theorists is the concept of marginal utility. *The marginal utility of a good (to a consumer when he has q units of it) is the additional utility gained by consuming one more unit of the good.* Thus,

$$MU(q) = \frac{\Delta TU(q)}{\Delta q}$$

where MU, TU, and q show the marginal utility, total utility, and the quantity of a good. The Δ sign represents a small change in the variable involved.[7] In other words, MU is the *rate of change* in TU.

The marginal utility of a good is a function of the amount of the good already possessed, and it is quite plausible that the smaller (larger) is the quantity on hand, the larger (smaller) is the additional utility gained from another unit of the same good. Thus, the marginal utility theorists argue, largely on introspective grounds, that the marginal utility of a good declines *eventually*. This is the well-known *law of diminishing marginal utility*.

The law of diminishing marginal utility merely states that, as more of a good is consumed, the marginal utility of the good will eventually decline. Therefore, the law is consistent with a constant or even an increasing marginal utility in an early stage. If a person enjoys his second glass of cocktail just as much as or even more than the first, it is not contrary to the law. It is also possible for

---

[6]Mathematically, such a utility function can be written

$$U = U_1(q_1) + U_2(q_2) + \ldots + U_n(q_n)$$

where $U_i(q_i)$ is the utility gained from q_i units of ith good. Total utility is the sum of individual utilities.

[7]When the quantity can be continuously changed,

$$MU(q) = dU(q)/dq$$

Thus, marginal utility is simply the rate of change in total utility with respect to the quantity of good x.

the marginal utility of a good to become negative, as in the case of excessive eating or drinking.

THE RELATIONSHIP BETWEEN TOTAL
AND MARGINAL UTILITIES

The graphic relationship between total and marginal utilities is shown in Figure 3-8. The height of each column in Figure 3-8a shows the total utility obtained by a consumer when he acquires the number of units indicated at the bottom of each column. The white blocks show marginal utilities, and are reproduced in Figure 3-8b. The smooth curves shown represent the continuous case—in which the amount consumed can increase in small units.

Some important quantitative relationships between the total and marginal utilities can be observed from Figure 3-8. First, the *marginal utility curve is the slope* (or *rate of change*) of the total

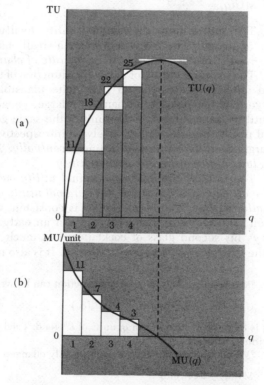

Figure 3-8 Total and marginal utilities; (a) total utility, (b) marginal utility

utility curve; this follows from the fact that MU shows $\Delta TU(q)/\Delta q$, the rate of change in TU. Observe that MU is positive as long as TU is increasing. When TU reaches its peak, where its slope is zero, MU is zero. When TU is declining, MU is negative.

Second, examine the difference between the total utility of 4 units, TU(4), and that of 1 unit, TU(1). As consumption is increased from 1 to 4 units, TU increases by 14 units (from 11 to 25). This *change in TU is* precisely *equal to the sum of the marginal utilities* of three additional units consumed, MU(2), MU(3), and MU(4). That is,

$$TU_{14} = MU(2) + MU(3) + MU(4) = 7 + 4 + 3 = 14$$

where the subscripts to TU, 1 and 4, show that consumption has increased from 1 to 4 units.[8] (The subscripts are read one, four, not fourteen). The continuous counterpart of the TU-MU relationship shows that the change in total utility is equal to the area under the marginal utility curve.[9]

3-5 THE BUDGET LINE

Consumer choices are made subject to budget constraints. Let us, therefore, see how the budget constraint can be introduced into our model. Assume that the prices of two goods x and y are given by the market, and that the amount of money income at the consumer's disposal is, for the time being, fixed. Then, the combinations of x and y that the consumer can purchase with his income are given by

$$xp_x + yp_y \leq M$$

where x and y are quantities of two goods, p_x and p_y are prices of the two goods, and M is the amount of money at the disposal of the consumer. This inequality merely states that the amount of money spent

---

[8]The above relationships between total and marginal utilities hold also for other quantities such as revenue, output, and variable cost. (Since fixed cost does not vary with output, the sum of marginal costs gives the total variable cost—that portion of the total cost which changes with output).

[9]By the definition of a marginal quantity, $M(x) = T'(x)$. Thus, the area under a marginal curve from a to b is

$$\int_a^b M(x)\, dx = T(x) \Big|_a^b$$

The right-hand member of the above equation shows the change in the value of the total function as quantity is increased from a to b.

on x plus the amount spent on y must be within the consumer's income. By rearranging the above equation we get

$$y \leqslant \frac{M}{p_y} - \frac{p_x}{p_y} x$$

The graphic representation of this inequality coupled with the assumption that economic quantities must be nonnegative (that is, $x, y \geqslant 0$) gives us Figure 3-9. *The white area in the figure shows the set of points in the commodity space that the consumer can afford, and is called the budget space or the budget set.*

Now consider the equation form of the above inequality

$$y = \frac{M}{p_y} - \frac{p_x}{p_y} x$$

This equation is the budget equation and its graphic representation is called the budget line. It is the northeast boundary line of the budget space, and *shows the locus of all combinations of x and y that can be purchased when the entire income is spent.* Because the consumer's goal is (by assumption) to maximize utility within his means, and because he can always reach a more preferable position by moving toward the budget line, he always chooses a combination that is on the budget line itself. Thus, the only relevant portion of the budget space is its northeast borderline; the consumer never settles for an interior point such as K in the budget space of Figure 3-9.

Note that the y-intercept of the budget line is given by M/p_y, which indicates the quantity of y that can be purchased if the consumer spends all his income on y only. Similarly, the x-intercept, M/p_x, shows the quantity of x that can be purchased if the entire

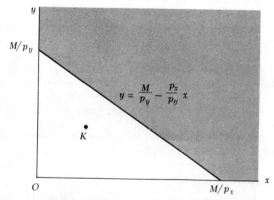

Figure 3-9   Budget space and budget line

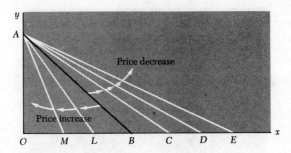

Figure 3-10   Changes in the price of *x*

budget is devoted to purchase *x* alone. The slope of the budget line
is $-p_x/p_y$, the negative inverse of the ratio of the prices of *y* and *x*.

3-6 SHIFTING THE BUDGET LINE

Changes in prices or money income shift the budget line.
First, let us assume that money income and the price of *y* remain
constant and examine the effect of *changes in the price of x*. In Figure
3-10, let the original price of *x* be represented by the budget line *AB*.
As the price of *x* is lowered successively, the budget line shifts from
AB to *AC*, *AD*, and *AE*. Similarly the budget lines *AL* and *AM* show
higher prices of *x*. Thus, changes in the price of *x*, while money income and the price of *y* are being held constant, are shown by *pivoting
the budget line* around point *A* on the *y* axis. At the risk of being
redundant, two easy explanations can be given. First, note that the
x-intercept of a budget line shows the quantity of *x* the consumer
can buy when he spends his total income on *x* only. The successively
longer *x*-intercept *OM*, *OL*, *OB*, etc., and corresponding budget lines
AM, *AL*, *AB*, etc., can be attained only if the price of *x* is consecutively
getting lower. Second, the absolute slope of the budget line is p_x/p_y.
As the budget line flattens (pivots counterclockwise), the numerical
value of its slope is getting smaller. Since the price of *y* is being held
constant, the price of *x* must be getting lower.

Let us now hold the relative price ratio of *x* and *y* constant[10] but relax the assumption of a given income and examine the
effect of *changes in real income*, or purchasing power, on the budget
line. The real income can be increased (1) by increasing the money
income and/or (2) by lowering prices of *x* and *y* proportionately (so
that the relative price ratio will not be disturbed). As shown in Figure

[10]In order to hold the price ratio, $-p_x/p_y$, constant, both p_x
and p_y must remain the same or change in equal proportions.

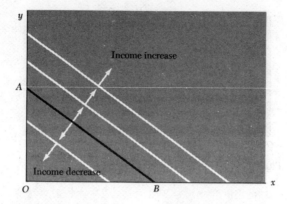

Figure 3-11 Changes in income (or proportionate changes in the prices of x and y)

3-11, changes in real income *shift the budget line parallel to itself.* Since the relative price ratio $(-p_x/p_y)$ does not change, the slope of the budget line, of necessity, remains the same. Clearly, increases in income shift the budget line upward and to the right, whereas decreases in income shift the line downward and to the left. This is also obvious from the budget equation,

$$y = \frac{M}{p_y} - \frac{p_x}{p_y}x$$

Changes in income merely affect the first term, and cause the y-intercept of the line to be higher or lower. Thus, the budget line moves parallel to the original line as income changes.

To sum up, when the prices of goods are given, the budget line is a straight line and its slope is $-p_x/p_y$. Changes in the price of x (while income and the price of y remain the same) are shown by pivoting the budget line around its y-intercept. Changes in income, on the other hand, are reflected in parallel shifts of the budget line.

3-7 CONSUMER CHOICE WITH A BUDGET CONSTRAINT

We are now in a position to combine the consumer's preference (given by his indifference map) and the information on his income and prices of goods (given by the budget line), and to examine how the consumer chooses the commodity bundle that maximizes his utility. The postulates of consumer behavior tell us that the consumer attempts to maximize his satisfaction. We also know that an indifference curve that lies to the right and above is preferred to any to its left. Thus, the consumer's task is to select from all combinations of goods within his means the one that lies on the highest indifference curve. Consider Figure 3-12. The consumer chooses combination E. Combination L is preferred to E but is beyond his budget limitation. Combinations J and K are on the budget line, but are inferior to combination E, because they are on a lower indifference curve. Combinations such as M and N can be immediately ruled out because we have already established that no interior point in the budget space will be chosen by the consumer. From the properties of the indifference curves, we know that there are an infinite number of indifference curves that could have been shown on the graph. But any indifference curve to the right of I_3 is beyond the reach of the consumer's budget, and any to the left of I_3 is less preferable than I_3. Thus, the combination E given by the *tangency* of indifference curve I_3 and the budget line is the best commodity bundle the consumer can purchase.

At the point of tangency, the slopes of the indifference curve and the budget line are equal. Thus,

$$\frac{\Delta y}{\Delta x} = \frac{-p_x}{p_y}$$

Since marginal rate of substitution MRS between x and y is defined as the negative of $\Delta y/\Delta x$, we multiply the above equation by -1 and obtain

$$\text{MRS} = \frac{-\Delta y}{\Delta x} = \frac{p_x}{p_y}$$

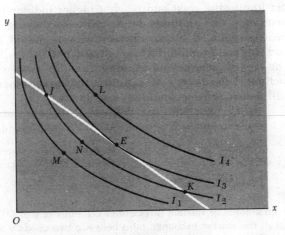

Figure 3-12   Optimal consumer choice

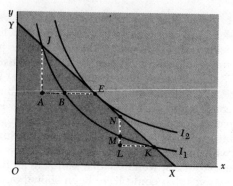

Figure 3-13 Equilibrium condition: MRS = p_x/p_y

In equilibrium, *the marginal rate of substitution must equal the ratio of prices.* The MRS can be interpreted as showing the rate at which the consumer is willing to exchange the two goods, while p_x/p_y shows the ratio at which the consumer is able to exchange the two goods in the market. If the two ratios were not the same, the consumer could better himself by moving to a new point on the budget line. For instance, consider Figure 3-13. Points J and B are on the same indifference curve. Thus, if the consumer were at point J and could get AB units of x in exchange for AJ units of y, he would be equally well off. But in the market he can exchange AJ of y for AE ($= AB + BE$) of x.[11] The consumer will, therefore, take advantage of this exchange opportunity available in the market and move along the budget line to the right and reach a higher indifference curve. This adjustment will continue for a utility-maximizing consumer until he reaches point E. For an entirely analogous reason, if the consumer were at point K he could move leftward until he finally reached E. Once he is at E, any movement away from the point will reduce his satisfaction. Thus, there is no incentive for the consumer to move, and the utility-maximizing condition is attained.

In Chapter One, we defined a situation, state, or configuration to be efficient or Pareto optimal if it is not possible to make

[11]From Figure 3-13, it can be seen that the numerical value of the slope of the budget line is equal to the ratio OY/OX. That is,

$$\frac{p_x}{p_y} = \frac{OY \text{ units of } y}{OX \text{ units of } x}$$

Since a given amount of income buys either OY units of y or OX units of x in the market, the market exchange ratio between two goods y and x must be given by $OY/OX = AJ/AE$.

someone better off without making someone else worse off. In the context of an individual consumer's consumption decision, a situation is efficient if it is impossible to make the consumer better off by reallocating his income among various goods or services. The solution *E* in Figure 3-12 is efficient because the consumer cannot make himself any better off given the budget constraint and his preference. But solutions such as points *J* and *K* are inefficient because he can make himself better off (without making anyone else worse off) by reallocating his income between *x* and *y*. For instance, by moving from point *J* to point *E*, the consumer moves to a higher indifference curve. But no one else is made worse off because they are trading at the market rate of exchange — the ratio at which people are engaging in voluntary exchanges.

Now consider the movement from *A* to *B* in Figure 3-14. The consumption of *x* increases by Δx and the resulting gain in utility is given by

$$(\text{marginal utility of } x)(\Delta x) = \text{MU}_x \cdot \Delta x$$

Similarly, the reduction in utility due to the loss of Δy of *y* is equal to $\text{MU}_y \cdot \Delta y$. Since the total change in utility along an indifference curve is zero by definition, we have

$$\text{MU}_x \cdot \Delta x + \text{MU}_y \cdot \Delta y = 0$$

which yields

$$\frac{-\Delta y}{\Delta x} = \frac{\text{MU}_x}{\text{MU}_y}$$

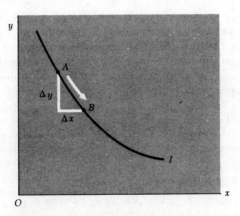

Figure 3-14 $\text{MRS} = -p_x p_y$

Thus, the marginal rate of substitution can be interpreted as the ratio of the marginal utilities of two goods x and y.[12] Combining this with the equation, $-\Delta y/\Delta x = p_x/p_y$, we have

$$\frac{p_x}{p_y} = \frac{MU_x}{MU_y}$$

or

$$\frac{MU_x}{p_x} = \frac{MU_y}{p_y}$$

The first equation says that when the consumer is maximizing his utility, the ratio of the marginal utilities of two goods x and y must be equal to the ratio of their market prices. The second equation states that in order to maximize his satisfaction the consumer must allocate his income between the two commodities in such a way as to *equalize the marginal utilities per dollar of expenditures on each good*. These are the conclusions that are usually derived by the cardinal utility analysis. But we have obtained the conclusion without assuming the cardinal measure of utility. (Appendix 3B shows that the above equilibrium condition can be derived by the mathematical technique known as the method of the Lagrange multiplier.)

3-8 CONVEXITY OF INDIFFERENCE CURVES

In order to see why indifference curves must be convex to the origin, let us examine what would happen if they were not, that is, if they were straight lines or curves concave to the origin.

In Figure 3-15, let the white line, LM, represent the budget line and the black straight lines, I_1, I_2, and I_3, be the indifference curves. In Figure 3-15a, the highest indifference curve that can be reached by the consumer is I_3. In order to do so the consumer must confine his purchase to good x only; he purchases M units of x and none of y. In Figure 3-15b, the consumer maximizes his utility by purchasing good y only; he buys L units of y on indifference curve I_2 and none of x. It is apparent that the optimal solution would be given by a corner solution (not by a tangency solution) if the indiffer-

---

[12]Let the utility function be given by $U = U(x,y)$. Then, an indifference curve — along which the utility remains constant — is shown by $U(x,y) = c$, where c is a constant. Taking total differentials of this equation, we get

$$U_x dx + U_y dy = 0$$

From this we readily obtain the expression for MRS in the continuous case:

$$\frac{-dy}{dx} = \frac{U_x}{U_y}$$

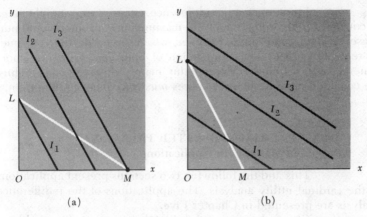

Figure 3-15 Straight-line indifference curves and the corner solutions:
(a) selection of x only, (b) selection of y only

ence curves were straight lines, and that the combination chosen
would contain only one of the goods (not both goods as in the case
of tangency solutions).

What would happen if indifference curves were concave
(rather than convex) to the origin as shown in Figures 3-16a and b?
Given the indifference curves and the budget lines shown, the optimal
solutions would again be corner solutions. In Figure 3-16a, the consumer would buy only good y, while he would purchase only good
x in Figure 3-16b. (If the tangency solution were selected in Figure
3-16b, it would have produced the utility-minimizing, not maximizing, solution.)

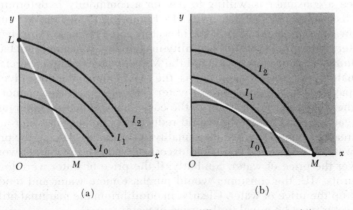

Figure 3-16 Concave-to-the-origin indifference curves and the corner solutions; (a) selection of y only, (b) selection of x only

In summary, if indifference curves were straight lines or concave to the origin, the utility-maximizing consumer would purchase a single good only. However, we observe that the consumer in real life purchases a combination of both goods (or, in a more general case, a bundle that contains many different goods.) Thus, we conclude that indifference curves *must be convex* to the origin.

3-9 THE DIAMOND-WATER PARADOX OF VALUE: An Application

This and the following two sections present applications of the cardinal utility analysis. The applications of the indifference analysis are presented in Chapter Five.

Classical economists knew that a commodity could not command value (price) unless there was some utility in it. But they were troubled with their inability to establish some clear-cut relationship between the utility of a good and its price. For instance, Adam Smith wrote about his famous diamond-water paradox in *The Wealth of Nations*. Nothing is more useful than water, according to Smith, but its price scarcely amounts to anything. On the other hand, a diamond has scarcely any value in use, but commands a high price. Unable to explain this paradox, classical economists simply distinguished the value in use of a commodity from its value in exchange and asserted that there is little relation between them.

Smith could not solve the paradox because the concept of marginal utility and the tools of demand and supply were not known to him. Today, we can solve the paradox immediately with the aid of the tool of marginal utility. A man cannot live without water, and the total utility of water to any man is very high. However, the price a consumer is willing to pay for a commodity is determined by its *marginal*, not total utility. In Figure 3-17, let the MU curve show the marginal utility, MU, of water, and PP' curve the price of water (in terms of utility). The utility-maximizing consumer purchases Q units of water per period, and the MU of water to him is precisely equal to the price of water; that is, the MU of money he must give up to pay for the marginal unit of water. The price of water cannot be higher than the MU of water to the consumer. If it were higher (as at Q' gallons per period), he would reduce his purchase of water until he reaches point E, where the equality between the MU and the price of water is restored. The unsold excess of water in the market would lower the price of water. Similarly, if the price of water were lower than its MU, the consumer would purchase more water and tend to bid up the price of water. Clearly, in equilibrium the marginal utility of water must be equal to the price of water.

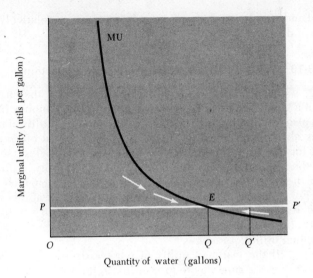

Figure 3-17　MU = price: the equilibrium condition

Now, water is relatively plentiful in many places, and consumers use it in large quantities. Whenever the consumer uses a large quantity of a commodity, its marginal utility declines due to the law of diminishing marginal utility. Water is very useful to the consumer, but its marginal utility is low because he consumes so much of it. Since the marginal utility of water is low, the price at which the market supply of water will clear the market has to be low.

Unlike water, diamonds are not essential to life. They may not be so useful and be of doubtful aesthetic value. However, most consumers possess few diamonds, and the marginal utilities of diamonds are high to them; accordingly, they are willing to pay high prices for diamonds (even though the total utilities of diamonds are much lower than that of water).

True, the market price is determined not only by demand — behind which lie the marginal utilities of individual consumers — but also by supply — behind which lies the cost of production. *The marginal cost — the additional cost of producing another unit of output —* of water is low because additional amounts of water can be produced relatively easily. Thus, the demand and supply curves of water — behind which lie the low marginal utilities of consumers and the low marginal cost of producers — intersect where the market price is low and the market volume is large. Diamonds, on the other hand, are rather scarce and their marginal costs are high. Therefore, the demand and supply curves for diamonds intersect at a relatively small volume and a high price.

3-10 WHY AVOID GAMBLING?: An Application

Neoclassical economists postulated that the marginal utility of a good declines. Does the marginal utility of money income decline also? While the proposition that the marginal utility of money declines also seems sensible, there is no firm logical or empirical support for the proposition. Many economists, nevertheless, seem to accept the hypothesis of diminishing marginal utility of income (though there is less agreement regarding the rate at which it declines). For instance, the popular interpretation that the ability-to-pay doctrine requires *progressive taxation—in which the tax rate increases as income increases—*is based on the assumption of diminishing marginal utility of income.[13]

If the marginal utility of income declines, as assumed, then gambling is a sure way to lose utility in the long run. In Figure 3-18, let the downward-sloping curve represent the marginal utility of income. Suppose that the individual possesses M and is contemplating a gambling activity that offers an even chance of winning or losing $100. Then, his expected gain in utility is shown by the white area, and his expected loss in utility by the crosshatched

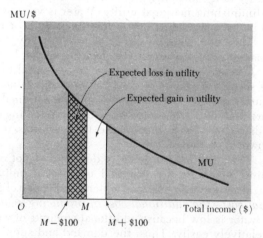

Figure 3-18 Gambling and the loss of utility

[13]Richard Musgrave, *The Theory of Public Finance* (New York: McGraw-Hill, 1959), pp. 98–105.

area. Since the expected gain is smaller than the expected loss in utility, a utility-maximizing consumer will never gamble at "fair" or even odds. He will not gamble $100 for a 1 percent chance of winning $10,000 but will spend $100 to insure against a 1 percent probability of losing $10,000.

Most students refuse to gamble $500, even if the odds given are quite favorable to them. Why? The utility of winning may be simply to have a few grand parties, etc., but the disutility of loss may be much greater, such as having to quit school.

3-11 CHOICES INVOLVING RISKS: INSURANCE AND GAMBLING: An Application[14]

We have seen in the previous section that if the marginal utility of money declines, a utility-maximizing individual will never gamble. This statement, however, is contradicted by a commonly observed phenomenon: individuals do gamble. Neoclassical economists such as Jevons and Marshall circumvented this difficulty by asserting that gambling must be explained not as a utility-maximizing act, but as an act due to the "love of gambling." In recent years, however, economists started to question the hypothesis of diminishing marginal utility of money. Even if the marginal utility of each and every commodity that money can purchase declined, it does not necessarily follow that the marginal utility of money income declines. With the abandonment of the hypothesis of the diminishing marginal utility of money, the Marshallian taboo against the utility analysis of gambling was also lifted. Economists have realized that it is possible to rationalize insurance and gambling by utility analysis if a special form of utility function (or curve) of money income is postulated. Two such hypotheses are explained below.

THE FRIEDMAN-SAVAGE HYPOTHESIS

Friedman and Savage have explained the existence of insurance and lotteries by assuming (1) that the total-utility-of-money curve for each individual is shaped like the one at the top of Figure 3-19 and (2) that the individual attempts to maximize his cardinal utility.[15] The marginal utility curve consistent with the Friedman-Savage total utility curve is shown at the bottom of Figure 3-19. Note that the total utility curve has, from the left to right, three

---

[14]Materials in this section are somewhat more difficult, and can be omitted without loss of continuity.

[15]Milton Friedman and L. J. Savage, "The Utility Analysis of Choices Involving Risk," *The Journal of Political Economy*, August 1948, pp. 279–304. Reprinted in *Readings in Price Theory* (Homewood, Ill.: Irwin, 1952), pp. 57–96.

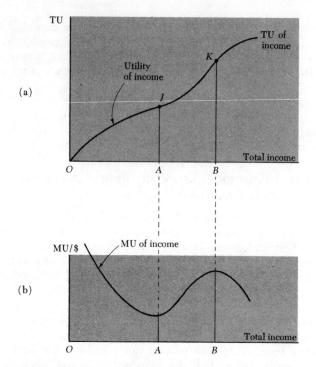

Figure 3-19 Friedman-Savage hypothesis; (a) total utility,
(b) marginal utility

segments that are first concave downward, then concave upward, and again concave downward. Points *J* and *K*, at which the curve changes from being concave downward to concave upward, or vice versa, are called *inflection points.* Accordingly, the marginal utility curve first diminishes, then increases, and diminishes again. Friedman and Savage believe that the three segments of the curve more or less represent the utility functions of the socioeconomic groupings; the poor, the middle-income group, and the rich. Referring to this total utility curve (the reader may find its corresponding marginal curve easier), Friedman and Savage explain the behavior of different income groups in buying insurance and lottery tickets as follows. A poor man whose marginal utility of income declines will be willing to buy a fair (or slightly unfair) insurance against any kind of risk; he will be averse to small fair gambles; he will, however, be attracted by fair gambles that offer a small chance of a large gain. A middle-income consumer will be attracted by a fair gamble; he is averse to insuring against small losses, but he may be attracted by insurance against relatively large losses. A high-income consumer may be willing to insure against small losses but will be averse to insuring against rather large losses; he will be averse to gambles of the lottery variety, but may be attracted to gambles that offer reasonably sure, though fairly small, gains with a small probability of sizable losses.

Thus, the Friedman-Savage hypothesis explains why an individual may simultaneously buy risk (gamble) and also buy certainty (insurance).

THE MARKOWITZ HYPOTHESIS

Harry Markowitz considers the Friedman-Savage hypothesis as one of the major contributions to the theory of consumer behavior involving risk, but finds that it contradicts common observations in major respects.[16] For instance, does not the claim that a rather poor or a rather rich person (one with income less than A or more than B in Figure 3-19) will be averse to a fair gamble sound peculiar? Do not poor people, as much as others, buy sweepstakes tickets and play horses? Do not rich people play roulette and the stock market? Markowitz shows that we can avoid these embarrassing contradictions and explains the symbiosis of insurance and gambling by postulating a slightly different form of a total utility curve.

Markowitz's total utility curve, reproduced in Figure 3-20a, has three inflection points. The marginal utility curve consistent with Markowitz's total utility curve is shown in the bottom section, Figure 3-20b. Now, according to Markowitz, the middle inflection point, O, is the present or customary level of income. The curve is concave upward immediately above present income; concave downward immediately below. The first inflection point, F, is located substantially below the customary income level, and the third inflection point, T, substantially above the customary income. The middle inflection point, O, shows the present level of income for *all* income groups. The distance between the first and third inflection points will be farther for the rich and closer for the poor.

An examination of Figure 3-20 — either the total utility curve or its marginal counterpart — shows that Markowitz's hypothesis is consistent with the existence of fair (or slightly unfair) insurance and fair (or slightly unfair) lotteries. The same individual will buy insurance and lottery tickets. He will take a large chance of a small loss (insurance premium or price of lottery tickets) for a small chance of a large gain (insurance payoff or lottery prize). The hypothesis implies that an individual will behave essentially the same way

[16]"The Utility of Wealth," *The Journal of Political Economy*, April 1952, pp. 151–158.

whether he is rich or poor, except the meaning of "large" and "small" will be different. Thus, the Markowitz hypothesis explains the simultaneous existence of insurance and gambling within the framework of the utility analysis without introducing the contradictions to which the Friedman-Savage hypothesis was subject.

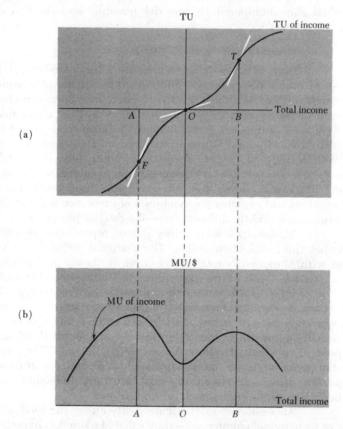

Figure 3-20 Markowitz hypothesis; (a) total utility, (b) marginal utility

APPENDIX 3

A. Utility Surface
and Indifference Curves

An indifference curve, it may be recalled, shows three things: the quantity of good x, the quantity of good y, and an index of utility. Indifference curves, indeed, are a two-dimensional representation of the three-dimensional utility surface. The purpose of this appendix is to show how indifference curves are derived from the utility surface.

A utility surface is shown in Figure 3-21. The quantities of goods x and y are shown along the x and y axes. The vertical axis

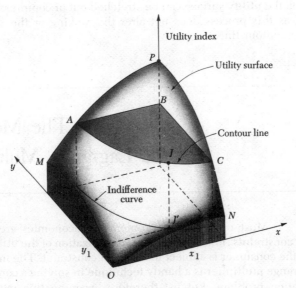

Figure 3-21 Utility surface

shows an *ordinal measure* (or index) of utility. Unlike the quantities along x and y axes, which can be cardinally measured, quantities along the vertical axis can only be ranked. We can say a point on the surface is higher, equal to, or lower than some other point on the surface. The amount of difference in utility between any two collections of goods, however, cannot be measured. Any point on the utility surface, *OMAPCN*, shows the quantities of x and y, and an ordinal measure of utility associated with this collection. For example, point J on the utility surface represents the collection of goods that contains x_1 units of x and y_1 units of y, and its utility index is given by the height, $J'J$, of the point. By slicing the utility surface parallel to the x-y plane at the height of point J, the contour line AJC is obtained. This contour line contains all combinations of two goods x and y that are equally satisfactory to the consumer as combination J. By projecting this contour line onto the x-y plane below, we secure an indifference curve – the locus of all combinations of x and y that yield a given level of satisfaction.

If the utility surface is sliced at many different altitudes, many contour lines are obtained. By projecting these contour lines onto the x-y plane, we acquire a set of indifference curves, that is, an indifference map. An indifference map avoids the cumbersomeness of dealing with a three-dimensional figure, and yet conveys all the relevant information contained in the utility surface.

Since the height of the utility surface has no cardinal meaning, the utility surface can be stretched out or compressed down as long as this process does not alter the ranking or the shapes of different contour lines.

B. The Method of the Lagrange Multiplier

Most optimization problems in economics are subject to some constraints. For instance, the maximization of the utility function by the consumer is subject to a budget constraint. The method of the Lagrange multiplier is a handy technique in solving a constrained optimization problem. Let us, therefore, examine this method by referring to the consumer maximizing his utility subject to a budget constraint.

The problem is to maximize the consumer's utility function subject to his budget constraint, that is,

Maximize $U(x,y)$

subject to $xp_x + yp_y = M$

In order to solve this problem by the method of the Lagrange multiplier, we form the Lagrangian function:

$$L(x,y,\lambda) = U(x,y) - \lambda(xp_x + yp_y - M) \qquad (3\text{-}1)$$

Note that the Lagrangian function is obtained by merely adding another term to the utility function. What is this additional term? What does this additional term do to the newly formed function? The additional term is obtained by multiplying the budget constraint by an artificial unknown λ (the Greek letter lambda), which is called *a Lagrange multiplier*. By taking the budget constraint, $xp_x + yp_y = M$, and bringing all the terms over to the left side, we obtain the expression in the parentheses, $xp_x + yp_y - M = 0$. If the budget constraint is satisfied (that is, if $xp_x + yp_y - M = 0$), the last term in (3-1) equals zero regardless of the value of the unknown; the value of the Lagrangian expression L will become identical to that of the utility function U. Whatever values of x and y that maximize L will automatically maximize U.

Now we treat λ merely as an additional variable and differentiate partially the Lagrangian function with respect to each of the three unknowns, x, y, and λ, and set the resulting partial derivatives equal to zero. For notational simplicity, let us use L_x, L_y, U_λ, etc. to denote $\partial L/\partial x$, $\partial L/\partial y$, $\partial U/\partial \lambda$, etc. Then,

$$L_x = U_x - \lambda p_x = 0$$
$$L_y = U_y - \lambda p_y = 0$$
$$L_\lambda = -xp_x - yp_y + M = 0 \qquad (3\text{-}2)$$

By multiplying the last equation by -1, we obtain $xp_x + yp_y = M$. Therefore, the last equation automatically guarantees that the budget constraint is satisfied. Since the constraint is satisfied, we have $L = U$ and the solution to the Lagrangian function also necessarily solves the original utility function. Note that, by incorporating the (budget) constraint in the Lagrangian function L and treating λ as an additional variable, we have solved the constrained maximization problem simply by checking the critical values of the Lagrangian function L.

Solving the first two equations of (3-2) for λ we get

$$\lambda = \frac{U_x}{p_x} \text{ and}$$

$$\lambda = \frac{U_y}{p_y}$$

Equating the right hand members of the above two equations, we have:

$$\frac{U_x}{p_x} = \frac{U_y}{p_y} \tag{3-3}$$

This is precisely the equilibrium condition given in section 3-7. If there are n commodities,

$$\lambda = \frac{U_1}{p_1} = \frac{U_2}{p_2} = \ldots = \frac{U_n}{p_n}$$

Since λ shows the marginal utility per dollar spent on any of the n commodities, λ can be interpreted as showing the marginal utility of income itself.

EXERCISES 3

Theory
of Consumer Behavior

3-1 Assume that the utility function of an individual is given by

$$U(x,y) = xy^2$$

1. Construct an indifference schedule by determining the combinations of x and y that yield 100 utils for the integer values of $x = 1, \ldots, 5$.
2. Construct another indifference schedule that yields the level of satisfaction of 50 utils.
3. From the above two schedules, plot the two indifference curves on graph paper, and label them I_{100} and I_{50}, respectively.

3-2 Examine Figure 3-22, which gives the budget line AB of a consumer who has \$300, and answer the questions below.

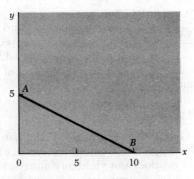

Figure 3-22

1. The algebraic expression for the above budget line is: _____
2. The price of x is $\$$_____per unit.
3. The price of y is $\$$_____per unit.
4. The slope of the budget line is _____.
5. The budget space is given by area _____.

3-3 Line A in Figure 3-23 shows the original budget line for Mr. Jones. Indicate the budget line that best describes the following changes in price(s) and/or income.

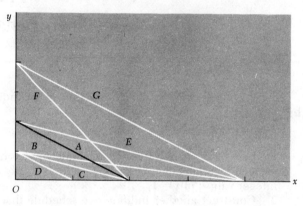

Figure 3-23

1. _____ The price of x, p_x, is reduced by 50 percent while the price of y, p_y, is held constant.
2. _____ p_y increases by 100 percent while p_x remains the same.
3. _____ p_y increases by 100 percent while p_x is reduced by 50 percent.
4. _____ Mr. Jones' budget for x and y is doubled.
5. _____ p_x and p_y are both increased by 100 percent.
6. _____ p_x and p_y are both reduced by 50 percent.
7. _____ p_y is reduced by 50 percent while p_x remains the same.
8. _____ p_x, p_y, and Mr. Jones' income all increase by 50 percent.

3-4 Given the indifference diagram of Figure 3-24, the consumer will not purchase combination J since it costs more than combination E and yet does not yield any more satisfaction. Assume that the cost of purchasing combination E is $100.

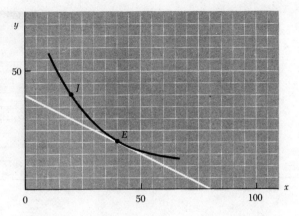

Figure 3-24

1. What are the prices of two goods x and y, respectively?
2. Show the difference in the cost of purchasing combination E and combination J.

3-5 Let a consumer's preference function be described by the following set of indifference curves:

I_1: $x + y = 10$

I_2: $x + y = 15$

I_3: $x + y = 20$

1. Draw the three indifference curves on graph paper.
2. Draw in the consumer's budget line represented by the equation, $2x + y = 20$.
3. Determine how many units of x and y are contained in the equilibrium bundle chosen by the consumer.
4. Suppose the budget line is $x + y = 20$. Discuss what happens to the optimal combination chosen.

3-6 Mr. Owen can buy his brand of gasoline from gas station A or gas station B. He considers the two stations identical in terms of accessibility, service, and gasoline and oil sold. However, the price of gasoline is 65¢ per gallon at station A and 60¢ per gallon at station B. Draw an appropriate budget line and indifference curves and show that Mr. Owen will purchase all his gasoline from station B.

3-7 Suppose a certain consumer's utilities, derived from the consumption of three goods, x, y, and z, are given by the following schedule:

NUMBER OF UNITS	TOTAL UTILITY			MARGINAL UTILITY			MU PER DOLLAR		
	x	y	z	x	y	z	x	y	z
0	0	0	0	—	—	—	—	—	—
1	27	30	12	—	—	—	—	—	—
2	45	50	22	—	—	—	—	—	—
3	60	62	30	—	—	—	—	—	—
4	72	70	36	—	—	—	—	—	—
5	81	72	40	—	—	—	—	—	—
6	87	72	43	—	—	—	—	—	—
7	90	72	45						

1. Assume that the prices of x, y, and z are \$3, \$2, and \$1, respectively, and complete the above table.

2. If the consumer has \$25 to spend, what is the utility-maximizing allocation of his income among the three goods?

3. If the consumer has only \$24, how should he allocate his income among the three goods?

3-8 Suppose a student is studying for his final examinations. If his goal is to maximize his average grade, how should he allocate his time among different subjects?

CHAPTER FOUR

THEORY
ONSUMER BEHAVIOR –
CONTINUED

We will now examine the manner in which consumer choices are affected by a change in money income or a change in the price of a good. This chapter will also show how the individual demand curve can be derived from the indifference analysis and examine the manner in which a change in price influences the consumer's purchase in two distinct ways. The last section gives an elementary account of the revealed preference analysis. This chapter has no section devoted to applications because the entire Chapter Five is devoted to the applications of the indifference analysis developed in Chapters Three and Four.

4-1 CONSUMER RESPONSES TO INCOME CHANGES

We are now ready to examine how variations in income and prices affect the consumer's purchases. We will start with the effect of changes in money income. To facilitate our exposition, let us assume that prices of goods x and y are constant. Given this assumption, a change in money income always means a change in real income.

As the income of the consumer increases, the budget line shifts to the right parallel to the original line. Thus; in Figure 4-1, M_1, M_2, M_3, and M_4 show budget lines representing successively larger income. As the income increases, the equilibrium combination chosen by the consumer shifts. At each level of income available,

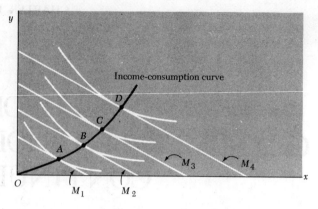

Figure 4-1   Income-consumption curve

the consumer selects the combination that is on the highest indifference curve attainable. The optimal combinations selected by the consumer, given the four different levels of the income constraint, are
shown by points A, B, C, and D. By connecting such points of equilibria, we obtain the income-consumption curve. *Thus, an income-
consumption curve shows the locus of various commodity bundles
purchased by the consumer as his income changes, while the commodity prices remain the same.*

Notice that the income-consumption curve begins at
the origin. This is understandably so: if the consumer had no income,
the quantities of x and y he could command in the market place must
be zero.

From an income-consumption curve an Engel curve for
each commodity can be derived. *An Engel curve describes the relationship between a consumer's income and his expenditure on a
specific good.*[1] Since commodity prices are assumed to remain constant, the quantity of a commodity purchased and the expenditure
for it are proportionally related. Thus, for our purpose, the Engel
curve may be taken as showing the relationship between the consumer's income and the number of units of the commodity purchased.

The income-consumption curve in Figure 4-2a shows
that the purchase of x increases from 10 to 20 to 28 to 32 as the consumer's total income increases from \$10 to \$20 to \$30 to \$40, successively. This information plotted on Figure 4-2b is the Engel curve
for good x. (The reader, on his own, may wish to draw the Engel curve
for good y.)

[1]Sometimes, the income-consumption curve itself is referred
to as an Engel curve.

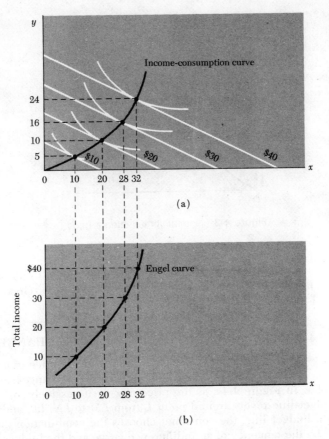

Figure 4-2 Derivation of an Engel curve; (*a*) income-consumption curve, (*b*) Engle curve

If a consumer purchases more (less) of a good as his income increases, the good is said to be a normal good (an inferior good) to the consumer. The slope of a consumer's income-consumption curve (with respect to the *x*-axis) reveals whether *x* is normal or inferior to the consumer. For example, examine Figure 4-3. In the lightly shaded region of the budget space (that is, when the consumer's income is less than $M), the income-consumption curve is positively sloped indicating that an increase in income increases the consumer's purchase of *x*. Thus, *x* is a normal good to the consumer when his income is less than $M per period. In the darkly shaded region of the graph, the income-consumption curve is negatively sloped: the consumer purchases less of *x* as his income increases. Thus, *x* is an inferior good to the consumer when his income exceeds $M per period.

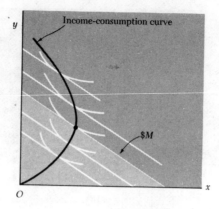

Figure 4-3 Normal versus inferior good

Note that the above statement with regard to the slope applies to the good shown on the horizontal axis only. Good y in Figure 4-3 is a normal good throughout the range shown.

4-2 CONSUMER RESPONSES TO PRICE CHANGES

Now let us hold money income and the price of y constant and examine how the consumer responds to changes in the price of x. In Figure 4-4a, as the price of x is successively lowered, the budget line pivots around point L from LM to LN, LP, and LQ. Given a budget line, the consumer chooses the combination that is shown by the tangency of an indifference curve and the budget line. Combinations A, B, C, and D represent such equilibrium bundles. The locus of all such points of equilibria is called a price-consumption curve. *Thus, a **price-consumption curve for good x** shows how changes in the price of x affect the quantity of x purchased, while the price of y and money income remain the same.*

Note that a reduction in the price of a good (which is purchased by the consumer) makes him better off. In Figure 4-4a, as the price of x is successively lowered, the consumer moves to a higher and higher indifference curve. A reduction in the price of x *(while his money income and the price of y remain unchanged)* widens his budget space and allows him to select combinations that were unattainable before the price reduction.

While the income-consumption curve started from the origin, the price-consumption curve starts at the pivot point L in Figure 4-4a. This is reasonable because as the price of x gets more · expensive (as indicated by the budget line pivoting clockwise), the

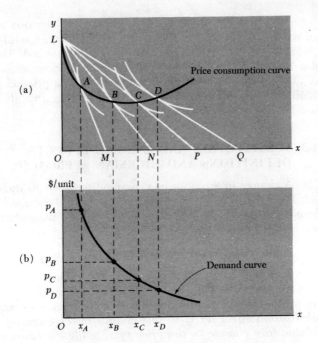

Figure 4-4 Derivation of a demand curve; (*a*) price-consumption curve, (*b*) individual demand curve

consumer would want to buy less and less of the good. Finally, the price of *x* may become so high that the consumer cannot afford and does not wish to buy any *x*; he thus ends up at point *L* spending all his income on *y* and none on *x*.

  The individual consumer's demand curve — which relates price and quantity of a good purchased by a consumer — can be derived from his price-consumption curve. Figure 4-4*b* shows such a demand curve derived from the price-consumption curve of Figure 4-4*a*. From the equilibrium points *A*, *B*, *C*, and *D*, the quantities of *x* that would be purchased, x_A, x_B, x_C, and x_D, can immediately be determined. Since the consumer's money income is fixed and the *x*-intercept of a budget line shows the maximum units of *x* that can be purchased, we can — simply by dividing the total money income by an appropriate horizontal distance — find the price of *x* applicable to each equilibrium quantity purchased. Thus, we can get the ordered pairs of price and quantity $A(x_A, p_A)$, $B(x_B, p_B)$, $C(x_C, p_C)$, and $D(x_D, p_D)$. Plotting these points and connecting them with a freehand curve, we derive the individual consumer's demand curve in Figure 4-4*b*.

Note that the demand curve shows how the quantities purchased would change as the price of the good changes, while the price of other goods and money income remain unchanged. This is the usual definition of the demand curve found in modern economic literature. (The change in quantity demanded when a price change is accompanied by a compensating change in money income will be discussed in the next section.)

4-3 SUBSTITUTION AND INCOME EFFECTS: DEFINITIONS AND HICKSIAN APPROACH

A change in the price of a commodity affects its quantity demanded. *The total effect—the change in quantity demanded that results from a change in the price of a good—can be viewed as the sum of two distinct effects, substitution and income effects.*

SUBSTITUTION AND INCOME EFFECTS

A reduction in the price of x, for example, makes x relatively more attractive than y. This makes the consumer substitute the now less expensive x for the now relatively more expensive y. *The substitution effect refers to this change in the quantity of x purchased due to a change in the price of x, while the consumer's real income is held constant.* (Shortly we will see different ways of holding the consumer's income constant.) The substitution effect of a price reduction (increase) is always to increase (decrease) the quantity demanded.

A reduction in the price of x affects the quantity demanded in still another way, by increasing the real income of the consumer. *The income effect is this change in the quantity of x purchased via a change in real income caused by a change in the price of x.* In order to isolate the income effect, we must hold the relative prices constant. (The method of holding the relative prices constant will be examined shortly.) The income effect of a price reduction will (1) increase the quantity of x purchased if x is a normal good and (2) decrease the quantity of x purchased if x is an inferior good.

In summary, both income and substitution effects refer to changes in the *quantity* of a good demanded initiated by a change in the price of a good. In Figure 4-5, the upper loop shows the substitution effect: the effect of a change in the price of a good on its quantity demanded, with the consumer's real income being constant. The lower loop shows the income effect. It shows how a change in the price of a good leads to a change in the consumer's real income, which in turn affects his quantity demanded. To measure the income effect, we hold the relative price constant.

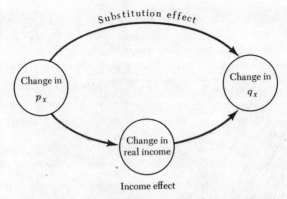

Figure 4-5 Two ways in which a price change affects quantity purchased

The substitution effect of a price reduction always increases the quantity demanded, and the income effect also increases the quantity demanded unless the good is inferior. Typically a consumer spends only a small fraction of his income on any single good, and this makes the income effect rather insignificant. Therefore, even though the commodity involved is an inferior good, the substitution effect generally overshadows the income effect and the law of demand holds. That is, a decrease in the price of x increases the quantity of x demanded. The only exception to the law of demand, Giffen's paradox, will be discussed later.

THE HICKSIAN APPROACH TO MEASUREMENT

Let us now refer to Figure 4-6 and secure a more precise understanding of the income and substitution effects. Let the original equilibrium position of the consumer be at E_1. As the price of x is reduced (as indicated by the shift of the budget line from AL to AM), the consumer moves to E_3. The total effect on the quantity purchased of this price reduction is $x_3 - x_1$. To isolate the substitution effect we must somehow hold the real income of the consumer constant. One way of accomplishing this, following J. R. Hicks, is to take away from the consumer an amount of money income just sufficient to *return him to the indifference curve he was on before* the price decrease. Graphically, this adjustment or "compensation" is accomplished by drawing in an imaginary budget line, $A'M'$, that is tangent to the original indifference curve I_1 and parallel to the new budget line (to reflect the new price ratio). The point of tangency is labeled E_2. Now the movement from E_1 to E_2 can be interpreted as showing the consumer's response to a change in the relative price

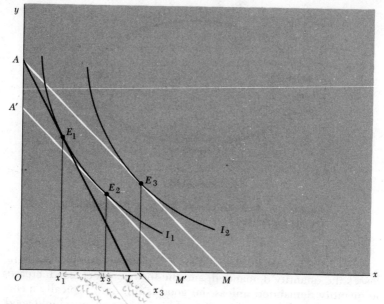

Figure 4-6 Substitution and income effects: Hicksian approach

ratio alone, while his real income is being held constant. The change in quantity demanded, $x_2 - x_1$, due to the movement from E_1 to E_2, is called the *substitution effect*—the change in quantity demanded when a price change is accompanied by a compensating income change.

The movement from E_2 to E_3 and the corresponding change in the quantity demanded, $x_3 - x_2$, show the income effect; the two budget lines at E_2 and E_3 are parallel, and the movement involves a change in real income while the relative prices are being held constant. The *income effect* of a change in the price of a good shows the change in quantity demanded via a change in real income, while the relative price ratio remains constant.

From Figure 4-6, it is clear that the total effect is the sum of the substitution and income effects:

$$x_3 - x_1 = (x_2 - x_1) + (x_3 - x_2)$$

Note that the substitution effect shows a change in quantity demanded due to a *compensated* price change (which makes the consumer move from E_1 to E_2 in Figure 4-6). On the other hand, a movement along the conventional individual demand curve (drawn on the price-quantity plane) shows a change in quantity demanded due to an *uncompensated* price change, that is, the total effect that makes the consumer move from E_1 to E_3 in Figure 4-6. These are the standard usages in modern economic literature.

4-4 SUBSTITUTION AND INCOME EFFECT: SLUTSKY'S METHOD

The Hicksian approach to hold real income constant is to shift the new budget line (parallel to itself) until it is tangent to the indifference curve on which the consumer was located before the price change. Thus, in the Hicksian approach the substitution effect is always measured by a movement along the original indifference curve. There is, however, another way of compensating the consumer for a change in his real income. In Figure 4-7, the consumer has moved from E_1 to E_3 following a reduction in the price of x. To measure the compensated change in quantity demanded, that is, to gauge the substitution effect, we must hold the consumer's real income constant. The needed compensation this time is obtained, following Eugen Slutsky, by allowing the consumer to retain the sum of money needed *if he were to purchase* (despite the change in relative prices of x and y) *the original combination E_1.* Thus, the imaginary budget line drawn in is $A'M'$, which goes through E_1 and is parallel to AM and tangent to I_2—a curve higher than the original curve I_1. Now the income and substitution effects can be read from the graph as before. The movement from E_1 to E_2 and the corresponding change in quantity demanded, $x_2 - x_1$, is the substitution effect, while the income effect is given by the movement from E_2 to E_3 and the corresponding change in quantity demanded, $x_3 - x_2$.

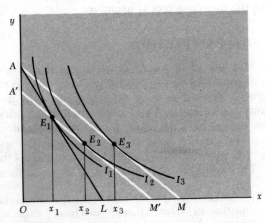

Figure 4-7 Substitution and income effects: Slutsky's method

HICKSIAN VERSUS SLUTSKIAN APPROACHES

Note that Slutsky's method is an attempt to hold the apparent real income constant. It holds the real income constant in the sense that the consumer is left with the income just sufficient to purchase the original combination if he so desires. The consumer's "real" (as opposed to apparent) real income, however, is higher as shown by the location of E_2 on indifference curve I_2 rather than the original I_1. Thus, the Slutskian measure is, in a sense, an approximation of the Hicksian measure and perhaps conceptually less satisfying. But the real advantage of the Slutskian measure is that it can be computed directly from observable phenomena—combination E_1 chosen when the p_x/p_y ratio is at the price ratio OA/OL, E_3 chosen at the price ratio OA/OM, and E_2 chosen when the price ratio is OA/OM and the income is so compensated that the budget line goes through point E_1. The Hicksian measure, on the other hand, cannot be obtained in the absence of the knowledge of the consumer's indifference map. Furthermore, it can be shown that the difference between the Slutsky measure and the Hicks measure is small when the change in price is small, and in the limit the two compensating changes yield an identical result.[2]

INCOME EFFECTS AND NORMAL OR INFERIOR GOOD

Depending on whether the income effect, taken by itself, is positive or negative (that is, whether the quantity purchased increases or decreases as real income increases), a good can be classified as a *normal* or an *inferior good*. For instance, in Figure 4-8, x is a normal good since the income effect $(x_3 - x_2)$ is positive. The increase in real income caused by the reduction in the price of x makes the consumer buy more of x. But in Figure 4-9, x is an inferior good because the income effect is negative.

4-5 GIFFEN'S PARADOX

The law of demand, which states that at lower prices greater quantities would be purchased, is a very general proposition. All normal goods as well as most inferior goods obey the law. The law of demand can be violated and a reduction in the price of a good can be accompanied by a decrease in quantity demanded *if* the income effect of an inferior good (which decreases the quantity demanded) exceeds its substitution effect (which increases the quantity demanded). This unlikely phenomenon is referred to as *Giffen's*

---

[2]For details, see J. L. Mosak, "On the Interpretation of the Fundamental Equation in Value Theory," in Oscar Lange, *et al.* (eds.), *Studies in Mathematical Economics and Econometrics* (Chicago: University of Chicago Press, 1942), pp. 69–74.

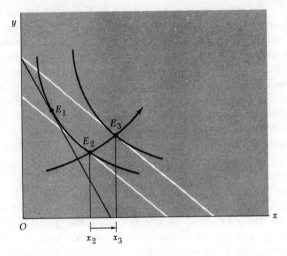

Figure 4-8 Normal good: a positive income effect

paradox. The name comes from the fact that Alfred Marshall attributed the origin of the paradox to Sir Robert Giffen.[3]

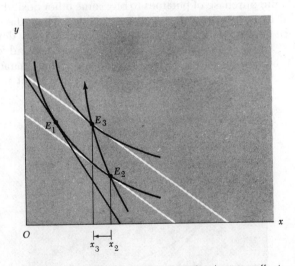

Figure 4-9 Inferior good: a negative income effect

[3]*Principles of Economics,* 8th ed. (New York: Macmillan, 1949), p. 132. No one, however, found the paradox among the voluminous writings of Giffen, and it is believed that Giffen might have stated the paradox orally.

A Giffen case is portrayed in Figure 4-10. As the price of x is lowered the consumer moves from E_1 to E_3 and the quantity of x purchased decreases by one unit. The movement from E_1 to E_3 can be decomposed into two parts: the substitution effect, which increases the quantity of x purchased by 3 units (from 4 to 7), and the income effect, which decreases the quantity purchased by 4 units (from 7 to 3). Since the decrease in quantity demanded due to the income effect is greater than the increase in quantity demanded due to the substitution effect, the total effect of the decrease in the price of x is negative. That is,

$$Total\ effect = Substitution\ effect + Income\ effect$$
$$-1\quad =\quad\quad 3\quad\quad +\quad\quad (-4)$$

Note that a Giffen case exists only if the negative income effect of an inferior good is greater than the substitution effect, which always reveals the inverse relationship between price and quantity demanded. Thus, a Giffen good is an exceptional subset of inferior goods.

For a Giffen case to exist, we must have an inferior commodity on which the consumer spends an important portion of his income. Suppose that poor inhabitants of some underdeveloped country subsist on potatoes. If the price of potatoes is reduced, the people will have to spend less on potatoes. They will use the money freed from the purchase of potatoes to buy some other desirable foods, which will in turn reduce the need for potatoes. Thus, the decrease in the price of potatoes leads to a reduction in its quantity demanded.

It is doubtful whether any market demand curve in advanced countries will actually demonstrate the characteristics of a Giffen good. Since a market demand is the sum of individual

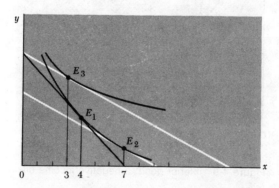

Figure 4-10   A Giffen good: an exceptional case of an inferior good

demands, Giffen's paradox has to apply to a large number of consumers before a market demand curve exhibits the characteristics of a Giffen good. This is very unlikely in most of today's economically advanced societies.

4-6 THE THEORY OF REVEALED PREFERENCE

Unlike the cardinal utility theory, the indifference analysis asks only for an ordinal measure of utility. Nevertheless, the amount of information required to draw a consumer's indifference map is enormous; we must be able to state the consumer's preference (and indifference) for all possible combinations of goods involved.

Professor Paul Samuelson has shown that all meaningful empirical implications of the theory of consumer choice can, in principle, be derived by confronting the consumer with various price sets and observing his purchases, without making any assumptions concerning either cardinal or ordinal utility. [4]

REVEALED PREFERENCE

When a consumer buys a set of commodities, he must do so either because he *likes* it better than other sets that are available to him, or because the set is *cheaper* than the others. *Therefore, if a consumer buys set A, rather than any other sets B, C, D, etc., which are no more expensive than A at the prevailing prices, the consumer has revealed his preference for A.* Accordingly, we say that set A is revealed to be preferred to the others (or that the others are revealed to be inferior to A). [5]

Let us clarify the concept of revealed preference further by referring to Figure 4-11. Suppose that the consumer purchases combination A when his income and the prices of two goods x and y are given by line LM. By the definition of a budget line, each combination on line LM costs the same amount as combination A. Any combination in the budget space OLM, that is not on LM, is less expensive than combination A. Since the consumer bought A when all other combinations in the budget space were no more expensive than A, A must be revealed preferred to all combinations in OLM (and all combinations on or to the left of LM must be revealed inferior to combination A). Since any combination to the right of LM is more expensive than A, the consumer's purchase of A cannot reveal them to be inferior to A.

[4] *Foundations of Economic Analysis* (Cambridge, Mass.: Harvard University Press, 1947), Ch. 5.
[5] When A is revealed preferred to B, we write this as ARB.

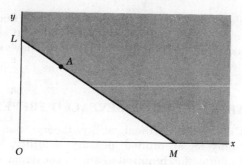

Figure 4-11   Revealed preference

THE ASSUMPTIONS OF THE REVEALED PREFERENCE THEORY

In order to present the theory of consumer choice without referring to the notion of cardinal or ordinal utility, the revealed preference theory makes the following basic assumptions.

1. The consumer's *tastes remain the same.*
2. The revealed preference relation is *antisymmetric.*
   If combination A is revealed preferred to combination B, B cannot be revealed preferred to A.
3. Revealed preference is *transitive.* If A is revealed preferred to B, and B is revealed preferred to C, then A is revealed preferred to C.
4. *Given any collection of goods, we can induce the consumer to purchase it by making its price appealing enough.* In terms of graphs such as Figure 4-11, this assumption states that for any combination of x and y in the commodity space, there is a price line that will induce the consumer to purchase it. By changing the prices of both goods in equal proportion, the budget line can be moved parallel to itself. By changing the relative price ratio, the slope of the budget line can be varied and the consumer can be induced to move up or down the budget line.

THE SUBSTITUTION AND INCOME EFFECTS

With the concept of revealed preference and its assumptions behind us, we are now in a position to derive some of the results of the theory of consumer behavior without the notion of cardinal or ordinal utility.[6] Let us first see how we can measure

[6]"The theory is formally independent of utility, but it is inconceivable that the right things would have been observed without guidance of the utility theory." George Stigler, *Price Theory*, 3rd ed. (New York: Macmillan, 1966), p. 68.

the substitution and income effects of a price change by using the revealed preference approach. Suppose the initial set of prices and the consumer's budget are given by the budget line *LM* in Figure 4-12, and the consumer purchases combination E_1. Next, we confront the consumer with a new price set *LN*, which shows a lower price of x and no change in the price of y, and observe that he buys combination E_3. To decompose the movement from E_1 to E_3 into the substitution and income effects, we use Slutsky's method of holding real income constant and reduce the consumer's money income in such a way that he is left with an income just sufficient to purchase the original combination E_1. In other words, we now confront the consumer with the prices and budget represented by the dotted line $L'N'$. Suppose we observe that the consumer chooses combination E_2. Then, the change in the quantity of x purchased, $x_2 - x_1$, that corresponds to the movement from E_1 to E_2 is the substitution effect of the change in relative prices. The increase, $x_3 - x_2$, that corresponds to the movement from E_2 to E_3 is the income effect of the change in relative prices. Notice that the substitution and income effects have been measured by confronting the consumer with various price sets and observing his purchases, without making any reference to cardinal or ordinal utility.

THE SLUTSKY THEOREM

*The **Slutsky** theorem states that the substitution effect taken by itself reduces (increases) the quantity demanded when the price of a good is increased (lowered).*[7] This proposition can be readily established by the revealed preference approach. Deleting some unnecessary details from Figure 4-12, we obtain Figure 4-13.

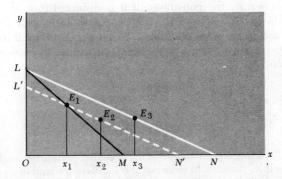

Figure 4-12   Substitution and income effects: the revealed preference approach

[7]This theorem is frequently stated as saying that the substitution effect taken by itself is "negative."

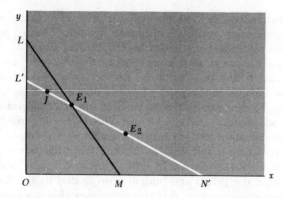

Figure 4-13 The Slutsky theorem: the revealed preference approach

We observed that the consumer chose combination E_1 when the prices and the budget were given by LM. Now let a decrease in the price of x, compensated for by the Slutskian construction, be shown by $L'N'$. In order to prove the Slutsky theorem, we must show that the new equilibrium combination E_2 on the budget line $L'N'$ lies, assuming that two points E_1 and E_2 are distinct, to the right of E_1. From the axioms of revealed preference, we know that any combination on $L'N'$ to the left of E_1 is revealed to be inferior to E_1. Thus, no point on $L'N'$ to the left of E_1 such as J would be chosen. This follows necessarily from the antisymmetry of revealed preference: if the consumer preferred E_1 to J once, he cannot subsequently prefer J over E_1 in a situation in which E_1 is also attainable. The new combination chosen by the consumer (if it is different from the original one) must lie to the right of E_1; that is, the quantity of x demanded must increase as its price decreases. Thus, a conventional individual demand curve must have a negative slope unless the commodity is a Giffen good.[8]

[8]Using the technique of the revealed preference analysis, it is also, in principle, possible to construct the indifference map of a consumer. The interested reader should consult William J. Baumol, *Economic Theory and Operations Analysis*, 3rd ed. (Englewood Cliffs, N.J.: Prentice-Hall, 1972), pp. 221–226.

EXERCISES 4

Theory
of Consumer Behavior–
Continued

4-1 Give an example of a good that used to be a normal good to you, but is now an inferior good.

4-2 Can you think of any good that may be a Giffen good to a particular consumer? Discuss why it is so difficult to find a good whose market demand exhibits the property of a Giffen good (that is, whose market demand curve is positively sloped).

4-3 Examine the income-consumption curve shown in Figure 4-14 and answer the questions by indicating the initial and ending letters of the appropriate curve segment(s).

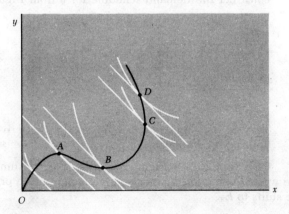

Figure 4-14

The range in which x is a normal good is _____.
The range in which x is inferior is _____.
The ranges in which y is normal are _____.
The range in which y is inferior is _____.

4-4 Examine Figure 4-15, and answer the following.

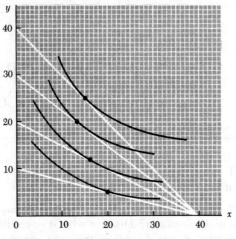

Figure 4-15

1. Draw in the price-consumption curve for good y.
2. Assuming the consumer's budget is limited to $400, construct the demand schedule for y from Figure 4-14.

Price				
Quantity				

3. Can the demand curve for good x be derived from the Figure? Explain your answer.

4-5 Suppose, in Figure 4-16, that the consumer's initial choice was combination E_1, but after a change in the price of y, his choice shifts to E_3.

1. If the initial prices of x and y were $p_x = \$2$ and $p_y = \$4$, the consumer's income must have been $_____.

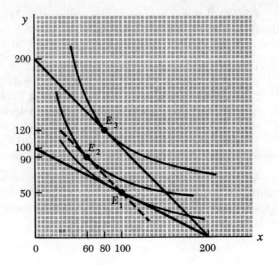

Figure 4-16

2. The prices of x and y shown by the new budget line are:

$p_x =$ _____ and $p_y =$ _____

3. To use Slutsky's method of measuring the substitution and income effects, we must compensate the consumer by taking away from him $_____. Show how you have obtained your answer.

4. If the Hicksian method of compensating the consumer to hold his income constant is employed, will the income taken away from the consumer be smaller or larger than your answer in (3)? Why?

5. A change in the price of y affects the purchases of x as well as y through the income and substitution effects. From the graph ascertain the income and substitution effects on both x and y, and complete the following table. (Make sure to furnish the sign for a negative quantity.)

	Substitution effect (S)	Income effect (Y)	Total effect (T = S + Y)
Good x			
Good y			

4-6 Paul is a junior at a state university. With $10 per week available to him for recreational purposes, he sees two movies (at $2 per show) and shoots 12 games of pool (at $.50 per game).

1. On graph paper, show Paul's allocation of his recreation budget in terms of an indifference diagram.
2. Assume now that the cost of shooting pool has risen to $.75 per game. Show in your graph how this will affect Paul's purchases of movies and pool games.
3. Explain in words the effect on Paul's purchases of the above increase in the price of pool games.

4-7 Suppose the prices of two goods x and y as well as the consumer's budget increase by 15 percent. How would this affect the equilibrium allocation of the consumer's income between the two goods? Explain precisely.

CHAPTER FIVE

APPLICATIONS OF
INDIFFERENCE ANALYSIS

The seemingly abstract tool of indifference analysis developed in the previous chapters has some important real world applications. In this chapter, we will apply indifference analysis to study the effects of many diverse subjects, such as wage rates and hours worked, social security, income versus excise tax, income versus price subsidy, single versus discriminatory prices, and biases involved in various price indexes.

5-1 THE EFFECT OF WAGE RATES AND NONLABOR INCOME ON HOURS WORKED

Let us apply indifference analysis to examine the effects of different wage rates as well as a nonwage income offer on a worker's willingness to work.

A worker's indifference map for income and leisure (the opposite of work) together with a series of straight lines representing different hourly wage rates are shown in Figure 5-1. Total wage per day is measured along the vertical axis, and the hours of work are measured along the horizontal axis from the origin to the right. We assume that 16 hours per day is the maximum number of hours available for work or leisure. The amount of leisure available to the worker per day (which is 16 hours minus the hours worked) is measured along the horizontal axis from the right to the left as indicated by the gray supplementary axis. Thus, the indifference curves of the worker for the two economic goods involved — daily income and daily leisure — are convex to the southeast origin.

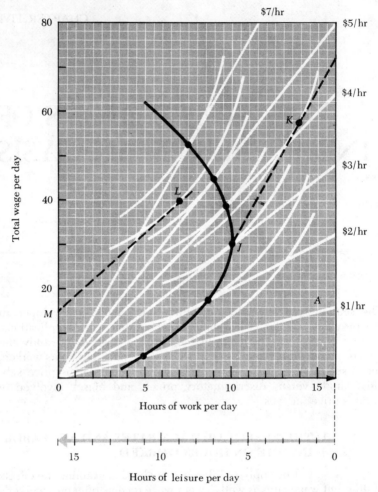

Figure 5-1 Derivation of a labor supply curve

Wage rate (or income opportunity) line *OA* is labeled $1 per hour. Since 10 hours of work bring in $10 of total income, the wage rate must be $1 per hour. The reader can readily verify that the successively steeper wage rate lines represent higher and higher wage rates as indicated. The point of tangency between each wage rate line and an indifference curve shows the hours of labor the worker is willing to supply given the wage rate. Let us connect these equilibrium points with a freehand curve, assuming that the worker is able to work as many hours as he wishes. This curve shows the relationship between wage rates and hours worked, and its tabular presentation gives the following labor supply schedule.

Wages per hour	$1	$2	$3	$4	$5	$7
Hours of work per day	5	8.2	10	9.7	9	7.5

Plotting this schedule on the traditional price-quantity axis will give the conventional labor supply curve of the worker. According to the above schedule, the hours the worker is willing to work decline as the wage rate increases beyond $3 per hour. Thus, the labor supply curve of this worker is *backward bending* at wage rates above $3. This is also clear from the negatively sloped segment of the price-consumption or *offer* curve in Figure 5-1.

Even though an individual worker's labor supply curve may be backward bending, the supply curve of labor faced by the firm is not backward bending. The firm can make an "all or nothing" offer that will always make its labor supply curve positive; that is, it can offer a package deal that gives a higher rate of pay only after the worker has put in a certain number of hours at a lower rate. The dotted line *JK* shows this situation in Figure 5-1. By offering the worker $3 per hour for the first 10 hours and $7 per hour thereafter, the worker is induced to work 14 hours per day.[1]

The effect of the *flow of nonlabor income* on the worker's willingness to work is also depicted in Figure 5-1. Assume the worker receives $3 per hour, and that he has $15 per day of nonlabor income. Then the wage rate line that will show the worker's total—labor and nonlabor—income per day is the dotted line *ML*. The worker will now work 7 hours per day instead of 10 hours per day. Thus, the effect of the nonlabor income for this worker was to reduce his willingness to work at a given wage rate.

Let us now refer to Figure 5-2 and examine what makes a labor supply curve positively or backward sloping. The worker moves from point E_1 to point E_3 following an increase in the wage rate indicated by the shift of the wage rate line from *OA* to *OB*. The movement from E_1 to E_3 and the corresponding change in hours worked can be decomposed into the substitution and income effects. The substitution effect of the wage increase makes the worker work W_1W_3 more hours (and reduces his leisure by the same number of hours): he substitutes work that is now relatively more remunerative for leisure that is now relatively more costly. But the increase in the wage rate increases the worker's real income, which makes him reduce his work by W_2W_3 hours: the income effect of the wage increase is negative. Because the substitution effect is greater than the negative income (or wealth) effect, the increase in the wage rate

[1]The line *JK* shows $7 per hour wage rate because it is parallel to the wage rate line labeled $7/hr.

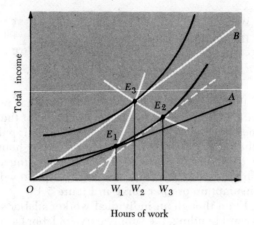

Figure 5-2 Substitution and income effects of a
wage increase

is accompanied by an increase in hours worked. The labor supply
curve is positively sloped in the relevant range.

In general, if the substitution effect is greater than the
income or wealth effect, an individual worker's labor supply curve
is positively sloped. On the other hand, if the substitution effect is
smaller than the income effect, his labor supply curve will be negatively sloped. As already mentioned, the labor supply curve facing
a firm need not be negatively sloped at all.

5-2 AN APPLICATION INVOLVING SOCIAL SECURITY BENEFITS

Quite frequently we hear an elderly worker saying that
he cannot work any more this year because if he does his social
security check will be reduced. In 1974, a person who was receiving
social security benefits was allowed to earn up to $2,400 without
having his benefits reduced. When his income exceeded this limit,
his benefits were reduced by $.50 for each $1 in earnings. [2]

[2]We use 1974 figures because they are convenient round
figures. Social security benefits as well as the amount that can be earned
without a reduction in benefits are increased automatically in accordance
with automatic cost-of-living provisions of 1972 legislation. Furthermore,
the social security recipient can get the full benefit for any month in which
he does not earn more than 1/12 of the wage income limit ($200 per month
in 1974) and he does not perform substantial services in self-employment.
For simplicity, we shall assume in our example that monthly
incomes are evenly distributed over a calendar year, and that social security
payments are reduced only after the allowable annual wage income is
reached.

To examine the effect of such reduction in social security payments on the amount of labor supplied by a worker who is on social security, consider the following simplified hypothetical situation. A worker receives $3,000 per annum in social security payments if he receives no wage or salary income at all. He is allowed to earn up to and including $2,400 per annum without having his social security benefits reduced by $.50 for each $1 in earnings.

His wage rate (or income opportunity) line *AECD* in Figure 5-3 graphically describes the above assumptions. When no work is performed, the worker receives $3,000 of social security benefits. Assuming the wage rate is $200 per week, the worker can earn and keep $2,400 for the first 12 weeks of work. For the next 30 weeks of work, the worker's social security payment is reduced by $1 for each $2 earned. Thus, though the worker earns $200 per week, his spendable income increases by only $100 per week: $200 of wage

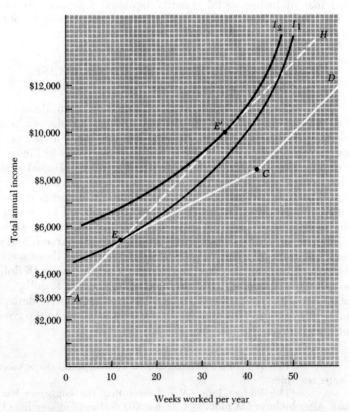

Figure 5-3 Reduction in social security payments and work effect

earnings minus $100 of loss in social security benefits. To show this fact, segment EC of the wage rate line is drawn only half as steep as segment AE. By the end of the 42nd week (= 12 + 30), the worker's social security benefits are reduced to zero. Thus, from the 43rd week on, the worker can again earn and retain all his income. The slope of his wage rate line in segment CD is again equal to the actual wage rate, $200 per week.

Since the worker's indifference curve I_1 touches the income opportunity line at point E, the optimal work-income combination chosen is 12 weeks of work and $5,400 of income. [3] For this worker the fact that his social security benefits will be reduced if he works more than 12 weeks per annum is enough deterrent to make him stop working as soon as he earns his first $2,400 in wages.

Now the dotted wage rate line AH shows the situation in which there is no penalty in terms of reduced social security payments when a worker earns wages or salaries. In the absence of the fear of losing social security benefits, according to Figure 5-3, the worker would choose combination E' on I_2 which contains 35 weeks of work and $10,000 dollars of income.

5-3 THE WELFARE EFFECT OF AN EXCISE VERSUS INCOME TAX

Using an indifference analysis, we can demonstrate that a given amount of tax in the form of an excise tax places a heavier burden on the taxpayer than the same amount of tax levied on him as an income tax. In order to see how this is done refer to Figure 5-4. We show *money* on the vertical axis and quantity of good x along the horizontal axis. Before the imposition of a tax, the consumer was in equilibrium at point E on the budget line LM. Let us now assume that the imposition of an excise tax — which is shifted in its entirety to the consumer — raises the price of x and the budget line shifts to LN. The consumer thus moves to E' on indifference curve I_1 and purchases OA units of x and pays $E'K$ dollars for it. [4] If there were no excise tax, the consumer could purchase OA units of x for JK dollars. The difference between what the consumer pays ($E'K$ dollars) and what he would pay in the absence of the excise tax (JK dollars) is equal to $E'J$ dollars. This sum is the revenue accruing to the government under the excise tax plan.

---

[3]This is a corner solution caused by the special shape taken by the wage rate lines.

[4]The budget line LN indicates that the consumer has OL dollars. After he buys OA units of x, he has OD dollars of money left. Thus, the amount of money spent must be DL (= $E'K$) dollars, which is the difference between OL and OD dollars.

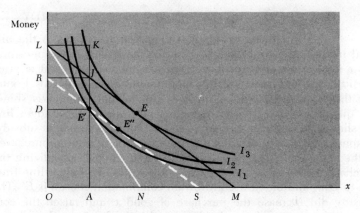

Figure 5-4   Excise versus income tax

Suppose the identical tax revenue ($E'J$ dollars) is imposed on the consumer as an income tax. The imposition of this income tax is shown by a parallel shift of the budget line from LM to RS. (The income tax reduces the money available to the consumer by RL dollars, which is equal to the amount of excise tax $E'J$ dollars). The optimal combination chosen by the consumer given the budget line RS is E'', which lies on indifference curve I_2. Since I_2 is preferred to I_1, it is clear that taxing a given amount of money in the form of an income tax produces a smaller amount of loss in utility or welfare to the consumer than the same sum imposed on him as an excise tax.

A few words of caution must accompany the foregoing analysis. First, we have assumed that the excise tax is imposed on a good that the consumer does purchase. Obviously, for a nonsmoker, a cigarette tax is far less painful than an income tax. Second, note that the foregoing analysis was in the tradition of partial equilibrium analysis: we have analyzed the effects of excise and income taxes assuming that other prices and production conditions remain the same. The appropriateness of such partial analysis depends on the smallness of interdependence between the market under study and other parts of the economy. When an excise tax is imposed on goods with important interdependence effects such as motor vehicles, we will have to consider the accompanying changes in production, other prices, etc. For instance, Friedman criticizes the foregoing analysis by taking into consideration changes in production conditions that are introduced by the excise tax.[5] Third, if excise taxes were placed on all goods in such a way as to keep relative prices unchanged, needless to say, the effect would be like an income tax.

[5]See Milton Friedman, *Price Theory: A Provisional Text* (Chicago: Aldine, 1962), pp. 56–67.

5-4 PRICE SUBSIDY VERSUS INCOME SUBSIDY

Employing an analytical technique similar to the one used in the preceding example, we can show why a consumer prefers a given amount of income subsidy to the same amount of price subsidy (such as rent subsidy and low-interest loans). In Figure 5-5, the vertical axis shows income and the horizontal axis shows the quantity of good x that is being subsidized. The budget line LM shows the market price of the good without a government subsidy. Suppose the society decides that the quantity of x being purchased at the going price is too small and passes a law subsidizing the purchase of the good. The subsidy of x shifts the budget line from LM to LM', and the new equilibrium combination chosen is E'. The subsidy did increase the purchase of good x, and raised the consumer's satisfaction from the level indicated by I_1 to that shown by I_2.

Now our problem is to identify the cost of subsidizing the purchase of good x and analyze the effect of giving the same sum as an income supplement to the consumer. Under the subsidy program, the consumer is paying $E'K$ dollars for OS units of x. In the absence of the price subsidy, the consumer would be paying JK dollars for OS units of x. Thus, the cost of the price subsidy to the society is JE' dollars.

Suppose we eliminate the price subsidy and give the consumer JE' dollars of income subsidy. This income subsidy will now shift the budget line from LM to AB. The equilibrium com-

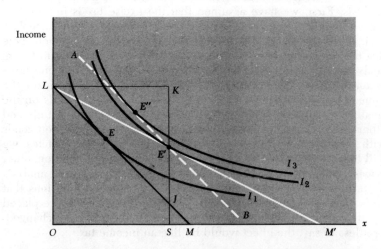

Figure 5-5 Price subsidy versus income subsidy

bination chosen, E'', lies on a higher indifference curve than E'. Thus, a given amount of income subsidy increases the utility of a consumer more than the same amount of price subsidy on a particular good.

The income subsidy is more efficient than the same sum given as a price subsidy because the former increases the consumer's utility more than the latter. However, real world economic policies are influenced not only by efficiency considerations but by value judgments as well. Taxpayers may be willing to provide a *food* subsidy, but not willing to give money that could be spent on, say liquor. The words of caution expressed with reference to the excise versus income tax analysis of the previous section apply to this section as well: the subsidy obviously has to be on the good the consumer purchases; and the interdependence effect between the subsidized product and others in the economy must be small.

5-5   GAINS FROM TRADE BETWEEN CONSUMERS

Let us now introduce an analytical tool known as the Edgeworth (Edgeworth-Bowley, or Pareto) exchange box, which is a convenient tool in evaluating the efficiency of allocating given amounts of goods (resources) between consumers (producers).[6] With the aid of the Edgeworth box diagram, we will examine how an exchange between two consumers may benefit both of them.

THE EDGEWORTH EXCHANGE BOX

Assume that the two consumers' names are Alice and Betty and that the total quantities of two goods x and y available are $O_A x$ and $O_A y$ units. The **Edgeworth exchange box** relevant for our problem is then given by Figure 5-6. The dimensions of the Edgeworth box are specified by the total quantities of two goods x and y available: the width shows the total units of x available and the height indicates the total units of y available (to both Alice and

[6]In economic literature, this analytical device is known as the Edgeworth or Edgeworth-Bowley box diagram. However, the box diagram does not appear in Edgeworth's writings, and Bowley was not the first to use the device. It was Vilfredo Pareto who first used the device in its now familiar form in his *Manuale d'economie politica* (Milano: Societa editrice libraria, 1906). Thus, genealogically speaking, the more appropriate tag for the device is the *Pareto box*. See Vincent J. Tarascio, "A Correction: On the Genealogy of the So-Called Edgeworth-Bowley Diagram," *Western Economic Journal*, June 1972, pp. 193–197.

We shall, however, use the term *Edgeworth box* because this is the shortest expression by which the box is commonly known among economists.

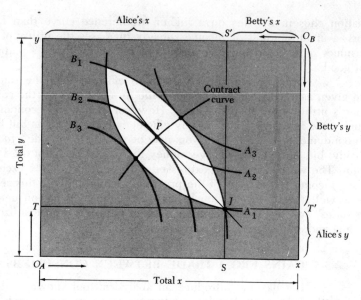

Figure 5-6 Exchange between two consumers

Betty). Alice's indifference map is shown as usual: the origin, O_A, is at the southwest corner; the quantity of x possessed by Alice is measured along the horizontal axis from left to right; the quantity of y, along the vertical axis from the bottom up, and her indifference curves are convex to the southwest origin. In order to show Betty's indifference map together with that of Alice's, we take Betty's usually shaped indifference map, rotate it 180°, and superimpose it on Alice's indifference map. Thus, Betty's indifference curves (white or gray curves) are convex to the northeast corner origin, O_B. Betty's possession of good x is measured along the horizontal axis from right to left, and the quantity of y available to Betty is measured along the vertical axis from top to bottom. (If the book is held upside down, Betty's indifference map will look as usual: convex to the southwest origin.)

The total quantities of x and y available specify the dimensions of an Edgeworth box. Since there are only two individuals involved, any point in the Edgeworth box, such as point J, indicates the manner in which the available x and y are allocated between the two consumers. For instance point J shows that Alice has $O_A S$ units of x and $O_A T$ units of y, while Betty has Sx ($= O_B S'$) units of x and Ty ($= O_B T'$) units of y.

GAINS FROM TRADE

Now assume that the initial amounts of goods x and y possessed by Alice and Betty when they first met were given by point J, where Alice's and Betty's indifference curves (A_1 and B_1, respectively) intersect. Keep in mind that the absolute slope of an indifference curve (the marginal rate of substitution) indicates the rate at which the consumer is willing to exchange the two goods. At point J, Alice's and Betty's indifference curves intersect, indicating that they attach *different relative valuations* to the two goods x and y. A magnified picture of the area around point J is shown in Figure 5-7. Combinations B and J are on the same indifference curve for Betty. Thus, in exchange for KJ units of x, Betty is willing to offer KB units of y. For Alice, the combinations J and A are equally preferable. Therefore, Alice is willing to offer only KA units of y for KJ units of x. Clearly, Alice attaches a higher valuation to y than Betty does.

Because Alice and Betty attach different relative valuations to two goods x and y, it is possible for both of them to gain by trading with each other. Suppose after some haggling, Alice and Betty agree to trade at the ratio indicated by the straight line JP in Figure 5-6. As they move from J to P along this *trading line JP*, both Alice and Betty move onto higher and higher indifference curves. At point P, for instance, Alice is on indifference curve A_2 and Betty is on indifference curve B_2. Alice and Betty have *both gained from exchange* and moved to preferred positions. Whenever two individuals' indif-

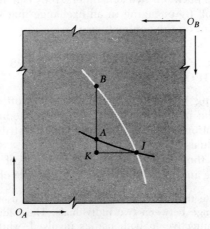

Figure 5-7 Different subjective valuations attached to good y

ference curves intersect, both of them can benefit by an exchange that will allow them to move to a point inside the football-shaped region marked off by indifference curves A_1 and B_1 in Figure 5-6.[7]

When two individuals are at a point like P where their indifference curves are tangent to each other, it is no longer possible to arrange an exchange that will make both of them better off. Moving along line JP to either side will reduce the welfare of both parties; moving in a northeast direction will increase Alice's utility at the expense of Betty's; and moving toward the southwest will increase Betty's utility at the cost of Alice's. *The curve labeled contract curve represents the locus of all points of tangency between Alice's and Betty's indifference curves.*[8]

All combinations of x and y on the contract curve are efficient: given any combination on the contract curve, it is not possible to increase the utility of one individual without reducing that of the other. *The term Pareto optimality or efficiency describes this situation in which the utility of an individual cannot be increased without reducing that of others, and the unshaded region in Figure 5-6 is referred to as the Pareto superior region relative to point J.* Both Alice and Betty prefer any combination in the interior of the football-shaped region marked off by the indifference curves through point J to combination J.

Combinations that are not located on the contract curve are suboptimal or inefficient in the sense that it is possible to increase the utility of either one or both parties without hurting anyone else. Whenever a point off the contract curve shows the current allocation of goods between two consumers, they can make one or both of them better off by engaging in an exchange that will allow them to move to a point on the contract curve.

5-6 PRICE DISCRIMINATION VERSUS UNIFORM PRICE

Using the apparatus of the Edgeworth exchange box introduced in the previous section, we can immediately show that price discrimination results in an inefficient distribution of goods between individuals.

Let the amount of money (or bundle of all other goods) available to Alice and Betty be shown by the height of the Edgeworth

[7]Note that a middleman can perform a useful service in arranging an exchange between two individuals. The middleman can offer exchange ratios attractive to both parties involved, while keeping some commission for his service.

[8]A contract curve is also referred to as a **conflict curve**, because moving along it creates conflict between the two individuals involved.

exchange box in Figure 5-8. The width of the box shows the quantity of medical service available to Alice and Betty. Suppose Alice and Betty go to the same physician, who practices price discrimination in the sense that he sells his service at different prices to different patients. The physician charges a higher fee to Betty, who is a wealthy person, and a lower fee to Alice, who is of modest means. In Figure 5-8, the lower price charged to Alice is shown by a flatter line p_a, and the higher price charged to Betty is shown by the steeper line p_b. Note that the lines p_a and p_b merely show the rates at which money and medical service can be exchanged for Alice and Betty, respectively. They are *not* the "budget lines" along which the consumer can move freely. The current allocation of money and medical service in Figure 5-8 is given by point J. Any change in the current allocation must be brought forward by a mutual agreement between Alice and Betty, and not by a unilateral action of either one alone.

Suppose the current purchases of medical services under the dual prices are indicated by point J, where Alice's and Betty's indifference curves are tangent to their price ratio lines. Since Alice's and Betty's indifference curves intersect at point J, from the discussion of the previous section, it is immediately clear that point J is inefficient or suboptimal. If any uniform price between p_a and p_b is chosen for both patients, the new trading line will emanate from J into the unshaded (Pareto superior) region where Alice and Betty can choose a combination preferable to both of them. If the uniform price is shown by line JS, the new equilibrium combination chosen by

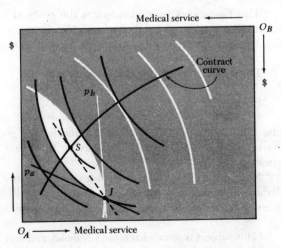

Figure 5-8 Price discrimination versus uniform price

Alice and Betty is S, and both will reach a higher indifference curve of their own. S is an efficient or Pareto optimal distribution since neither party's utility can be increased without reducing the other's utility.

Note that point S on the contract curve is clearly preferred to point J. S is an optimal or efficient solution, while J is a suboptimal or inefficient solution. However, we must also note that an efficient or optimal solution says nothing about the inequities stemming from unequal income distribution. *Given* the existing income and wealth distributions—from which the consumers' purchasing powers arise—the optimal or efficient solution is to let rich Betty purchase more medical service and not-so-fortunate Alice use less medical service. Whether the existing income and wealth distributions are ethically ideal or not is not a question that positive or scientific economics can answer.

5-7 PRICE INDEXES AND THE COST OF LIVING[9]

The two well-known approaches to the measurement of price level change are given by the Laspeyres price index and the Paasche price index. *The Laspeyres price index is defined by*

$$L = \frac{\Sigma p_1 q_0}{\Sigma p_0 q_0}$$

where p and q stand for price and quantity, and the subscripts 0 and 1 refer to the base (earlier or year 0) period and the given (later or year 1) period.

The Laspeyres index compares the costs of purchasing a particular market basket of goods and services in the *base* period $(\Sigma p_0 q_0)$ with the cost of buying the identical basket in a given year $(\Sigma p_1 q_0)$.

The Paasche price index is defined by

$$P = \frac{\Sigma p_1 q_1}{\Sigma p_0 q_1}$$

The Paasche index compares the cost of purchasing the *given* period (year 1) market basket with that of purchasing the same basket in an earlier period (year 0).

Neither of the above two indexes, however, is a completely satisfactory measure of the change in the cost of living. While the Laspeyres index tends to overestimate the cost of living change,

[9]This subject is somewhat more advanced, and may be omitted without any loss of continuity.

the Paasche index tends to underestimate it. Let us first examine the upward bias involved in the Laspeyres index.

UPWARD BIAS INVOLVED IN THE LASPEYRES INDEX

Let us assume that the consumer purchases only two goods x and y. (This restriction to two goods is necessary for a two-dimensional graphic analysis, but the result can be extended to any number of goods.) The consumer's tastes, which are assumed to remain the same in periods 0 and 1, are described by the indifference curves shown in Figure 5-9. The budget line $m_0 m_0$ shows the relative prices prevailing in year 0 and the amount of income that was available to the consumer in year 0 ($M_0 = \Sigma p_0 q_0$): the slope of the budget line shows the relative price ratio, and its location indicates various combinations of x and y that can be purchased with a given amount of income. The utility-maximizing combination chosen by the consumer in year 0 is C_0, where the budget line is tangent to indifference curve I_0.

The cost of year 0 basket in year 1 prices.   Now assume that the relative prices change from year 0 to 1, as shown by the slope of the new budget line $m_1 m_1$. How much does it cost to purchase the base period market basket, C_0, in year 1, in which relative prices are different? The answer is offered by the dollar value associated with the budget line $m_1 m_1$: this budget line shows (1) the ratio of prices prevailing in period 1, and (2) the expenditure needed to purchase C_0 (which is located on the budget line $m_1 m_1$). Let $\$M_1$ represent the expenditure associated with the budget line $m_1 m_1$. Since this expenditure allows the purchase of period 0 market basket at period 1 prices, it follows that $\$M_1 = \Sigma p_1 q_0$.

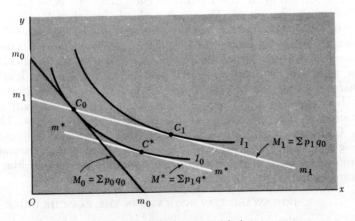

Figure 5-9   Upward bias of the Laspeyres index

109

The Laspeyres index and the cost of living. The Laspeyres index compares M_1 and M_0 (the costs of purchasing year 0 basket in year 1 and year 0) and assumes that the following changes in the cost of living have taken place from year 0 to year 1:

$$L = \frac{M_1}{M_0} = \frac{\Sigma p_1 q_0}{\Sigma p_0 q_0} \begin{cases} > 1 \Rightarrow \text{An increase in the cost of living} \\ = 1 \Rightarrow \text{No change in the cost of living} \\ < 1 \Rightarrow \text{A decrease in the cost of living} \end{cases}$$

Suppose M_1 is actually equal to M_0. Then, the Laspeyres index concludes that the cost of living has not changed; the consumer can still purchase the base period basket in the given period at the same cost. However, we notice from Figure 5-9 that given the budget constraint $m_1 m_1$, the consumer will choose combination C_1 (which is on a higher indifference curve I_1). By substituting more of now relatively cheaper commodity x for now relatively expensive y, the consumer has increased his level of satisfaction to I_1.

The true indicator of the cost of living. The expenditure needed in year 1 to keep the consumer on the original indifference curve (that is, the true cost of living in year 1, that is required to keep the consumer just as well off as he was in year 0) is shown by the dollar value associated with the budget line $m^{\circ} m^{\circ}$. Let us call this sum M° dollars. It then follows that if $M^{\circ} = M_0$, the cost of living between year 0 and year 1 has not changed. Similarly, if $M^{\circ} > M_0$ the cost of living has increased; and if $M^{\circ} < M_0$ the cost of living has decreased. In other words, the true cost of living has increased (decreased, remained the same) if M°/M_0 is greater than (less than, equal to) 1.

The upward bias of the Laspeyres index. Now the budget lines $m_1 m_1$ and $m^{\circ} m^{\circ}$ are parallel to each other and $m^{\circ} m^{\circ}$ is closer to the origin than $m_1 m_1$. Thus, M° is clearly less than M_1. The true cost of living index, which has to be determined by the ratio M°/M_0, must, therefore, be smaller than the Laspeyres index, which is determined by the ratio M_1/M_0. The Laspeyres index has an upward bias! The true cost of living in year 1 (needed to maintain the level of satisfaction enjoyed in year 0) will be as high as what is indicated by the Laspeyres index only if the consumer fails to make any substitution to take advantage of the changed relative prices. Thus, the Laspeyres index shows the *upper limit* of the cost of living in the given year. Since we do not know the shape of the consumer's indifference map, it is not possible to quantify the upward bias inherent in the Laspeyres index.

DOWNWARD BIAS INVOLVED IN THE PAASCHE INDEX

Now let us turn our attention to the downward bias involved in the Paasche index. We do not even need a new graph;

all that is needed is to take Figure 5-9 and relabel the curves. Figure 5-10 differs from Figure 5-9 only in labels. Since the Paasche index compares the costs of purchasing year 1 basket in year 1 and year 0, let us show the original combination chosen in year 1 by C_1. Year 1 prices and expenditure ($\Sigma p_1 q_1 = M_1$) are thus represented by the budget line $m_1 m_1$ and the consumer attains the level of satisfaction given by I_1.

Now the question asked by the Paasche index is: What was the cost of purchasing year 1 basket in year 0? The budget line $m_0 m_0$ that goes through C_1 holds the key to this question; it shows the year 0 prices and the expenditure that would have enabled the purchase of combination C_1 in year 0 ($\Sigma p_0 q_1 = M_0$).

Implicit in the Paasche index are the following assumptions regarding the change in the cost of living from year 0 to year 1:

$$P = \frac{M_1}{M_0} = \frac{\Sigma p_1 q_1}{\Sigma p_0 q_1} \begin{cases} > 1 \Rightarrow \text{An increase in the cost of living} \\ = 1 \Rightarrow \text{No change in the cost of living} \\ < 1 \Rightarrow \text{A decrease in the cost of living} \end{cases}$$

According to the Paasche index, if the expenditure represented by the budget line $m_0 m_0$ is equal to that represented by the original budget line $m_1 m_1$, the cost of living and the consumer's welfare have not changed: the consumer could have purchased the year 1 market basket in year 0 at the same expense. Given the budget constraint of $m_0 m_0$ dollars, however, the utility-maximizing consumer takes advantage of the new price situation and selects combination C_0, which lies on a higher indifference curve.

The budget constraint that keeps the consumer on the original indifference curve I_1 when he is purchasing at year 0 prices

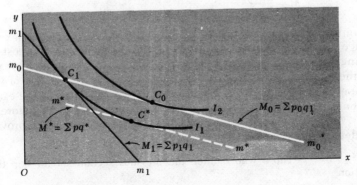

Figure 5-10 Downward bias of the Paasche index

is given by the dotted line m^*m^*. Let M^* show the expenditure associated with this budget line. Now, the true relevant cost M^* dollars is clearly less than the M_0 dollars used in computing the Paasche index. Therefore, the Paasche index, which is determined by the ratio M_1/M_0, must be smaller than a true cost of living index given by the ratio M_1/M^*. Clearly, the Paasche index has a downward bias and shows the *lower limit* of the cost of living. The cost of living in year 1 would be as low as what is indicated by the Paasche index only if the consumer failed to take advantage of the prices prevailing in year 0 and insisted on purchasing the year 1 basket in year 0.

COST OF LIVING AND THE PRICE INDEXES

Most price indexes are computed by the Laspeyres method, and are subject to upward biases. Because of such upward biases, it is not possible to claim that our price indexes measure "true" changes in the cost of living. This is the reason why contemporary price indexes have such titles as "prices paid by consumers" rather than a misleading title such as "cost of living."

In peacetime the upward bias of the Laspeyres index tends to be enhanced by the failure to take into account improvements in the qualities of goods. On the other hand, during national emergencies such as World War II, the deterioration and unavailability of goods will tend to counterbalance the upward bias.

5-8 PRICE INDEXES AND CONSUMER'S WELFARE[10]

No discussion of price indexes as the measure of cost of living will be complete without a reference to the relationship between changes in price indexes and changes in the individual's real income over time. Let the changes in money income (the entire sum of which is assumed to be spent on goods and services) be shown by the following index:

$$M = \frac{\Sigma p_1 q_1}{\Sigma p_0 q_0}$$

Compare this index of money income with the Laspeyres index, L. Since we know that L shows the maximum by which the cost of living could have increased, $M > L$ would imply a definite increase in the consumer's welfare. In the absence of the knowledge of the shape of an individual's indifference map, we do not know the exact amount of upward bias involved in Laspeyres index. Therefore if $M < L$, we cannot tell whether the individual's welfare has improved or deteriorated.

[10]Those who omitted the previous section should skip this section.

The Paasche index, P, has a downward bias and represents the lower limit of the change in the cost of living. Therefore, following the similar reasoning used in evaluating the Laspeyres index, we conclude that $M < P$ implies that the consumer's welfare has diminished; however, $M > P$ leaves us with inconclusive answers.

EXERCISES 5

Applications
of Indifference Analysis

5-1 Given a wage increase, the income effect may decrease the hours of work. Whether this negative income effect is substantial or not depends on individual preferences.

1. Cite an example of a group of people for whom the negative income effect may be quite small or zero and explain why you think so.
2. Give an example of a group of people for whom the negative effect may be large and explain why.

5-2 Suppose the worker has no choice but to work 40 hours per week, if he is to work at all. Illustrate the choice involved under this situation in a graph that shows weekly income on the vertical axis and hours worked on the horizontal axis. Is your solution a tangency or corner solution? Why?

5-3 Suppose the worker chooses to work every week until he earns $200. Illustrate this case graphically and explain.

5-4 The following is quoted from a local daily paper.

WILLIAMSBURG, Va., April 19, 1972—(UPI)—President Nixon, appealing anew for enactment of his welfare reform proposals, told the nations's Republican governors Monday that the time has come to stop rewarding people for doing nothing.

"It is incredible that we have allowed a system of laws under which one person can be penalized for doing an honest day's work and another person can be rewarded for doing nothing. It can happen and does happen under the present system. The person on welfare can often have a higher income than his neighbor who holds a low-paying job."

Describe what President Nixon is saying in terms of wage rate (income opportunity) lines and indifference curves for income and work (or leisure).

5-5   Let us infer the welfare implications of various areas in the following Edgeworth box diagram relative to the original bundle *J*.

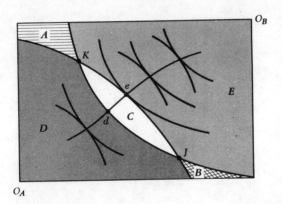

1.   The Pareto superior area(s) relative to *J* is _____.

2.   The Pareto inferior area(s) relative to *J* is _____.

3.   The Pareto optimal combinations relative to *J* are those on _____.

4.   The combination that is equivalent to *J* is _____.

5.   The combination(s) that are not comparable to *J* are in area(s) _____.

5-6   From the Social Security Office nearest you, find out the current social security payments and the way these payments are reduced as the pensioner's income increases. Assume that monthly wage incomes are evenly distributed throughout the year, and draw (and explain) his income opportunity line on graph paper.

5-7   Using the Edgeworth box diagram, show how a middleman may benefit two individuals interested in trading as well as himself.

CHAPTER SIX

MARKET DEMAND AND ELASTICITY OF DEMAND

This chapter provides a transition from the study of consumer behavior to the theory of markets, which will commence in Chapter Eleven. In the first several sections, we examine the process of deriving the market demand curve by summing individual consumers' demand curves, and study various concepts of demand curves and the relationship among various revenue concepts. In sections 6-5 through 6-8, we shall study the price elasticity of demand and other related concepts and examine the determinants of such elasticities. Sections 6-9 through 6-11 introduce the graphic technique of measuring an elasticity coefficient and explore the relationships between the price elasticity of demand and average, marginal, and total revenues. The remainder of the chapter deals with applications.

6-1 THE MARKET DEMAND

In Chapter Two, we observed the important role played by market demand in determining equilibrium price and output and allocating resources among different industries. We used the concept there without asking how it was obtained. Now we show how the market demand curve is obtained by summing individual consumers' demand curves.

In section 4-2, we saw that an individual consumer's demand curve can be derived from his price-consumption curve. Recall that *an individual consumer's demand curve shows the relationship between quantities purchased and the price of the good, while prices of other goods and money income remain unchanged.*

The market demand curve shows the relationship between total quantities purchased in the market and the price of the good, while other variables such as prices of other goods and consumers' incomes and tastes remain unchanged. As the similarity of the two definitions may suggest, the market demand can, at least conceptually, be obtained by adding individual consumers' demands.[1] (In practice, the market demand of a good is directly estimated from aggregate market data.) Graphically, the market demand curve is obtained by summing laterally individual consumers' demand curves.

Table 6-1 The Market Demand as the Sum of Individual Demands

PRICE	q_1	q_2	q_3	Q[†]
$5	0	2	4	6
4	1	4	6	11
3	2	6	8	16
2	3	8	11	22
1	4	9	14	27

[†] $Q = q_1 + q_2 + q_3$

The demand schedules and demand curves of three individuals that make up a hypothetical market are shown in Table 6-1 and Figure 6-1. The aggregate or total quantity demanded in the market, Q, column is obtained by adding the quantities demanded by three individual consumers (q_1, q_2, and q_3) at each price. Since most markets are made up of more than three consumers, the total quantity demanded in the market at each relevant price is given by $Q = q_1 + q_2 + \ldots + q_n$. In Figure 6-1, the market demand curve labeled D is obtained by the horizontal summation of the individual demand curves, d_1, d_2, and d_3. For instance, the point K on the market demand curve is obtained by the lateral or horizontal additions of the distances AB, AC, and AE.

6-2 DIFFERENT KINDS OF DEMAND CURVES

When we talk of a demand curve, we may refer to (1) an individual consumer's demand curve, (2) a market (or aggregate)

[1] The procedure of obtaining the market demand curve as the sum of individual consumers' demand curves assumes that (1) an individual consumer's demand is not affected by those of other consumers and (2) a single price prevails in the market and everyone pays the same price.

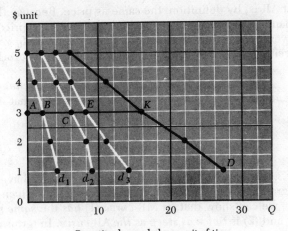

Figure 6-1   Market demand curve as the horizontal
sum of individual demand curves

demand curve, or (3) a demand curve faced by a firm. In general,
the context in which the demand curve is referred to should make
it clear which demand curve is being considered.

An *individual (consumer's) demand curve shows quantities of a good that would be purchased by a single buyer at various
prices. The market demand curve shows quantities of a good that
would be purchased at various prices by all buyers in the market,*
and is obtained by horizontally summing individual demand curves.
*The demand curve faced by a firm shows total quantities of the
firm's product demanded by all of its customers at various prices.*
In other words, the demand curve faced by a firm represents the
sales rates the firm can attain at various possible prices.

6-3 TOTAL, AVERAGE, AND MARGINAL REVENUES

The *total revenue or total sales receipts of a firm is
obtained by multiplying the price per unit of its product by the
quantity sold at the price.* That is,

$$TR = pq$$

The *average revenue is simply the total revenue divided
by the quantity, or the rate of output.* That is,

$$AR = TR/q = pq/q = p$$

Note that AR is, by definition, the same as price. Because the height of a demand curve at any given output rate shows the price per unit or the average revenue, *a demand curve is frequently referred to as an average revenue curve.* We shall use the two terms synonymously.

The marginal revenue is the amount of change in the total revenue when output is increased by one unit.[2] That is,

$$MR = \Delta TR/\Delta q$$

THE RELATIONSHIP BETWEEN LINEAR AR AND MR CURVES

Average and marginal revenue curves have a well-defined graphical (and mathematical) relationship. *Given a linear AR curve,* we can show that *its* MR *curve* (1) *has* the *same price-axis intercept* and (2) is *twice as steep* as the AR *curve.* In terms of Figure 6-2, this relationship says that the line segments AC and CB are equal (or that $AJ = NB$). This proposition makes it quite easy to draw in the MR curve corresponding to any linear AR curve: Find the midpoint of any horizontal line segment between the price axis and the AR curve, then connect this midpoint and the point at which the AR curve intersects the price axis by a straight line. This straight line is the desired MR curve.

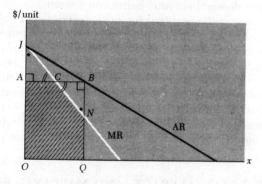

Figure 6-2 Relationship between average and marginal revenue curves

[2]In the continuous case, marginal revenue shows the rate of change in the total revenue with respect to output. That is,

$$MR = d TR/dq$$

MR is simply the first derivative of TR, and graphically shows the slope of the TR curve.

Referring to Figure 6-2, let us prove the above proposition geometrically.[3]

Steps	Reasons
1. $OABQ$ = Total Revenue (TR)	1. TR = (Price) (Quantity)
2. $OJNQ$ = TR	2. Area under the MR curve from O to Q = TR(Q)
3. Area of $\triangle AJC$ = Area of $\triangle CBN$	3. Both areas are obtained by subtracting $OACNQ$ from TR
4. $\triangle AJC \simeq \triangle CBN$	4. They are congruent because:
	(a) Area of $\triangle AJC$ = Area of $\triangle CBN$
	(b) $\angle ACJ = \angle BCN$ (vertical angles)
	(c) $\angle JAC = \angle CBN$ (right angles)
5. $\therefore AC = CB$ and $AJ = NB$	

THE RELATIONSHIP AMONG AR, MR, AND TR

Figure 6-3 summarizes the relationship between TR, AR, and MR. To show that the demand curve and the AR curve are the same, we labeled the AR curve AR = D. Note that the MR curve is twice as steep as the AR curve and $OA = 2(OM)$. The MR curve shows the slope of the TR curve. As long as MR is positive, TR increases with output; when MR = 0, TR is at its maximum; and when MR is negative TR declines. The horizontal axis for TR as well as AR and MR curves are the same. The vertical axes, however, are in different dimensions for the TR curve and the AR-MR curves. The TR axis shows *dollars* of sales, but the AR-MR axis shows *dollars*

[3]Mathematically, a general expression for a linear AR curve is given by

$$AR = p = a - bq$$

where p is price, q is quantity demanded, and a and b are positive constants. Now the total revenue function is

$$TR = pq = aq - bq^2$$

Differentiating this with respect to q, we obtain the MR function,

$$MR = \frac{d(pq)}{dq} = a - 2bq$$

Comparing the equations for AR and MR, we note that the MR curve has the same price axis intercept as the AR curve, but its absolute slope is twice as steep as that of the AR curve.

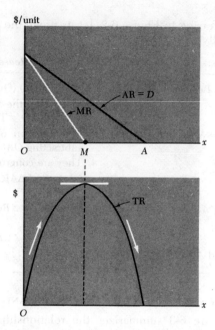

Figure 6-3 Relationships among AR, MR, and TR

per unit of output. When TR, AR, and MR curves are shown in the same graph to save space (or for the sake of comparison), the reader should remember that the vertical axes are in different dimensions for the TR curve and the AR-MR curves.

6-4 THE RELATIONSHIP BETWEEN CURVILINEAR AVERAGE AND MARGINAL REVENUE CURVES

The technique of drawing the MR curve can be readily extended to the case of a curvilinear demand curve. In Figure 6-4, the demand curve is shown by AR = D. To draw the corresponding MR curve, we select a few points on the AR curve and determine the values of MR that correspond to these values of AR.

To find the MR corresponding to point *A*:

1. Draw a line tangent to the AR curve at point *A* and let it intersect the price axis at *T*. (The tangent line gives the slope of the AR curve at *A*.)
2. Draw a horizontal line that goes through point *A* and cuts the price axis at *R*.

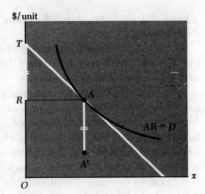

$/unit

Figure 6-4   Relationship between curvilinear average and marginal revenue curves

3.   Mark off the vertical line segment $A'A$ (whose length is identical to RT) directly below point A.

Point A' thus obtained is on the MR curve, and the height of the point is the value of the MR corresponding to point A on the AR curve.

We can repeat the above steps for a few selected points on the AR curve and secure additional points on the MR curve. When these points are connected by a freehand curve, we have the desired MR curve. The reader should locate several more points and draw the MR curve in Figure 6-4.

6-5   PRICE ELASTICITY OF DEMAND AT A POINT

From the law of demand, we know that price and quantity demanded are inversely related. The direction of change in quantity demanded following a given price change is clear. What is not clear is the extent by which quantity demanded will respond to a price change. But such information is precisely what businessmen and public policy makers are frequently interested in. The concept of price elasticity of demand (devised by Alfred Marshall) furnishes us with a convenient measure of responsiveness in quantity demanded when price is changed. *The price elasticity of demand, η, is defined as*:

$$\eta = \frac{\text{relative change in quantity demanded}}{\text{relative change in price}}$$

$$= \frac{\Delta q/q}{\Delta p/p} = \frac{\Delta q}{\Delta p} \cdot \frac{p}{q}$$

where Δq and Δp stand for small changes in price and quantity demanded.[4]

The price elasticity of demand as defined above is called the point elasticity of demand because it measures the elasticity at a point on the demand curve.

The price elasticity of demand (or elasticity coefficient) is a *pure ratio* independent of the units in which price and quantity are quoted. If the price quotation is changed from dollars to cents, both the price and the change in price will be increased a hundredfold, leaving the relative change in price unchanged. Likewise, a change in the units in which the quantity is measured (say, from pound to ounce) will not affect the relative change in quantity demanded. Clearly, an important advantage of the elasticity of demand is that it is *not influenced by an arbitrary choice of units.* Furthermore, being pure ratios, elasticity coefficients of different commodities *can be compared* even though commodities are quoted in different units and prices.

Because a demand curve has a negative slope, price and quantity move in opposite directions. Thus, the sign of a price elasticity (of demand) coefficient is always negative. In tabulating price elasticity coefficients, we usually add the negative signs. However, in comparing the magnitudes of elasticity coefficients, we think in terms of the absolute values; and classify price elasticity of demand into the following three categories on the basis of the absolute (or numerical) value of the elasticity coefficients.

$$|\eta| > 1 : \text{Elastic}$$
$$|\eta| = 1 : \text{Unitary}$$
$$|\eta| < 1 : \text{Inelastic}$$

Frequently, economists take the absolute value signs for granted, and talk of -2.8 being more elastic than -0.9. We may also follow this convention, and omit the absolute value signs when there is no danger of confusion.

SLOPE AND PRICE ELASTICITY

Note that $\eta = \dfrac{\Delta q}{\Delta p} \cdot \dfrac{p}{q}$. That is, η is the product of the reciprocal of the slope of a conventional demand curve, $\Delta q/\Delta p = 1/(\Delta p/\Delta q)$, and p/q whose value is determined by a point on the demand curve. In Figure 6-5, the elasticity coefficient measured

[4]In calculus notation,

$$\eta = \frac{dq/q}{dp/p} = \frac{dq}{dp}\frac{p}{q}.$$

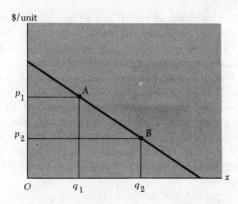

Figure 6-5 Elasticity coefficients of a linear demand curve differ at every distinct point

at point A is quite different from that at point B. The slope of the demand curve (and hence its reciprocal) is the same but the ratio p/q declines as we move from A to B, causing η at B to be numerically much smaller. Clearly, an elasticity coefficient is *not equal to* (the reciprocal of) *the slope;* elasticity coefficients of a (downward-sloping) *linear* demand curve differ at every distinct point on it.

Given a downward-sloping demand curve, you cannot tell the price elasticity of demand from its slope alone. Figure 6-6*a* shows two exceptions. If the demand curve is a horizontal line, η is infinite or undefined and demand is said to be *perfectly elastic.*

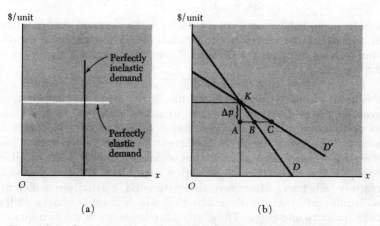

Figure 6-6 Special cases in which slopes reveal price elasticities

Similarly, when the demand curve is a vertical line, η is zero and demand is said to be *perfectly inelastic*. When two demand curves intersect, we can also say something about the price elasticities of the two curves at the particular point of intersection. In Figure 6-6b, at point K the flatter demand curve D' is more elastic than the steeper demand curve D. Let us see why. By definition, $\eta = (\Delta q/\Delta p)(p/q)$. At point K, price and quantity are the same for both demand curves. Now, for a given amount of change in price, Δp, the corresponding Δq for the flatter curve D' is AC units, while for the steeper curve D, it is only AB units. Thus, $\Delta q/\Delta p$ is larger for the flatter curve; and η (which equals $\Delta q/\Delta p$ times p/q) must be numerically larger for the flatter curve.

To repeat, in general, it is not possible to determine the elasticities of demand by looking at the slopes of demand curves alone. The only exceptions are when a demand curve is vertical or horizontal or when examining the relative elasticities of two or more demand curves at a common point of intersection.

6-6 ARC ELASTICITY OF DEMAND

Since the point elasticity of demand is defined for small changes in price and quantity, it should not be used unless relative changes involved are extremely small. In order to compute the elasticity coefficient from discrete recorded data, we employ the concept of *arc elasticity of demand*, Arc η, *which is defined as follows*:

$$\text{Arc } \eta = \frac{\dfrac{q_1 - q_2}{(q_1 + q_2)/2}}{\dfrac{p_1 - p_2}{(p_1 + p_2)/2}} = \frac{\Delta q/(q_1 + q_2)}{\Delta p/(p_1 + p_2)}$$

where p_1 and p_2 are any two prices on the demand schedule and q_1 and q_2 are the corresponding quantities. (The right-hand expression follows because the divisers "2" cancel out, $\Delta q = q_1 - q_2$, and $\Delta p = p_1 - p_2$).

Note that the only difference between this formula and the point elasticity formula is the use of the average quantities and average prices (instead of single price and quantity) as the bases in computing relative changes. Refer to Figure 6-7. We want to estimate the price elasticity coefficient between two points A and B on the demand curve. Can we tell which one, A or B, makes a better base for the estimation of the price elasticity? No, the choice is entirely arbitrary. However, the estimated elasticity coefficients will differ substantially depending on which point is chosen as the base quantity and price. Thus, using the averages of the two quanti-

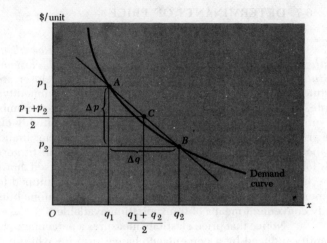

Figure 6-7 Arc elasticity of demand

ties and the two prices as the base quantity and price is a good compromise. In Figure 6-7, the arc elasticity is measured by

$$\frac{\Delta q}{(q_1 + q_2)/2} \div \frac{\Delta p}{(p_1 + p_2)/2}$$

Graphically, the arc elasticity of demand coefficient is identical to the point elasticity of demand coefficient measured at the midpoint of the straight line or chord connecting two points A and B.

The arc elasticity coefficient is interpreted just like the point elasticity coefficient and classified into elastic, inelastic, and unitary categories in an identical manner.

As an example of a numerical computation of the arc elasticity coefficient, consider a hamburger store that raised its price from 50 cents to 60 cents and found the daily sale of hamburgers to decline from 2,000 to 1,500. The magnitudes of changes involved are far from being small, and the proper elasticity measure to use is Arc η. Applying the arc elasticity formula, we find that

$$\text{Arc } \eta = \frac{\Delta q/(q_1 + q_2)}{\Delta p/(p_1 + p_2)} = \frac{-500/(2,000 + 1,500)}{10/(50 + 60)}$$

$$= \frac{-1/7}{1/11} = \frac{-11}{7}$$

The elasticity of demand for hamburgers thus is found to be $-11/7$ or -1.57.

6-7 DETERMINANTS OF PRICE ELASTICITY OF DEMAND

Whether demand for a commodity is price elastic or inelastic is largely determined by the number and closeness of substitutes available. The more numerous and the closer are the substitutes, the more elastic the demand for the commodity. For example, the demand for Texaco gasoline—which has a number of close substitutes in other brands of gasoline—will be highly elastic. If the price of Texaco gas is raised while those of other brands remain the same, a large number of demanders will substitute other brands for the Texaco brand. The demand for gasoline itself, however, will be highly inelastic because most cars are not equipped to use any other fuel as a substitute, and for many people automobiles are the only convenient means of transportation available.

Notice that price elasticity measures a percentage change in quantity induced by a percentage change in price while holding other variables constant. Such measures of relative responses, however, are affected greatly by the length of *time* involved. In general, the longer the time period involved, the more elastic is the demand for a commodity. There are several obvious reasons for this. First, it takes time for people to learn about a price change and the characteristics of the good involved. Thus, the imperfection of knowledge tends to make demand more elastic over a longer period of time. Second, there is the matter of inertia. It takes time and planning to change habitual patterns of consumption. For instance, a recent study shows that the demand for foreign travel becomes far more price elastic over a longer period of time.[5] Third, there is a technological consideration. Suppose the price of a major appliance is reduced. Even though the consumer may consider the appliance an attractive buy, it takes time for him to wear out the one he already owns. Even if there were a substantial reduction in the price of electricity, the consumers cannot increase kilowatt-hours consumed substantially in a short period of time. However, given time, the lower electric rate is likely to induce more use of electrical appliances, such as dishwashers, electric heaters, air-conditioners, and freezers. As new houses are built, they are likely to contain more features that take advantage of lower electric rates.

Several other factors are claimed to influence the demand elasticity. It is asserted that *if the price* of the commodity relative to the consumer's income *is low* the demand for the commodity is inelastic. Matchbooks and salt are frequently cited examples. Note, however, that demand for a particular brand of matches or salt—whose cost is but a small portion of the consumer's budget—

[5] See Table 6-3 on p. 137.

will be highly elastic. As long as there is a ready substitute available, the price elasticity of demand for a commodity will be highly elastic even if its price is a small fraction of the consumer's income.

The greater the *number of uses* to which a commodity can be put, it is argued, the more elastic is the demand for the good. There is something uneasy about this claim. A large number of relatively unimportant uses put together would not necessarily be as significant as a few major uses combined. We can explain this so-called number-of-uses argument in a much more convincing manner in terms of substitutability. If a resource (or good) is a good substitute for other resources or goods, demand for this resource will be elastic. A decline in the price of this resource must increase its quantity demanded substantially because this resource will now be substituted for other resources. Thus, we may conclude that the more numerous (or important) are the uses for which a good can serve as a close substitute, the more elastic the demand for this good.

6-8 DIFFERENT KINDS OF ELASTICITY

The elasticity of demand we have been discussing thus far is the *price* elasticity of demand, which shows a relative change in quantity demanded in response to a relative change in price. There are many other kinds of elasticities. The following are some of the more frequently used elasticity types.

Income Elasticity of Demand, $\eta_y = \dfrac{\Delta q/q}{\Delta y/y}$

Demand for some goods is closely related to the level of income, y. For example, expenditures for more expensive home furnishings, such as carpeting, and the amount spent for recreation are highly correlated to the level of income. If an increase in income results in an increased (decreased) purchase of a good, the sign of the income elasticity coefficient will be positive (negative). From the sign of the income elasticity coefficient, therefore, it is possible to tell whether a good is normal or inferior. *Goods whose income elasticities are positive (that is, goods that are purchased more as income increases) are* **normal goods.** *On the other hand, goods whose income elasticities are negative (that is, goods that are purchased less as income increases) are* **inferior goods.**

Cross Elasticity of Demand, $\eta_{BA} = \dfrac{\Delta q_B/q_B}{\Delta p_A/p_A}$

Use of two goods A and B may be related. *Two goods A and B are said to be complements if an increased use of A induces an increased use of B. On the other hand, if an increased use of A results in a decreased use of B, they are said to be substitutes.*

Cross elasticity of demand measures the relative change in the quantity of good *B* purchased as a consequence of a relative change in the price of *A*, while the price of *B* remains the same. For example, consider the case of bus and subway transportation in a city. Suppose the subway fare is raised by 25 percent while bus fare is not altered, and that because of the subway fare increase, the number of bus commuters increases by 10 percent. Here the cross elasticity of demand (for bus transportation with respect to the subway fare) is:

$$\eta_{BS} = .10/.25 = +.40$$

In general, the *cross elasticity coefficient is positive if two goods are substitutes*. On the other hand, the cross elasticity coefficient for complementary goods (such as slacks and sport coats) is *negative*. If two goods are unrelated, the quantity demanded of *A* will not be influenced by a change in the price of *B*. Thus, the cross elasticity coefficient for unrelated goods is *zero*.

Price Elasticity of Supply, $\eta_s = \dfrac{\Delta q_s/q_s}{\Delta p/p}$

Price elasticity of supply shows the relative change in quantity supplied, q_s, of a good corresponding to a relative change in its price. For example, an increase in the price of beef tends to encourage ranchers to raise more cattle and increase the supply of beef in the market. Some products may have rather high price elasticities of supply, while others have relatively low supply elasticities. Thus, the knowledge of supply elasticities is important for businessmen as well as for public policy makers. Time may importantly influence the supply elasticities. For instance, price or income elasticity of supply for engineers may be quite low in a short period of time because it takes time to train new engineers. Over a longer period of time, however, higher wages and plentiful job opportunities induce more young people to enter the engineering profession and increase the supply of engineers. Accordingly, we will often talk of short-run and long-run supply elasticities. We shall have more to say about the elasticities of supply in later chapters.

Many other kinds of elasticity coefficients can be considered. Generally speaking, whenever a relative change in variable *y* is compared with a relative change in variable *x*, while other variables remain the same, we have an elasticity coefficient.[6] Thus,

[6]In general, given a function $f(x_1, x_2, \ldots, x_n)$, its elasticity with respect to variable x_i is defined as

$$\eta_i = \frac{\partial f/f}{\partial x_i/x_i} = \frac{\partial f}{\partial x_i} \frac{x_i}{f}$$

we may speak of income elasticity of import, elasticity of grade point average with respect to hours studied, etc.

6-9 GEOMETRIC MEASUREMENT OF POINT ELASTICITY OF DEMAND

The following proposition provides a simple method of measuring the point elasticity of demand. *Given a linear demand curve that intersects the price axis at A and the quantity axis at B, the point elasticity of demand at any point C on the demand curve is given by CB/CA.*

Let us prove this proposition referring to Figure 6-8.

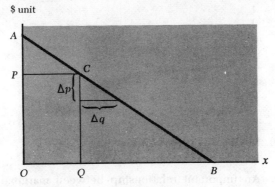

Figure 6-8 Geometric measurement of elasticity coefficient

Steps	Reasons
1. We want to show that	
$\eta = \dfrac{\Delta q}{\Delta p}\dfrac{p}{q} = CB/CA$	1. By the definition of η
2. $\dfrac{\Delta q}{\Delta p} = \dfrac{QB}{CQ} = \dfrac{QB}{PO}$	2. $CQ = PO$
3. $\eta = \dfrac{\Delta q}{\Delta p}\dfrac{p}{q} = \dfrac{QB}{PO}\cdot\dfrac{OP}{OQ}$	3. When directed distance is considered, $OP = -PO$
$= \dfrac{QB}{PO}\cdot\dfrac{PO}{QO} = \dfrac{QB}{QO}$	$\therefore \dfrac{OP}{OQ} = \dfrac{-PO}{-QO} = \dfrac{PO}{QO}$
4. $\therefore \eta = \dfrac{QB}{QO} = \dfrac{CB}{CA} = \dfrac{PO}{PA}$	4. A line parallel to a side of a triangle bisects the other two sides in equal proportions.

Note that the directed line segments CB and CA are opposite in sign. The price elasticity coefficient remains negative by this mathematical convention.

The ratio CB/CA in Figure 6-8 is zero at point B, unitary at the midpoint between B and A, and infinitely large (or undefined) at point A. Clearly, the point elasticity of demand along a downward-sloping linear demand curve is different for every distinct point on the curve. Again, it is obvious that the slope of a demand curve does not show its price elasticity of demand.

In order to measure the elasticity of demand of a curvilinear demand curve at a point, we simply draw a tangent line to the curve at that point, and apply the above geometric technique.

6-10 MARGINAL REVENUE AND POINT ELASTICITY OF DEMAND

An important relationship between marginal revenue, MR, price elasticity of demand, η, and price, p, is given by the following equation.

$$MR = p(1 + 1/\eta)$$

This relationship can be readily established by simple geometry. In Figure 6-9, given the AR and MR curves, we want to show that MR at output OM is related to the point elasticity of demand at output OM by the above equation. The following steps provide the needed geometric proof.[7]

[7]Mathematically, marginal revenue is the first derivative of the total revenue. That is,

$$MR = \frac{d(pq)}{dq} = p + q\frac{dp}{dq}$$

In order to obtain the desired expression, we simply rearrange the right-hand members of the equation.

$$MR = p\left(1 + \frac{q}{p}\frac{dp}{dq}\right)$$

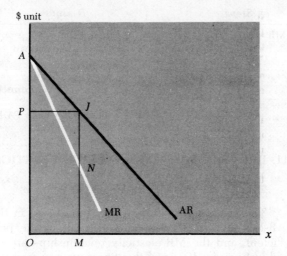

Figure 6-9 Marginal revenue and price elasticity:
$MR = p(1 + 1/\eta)$

$$= p\left(1 + 1/\frac{dq}{dp}\frac{p}{q}\right)$$
$$= p(1 + 1/\eta)$$

   This relationship among η, MR, and p applies equally well to nonlinear demand curves, because the above mathematical proof is independent of any linearity assumption.

   By replacing MR by M, any marginal quantity, and p by A, any average quantity, we can write the above relationship as

$$M = A(1 + 1/\eta)$$

This is a general formula that applies to the relationship between any marginal quantity and its elasticity coefficient. The reader must be careful *not to ignore* the sign of the elasticity coefficient in the above formula. For instance, it is negative for demand elasticity and positive for supply elasticity.

   Some textbooks will show the MR-elasticity relationship as $MR = p(1 - 1/\eta)$. In this formulation, η is treated as positive by taking the absolute value. We chose to define the way we did in order to provide an easier transition to the more general result, which applies to any marginal and average relationship and is not restricted to the MR-AR relationship alone.

Steps	*Reasons*
1. MR $= MN = MJ - NJ$	1. By definition
2. $\quad = OP - PA$	2. $NJ = PA$ by the AR-MR proposition.
3. $\quad = OP(1 - PA/OP)$	3. By factoring OP out
4. $\quad = p(1 + PA/PO)$	4. $p =$ Price $= OP$ and directed distance $OP = -PO$
5. $\quad = p(1 + 1/\eta)$	5. $\eta = PO/PA$ and $1/\eta = PA/PO$

6-11 RELATIONSHIP AMONG PRICE ELASTICITY, MARGINAL REVENUE, AND TOTAL REVENUE: A SUMMARY

The quantitative propositions introduced in this chapter—the AR-MR-TR relationship, measurement of the point elasticity coefficient, and the MR-elasticity relationship—are concisely summarized in Figure 6-10. From this figure, we can readily observe the relationships among the price elasticity coefficient, marginal revenue, and total revenue (or expenditure from the buyers' point of view) summarized in the following table.

Table 6-2 Relationships among Price Elasticity, Marginal Revenue, and Total Revenue

PRICE ELASTICITY OF DEMAND	MARGINAL REVENUE	TOTAL REVENUE WHEN PRICE IS LOWERED
Elastic	Positive	Increases
Unitary	Zero	Remains constant
Inelastic	Negative	Decreases

Note from Figure 6-10 that if demand is elastic and price is being lowered, the corresponding total revenue increases. If the price is being raised (that is, if we move along the demand curve to the left), however, an elastic demand implies a decreasing total revenue. Therefore, it is necessary to specify whether the price is being lowered or raised when discussing the relationship between the elasticity coefficient and the direction of change in total revenue.[8]

[8]*If price is being raised,* the direction of change in TR will be reversed. That is, TR decreases for elastic demand, increases for inelastic demand, and remains constant for unitary demand. The reader will be less confused if he focuses his attention on one price situation alone (and remembers that the direction of change in TR is reversed as the direction of change in price is reversed.)

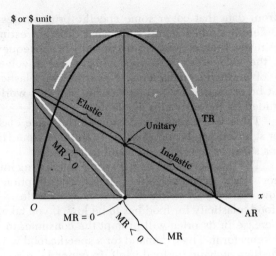

Figure 6-10   Relationships among price elasticity, marginal revenue, and total revenue

If the price elasticity of demand is unitary throughout the relevant range of a demand curve, the total revenue must remain constant even though the price is changed. Thus, the demand equation must be of the form, $pq = k$, where k is a constant. The graph of such an equation is a rectangular hyperbola, as shown in Figure 6-11.

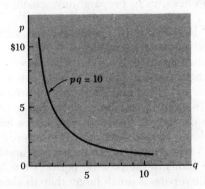

Figure 6-11   Demand curve having a unitary elasticity

6-12   EMPIRICAL ESTIMATES OF ELASTICITIES:
An Application

Let us now look into some empirical estimates of elasticity coefficients. Elasticity coefficients are *estimates* that must be obtained from data that cover some specific price ranges and time periods. Different studies report somewhat different estimates, and researchers revise their estimates substantially in subsequent studies, indicating the difficulties and inconclusiveness involved in the estimation of elasticity coefficients. Nevertheless, elasticity coefficients must be estimated as best as we can, and real world policies must be guided by the estimates available.

Table 6-3 contains estimates of the price elasticities of demand for selected goods and services in the U.S. from Houthakker and Taylor's study on consumer demand in the U.S.

The table provides us with some interesting information. Demand for *broad aggregates* like "home consumption of food" has very low elasticity of demand. Since there is little we can substitute for food, elasticity for food has to be low. If you take a specific food, an increase in its price will prompt the consumer to substitute other food items for it. Thus, demand for a specific food will be much more elastic than demand for food itself. In general, broad aggregates like food, clothing, gasoline and oil, automobiles (new and net purchase of used ones), tobacco products, and shoes have low elasticities; while specific goods such as T-bone steaks, Kuppenheimer suits, and Texaco gasoline have high elasticities. Many entries in the table represent broad aggregates, and for that reason their elasticities are rather low. Whenever a good is defined in broad aggregates, it becomes difficult to find a substitute for it. Such unavailability of substitutes is the major reason for low price elasticities for physicians' services, drug preparations, gasoline and oil, water, etc.

The low elasticity coefficient for airline travel suggests that demand for air transportation is influenced by the level of income rather than its price. Note the difference between short-run and long-run elasticities for foreign travel, intercity railway and bus transportation, and radio and TV repairs. Foreign travel and use of railways and intercity buses tend to be habit forming; since it takes time to change habits, the price elasticities for these services tend to be much lower in the short run. (It is interesting to note that Houthakker and Taylor found intercity railway and bus transportation were inferior goods in the postwar period.) The long-run elasticity for TV and radio repairs is much larger than its short-run elasticity, suggesting that in the short run consumers do not have much alternative but to have their sets repaired.

Elasticities for what are loosely called *necessities* such as food, clothing, water, gasoline and oil, automobiles, and physicians' services are noticeably lower than elasticities for so-called *luxuries* such as jewelry and watches, china and tableware, and toilet articles.

Table 6-3 Price Elasticities of Demand
for Selected Goods in the U.S.

ITEM	SHORT-RUN	LONG-RUN	ITEM	SHORT-RUN	LONG-RUN
Home consumption of food	n.s.	n.s.	Shoes	− .9	n.s.
Clothing	n.s.	n.s.	Jewelry and watches	− .4	− .7
Furniture	n.s.	n.s.	Toilet articles and preparations	− .2	−3.0
Cars (new and old)	n.s.	n.s.	China and tableware	−1.5	−2.6
Tobacco products	n.s.	n.s.	Electricity	− .1	−1.9
Physicians	n.s.	n.s.	Water	− .2	− .1
Drug preparations	n.s.	n.s.	Tires and tubes	− .9	−1.2
Gasoline and oil	n.s.	n.s.	Intercity railways	−1.4	−3.2
Education	n.s.	n.s.	Intercity bus	− .2	−2.2
Airline travel	n.s.	n.s.	Newspapers and magazines	− .4	n.s.
Foreign travel	− .1	−1.8	Radio and TV repairs	− .5	−3.8
			Motion pictures	− .9	−3.7

n.s.: No significant response in consumer purchases to price changes
was observed.

Source: H. S. Houthakker and L. D. Taylor, *Consumer Demand in the
United States: Analyses and Projections* (Cambridge, Mass.: Harvard University Press,
1970), pp. 60–144.

However, it must be warned, the concepts of necessities and luxuries
are rather nebulous; their meanings vary from people to people, from
place to place, and from time to time.

INCOME AND CROSS ELASTICITIES
FOR SELECTED GOODS IN THE U.K.

Richard Stone's estimates of income, price and cross
elasticities for selected commodities in the United Kingdom are
reproduced in Table 6-4.

The various elasticity coefficients found by Stone
correspond surprisingly well to our *a priori* expectations. Most goods
are normal, but such commodities as flour, bread, margarine, and beer
are found to be inferior. The cross relationships shown also conform
rather well with our expectations. Most related goods shown are substitutes. The cross elasticity of demand for butter with respect to
the price of flour, however, is negative, suggesting that there is a
complementary relationship between the two commodities. Com-

Table 6-4 Income, Price, and Cross Elasticities for Selected
Commodities in the United Kingdom
(based on budget surveys, 1937–39, or time series, 1920–38)

COMMODITY	INCOME ELASTICITY	PRICE ELASTICITY	CROSS ELASTICITY WITH RESPECT TO PRICE OF SPECIFIED COMMODITIES	
Flour (1924–38)	−0.15	−0.79		
Bread	−0.05	−0.08		
Beef and veal			Imported mutton	
(domestic)	0.34	−0.41	and lamb	0.50
Poultry	1.17	−0.27	Mutton and lamb	
			(domestic)	0.73
Eggs	0.54	−0.43		
Fresh milk	0.50	−0.49	Beef and veal	
			(domestic)	0.73
Butter	0.37	−0.41	Flour	−0.21
Margarine	−0.16	0.01	Butter	1.01
Apples (domestic)	1.33	−1.67	Fresh fruit	2.77
Sugar	0.09	−0.44	Chocolate and	
			confectionery	1.06
Tea	0.04	−0.26	Coffee	0.14
Coffee	1.42			
Beer	−0.05	−0.87		
Tobacco (as a whole)	0.25	−0.27		
Electricity	0.15	−0.06		

Source: Richard Stone, *The Measurement of Consumers' Expenditure
and Behavior in the United Kingdom,* 1920–38, Vol. 1 (Cambridge: Cambridge University Press, 1954), pp. 322–337, 390, 400.

paring the income elasticities of demand for coffee and tea makes it
clear that the British are tea drinking (rather than coffee drinking)
people.

6-13 CROP LIMITATION: An Application

Often a farmer may wonder why the federal government, which purports to aid the farmers, restricts the acreages for many agricultural commodities. With our knowledge of elasticity of demand and of the fact that demand for many agricultural goods is *inelastic* over the relevant range of prices, we are in an excellent position to answer the farmer's question.

Suppose the demand and supply curves for a crop, in the absence of any government interference, are as shown in Figure 6-12. The competitive equilibrium is given by point E and the total revenue received by the farmers growing this crop is $OPEQ$ dollars. Suppose we Americans consider that this revenue is insufficient for the farmers, and that the farmers must be aided by a federal action. One way to aid the farmers is to restrict crop production to Q' units per annum. This legal crop restriction changes the shape of the supply curve to the dotted line ABC: the vertical segment BC shows that the quantity supplied cannot be greater than Q' units no matter how high the price is. The intersection of the dotted supply curve and the demand curve establishes the market price at $\$P'$ per bushel, and the farmers' total revenue increases to $OP'E'Q'$. How do we know that $OP'E'Q'$ is greater than $OPEQ$—the farmers' total revenue in the absence of the crop limitation program? We know it because an increase in price when demand is inelastic is accompanied by an increase in total revenue. Thus, it is clear that when demand for a crop is inelastic—as is true for most agricultural commodities— a crop limitation program increases the total revenue received by the crop growers. Since it must cost less to produce a smaller quantity, the net gain to the farmers must be even greater.

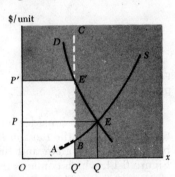

$/unit

Figure 6-12 Crop limitation and farmers' revenue

Note that the consumers are worse off: they pay a higher price, and consume a smaller quantity. Since all the output produced is sold in the market, there is neither a surplus nor a shortage.

6-14 PRICE SUPPORT PROGRAM VERSUS SUBSIDIZING CONSUMER-PRODUCER PRICE DIFFERENTIAL: An Application

Let us consider two more forms of aid to agriculture and compare their costs to the government. First, there is the *price support* program. In order to see how this program works refer to

Figure 6-13. We have assumed a vertical supply curve in order to simplify our argument. In view of the demand and supply conditions portrayed in the graph, the equilibrium price in the absence of any government interference is P and the total revenue received by the farmers is $OPEQ$. Suppose now the government guarantees to support the price at P' per unit, then consumers will purchase only $P'T$ units at this higher price, but the suppliers will be happy to produce $P'E' = OQ$ units. Because of the price support program, the farmers' total revenue jumps to $OP'E'Q$ per period. The consumers are again adversely affected: they pay a higher price per bushel and consume a smaller quantity. The consumers' total expenditures are $OP'TR$ dollars. The difference between the farmers' total revenue and the consumers' total expenditure, $RTE'Q$, shows the cost to the government of purchasing the unsold surplus at the support price. This area is shaded and labeled G in the figure. The government must, in addition, incur the cost of storing this surplus.

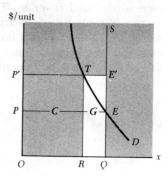

Figure 6-13 Price support program

Now consider an alternative scheme of aiding agriculture referred to as the *Benson-Brannan plan*. To facilitate a comparison between this program and that of the price support, we introduce Figure 6-14, which contains the identical demand and supply curves of Figure 6-13. This plan works something like this. Farmers are told to sell all they can at the price established by the market, and promised that the government will pay them, for each bushel of the crops sold, the difference between the market price and the government support price. In terms of Figure 6-14, farmers sell Q units at the price of P per unit and receive $OPEQ$ from the consumers. The government subsidizes the farmers EE' per bushel for Q units sold, and adds $PP'E'E$ to the farmers' receipts. The cost to the government, G', under the Benson-Brannan plan must be larger than the government cost, G, under the price support program. Visual impression aside, how do we know that this assertion is true? To answer this question, we must again rely on our knowledge of the

140

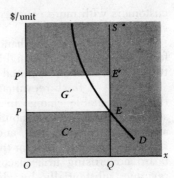

Figure 6-14 Consumer-producer
price differential subsidy

relationship between price elasticity and total revenue. By the very construction of the graphs, the total revenues received by the farmers in both graphs are identical. Therefore, if we can show that C (consumer payments under the price support program) is larger than C' (consumer payments under the Benson-Brannan plan), we will succeed in showing that G is smaller than G'. Since demand is assumed to be inelastic over the relevant range of prices, and the price charged consumers is higher under the price support program, it is obvious that C is greater than C'.

The reader, however, should not jump to the conclusion that the price support program is cheaper and superior to the Benson-Brannan plan. Note that a price support program creates a surplus and a myriad of storage problems associated with it. Consumers who have to pay the higher support price and consume a smaller quantity under a price support program will definitely prefer the Benson-Brannan plan, which offers them a much lower competitive price.

6-15 ELASTICITY AS A BASIS FOR PRICE POLICY

When a new product is introduced, how do we determine its price? Should the product be launched with a high price in order to skim off the cream of demand or with a low price in order to penetrate the mass market early? To answer this question, we must evaluate the price elasticity of demand for the product. Introducing a new product with a high initial price, for instance, is an effective way of segmenting the total market into submarkets that differ in elasticities. The initial high price skims the cream off the market; successively lower prices capture submarkets with higher elasticities. Deluxe, hard cover, and paperback editions of a book represent such a pricing policy. Introduction of color television receivers at high initial prices, and subsequent lowering of their prices to capture customers with more elastic demands also exemplify such a pricing strategy.

On the other hand, if market research reveals the demand for a new product to be highly elastic, a bold program of launching the product with a low initial price may be undertaken.

A fresh reevaluation of price elasticity may often introduce a profitable change in price policy of a firm. For instance, a service station owner's monthly revenue from fixing flat tires, balancing and rotating tires, and greasing has increased substantially since he lowered prices for those services. On the other hand, a billboard advertising firm discovered that it could increase its sales revenue substantially by charging higher rates for its billboard advertising; the demand for billboard advertising was inelastic in the relevant range.[9]

[9]W. W. Haynes and W. R. Henry, *Managerial Economics*, 3d ed. (Dallas, Texas: Business Publication, 1974), pp. 370–371.

APPENDIX 6

A. Demand Curves
with Constant Elasticities

The purpose of this appendix is to examine the form of demand function that has constant elasticities. As a preliminary step, we note the following rather useful way to show the price elasticity coefficient.

Using the chain rule of differentiation,

$$\frac{d(\ln q)}{d(\ln p)} = \frac{(d \ln q)}{(dq)} \cdot \frac{(dq)}{(dp)} \cdot \frac{(dp)}{(d \ln p)}$$

$$= \left(\frac{1}{q}\right)\left(\frac{dq}{dp}\right)\left(\frac{1}{1/p}\right)$$

$$= \frac{dq}{dp}\frac{p}{q} = \eta$$

Thus, the elasticity coefficient is equal to the derivative of $\ln q$ with respect to $\ln p$.

Now we are ready to introduce and prove the following proposition on demand curves with constant elasticities.

If the demand equation takes a hyperbolic form such as $q = k \, p^e y^j$, the exponents of the independent variables are elasticity coefficients, which are constant at every point on the demand curve.

Proof: Let the demand equation be given by

$$q = k \, p^e y^j$$

where k, e, and j are constants, $p = $ price, and $y = $ income.

We want to show that e is the price elasticity coefficient and j is the income elasticity coefficient. Writing the demand equation in the logarithmic form we get

$$\ln q = \ln k + e \ln p + j \ln y$$

The partial elasticities for price η and income η_y are

$$\eta = \frac{\partial \ln q}{\partial \ln p} = \frac{\partial(\ln k + e \ln p + j \ln y)}{\partial(\ln p)} = 0 + e(1) + 0 = e$$

$$\eta_y = \frac{\partial \ln q}{\partial \ln y} = \frac{\partial(\ln k + e \ln p + j \ln y)}{\partial(\ln y)} = 0 + 0 + j(1) = j$$

Thus, $\eta = e$ and $\eta_y = j$.

Example: If the demand function is $q = 3p^{-2}y^3$, then the partial elasticities are:

$$\eta = \frac{\partial \ln q}{\partial \ln p} = \frac{\partial}{\partial \ln p}(\ln 3 - 2 \ln p + 3 \ln y) = -2$$

$$\eta_y = \frac{\partial}{\partial \ln y}(\ln 3 - 2 \ln p + 3 \ln y) = 3$$

In section 6-11, we noted that when total revenue does not change as price changes, the elasticity of demand is unitary. This can be readily verified by the proposition we have just proved. If the total revenue (pq) is constant, the demand equation is

$$pq = k \text{ or } q = k \, p^{-1}$$

From our proposition on constant elasticities, we know immediately that the price elasticity coefficient is -1 (unitary).

If the demand equation is given by $q = ap^{-b}$, the price elasticity coefficient is $-b$ by our proposition. The equation $q = ap^{-b}$, however, can be written in logarithm as $\ln q = \ln a - b \ln p$ which is the equation of a straight line on a double-log graph with a slope of $-b$. Thus, the price elasticity coefficient is given by the slope of

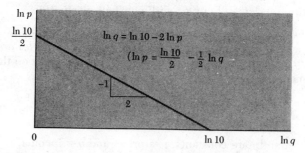

Figure 6-15   Elasticity measurement on a double-logarithmic scale

the demand curve with respect to the ln p axis *if* the curve is plotted on a double-logarithmic scale. As an example consider the demand equation given by $q = 10\,p^{-2}$. Then $\ln q = \ln 10 - 2 \ln p$. Plotting this on a double-log scale we get Figure 6-15. The reciprocal of the slope (or slope with respect to ln p axis) is -2 and shows the price elasticity of demand. The reason we have to take the reciprocal of the slope (rather than the slope of the curve) is due to the convention in economics of reversing the price and quantity axes.

B. Price-Consumption Curve and Price Elasticities

By showing the amount of money on the vertical axis and the quantity of a good on the horizontal axis of an indifference diagram, we can determine whether the demand for the good is elastic, unitary, or inelastic simply by observing the slope of the price-consumption curve.

Three graphs are shown in Figure 6-16a, b, and c. In each of these graphs, the total amount of money available to the consumer is shown by OL along the vertical axis, and the original budget line is given by LM. The initial equilibrium combination chosen by the consumer in each graph is, therefore, given by point E.

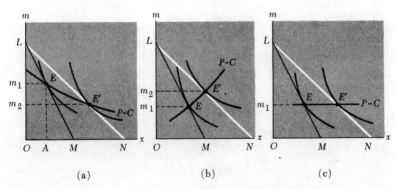

Figure 6-16 Price elasticities as measured by the slopes of the price-consumption curves

In Figure 6-16a, the consumer's equilibrium bundle, E, contains Om_1 dollars of money and OA units of x. The difference between the original sum held by the consumer and the current sum held by him ($OL - Om_1 = m_1L$) shows the amount spent by the consumer. Note that the amount of money spent on good x is measured by the vertical distance m_1L, *not* by line segment Om_1 — which shows the amount of money remaining. Now a reduction in the price of x shifts the budget line from LM to LN. The new equilibrium combination chosen by the consumer following this price reduction is E'. In purchasing this combination, the consumer spends m_2L (which is equal to $OL - Om_2$) dollars. Thus, the consumer's expenditure on x has increased by m_2m_1 dollars as the price of x is reduced. From the TR-elasticity relationship of section 6-11, we conclude that the demand for good x is elastic in the observed range. Notice that the price-consumption curve in Figure 6-16a is negatively sloped. *A negatively sloped price-consumption curve, thus, indicates an elastic demand.* This conclusion is valid, however, only if income (or its equivalent, the bundle of all other goods) is shown on the vertical axis.

In Figures 6-16b and c, line LN indicates a lower price for good x, and E' shows the new equilibrium combination chosen by the consumer following the price reduction. The price-consumption curve in Figure 6-16b is positively sloped, indicating that the consumer has reduced his expenditure on good x by m_1m_2 dollars as the price of x is reduced. Therefore, we conclude that *a positively sloped price-consumption curve shows an inelastic price elasticity of demand.* In Figure 6-16c, the price-consumption curve is horizontal: the expenditure on good x remains unchanged as the price of x is reduced. Accordingly, we know that *a horizontal price-consumption curve indicates a unitary price elasticity of demand.*

EXERCISES 6

Market Demand
and Elasticity of Demand

6-1 The demand equations of three individual consumers that make up the total market are $q_1 = 10 - p$, $q_2 = 12 - 1.5p$, and $q_3 = 20 - 2p$.

1. Complete the following table and show three individual demand schedules as well as the market demand schedule. (For any given price, $Q = q_1 + q_2 + q_3$.)

Price	q_1	q_2	q_3	Q
\$12	____	____	____	____
10	____	____	____	____
8	____	____	____	____
6	____	____	____	____
4	____	____	____	____
2	____	____	____	____

2. Plot the individual demand curves on graph paper and label them d_1, d_2, and d_3.
3. Obtain the market demand curve as the horizontal sum of individual curves and label it D.

6-2 The relationship between linear AR and MR curves can be readily translated into the relationship between linear average variable cost (AVC) and marginal cost (MC) curves. (VC is the cost that varies as output changes, and MC is the additional cost incurred in producing one more unit of output.) Demonstrate your mastery of the relationship between linear AR and MR curves by proving that $\overline{AB} = \overline{BC}$ in Figure 6-17, which shows an AVC curve and its corresponding MC curve.

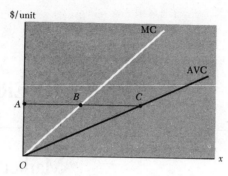

Figure 6-17

6-3 Complete the following table, which shows the relationships among TR, MR, and arc elasticity coefficient. Check whether your answers are consistent with TR-MR-elasticity relationships discussed in the text.

p	q	TR	MR	Arc elasticity	Elasticity category
$12	8	$96		$\dfrac{2/18}{-2/22} = \dfrac{-11}{9}$	
			$2		elastic
10	10	100		_____	_____
8	16	____	—	_____	_____
6	20	____	—	_____	_____
4	30	____	—	_____	_____

6-4 Suppose the price elasticity for automobiles is −1.5. Would it then be in the interest of the auto industry to lower prices? Explain.

6-5 Suppose the price elasticity of demand for beef is −0.8. Would the price elasticity for meat (including poultry, fish as well as beef) be larger or smaller than that for beef? Explain.

6-6 Asked to furnish an exception to the law of demand, a student cited cattle ranchers who consume more beef steaks when the price of beef is high. Do you agree that this is an exception to the law of negatively sloping demand curve? Or do you have a better explanation?

6-7 The Johnsons are a middle-income American family who live in a small city. The price of salt in the town in which the Johnsons live is 20 cents per pound, and the Johnsons consume 10 pounds of salt per annum. Now all the stores that sell salt have raised their price to 30 cents per pound.

1.   Would the Johnsons' purchases of salt be affected by the price increase? Why or why not?

2.   In view of your answer to (1), what can you say about the price elasticity of demand for salt?

3.   Suppose the Johnsons' income doubles, how would this affect the quantity of salt consumed by this family? What can you say about the income elasticity of demand for salt?

4.   Suppose only the price of brand M salt is increased by 10 cents per pound while brands X and Y maintained the old price of 20 cents per pound. How would this affect the Johnsons' purchase of salt?

5.   Can you think of a commodity with respect to whose price the cross elasticity of demand for salt may be significant?

6.   Why do you think that in olden days monarchs frequently taxed salt?

6-8   The following table shows prices and quantities of beef and pork consumed per family in a certain city for three periods of time.

PERIOD	BEEF		PORK	
	p	q	p	q
I	.90	4.0	.80	2
II	1.00	3.2	.80	3
III	1.00	3.5	.88	2.5

1.   For beef, using the information given in the table, compute the price and cross elasticities.

2.   For pork, compute the price elasticity and cross elasticity.

3.   Explain why the cross elasticities in (1) and (2) are different.

CHAPTER SEVEN

THE THEORY OF PRODUCTION: PHYSICAL ASPECTS

The business firm is the decision unit that governs the supply side of the market mechanism. The firm hires various resources, transforms them into goods and services, and makes them available to consumers. To analyze business firms' behavior, we begin this chapter with an examination of production. The theory of production forms the cornerstone of the theory of cost, which in turn controls the supply side of the price mechanism.

The main tasks that lie ahead of us in this chapter are to: (1) show how economists represent the state of technology that constrains the production processes; (2) examine production with a single variable input, that is, what happens to output when increasing amounts of an input are combined with other inputs whose quantities are fixed. In Chapter Eight, which is a continuation of this chapter, we will evaluate production with two inputs, that is, the effect on output of substituting one input for another or increasing all inputs proportionately. Estimates of some empirical production functions will also be presented toward the end of the next chapter.

7-1 PRODUCTION

Generally, production may be defined as a process by which inputs are transformed (produced, or processed) into an output. An input is any good or service that goes into production, an output is any good or service that comes out of the production process. Production does not necessarily mean a physical conversion of raw materials into a commodity as in manufacturing. Such processes as transportation and storage are just as good examples of production as is the manufacturing process. Transportation increases the utility of a good by bringing it to the place of need, whereas storage provides the good when it is needed.

Production is a *process*, not an act. Thus, inputs and output are rates of flow per unit of time; bushels per week, tons per month, and so on. The selection of a particular time period is arbitrary. It is only for economy of time and space that economists, including this author, do not constantly refer to the phrase "per unit of time." Whenever there is any ambiguity, the time period involved should be stated explicitly.

To simplify our study of production, we introduce the following *assumptions*. First, current technological know-how is perfectly known among the firms that are engaged in the particular line of production. Any modern industrialized society possesses a vast amount of technical know-how, and no single individual producer is capable of knowing all such technology. But it is reasonable to assume that a firm knows the current technology of the field in which it operates.

Second, in order to facilitate the two-dimensional graphical analysis, we assume there are only *two inputs* (labor and capital) and one output. This amounts to assuming that production processes do not require such other inputs as raw material or that they all require the same amounts of other inputs per unit of output.

Third, an inefficient production process will never be used. *A process is inefficient if it uses more of some inputs without using less of any input in producing a given amount of output.*

7-2 PRODUCTION FUNCTION

In order to describe the technological relationship between inputs and output, economists rely on the concept of the production function. *The production function shows the maximum quantity of output, q, that can be produced as a function of the quantities of inputs, labor and capital, used in the production processes.* In equation form, we write

$$q_{max} = f(l, k)$$

More generally, the production function with n variables is defined as

$$q_{max} = f(v_1, v_2, v_3, \ldots, v_n)$$

where v_i is the rate at which input i is used.

To emphasize the fact that technical efficiency is presupposed (that is, an inefficient process is never used), the subscript "max" is attached to the amount of output q. Since only efficient input combinations are used, the production function associates a unique maximum level of output to each combination of inputs.

The production function shows only the *physical* relationship between inputs and output, and says nothing about the optimal combination of inputs. Selecting the optimal input combination is an economic decision that requires such additional information as the prices of inputs and the demand for output.

7-3   THE PRODUCTION SURFACE AND ITS SLICES

THE PRODUCTION SURFACE

The relationship between two inputs and one output is described graphically by the production surface of Figure 7-1. The quantities of labor and capital—which we shall use as representative inputs—are shown along the two horizontal axes, and the output is shown along the vertical axis.

The reader will no doubt recognize the similarity of this surface to that of the utility surface encountered in Chapter Three. However, there are some important differences between the two surfaces. First, unlike the case of utility surface where the vertical axis shows the ordinal magnitude only, the vertical axis of the production surface shows units of output that are *cardinal* magnitudes.

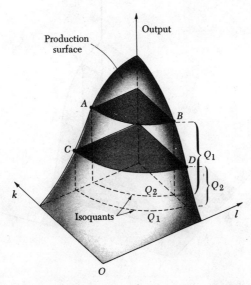

Figure 7-1 Production surface and its horizontal slices

Second, the utility surface of Appendix 3A assumes that as the consumer acquires more of x or y while purchasing none of the other, his utility increases. The tacit assumption involved is to treat the two commodities as ones that the consumer can enjoy separately. The production surface of Figure 7-1, unlike the utility surface, does not rise if only labor or capital employed increases. The presumption of the model here is that it takes labor as well as capital to produce this product.

Third, the production surface need not be smooth as shown in Figure 7-1. If inputs must be increased in discrete steps (such as the number of machines installed) and/or output increases in discrete units, the production surface may be quite discontinuous, and may even contain substantial gaps.

VARIOUS SLICES OF THE PRODUCTION SURFACE

We can study different properties of production by slicing the production surface in different manners.

In Figure 7-1, we slice the production surface *horizontally* at the heights of Q_1 and Q_2 units. The two curves or contour lines, AB and CD, on the production surface thus created show various labor-capital combinations that will produce Q_1 and Q_2 units

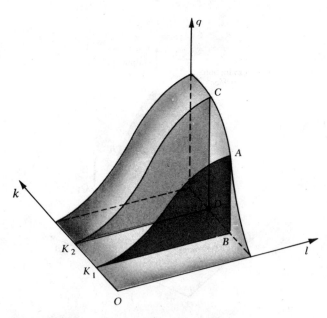

Figure 7-2 Returns to variable proportions

of output. By projecting the two curves onto the labor-capital plane, the two dotted isoquant curves are obtained. *An isoquant shows, on a two-dimensional graph, various combinations of two inputs that produce a given level of output.* The numbers attached to the isoquants, Q_1 and Q_2, stand for actual units of physical output that can be attained by labor-capital combinations on the curves. *A set of isoquants is called an isoquant map.* An isoquant map, therefore, is a two-dimensional representation of a production function with two inputs and one output.

By slicing the production surface in Figure 7-2 *vertically along the labor axis,* a vertical slice such as K_1AB is obtained. Such a slice shows the manner in which the total output varies when different amounts of labor are combined with a fixed amount of capital. If the production surface is sliced vertically parallel to the capital axis, the resulting vertical slice will show returns to capital input, with the quantity of labor held constant.

By slicing the production surface *vertically along a ray* from the origin in Figure 7-3, we obtain the vertical slice *OJD,* which shows the relationship between proportionate changes in both labor and capital and the resulting output.

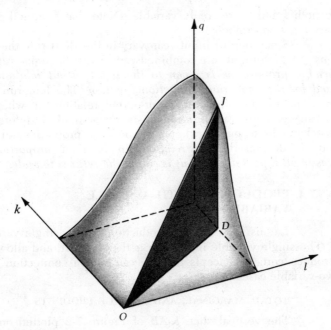

Figure 7-3 Returns to scale

SHORT-RUN VERSUS LONG-RUN PRODUCTION FUNCTION

The vertical slices of Figure 7-2 show the cases in which only one input can be varied, while the vertical slice in Figure 7-3 shows the case in which all inputs are varied. *When all inputs are freely variable, we are said to be in the long run. When one or more inputs are fixed in quantity, we are said to be in the short run.* The long run and short run are, therefore, analytical (not calendar) time periods; the concept of time is only incidental, and the crucial determinant of the so-called time periods is the existence or nonexistence of a fixed input(s). It is quite possible for the short run of a firm or industry to be much longer than the long run of another firm or industry. For instance, changing the rate of operation of a fixed plant in the steel industry may take much longer than building and operating a small grocery store.

In terms of the two-inputs, one-output production function, the short-run production function is given by:

$$q_{max} = f(l, \bar{k}) \text{ or } q_{max} = g(\bar{l}, k)$$

where the horizontal bar over l or k shows that the quantity of that input is fixed. The long-run production function is given by:

$$q_{max} = \phi(l, k)$$

where both l and k are freely variable. (Note that f, g, and ϕ are arbitrary function symbols.)

Since not all inputs can vary in the short run, the proportions at which inputs are combined vary. *Thus, the name **returns to variable proportions** is given to the input-output relationship depicted by the short-run production function.* The long-run production function describes the input-output relationship when all inputs can be freely varied. Economists are particularly interested in what happens to output when all inputs are proportionately increased or decreased. *The relationship between proportionate changes in all inputs and output is called the **returns to scale**.*

7-4 PRODUCTION WITH A SINGLE VARIABLE INPUT

Let us now discuss production with a single variable input. The single variable input case is the simplest, and allows us to introduce certain concepts that we can use in connection with the two-variable cases.

TOTAL, MARGINAL, AND AVERAGE PRODUCTS

The vertical slice K_1AB of Figure 7-2 plotted on the labor-output plane gives the conventional *total product*, TP, *curve,*

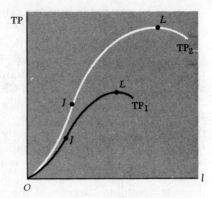

Figure 7-4   Total product curves

which shows the technological relationship between a variable input and TP *(assuming other inputs to remain the same).* The shape and position of the TP curve describe the state of technology. For instance, in Figure 7-4, the productivity of labor represented by TP_2 is much higher than that shown by TP_1. The availability of more and/or better cooperating inputs will shift the TP curve upward.[1] Thus, a TP curve always presupposes a given state of technology and given amounts of other resources used in the production process.

The TP curves of Figure 7-4 have the shape most commonly assumed in economic literature. Each TP curve is concave upward and increases at an increasing rate from the origin to point *J*, which is the point of inflection. From *J* to *L*, each curve is concave downward, and TP increases at a decreasing rate. Beyond *L*, TP decreases.

The marginal product (or marginal physical product) of labor is the increase in TP *when labor is increased by one unit.*[2] Graphically, it shows the slope of the TP curve. *The average product of labor shows the output per unit of labor, and is obtained by dividing the* TP *by the quantity of labor.* In equation form,

$$MP = MPP = \Delta TP/\Delta l \text{ and}$$
$$AP = TP/l$$

[1]TP_2 may well lie below TP_1 for small amounts of labor because of greater redundance of the fixed factor(s) for small amounts of labor.

[2]In the continuous case, the marginal product of labor is the rate of change in the TP with respect to the rate of labor usage, that is,
$$MP_l = dTP/dl$$

157

QUANTITATIVE RELATIONSHIPS AMONG TOTAL, MARGINAL, AND AVERAGE PRODUCTS

Given a TP curve, there are unique MP and AP curves that correspond to the TP curve. The MP curve depicts the slope of the TP curve, just as the marginal utility curve represented the slope of the total utility curve in Chapter Three.

The relationship between TP and AP is shown by Figure 7-5. From the definition of AP, it is clear that AP's corresponding to points A, B, and C on the TP curve are given by L_1A/OL_1, L_2B/OL_2, and L_3C/OL_3. These ratios are nothing but the slopes of the rays through the origin to the point in question on the total curve. Thus, the average quantities at A, B, and C can also be measured by the corresponding tangents of the angles, $\tan \theta_1$, $\tan \theta_2$, and $\tan \theta_3$, respectively. For instance, the AP's at points B and D are the same, since both can be measured by $\tan \theta_2$. The AP $(= \tan \theta)$ is *at maximum* when the ray from the origin is just tangent to the TP curve.

The average and marginal products have this important relationship: the *AP increases* (remains constant, decreases) *if the MP is greater than* (equal to, less than) *the AP*.

For an intuitive explanation of the above theorem,[3] consider an economics class in which students' average height is 5′9″. Now an additional (marginal) student whose height is 6′10″ joins the class. Because this marginal student's height is greater than the average height, the class average height increases. Similarly, if a coed whose height is 5′3″ subsequently joins the class, this marginal height smaller than the average height will lower the class average height. If the third student that joins happens to have a height equal to the class average height, the average must remain the same.

Graphically the AP and MP relationship is illustrated in Figure 7-6. In the unshaded region, MP is greater than AP, and AP increases. In the shaded region, MP is smaller than AP, and AP decreases. At the borderline MP and AP are equal and MP is at its maximum, that is, it neither increases nor decreases.

---

[3]Since this proposition applies to any marginal-average quantity relationship, we give the following mathematical proof. Letting $T(x)$ stand for any total quantity, the slope of the average curve is given by

$$\frac{d}{dx}\left[\frac{T(x)}{x}\right] = \frac{xT'(x) - T(x)}{x^2} = \frac{1}{x}\left[T'(x) - \frac{T(x)}{x}\right]$$

$$\gtreqless 0 \text{ according as } T'(x) \gtreqless \frac{T(x)}{x}$$

The slope of the average curve is positive (zero, negative) according as the marginal quantity is greater than (equal to, smaller than) the average quantity.

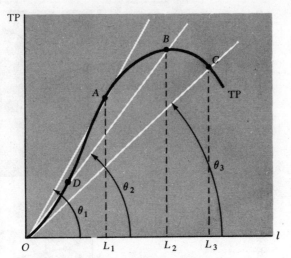

Figure 7-5   Relationship between TP and AP

The relationships among the total, average, and marginal product curves are summarized in Figure 7-7. Note the correspondence between points J, K, and L on the TP curve and points J', K', and L' in the lower panel. The slope of the TP curve increases until it reaches point J, decreases beyond point J, and becomes negative beyond point L. Therefore, its MP curve increases until it reaches J'; beyond point J', it declines and becomes negative beyond L'. The AP curve reaches its maximum at K', AP declines but remains

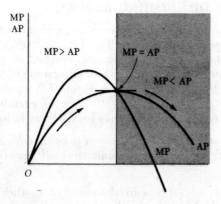

Figure 7-6   Relationship between MP and AP

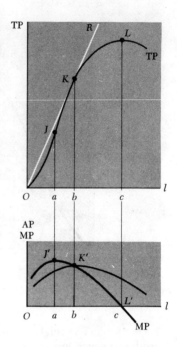

Figure 7-7 Relationships among
TP, AP, and MP

positive as long as TP is positive. Observe that the ray from the origin *OR*, touches the TP curve at *K*, indicating that AP is largest at this level of labor usage. Also note that where AP is largest, AP = MP.

7-5 THE LAW OF VARIABLE PROPORTIONS OR DIMINISHING RETURNS

The relationship between the amount of labor used and its TP was shown in Figure 7-7. The TP increased at first at an increasing rate, then at a decreasing rate, reached its peak, and then started to decline. The fact that the rate of increase in TP slows down (or that MP declines) from point *J* in Figure 7-7 is an important technological phenomenon known as *the law of variable proportions or diminishing returns.* The law may be stated as follows:

The MP of a variable input (which is being added to other inputs that are fixed in quantity) will eventually decline.

As more labor is added to a fixed amount of another input, capital, the proportion of labor to the fixed input (the labor/capital ratio) becomes such that the MP of labor starts declining. For instance, as more farm laborers are added to a given size farm, the extra output or the MP of an additional worker becomes smaller.

The following are some important features of the law of diminishing returns. (1) The law requires that there be *at least one fixed input* so that the ratio at which inputs are combined varies as the variable input is changed in quantity. The crucial factor that makes the law work is variable proportions; hence the name, the law of variable proportions![4] (2) The law refers to the MP (not TP or AP). Thus, the law may be at work while the TP or AP is still increasing. For instance, in Figure 7-7, the law is at work when the amount of labor exceeds *a* units per period; but the TP keeps increasing until it reaches *c* units per period, and the AP until it reaches *b* units per period. (3) The law assumes a *given state of technology*. Thus, the law should not be misapplied in situations in which technological conditions are changing. (4) The law is a rather *general* statement; it states that the MP of an input will eventually decline but says nothing about how soon or how fast. Thus, the law is entirely consistent with the initial increasing return to labor (from the origin to *J* in Figure 7-7), which occurs as additional labor makes the labor/capital ratio more favorable. However, the law does say that, as the labor/capital ratio keeps increasing, the MP will eventually decline.

7-6 THE THREE STAGES OF PRODUCTION

In Figure 7-7, we showed the TP curve separately from the AP and MP curves because while the TP curve showed physical units of output the AP and MP curves showed output *per* unit of input. For the sake of easy comparison, we have drawn all three curves in a single graph in Figure 7-8. To overcome the difficulty caused by different units of measurement, we show TP on the left vertical axis, and AP and MP on the right vertical axis. Thus the heights of TP and AP-MP curves are not comparable.

Using the relationships among the TP, MP, and AP, *the three stages of production are defined as shown in Figure 7-8.*

Stage I: From the origin to a_1

This is the stage in which AP continues to increase. Note that MP is greater than AP in this stage and MP reaches its maximum within this stage.

[4]The "law" of variable proportions is a synonym for the law of diminishing returns. However, the phrase "variable proportions" describes all situations in which input (labor/capital) ratio changes. In terms of Figure 7-7, variable proportions are presupposed for all levels of labor usage; while the *law* of variable proportions is at work only for the level of labor usage exceeding *a* units per period.

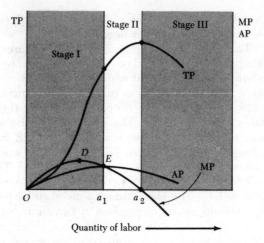

Figure 7-8   The three stages of production

Stage II: From a_1 to a_2

This is the stage in which both AP and MP decline but
remain positive. AP is at its maximum at the beginning of this
stage and MP is zero at the end of this stage. TP increases
in this stage.

Stage III: To the right of a_2

This is the stage in which MP is negative, and TP is declining.

Since no profit-maximizing entrepreneur will hire an
additional amount of labor when its MP is negative and the TP declines, it is clear that Stage III is an economically meaningless
region. This is the stage in which, say, the labor/capital ratio is so
high that as more labor is applied the TP declines. In Appendix 7c,
it is shown that Stage I for the variable input corresponds to Stage
III of the fixed input, capital. The labor/capital ratio showing too
few units of labor applied to a fixed amount of capital is equivalent
to that of too much capital combined with a fixed amount of labor.
In Stage I, the capital/labor ratio (the reciprocal of the labor/capital
ratio) is so high that the MP of capital is negative. Thus, Stage I is
economically meaningless as well. Clearly, *the producer operates
only in Stage II, in which the marginal products of both inputs are
positive.* Stage II is the only economically meaningful stage. Even if
labor is free, the producer will not hire more than a_2 units of labor;
even if land is free he will not go below a_1, the beginning of Stage II.

If the output desired is smaller (larger) than the output attainable by operating in Stage II, the amount of fixed input employed must be reduced (increased). Only in this way, can we avoid excessive amounts of fixed input in Stage I or the use of too much variable input in Stage III.

If we assume that the producer can sell all his output at the going market price, the labor/capital ratio he will select in Stage II depends on the prices of the two inputs. If the price of labor is free, the labor/capital ratio that maximizes profit is attained at the end of Stage II. If the price of land is zero, the best input ratio is obtained at the beginning of Stage II. We may deduce from this that, given the productivities of capital and labor, the lower the price of labor relative to that of land, the closer to the end of Stage II will be the desired labor/capital ratio. Similarly, a relatively inexpensive price of land will imply the use of a labor/capital ratio closer to the beginning of Stage II.

Note that the law of variable proportions or diminishing returns starts at point *D* in Figure 7-8; but the *economically relevant point is where the* AP *starts declining*, that is, point *E*.

APPENDIX 7

Symmetry of the Stages
of Production

In order to demonstrate the symmetry of the stages of production referred to in section 7-6, consider the following hypothetical example. Assume that two inputs, labor and land, are required to produce corn — we assume away such factors as seeds, fertility of land, rainfall, temperature, and fertilizers. We would like to know how varying the amount of labor applied to a given amount of land will affect the yield of corn. To establish this relationship, let us set up an experiment using nine identical adjoining one-acre lots. On lot one, 1 man-year of labor is applied; on lot two, 2 man-years of labor are applied; and so on until on lot nine, 9 man-years of labor are applied. The result of this experiment is summarized in part A of Table 7-1. The total product that is shown in column (4) increases as the amount of labor added to the given size plot increases. The average and marginal products of labor (columns 5 and 6) are computed from the input-output relationship recorded in columns (2) and (4). Next to column (6) the three stages of production for labor are shown. The reader should check whether this classification is consistent with the definitions of the three stages given in section 7-6.

The effects of applying varying amounts of labor to a given amount of land are shown in part A. Now we want to derive from this table the table in part B, which shows labor as the fixed input and *land as the variable input*. In order to achieve this transformation, we assume that the constant returns to scale exist. That is, a reduction in labor and land of, say, 50 percent will reduce the output by 50 percent as well. Now divide the entries in labor, land, and total product columns of part A by the units of labor in each row, and record the results in the corresponding columns and row of part B. For instance, the entries for lot nine of part B are obtained as follows:

164

Table 7-1   Symmetry of the Stages of Production

A. PRODUCTION WITH LABOR AS THE VARIABLE*

(1) Lot	(2) Labor	(3) Land	(4) TP_l	(5) AP_l	(6) MP_l	Stage
1	1	1	10	10	14	} Stage I
2	2	1	24	12	21	
3	3	1	45	15	15	
4	4	1	60	15	10	} Stage II
5	5	1	70	14	8	
6	6	1	78	13	5	
7	7	1	83	11.9	−8	} Stage III
8	8	1	75	9.4	−15	
9	9	1	60	6.7		

*TP_l, AP_l, and MP_l stand for total, average, and marginal products of *labor*, respectively.

B. PRODUCTION WITH LAND AS THE VARIABLE**

(7) Labor	(8) Land	(9) TP_k	(10) AP_k	(11) MP_k	Stage
1	1	10	10	−4	} Stage III
1	1/2	12	24	−18	
1	1/3	15	45	0	} Stage II
1	1/4	15	60	20	
1	1/5	14	70	30	
1	1/6	13	78	48	} Stage I
1	1/7	11.9	83	139	
1	1/8	9.4	75	195	
1	1/9	6.7	60		

**TP_k, AP_k, and MP_k show total, average, and marginal products of *land*.

Amount of labor: $9 \times 1/9 = 1$

Amount of land: $1 \times 1/9 = 1/9$

Total product: $60 \times 1/9 = 6.7$

In a similar manner, we can divide part A entries for lot eight by 8, for lot seven by 7, etc., and obtain the entries for labor, land, and TP_k columns of part B. Note that our transformation process is justified by the assumption of the constant returns to scale.

Now read part B from the bottom up, and you will see what happens to the total product of land, as more land (1/9, 1/8, 1/7, . . .) is applied to a fixed amount of labor (1 man-year). From this data on the TP of land, we can readily calculate the entries for the average product of land, AP_k, and the marginal product of land, MP_k.

The three stages of production for land (with labor as the fixed input) are marked off in part B. Stage I is the region in which the AP of land is increasing, Stage II is the region in which the MP of land is positive and the AP of land is decreasing, and Stage III is the region in which the MP of land is negative.[5] Comparing these stages of production for land with those for labor shown in part A, we can readily observe the following symmetry of the stages for the two inputs.

1. Stage I of labor corresponds to Stage III of land
2. Stage II of labor corresponds to Stage II of land
3. Stage III of labor corresponds to Stage I of land

[5]Note that, with discrete data, the stages cannot be established unequivocably. For instance, we cannot be really sure whether the peak of the average product of land curve occurs between the second and third rows from the bottom of the average product column in Table 7-1B, or between the third and fourth rows, or at the third row itself. The reason for this is that the discrete case differs from the continuous case because we are dealing with ΔQ in the first and dQ in the second.

EXERCISES 7

The Theory of Production:
Physical Aspects

7-1 "A mechanical tractor that requires a single operator can till, fertilize, and plant 50 acres of land per day. A peasant with no machinery, on the other hand, can do the same for only one acre per day. Clearly, peasant labor in agriculture is economically inefficient."
Do you agree that peasant labor is "inefficient" in the sense used in the theory of production?

7-2 Different properties of production—production with a single variable input, returns to scale, and isoquants—can be portrayed by slicing the production surface in different manners. Explain.

7-3 Draw a traditional (cubic) TP curve. Below this TP curve, in a separate graph draw the AP and MP curves that are consistent with the TP curve. Explain why it is advisable to draw the AP and MP curves on a separate graph, rather than on the same graph on which the TP curve appears.

7-4 The law of diminishing returns is also referred to as the law of eventually diminishing marginal products. What are the advantages associated with this latter expression?

7-5 Explain why the producer will choose to operate only in Stage II.

7-6 Indivisibilities may produce a discontinuous total product curve pictured in Figure 7-9. Below the TP curve (shown by three black discontinuous line segments), draw in the AP and MP curves that are qualitatively consistent with the TP curve shown.

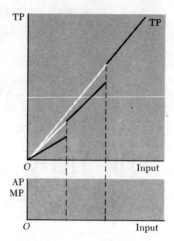

Figure 7-9

CHAPTER EIGHT

THE THEORY
OF PRODUCTION:
PHYSICAL ASPECTS—
CONTINUED

In this chapter we continue the study of production by examining the properties of production with two inputs. More specifically, we shall examine the properties of isoquants, the marginal rate of technical substitution, and returns to scale, and take a look at some empirical production functions. The appendixes contain some additional topics in production.

8-1 PROPERTIES OF ISOQUANTS

There is a great deal of similarity between isoquants and indifference curves. An isoquant shows a given amount of output produced by various combinations of two inputs, while an indifference curve shows various combinations of two goods that yield a given amount of satisfaction. The similarity is so great that isoquants are frequently referred to as *production indifference curves*. The role of isoquants in production theory is quite analogous to that of indifference curves in consumer theory, and the properties of isoquants resemble those of indifference curves rather closely.

First, an isoquant must be *negatively sloped* in the relevant range. The relevant range or the economic region is the range in which a profit-maximizing producer will operate, and is disussed in detail in Appendix 8c. In Figure 8-1, combination B uses less capital than combination A; but combination B also uses more labor than combination A. In general, to maintain a given output,

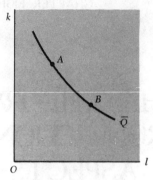

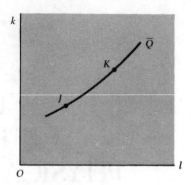

Figure 8-1 An isoquant must be negatively sloped

Figure 8-2 An isoquant cannot be positively sloped

$\overline{Q}$, a reduction in the use of an input must be offset by an increased use of another input. Suppose an isoquant is positively sloped as shown in Figure 8-2, and compare two points J and K on it. Both combinations produce the same output. But combination K uses more of both labor and capital than combination J, and is clearly *inefficient*. Since by assumption an inefficient production process is ruled out, we confine our attention to negatively sloped isoquants only.

Second, an isoquant must be *convex to the origin*. This property of isoquants, which follows from the fact that two inputs are not perfect substitutes, will be explored in detail in section 8-3.

Third, isoquants *cannot intersect or be tangent to each other*. Suppose two isoquants intersected as shown in Figure 8-3. The curve labeled Q_{100} shows 100 units of output produced by various combinations of inputs and the curve Q_{200}, 200 units of output. Now,

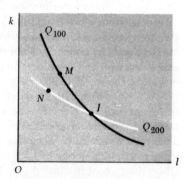

Figure 8-3 Isoquants cannot intersect

examine the outputs represented by points J, M, and N in Figure 8-3. On Q_{100}, $J = M$, because they are on the same isoquant. Similarly, on Q_{200}, $J = N$. Therefore, $M = N$. However, this is inconsistent since $M = 100$ and $N = 200$. Clearly, isoquants cannot intersect. The argument for the nontangency requirement is entirely analogous.

Fourth, isoquants show *cardinal magnitudes.* Unlike the indifference curves of consumer theory, isoquants indicate physical magnitudes that are cardinally measured as 100, 200, 300, etc. An isoquant that lies further away along the ray from the origin represents a greater output, but the distance from the origin *need not* show the output. The outputs come from the third dimension of the production surface and are identified by the numbers attached to isoquants. In Figure 8-4, for instance, the outputs represented by isoquants are not proportional to their distances from the origin.

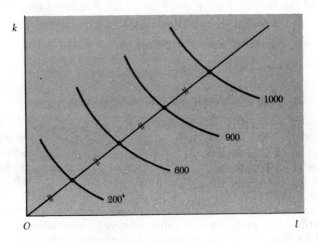

Figure 8-4 Spacing of isoquants

8-2 MARGINAL RATE OF TECHNICAL SUBSTITUTION

An isoquant shows various input combinations that produce a given output, and the slope of the isoquant shows the rate at which one input can be substituted for another without changing the given output. Consider the movement from A to B along the isoquant in Figure 8-5. The amount of capital used is reduced by Δk and that of labor is increased by Δl. The slope of the isoquant between two points A and B, $\Delta k/\Delta l$, therefore, shows the rate at which two inputs can be substituted for each other without affecting the

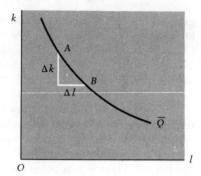

Figure 8-5 Marginal rate of technical substitution

output. By attaching the minus sign to the slope $\Delta k/\Delta l$, which is a negative quantity, a positive magnitude is obtained. *This absolute slope of the isoquant for a small Δk or Δl is referred to as the marginal rate of technical substitution*, MRTS, *between two inputs*:

$$\text{MRTS} = -\Delta k/\Delta l = |\Delta k/\Delta l|$$

where Δ shows a small change.[1]

8-3 THE CONVEXITY OF ISOQUANTS

In section 8-1, we said that an isoquant must be convex to the origin. This is essentially an assumption. Let us see why this assumption is reasonable by referring to the convex-to-the-origin isoquant shown in Figure 8-6 and exploring the economic implication of this convexity requirement. As we move from left to right along the isoquant in Figure 8-6, its absolute slope, MRTS, declines. This has a very plausible economic implication. As we move from production processes that require relatively less labor and more capital to those that require higher labor/capital ratios, labor gradually becomes a poorer substitute for capital; and, therefore, we must

[1]In calculus notation, MRTS $= -dk/dl$. It is the absolute slope of the isoquant at a point.

Doing a short library research on the concept of MRTS, the reader will immediately find that many textbooks define the absolute slope of an isoquant as MRTS *of labor for capital*, while many others define the same slope as MRTS *of capital for labor*. If the movement along the isoquant is from left to right, labor is being substituted for capital. However, if the movement is from right to left — and there is no reason why it should not be — capital is being substituted for labor. This explains the confusing terminologies. In order to avoid the confusion, we will simply talk of MRTS *between inputs*. From the context of the discussion, the reader should have no difficulty in ascertaining which input is which.

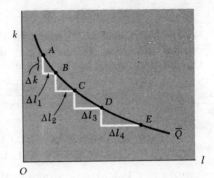

Figure 8-6   Convexity of an isoquant

substitute a progressively larger amount of labor for a given amount of capital in order to maintain a given output. In Figure 8-6, as we move along the isoquant from A to B, . . . , to E the amount of labor that must be substituted for a given amount of capital (Δk) becomes progressively larger as indicated by the lengthening line segments Δl_1, Δl_2, . . . , Δl_4. For an entirely analogous reason, the MRTS increases as we move along the isoquant from right to left. Again, the economic implication is clear. As more capital is substituted for labor, capital becomes progressively a poorer substitute for labor. This phenomenon of input substitution is generally referred to as the *diminishing marginal rate of technical substitution* in economic literature. However, if the movement along the curve were from right to left, the slope of the isoquant would increase; and one may even talk of the increasing MRTS. Here again, as with the case of the marginal rate of substitution between goods in consumption theory, it may be better to avoid either terminology and describe the situation merely as one of *convex isoquant*. Furthermore, the MRTS at any point is the same for movement in either direction.

8-4 MARGINAL RATE OF TECHNICAL SUBSTITUTION AND MARGINAL PHYSICAL PRODUCTS OF TWO INPUTS

We are now ready to show that the MRTS is equal to the ratio of the marginal physical product, MPP, of labor to the MPP of capital. Refer back to Figure 8-5, and consider the movement from A to B along the isoquant. As we move from A to B, the amount of capital used is reduced by Δk and that of labor is increased by Δl. Since the output must remain constant for any movement along a given isoquant, the contribution to the output of the change in capital, $\Delta k \cdot \text{MPP}_k$, must be precisely offset by the contribution of labor to the output, $\Delta l \cdot \text{MPP}_l$. That is,

$$\Delta k \cdot \text{MPP}_k + \Delta l \cdot \text{MPP}_l = 0$$

where MPP_k and MPP_l stand for the marginal physical products of capital and labor. By rearranging this equation, it can be seen that the MRTS is equal to the ratio of the MPP of the two inputs.[2]

$$\text{MRTS} = \frac{-\Delta k}{\Delta l} = \frac{\text{MPP}_l}{\text{MPP}_k}$$

8-5 RETURNS TO SCALE: PROPORTIONATE CHANGES IN ALL INPUTS

Let us now examine the responses in output when all inputs are varied in equal proportions. This property of production is called *returns to scale;* the returns to variable proportions, on the other hand, describes the response in output when a single input is varied.

In section 7-3 (Figure 7-3), we saw that the returns-to-scale property of the production surface was shown by the vertical slice going through the origin. In terms of an isoquant map, the returns-to-scale property is shown by a ray from the origin, such as the ray OS in Figure 8-7. Along ray OS, the capital/labor ratio remains the same. Thus, movement from A to B to C to D shows proportionate increases in both labor and capital.[3]

Depending on whether the proportionate change in output equals, exceeds, or falls short of the proportionate change

---

[2]The MRTS can be easily derived from the production function $Q = f(l, k)$. Taking the total differential of the function:

$$dQ = f_l dl + f_k dk$$

where f_l and f_k are partial derivatives of the function with respect to l and k. Now for any movement along an isoquant dQ is zero. Thus,

$$dQ = f_l dl + f_k dk = 0$$

and

$$\text{MRTS} = \frac{-dk}{dl} = \frac{f_l}{f_k}$$

The economic meanings of the partial derivatives f_l and f_k are the MPP_l and MPP_k.

[3]The case of production with a single variable input discussed in section 7-5 can also be handled in terms of an isoquant map. For instance, the horizontal line VP in Figure 8-7 shows how TP increases as more labor is applied to a given amount of capital. Similarly, a vertical line on an isoquant map will describe the relationship between capital and output while holding the amount of labor constant.

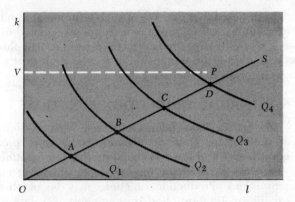

Figure 8-7 Returns to scale

in both inputs, a production function is classified as showing constant, increasing, or decreasing returns to scale. The ratio of the proportionate change in output to a proportionate change in all inputs is called the function coefficient, ϵ. That is,

$$\epsilon = \frac{\Delta q/q}{\Delta \lambda/\lambda}$$

where the proportionate changes in output and *all* inputs are shown by $\Delta q/q$ and $\Delta \lambda/\lambda$. Then the returns to scale is classified as follows:

$\epsilon > 1$: Increasing returns to scale

$\epsilon = 1$: Constant returns to scale

$\epsilon < 1$: Decreasing returns to scale

There are several technological factors that contribute to increasing returns to scale:

1. *Increasing specialization of labor.* As the scale of operation increases, each man can be trained and assigned to the specialized task for which he is best suited, where he acquires additional expertise by repetitive experiences.
2. *Use of more specialized machine.* Specialized machines are generally far more productive than less specialized machines. However, the capacities of specialized machines are very often large and *indivisible—in the sense that it is technically impossible to use the machine for small output or prohibitively expensive to do so.* Use of hand shovel versus bulldozer in removing earth is a case in point.
3. For some production processes, it is a *matter of geometric necessity* that a larger scale of operation is more efficient. En-

gineers have noted that the cost of such equipment as tanks, gas holders, columns, or compressors is frequently related to its surface area, while its capacity is directly related to its volume. For instance, doubling the dimension of a cube requires four times as much materials but increases its volume eightfold.

8-6 EMPIRICAL PRODUCTION FUNCTIONS

So far we have been concerned with theoretical discussions of production. How do economists measure production functions empirically, and how do actual production functions look? Basically, there are three main approaches to obtaining empirical production functions. Production functions may be obtained from (1) technical information supplied by engineers, (2) data obtained by experiments as in agriculture, and (3) statistical analysis of cross-section or time series data. (*Cross-section data record various amounts of inputs used to produce output for a firm, industry, or country at a given period of time;* while *time series data record various amounts of inputs used and output produced over some periods of time,* such as from 1950 to 1970.)

PRODUCTION FUNCTIONS DERIVED
FROM TECHNICAL INFORMATION

Some production processes may be characterized by fairly simple relationships between inputs and output. For instance, the annual output of timber is, *ceteris paribus*, the function of the number of saplings planted per year and the amount of land used to cultivate trees.[4] To obtain a given output of timber, we can cut down the trees sooner and use less land and more saplings, and vice versa. Thus, the number of saplings and the amount of land are substitutes in the production of timber, and the selection of an appropriate saplings/land ratio is an important part of planning for a long-range timber production program.

As another example, consider the transmission of electrical energy via a power line from a hydroelectric dam to a city. The two major substitutable inputs involved in the transmission process are electrical energy (at the power plant source) and the weight or size of transmission cable. The heavier the cable weight, the less is energy loss in transmission. Thus, the input substitution involved is between the weight of cable and the size of generators. A given amount of electric energy can be supplied to the city by heavier cable and smaller generators or by lighter cable and larger generators.

[4]This and two following examples of technical production functions are taken from Vernon L. Smith, *Investment and Production* (Cambridge, Mass.: Harvard University Press, 1966), pp. 17–61.

Transmission of heat, gas, or oil is another example of a technical production function in which substitution between two inputs is involved. Consider the problem of transmitting gas via a pipeline. The substitution possibilities involved are between the diameters of pipes and the sizes of compressors. Since the energy loss in the pipe due to friction in transmission decreases with the pipe size, the greater the pipe diameter, the smaller the required compressor capacity to pump any given amount of gas a specified distance.

For many simple production processes such as those discussed in the preceding paragraphs, production functions can be analytically developed from the technical information available. For example, Vernon L. Smith obtained the production function for the transmission of electricity as follows:

$$\text{Electricity: } x_2(x_1 - y) - 218.44 \times 10^{-6}y^2 = 0$$

where x_1 is the electrical energy input (kwh), x_2 is cable input (lb), and y is the kilowatt hours of electricity delivered at the destination. (This function assumed that the cable was made of copper, the distance between the power source and the destination was 100 miles, and the voltage at the power source was 50,000 volts.) Figure 8-8 shows the isoquant map of this production function.[5]

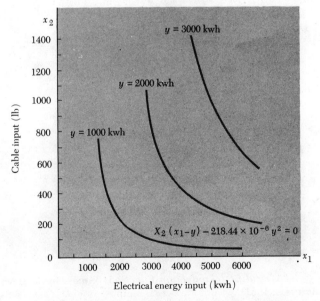

Figure 8-8 Isoquant map for the transmission of electricity

[5]*Ibid.*, pp. 24–30.

PRODUCTION FUNCTIONS DERIVED FROM
STATISTICAL EXPERIMENTATION

Agricultural economists have extensively relied on statistical experimentation in measuring production functions. For example, Earl O. Heady and John L. Dillon report production functions obtained from statistical experimentations for such products as pork, broilers, turkeys, milk, beef, and corn.[6] Figure 8-9 shows Heady and Dillon's pork isoquant map, which shows the combination of corn and soybean meal that will produce 100 pounds of gain for pigs of 60, 110, and 175 pounds.[7] Note that isoquants get flatter as a pig increases in weight. This indicates that while soybean meal protein is a good substitute for corn in the early growing stage, it becomes a poorer substitute in later stages (as the growing stage merges into fattening stage).

PRODUCTION FUNCTIONS OBTAINED
BY CROSS-SECTION ANALYSES

Manufacturing production functions are frequently obtained by cross-section analyses of data. Many works along these lines assume the Cobb-Douglas production function, which is explained in Appendix 8B. In its best known form, we write

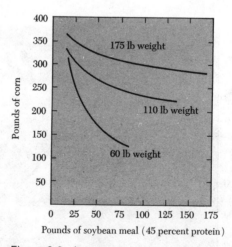

Figure 8-9 Isoquant map for pig production

[6]*Agricultural Production Functions* (Ames, Iowa: Iowa State University Press, 1961).

[7]*Ibid.*, p. 288.

$$Q = Aa^{\alpha}b^{\beta}c^{\gamma}, \; Q, A, a, b, c > 0 \text{ and } \alpha, \beta, \gamma \geqslant 0$$

where Q is output and a, b, and c are three inputs, and A, α, β, and γ are parameters that must be estimated from empirical data. As shown in Appendix 8B, several important interpretations can be attached to the exponents of the production function. First, the sum of the exponents $(\alpha + \beta + \gamma)$ shows the nature of the *returns to scale.* If the sum is greater than (less than, equal to) 1, the production function displays increasing (decreasing, constant) returns to scale. Second, each exponent can be interpreted as indicating the *percentage change in total output brought about by 1 percent increase in that input,* that is, the *output elasticity coefficient.*

George H. Hildebrand and Ta-Chung Liu's estimates of Cobb-Douglas production function coefficients for selected manufacturing industries in the U.S. for 1957 are partly reproduced in Table 8-1.

Note that the sum of the exponents, $\alpha + \beta + \gamma$, shows the returns-to-scale property of the production function. Thus, according to Table 8-1, there is increasing returns to scale in food products and chemicals, constant returns to scale in petroleum and coal products,

Table 8-1 Cross-Section Estimates of Production Function Coefficients

INDUSTRY	PRODUCTION WORKER OUTPUT ELASTICITY (α)	NON-PRODUCTION EMPLOYEE OUTPUT ELASTICITY (β)	CAPITAL OUTPUT ELASTICITY (γ)	RETURNS TO SCALE ($\alpha + \beta + \gamma$)
Food products	0.31	0.40	0.53	1.24
Chemicals	0.34	0.57	0.27	1.18
Transportation equipment	0.41	0.28	0.32	1.01
Petroleum and coal products	0.27	0.50	0.23	1.00
Electric machinery	0.41	0.24	0.30	0.95
Leather products	0.85°		0.07	0.92

°This is the combined (production and non production) Labor output elasticity.

Source: G. H. Hildebrand and Ta-Chung Liu, *Manufacturing Production Functions in the United States,* 1957 (Ithaca, N.Y.: Cornell University, 1965), p. 109.

and decreasing returns to scale in electric machinery and leather products.

Since each exponent shows the output elasticity coefficient, we know that in the case of food products a 1 percent increase in production workers increases output by 0.31 percent, while a 1 percent increase in nonproduction workers and capital will increase the output by 0.40 percent and 0.53 percent, respectively. A one percent increase in all three inputs will increase the output by 1.24 percent; hence, an increasing returns to scale![8]

[8]Those who wish to pursue the subject of empirical production functions further should read an excellent survey article by A. A. Walter, "Production and Cost Functions: An Econometric Survey", *Econometrica*, January–April 1963, pp. 1–66.

A. Production Processes

We may start the discussion of production with production processes and introduce "kinked" isoquants rather than the traditional smooth isoquants. This approach introduces some realism into the theory of production, since businessmen and production engineers view production as processes.

· Consider production process A, which uses 2 machine-hours of capital and 1 man-hour of labor to produce a unit of output. This production process is shown in Figure 8-10 by the ray from the origin, OP_A. The horizontal axis shows the number of man-hours; and the vertical axis, the amount of machine-hours. Point A_1 on the *process* (or activity) *ray* OP_A indicates that 1 man-hour of labor and 2 machine-hours of capital are required to produce a unit of output. Similarly,

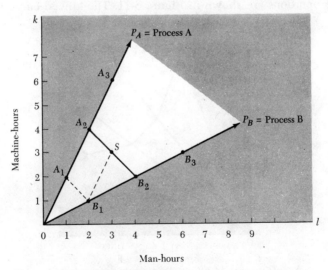

Figure 8-10 Production processes

points A_2 and A_3 show the amounts of labor and machine-hours needed to produce 2 and 3 units of output. (We assume that constant returns to scale prevail.) Alternately, points A_2 and A_3 show the use of process A at the levels of 2 and 3.

Now let us introduce another production process. Production process B requires 2 man-hours of labor and 1 machine-hour of capital to produce a unit of output. This production process is depicted by process ray OP_B. Points B_1, B_2, and B_3 show 1, 2, and 3 units of output that can be obtained by operating the process at the unit level, at the level of 2, and at the level of 3.

By introducing the second production process, we can show that a given output can be produced by either process A or B, or by using a combination of both processes A and B at certain levels. In order to show this latter point, let us assume that fractional units of labor and capital can be employed. In Figure 8-10 points A_2 or B_2 show 2 units of output produced by using process A or B. Now the line segment A_2B_2 shows various combinations of processes A and B that will produce 2 units of output. For instance, point S indicates 2 units of output produced by using processes A and B at the unit level. Moving along process ray B from the origin to B_1—that is, by using process B at the unit level—a unit of output is produced. Now, moving along the dotted line B_1S is equivalent to, by the very construction of the graph, moving along process ray A from A_1 to A_2 or from the origin to A_1—that is, using process A at the unit level. The combined output of processes A and B thus is 2 units as was claimed.

Four processes that combine labor and capital in different proportions are shown in Figure 8-11. The kinked curve JKLM,

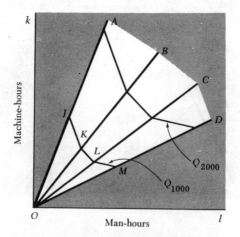

Figure 8-11 Kinked isoquants derived from four processes

Q_{1000}, shows 1000 units of output that can be produced by either one of the four processes or some combination of the two adjoining processes. Similarly the kinked curve labeled Q_{2000} shows 2000 units of output produced by various combinations of capital and labor. Clearly, these curves are isoquants. If the number of processes available is large, the kinks of an isoquant will become less pronounced as shown by an isoquant in Figure 8-12, in which there are ten production processes. The smooth isoquants postulated by traditional production theory can be considered as a limiting case in which the number of production processes available increases without limit. The unshaded regions in Figures 8-10, 8-11 and 8-12 show that feasible input combinations lie only in those areas.

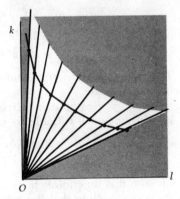

Figure 8-12   An isoquant with ten
processes

B. Linearly Homogeneous Production Functions

HOMOGENEOUS FUNCTIONS

A function is said to be **homogeneous** *of degree r if multiplying each independent variable by a constant k changes the value of the function by the multiple, k^r. Thus, if a function q = f(x,y) is homogeneous of degree r,* then

$$f(kx, ky) = k^r f(x,y) = k^r q$$

A few examples should make the concept of homogeneity clear.

Example 1:   Given the function $f(x,y,z) = 2x/y + y/z$, multiplying each variable by constant k will result in

$$f(kx,ky,kz) = \frac{2kx}{ky} + \frac{ky}{kz} = 2x/y + y/z$$

$$= f(x,y,z) \quad = k^0 f(x,y,z)$$

The value of the function does not change as all its independent variables are multiplied by k. This situation may be described as one in which the value of the function changes by k^0 times. Thus, the function is said to be homogeneous of degree zero.

Example 2:   Suppose the production function is given by $q(a,b) = 3a^{3/4}b^{1/4}$, then

$$q(ka,kb) = 3(ka)^{3/4}(kb)^{1/4}$$

$$= 3k^{3/4}k^{1/4}a^{3/4}b^{1/4}$$

$$= k^1(3a^{3/4}b^{1/4}) = k\ q(a,b)$$

The given production function is homogeneous of degree 1 (linearly homogeneous).

Example 3:   Given the function $q(a,b) = 3a^2 + 2ab + b^2$, multiplying each variable by k, we get

$$3(ka)^2 + 2(ka)(kb) + (kb)^2$$

$$= k^2(3a^2 + 2ab + b^2) = k^2 q(a,b)$$

Clearly, this function is homogeneous of degree 2.

Note that the *returns to scale* can be classified in terms of the degree of homogeneity r. Given the homogeneous production function

$$f(ka,kb,kc, \ldots) = k^r f(a,b,c, \ldots)$$

where $k > 1$, we have

$$\left.\begin{array}{l} \text{constant returns to scale} \\ \text{increasing returns to scale} \\ \text{decreasing returns to scale} \end{array}\right\} \quad \text{according as} \quad \left\{\begin{array}{l} r = 1 \\ r > 1 \\ r < 1 \end{array}\right\}$$

LINEARLY HOMOGENEOUS PRODUCTION FUNCTIONS

Production functions homogeneous of the first degree are commonly referred to as linearly (or linear) homogeneous production functions. Note that the word *linearly* or *linear* modifies the adjective, *homogeneous*. The production function itself need not be linear at all. For example $f(x, y) = 3x^2/y + y^3/x^2$ is definitely not a linear function. However, the independent variables multiplied by a constant k will give

$$f(kx,ky) = \frac{3(kx)^2}{ky} + \frac{(ky)^3}{(kx)^2} = k\left(\frac{3x^2}{y} + \frac{y^3}{x}\right)$$

which shows that the function is linearly homogeneous.

Linearly homogeneous production functions are widely used in economic literature. They are not only mathematically simple but also possess some important properties. If $Q = f(l,k)$ is a linearly homogeneous function, then it possesses the following properties:

1. The function shows *constant returns to scale*. This is easy to see since for any value of c, $f(cl, ck) = c f(l,k)$ by the definition of linear homogeneity. A proportionate change in all inputs results in an equal proportionate change in output. And this is precisely what is meant by constant returns to scale.

2. The *average product* (of either input) *depends upon the* capital/labor ratio (k/l) alone, and is independent of the absolute amounts of inputs used.

    Proof: Multiplying each variable of the production function by $1/l$, we get

    $$\frac{Q}{l} = f\left(\frac{l}{l}, \frac{k}{l}\right) = f(1, k/l)$$

    Since Q/l is the average product of labor, we have

    $$AP_l = f(1, k/l) = \phi(k/l)$$

    That is, AP_l depends on the capital/labor ratio alone. Similarly, by multiplying $f(l,k)$ by $1/k$, we get

    $$AP_k = \frac{Q}{k} = f\left(\frac{l}{k}, 1\right) = \psi(l/k)$$

    which is again the function of the capital/labor ratio alone.

3. The *marginal product* (of either input) *is the function of the capital/labor ratio only*.
    Proof: Multiplying the equation $Q/l = \phi(k/l)$ by l we get $Q = l \phi(k/l)$. Partially differentiating this expression with respect to l yields

    $$\frac{\partial Q}{\partial l} = \frac{\partial}{\partial l}\left[l\phi(k/l)\right] = \phi(k/l) + l\phi'(k/l)(-k/l^2)$$

    $$= \phi(k/l) - (k/l)\,\phi'(k/l)$$

    which shows the marginal product of labor (MP_l) as the function of k/l only.

Similarly,

$$\frac{\partial Q}{\partial k} = \frac{\partial}{\partial k} [l \; \phi(k/l)]$$

$$= l \; \phi'(k/l)(1/l) = \phi'(k/l).$$

The MP_k depends upon the input ratio alone.

4. *Euler's Theorem for homogeneous functions holds.* That is,

$$k \frac{\partial Q}{\partial k} + l \frac{\partial Q}{\partial l} = Q.$$

Proof: Substituting the expressions for $\frac{\partial Q}{\partial k}$ and $\frac{\partial Q}{\partial l}$ obtained in (3) into the left member of the Euler's theorem, we get

$$k \frac{\partial Q}{\partial k} + l \frac{\partial Q}{\partial l} = k \; \phi'(k/l) + l \; \phi(k/l) - k \; \phi'(k/l)$$

$$= l \; \phi(k/l) = Q$$

Mathematically, Euler's theorem says that the value of a linearly homogeneous function can be shown as the sum of the terms, each of which shows the product of the value of a variable and the partial derivative of the function with respect to the same variable. Economically, the theorem states that total product is the sum of the quantities of each input multiplied by their respective marginal products.

THE COBB-DOUGLAS FUNCTION

Probably the best known production function in economics is the Cobb-Douglas function (named so after the pioneering study in which Douglas fitted a function suggested by Cobb to U.S. data). The function takes the form,

$$Q = Aa^{\alpha}b^{\beta}$$

where Q is output, a and b are inputs, A is a positive constant, and α and β are positive fractions. There are several features of the Cobb-Douglas function that make it so popular.

1. Being in a log-linear form, it is *simple to handle.* (In logarithmic form, the function is $\log Q = \log A + \alpha \log a + \beta \log b$.)
2. Often the function is used in the form

$$Q = Aa^{\alpha}b^{1-\alpha}$$

In this special case *where $\alpha + \beta = 1$, the function shows constant returns to scale.*

That is,

$$A(ka)^\alpha(kb)^{1-\alpha} = k(Aa^\alpha b^{1-\alpha}) = kQ$$

It is not necessary that $\alpha + \beta = 1$ in the Cobb-Douglas function. If the function is homogeneous of degree 1, the constant returns to scale prevails. If it is of degree less than 1, decreasing returns to scale exists. Similarly, if it is of degree greater than 1, there is an increasing returns to scale.

3.   The function *yields diminishing returns to each input.* This can readily be shown. Consider input a.

$$Q = Aa^\alpha b^\beta$$
$$\partial Q/\partial a = \alpha Aa^{\alpha-1}b^\beta$$
$$\partial^2 Q/\partial a^2 = \alpha(\alpha-1)Aa^{\alpha-2}b^\beta > 0$$

Since α is a positive fraction, $(\alpha - 1)$ is negative. Thus the rate of change of the marginal product of input a is negative, and MP_a declines.

4. α *and* β *show the output elasticity coefficient for inputs* a *and* b. The *output elasticity* (ξ) *is defined as the ratio of the relative change in output over a relative change in an input.*

In formula, the output elasticity of factor a is

$$\xi_a = \frac{\partial Q}{Q} \Big/ \frac{\partial a}{a} = \frac{\partial Q}{\partial a} \frac{a}{Q}$$

In order to show that α is the output elasticity of factor a, we simply need to substitute the values of $\partial Q/\partial a$ and Q from (3) into the output elasticity formula.

$$\xi_a = \frac{\partial Q}{\partial a} \frac{a}{Q} = \frac{\alpha Aa^{\alpha-1}b^\beta \cdot a}{Aa^\alpha b^\beta} = \alpha$$

Clearly, the same procedure holds for factor b.

5. α *and* β *show the relative distributive shares of inputs* a *and* b.

The relative distributive share of input a is given by

$$\frac{\frac{\partial Q}{\partial a} \cdot a}{Q}$$

where a is the quantity of input a.

Substituting the values of $\partial Q/\partial a$ and Q into this expression, we have

$$\frac{\frac{\partial Q}{\partial a} \cdot a}{Q} = \frac{\alpha Aa^{\alpha-1}b^\beta \cdot a}{Aa^\alpha b^\beta} = \alpha$$

Clearly, α is the relative distributive share of factor a.

CES PRODUCTION FUNCTION

Another widely used production function is the class of function known as the CES (for constant elasticity of substitution) production function. The equation of this function is

$$A[\delta l^{-\rho} + (1 - \delta)k^{-\rho}]^{-1/\rho}$$

$$(A > 0, 0 < \delta < 1, \rho > -1)$$

where A, δ and ρ (Greek letter rho) are three parameters and l and k represent two inputs.

Let us show that this function is homogeneous of degree 1. By increasing inputs l and k m-fold, we get

$$A[\delta(ml)^{-\rho} + (1 - \delta)(mk)^{-\rho}]^{-1/\rho}$$

$$= A\{m^{-\rho}[\delta l^{-\rho} + (1 - \delta)k^{-\rho}]\}^{-1/\rho}$$

$$= (m^{-\rho})^{-1/\rho} \cdot A[\delta l^{-\rho} + (1 - \delta)k^{-\rho}]^{-1/\rho} = mQ$$

The CES production function, thus, possesses the properties of a linearly homogeneous function. Given a CES production function:

1. It shows constant returns to scale.
2. Average product of either input depends on the input ratio alone.
3. Marginal product of either input depends upon the input ratio alone.
4. Euler's Theorem (for homogeneous functions) holds.

C. The Economic Region of Production on an Isoquant Map

Given a production function that is characterized by a few processes, such as the one shown in Figure 8-11, it is immediately clear that the feasible input combinations lie in the unshaded region only. There simply is no process that will allow us to provide the product using labor-capital combinations located in the shaded regions.

Given a conventional isoquant map with smooth curves, we can also indicate the *economic region* of production in which production is efficient and uneconomical regions in which production is inefficient. The curve OK in Figure 8-13 is obtained by connecting the point on each isoquant at which its slope is vertical (or undefined). Similarly, the curve OL shows the locus of the points on each isoquant at which its slope is zero. *Since both curves are secured by connecting the points on isoquants that have equal slopes, they are referred to as isoclines.* The isoclines OK and OL, however, are very special kinds of isoclines called *ridge lines* and serve to separate the economic region of production from the uneconomic region. To see how this is done, assume that 200 units of output are produced by using input combinations $S - a_2$ of l and b_2 of k. Since the isoquant bends back up at point S, combining any more labor with b_2 units of capital will result in a reduction in total output, as seen by movement to a lower isoquant curve. When the amount of labor (combined with b_2 of capital) exceeds a_2, its marginal product becomes negative. Clearly, no producer would voluntarily employ more than a_2 units of labor. If more labor is combined with more capital as well (such as at combination J) 200 units of output can be maintained. Such an input combination, however, would be inefficient since combination J is a more expensive way of producing the given output.

If the producer is initially at T, employing more than b_1 units of capital with the given amount of labor will reduce the total

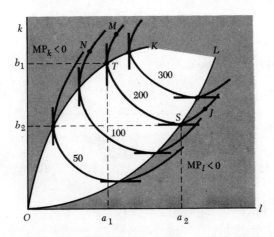

Figure 8-13   Ridge lines

product. *T* thus shows the point above which the marginal product of capital will turn negative. Obviously, combinations such as *M* and *N* are uneconomic ways of producing the outputs involved. In general, any combination of inputs given by the segments of isoquants above isocline *OK* or below isocline *OL* represents waste of inputs, which a producer will normally try to avoid. Since the isoclines show the limits or "ridges" beyond which a producer would not go, if he could help it, they are generally referred to as the *ridge lines. The economic region of production is confined to the input combinations within the ridge lines where the marginal products of both inputs are positive, and isoquants are negatively sloped.*

Sometimes, a producer must operate in Stage III for capital due to indivisibility of the capital equipment. This fact explains why many giant producers farm out some of their work to smaller specialized firms.

The unshaded area bounded by isoclines *OK* and *OL* (the economic region) is, in the language used in section 7-6, Stage II for both labor and capital. The area below isocline *OL* corresponds to Stage III of labor (and Stage I of capital). The area above isocline *OK* is equivalent to Stage III of capital (and Stage I of labor).

EXERCISES 8

The Theory of Production:
Physical Aspects — Continued

8-1 Two basic inputs required in the construction of a pipeline are the pipe and the amount of hydraulic horsepower (the pumping stations). Two inputs may be combined in a variety of ways to achieve any given capacity (which is defined as barrels per day of "throughput"). Any given throughput can be carried by substituting additional horsepower for a certain number of inches of diameter of pipe. A Rice University research team under a government contract, for example, found that a throughput of 125,000 barrels per day (60 SUS oil over 1,000 miles) can be obtained by any of the following combinations of pipe and horsepower:

Outside diameter of pipe	Horsepower (approximate)
30	2,000
26	4,000
22	8,500
18	22,500
16	37,500

Source: F. T. Moore, "Economies of Scale: Some Statistical Evidence," *Quarterly Journal of Economics*, May 1959, p. 238.

1. From the above table, plot an isoquant on graph paper.
2. Is the isoquant convex to the origin?
3. Are all combinations efficient?

4.   Which one, a smooth isoquant or an isoquant with kinks, is a better approximation to a real production function? Why?

8-2   How would the isoquant map look if there is only one process of producing a good? Would it be a straight line, a series of isolated points, or a series of convex (to the origin) curves with 90° angles in them? Explain your answer.

8-3   In Figure 8-14, isoquant Q_b is twice as far away from the origin as isoquant Q_a. Does it then follow that Q_b must represent an output level twice as large as Q_a? Why or why not?

8-4   Assume that there are constant returns to scale. Given the isoquant that shows 100 units of output in Figure 8-15, what are the outputs represented by other isoquants? On each isoquant, attach a proper number that indicates its output level.

8-5   Compare the concept of the marginal rate of technical substitution (MRTS) with the marginal rate of substitution (MRS) encountered in Chapter Three, and disuss the similarities and differences between them.

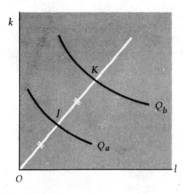

Figure 8-14

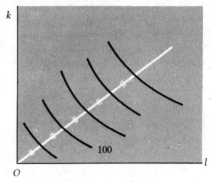

Figure 8-15

CHAPTER NINE

PRODUCTION DECISIONS AND COSTS

In this chapter, we combine our knowledge of production with input prices and examine how optimal input decisions are made. We shall also examine how cost schedules can be constructed from the data on physical production, and introduce the concept of opportunity cost. Applications of opportunity cost in analyzing the significance of historically incurred cost and the issue of draft versus volunteer army conclude the chapter.

To simplify our analysis, we will assume, unless otherwise mentioned, that (1) two inputs (labor and capital) are used to produce one output; (2) input prices are not affected by the rate of purchase; and (3) there is no inventory cost (or that inputs can be purchased as they are needed).

9-1 THE ISOCOST LINE

The production counterpart of the consumer's budget line is the isocost line. *An isocost line shows the locus of input combinations that can be purchased with a given amount of expenditure.* Assume that the prices of inputs, p_l and p_k, are not affected by any single producer's purchases. Then, given the amount of production budget, C, and the prices of two inputs, the isocost equation is given by

$$p_l \cdot l + p_k \cdot k = C$$

where l and k show the quantities of labor and capital. Rearranging this equation, we get

$$k = \frac{C}{p_k} - \frac{p_l}{p_k} \cdot l$$

The graphic representation of this equation yields the isocost line shown in Figure 9-1. The shaded area shows all combinations of labor and capital that can be purchased with C or less dollars.

The reader should notice the essential similarity of the isocost line with the budget line of Chapters Three and Four. The vertical and horizontal intercepts, the slope, parallel shifts, and pivoting of an isocost line have the identical meanings as the corresponding counterparts of the budget line.

9-2 OPTIMAL INPUT COMBINATIONS

How can a firm minimize the cost of producing any output it wishes to produce? This question can now be answered by combining isoquants of the previous chapter with isocost lines of section 9-1. In Figure 9-2, the desired level of output is indicated by isoquant $\overline{Q}$. The slopes of the isocost lines show the ratio of input prices p_l/p_k; the three isocost lines are parallel because the producer's purchase rate does not affect the input prices. In order to minimize the cost of production, the producer must use the input combination that is located on the lowest isocost line that enables the production of $\overline{Q}$ units. Thus, *the cost-minimizing or optimal input combination is shown by point E, where the isoquant is tangent to an isocost line.*

THE LEAST-COST CONDITION

At the point of tangency between the isoquant and the isocost line, the slope of the isoquant, $\Delta k/\Delta l = -\text{MPP}_l/\text{MPP}_k$, is equal

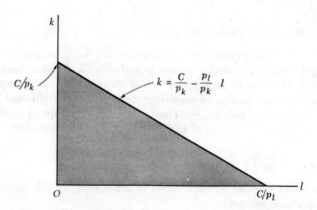

Figure 9-1   Isocost line

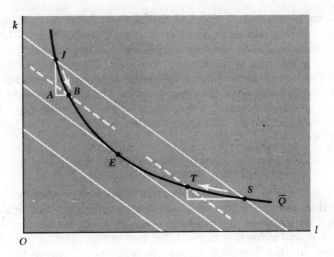

Figure 9-2 Cost-minimizing input combination

to the slope of the isocost line, $-p_l/p_k$. Thus, in equilibrium (that is, when the optimal input combination is attained),

$$-\frac{\Delta k}{\Delta l} = \frac{\text{MPP}_l}{\text{MPP}_k} = \frac{p_l}{p_k}$$

or

$$\frac{\text{MPP}_l}{p_l} = \frac{\text{MPP}_k}{p_k}$$

  Referring to Figure 9-2, let us see why the first equation — which requires the *equality of the slopes of the isoquant and isocost line* — must hold in equilibrium. The movement along the isoquant from J to B indicates the substitution of AB units of labor for AJ units of capital, which leaves the output unchanged. However, the input combination B is less expensive than combination J, as indicated by the dotted isocost line going through it. As long as the numerical slope of the isoquant is steeper than the slope of the isocost line, substitution of labor for capital reduces the cost of production. Similarly, when the numerical slope of the isoquant is less steep than that of the isocost line as at point S, production cost is reduced by substituting more capital for labor. Once at point E, where the slopes of isoquant and isocost line are equal, any movement away from E will increase the cost of producing the output.

  The second equation above can be interpreted as saying that the producer must, in order to minimize the cost of production, allocate his production budget among the two inputs in such a way as to *equalize the marginal physical product per dollar of each input.* If the current input combination chosen is such that $MPP_l/p_l > MPP_k/p_k$, the producer should employ more labor and less capital in order to minimize his cost of production. Similarly, the producer must substitute more capital for labor if the marginal physical product per dollar of capital is greater than that of labor. Thus, the cost-minimizing input combination requires that marginal physical product per dollar of input be equal for all inputs that are employed.[1] (This holds for *n* inputs.)

OUTPUT MAXIMIZATION WITH A GIVEN PRODUCTION BUDGET

The selection of optimal input combination can be analyzed in terms of maximizing output with a given production budget. In this formulation, the producer wants to select the input combination that will allow him to reach the highest isoquant, given his production budget. Needless to say, the optimal solution is shown by the tangency of the given isocost line and an isoquant. Any isoquant that represents a higher output than the chosen isoquant will be unattainable due to the budget constraint; any isoquant showing a smaller output is less desirable.

EFFECT OF CHANGING INPUT PRICES

Let us now refer to Figure 9-3 and consider the effect of changing input prices. Any proportionate change in both input prices will not alter the slope of the budget line. Therefore, the cost-minimizing input combination required to produce the given output remains the same; only the cost of production changes. On the other hand, a change in price that makes the price of labor more expensive relative to that of capital will increase the numerical slope of the budget line. In order to take advantage of this new price situation, the producer will employ more of the now relatively cheaper capital and less of the now more expensive labor, as indicated by point E' in Figure 9-3. A change in price that makes labor relatively cheaper will make the budget line flatter; taking advantage of this new input price situation, the producer will employ more labor and less capital as indicated by point E''. Given a smooth isoquant, any change in the p_l/p_k ratio will necessarily alter the optimal input combination.

9-3 THE EXPANSION PATH

Let us now examine how the optimal input combinations for various levels of production are chosen by referring to Figure 9-4.

---

[1]For a mathematical treatment of production decisions, see Appendix 9A.

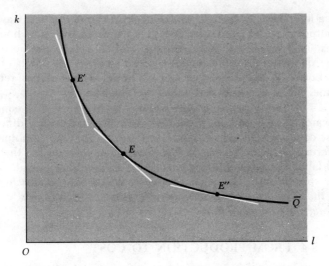

Figure 9-3 Optimal input combination affected by changing input prices

Assume that input prices remain constant as shown by the parallel isocost lines. As the outlay for production increases from C_1 to C_2 to C_3, the optimal combination chosen shifts from E_1 to E_2 to E_3. The equilibrium path along which production expands as the production budget is increased is called the expansion path. *An expansion path, therefore, shows the locus of the least-cost input combinations for producing various levels of output assuming that input prices remain constant.* The expansion path does *not* show the historical path along

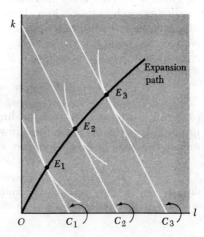

Figure 9-4 Cost-minimizing expansion in output

197

which a firm does, in fact, expand. Rather, it shows the best way various outputs can be produced at a given time in which technology and resource prices are held constant, and all inputs can be freely varied. All points on the expansion path represent the points of tangency between isoquants and isocost lines, whose slopes remain the same. *Thus, an expansion path is an isocline.*

The expansion path shown in Figure 9-4 is concave downward. In general, an expansion path may take many different shapes; concave upward or downward, linear, or some combination of different shapes. A straight-line expansion path means that the capital/labor ratio remains unchanged for all levels of output. *Thus, in this special case, the expansion path shows the relationship between the output and proportionate increases in both inputs, and is, therefore, called a scale line.*

9-4 FROM PRODUCTION TO COST

Given an expansion path that shows the least cost combinations required to produce various levels of output, we can immediately derive the associated cost schedule. In discussing cost, we presuppose efficient production; that is, all costs refer to the minimum costs of producing the indicated outputs.

Let us now see how a cost schedule can, in theory, be derived from an expansion path.[2] Examine Figure 9-5a, which shows an expansion path. The points of tangency, A, B, C, etc., associate each level of output with the least cost of producing it when both inputs can be freely varied. For instance, point A shows that the minimum cost of producing 10 units of output is $100. By ascertaining the cost-output pair for each tangency solution, we can immediately obtain the *long-run total cost*, LTC, entries shown in the first two columns of Table 9-1. This LTC schedule indicates the lowest total cost of producing each output when all inputs are variable. The LTC schedule of Table 9-1 is plotted in Figure 9-5b as a conventional LTC curve. Notice that points A', B', C', etc., on the LTC curve in Figure 9-5b correspond directly to points A, B, C, etc., on the expansion path in Figure 9-5a.

We have just seen how costs are related to efficient production. Before we start exploring various concepts of short-run and long-run costs and the relationships between them, however, it is important for us to pause for a few moments and ask what is really meant by cost. Let us, therefore, devote the rest of this chapter to

---

[2]In practice, it is more convenient to measure the cost function directly rather than measuring it from the production function, since the accounting data are usually given in money terms.

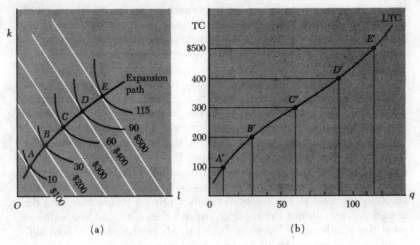

Figure 9-5 Derivation of the total cost curve (*b*) from the expansion path (*a*)

exploring the nature of cost itself and postpone the detailed study of short-run and long-run costs to the next chapter.

9-5 THE ALTERNATIVE OR OPPORTUNITY COST

Scarcity is basic to economic resources. Using scarce resources to produce good A, therefore, means forgoing some other goods that could have been produced using those resources. If a given amount of resources can be used to produce either military hardware or consumer goods, the cost of using the resources to produce weapons is the consumer goods that must be forgone. If a certain amount of money is being used to finance the proprietor's business, the cost of using the money in his business is the *highest* rate of return the money could have earned in its alternative use. The cost of reading

Table 9-1 Long-Run Cost Schedule

OUTPUT	LTC ($)	LMC ($/UNIT)	LAC ($/UNIT)
10	100		10.00
		5.00	
30	200		6.67
		3.33	
60	300		5.00
		3.33	
90	400		4.44
		4.00	
115	500		4.35

199

this book at this time is the best alternative you are giving up (such as getting an extra hour of sleep). We may even say that one of the costs of marrying a woman is the forgone opportunity of marrying another woman; a young man in love, however, may consider this cost negligible.

In order to make various forgone alternatives comparable, we must consider their monetary values. *Thus, the alternative or opportunity cost of using resources to produce A is the value of the best alternative or opportunity forgone.* Whenever an assessment of cost is required for decision making, the relevant cost is the alternative cost. For instance, a fixed input has no alternative use in the short run; thus, the alternative cost of using the fixed input in the short run is zero even though the so-called historical cost was substantial. The cost to the society of conscripting a young man into the armed services is not the meager pay it offers him, but the value of what the youth could have produced in his civilian life. A man who owns and operates a small firm must not forget to include in his costs such items as wages, interest, and rent that could have been received if he had used his labor, money, and building in their best alternative uses.

Suppose that active competition for productive resources prevails in the market. Then, every variable resource must be paid what it can receive in its next best alternative, that is, the opportunity cost. Otherwise, the resource cannot be retained in its current employment. Thus, under competition, the money outlay for a resource represents the opportunity cost of the resources.

Alternative or opportunity costs include both explicit and implicit costs. *Explicit costs are those readily observed, such as wages and salaries paid to employees, costs of merchandise, utility bills, license fees, insurance premiums, and depreciation charges. Implicit costs are what self-owned and self-employed resources could have earned in their best alternative uses.* For instance, implicit wages, implicit rent, and implicit interest refer to the highest wage, rent, and interest the owner could have received for his labor, his building, and his money had he let someone else (rather than himself) use his labor service, buildings, and money. Students occasionally make the error of equating opportunity costs with implicit costs. However, the opportunity or alternative costs of undertaking any action must be composed of all opportunities or alternatives sacrificed, whether they be implicit or explicit. Clearly, opportunity costs must include *both implicit and explicit costs.*

9-6 PRIVATE, EXTERNAL, AND SOCIAL COSTS

Sometimes, there is a discrepancy between the cost incurred by a firm (or individual or group) and the cost that must be incurred by the society as a whole. For example, a factory may dispose its untreated waste into a river or an ocean. Such a method of waste disposal may minimize the private cost, but it does impose a cost to the society in the form of polluted waterways. *A cost that is not borne by the firm, but is incurred by others in society is called an external cost.* The true cost to the society must include all costs regardless of who bears them. *Thus, the social cost is the sum of private and external costs.* That is,

Social cost = private cost + external cost

or

External cost = social cost − private cost

A firm may also create, in the process of production, some benefits to society for which it is not directly paid. For example, there is the celebrated example of apple blossoms and honey bees. The apple blossoms increase the output of nearby honey producers. Thus, the apple growers create *external benefits* to the honey producers. Similarly, a firm's manpower training program may provide skilled labor to other firms.

In general, externalities are said to exist whenever the actions of an individual or group affect (benefit or hurt) other(s) in society. If the social cost is greater than the private cost, there is an external cost or *negative externality*. If the social cost is smaller than private cost, there is an external benefit or a *positive externality*.

When there are no interactions that cause externalities, economic efficiency calls for the production of a good if its benefit exceeds its cost (both measured in monetary terms). However, when externalities exist, private benefit-cost calculations fail to produce efficient allocation of resources. Private producers tend to overproduce when there are external costs; while they tend to underproduce when there are external benefits.

Externalities are an important concern in modern economic discussions, and will be examined in some detail in Chapter Nineteen. But, in the remainder of the chapter, we will assume that all costs and benefits are private and that there are no externalities.

9-7 OPPORTUNITY COST VERSUS HISTORICAL COST: An Application

In order to appreciate the significance of opportunity cost and the irrelevance of historical cost in decision making, consider the following examples. Suppose you bought a piece of pretty stone for $5 while touring in a foreign country. After you returned home, you had the stone polished and discovered that it was a good quality emerald. In trying to get this stone priced for sale, which one would you consider, the historical cost paid to the native or the maximum price the stone can command in the market—the alternative or opportunity cost? As another example, let us consider the purchase and sale of a stock. Suppose you bought AT & T (American Telephone and Telegraph) shares at $75 per share. Should you sell this stock to your old aunt at $50 per share and tell her that you are doing her a great favor because you are giving her a highly rated stock at below your historical cost? (For your information, it so happens that the market price of the stock at the time of this offer was around $40 per share.) In both of these examples, it is clear that the relevant cost is the alternative cost—the maximum price the item can command today—not the historical cost that happened to be incurred in the past.

If you agree with the above arguments, consider this. A friend of yours is offering you $40,000 for your house, which you purchased a year ago for $30,000. Should you accept this offer? The answer depends on the opportunity cost or the current market price of the house. If you did not know that the market price of the house was $45,000 and sold it to your friend for $40,000, you have really come out $5,000 short in the transaction, even though the Internal Revenue Service wants you to pay a capital gains tax and some of your friends may frown upon your "profiteering."

In using accounting cost for economic analysis, economists frequently encounter some difficulties. For instance, recorded accounting cost is usually in terms of historical cost. Recorded depreciation allowances tend to represent legal rather than economic considerations. Cost of producing **joint products**—*products that are produced together such as beef and cowhide*—and overhead costs are frequently allocated rather arbitrarily.

9-8 DRAFT VERSUS VOLUNTEER ARMED FORCES: An Application

For quite some time we have been faced with the complex moral-social-economic issue of the draft versus volunteer armed forces. Though an economist does not have any special competence to analyze moral or social issues involved in this difficult question, he can offer a great deal of insight into the economics of this issue.

The demand and supply curves for military manpower are shown in Figure 9-6. Since more young people will be induced to join the military services at higher wage rates, the supply curve has a positive slope. The military must also function under a budget constraint. If the wage rate it has to pay is low, it can afford to hire more. If the wage rate is high, it is forced to hire less or to look for the possibilities of substituting capital for manpower. Thus, its demand curve must be negatively sloped. In drawing the demand curve, however,

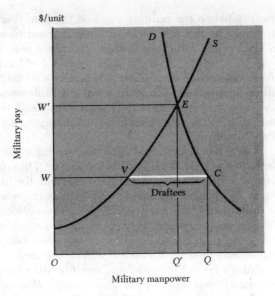

Figure 9-6   Draft versus volunteer systems

we have assumed that the demand for military manpower is inelastic in the relevant range.

Under the draft system, the government fixes both the wage rate paid to draftees and the number of young people to be drafted. Suppose the military wants WC ($=OQ$) persons and sets the wage rate at W dollars per draftee per month. At this wage rate WV persons will volunteer and VC persons must be drafted. The total wage bill that must be paid by the military is $OWCQ$ dollars.

Given the demand and supply curves in Figure 9-6, the equilibrium price and quantity under the voluntary system must be W' dollars and Q' persons per unit of time. Given the inelastic demand for the military manpower in the relevant range, the total wage bill under the voluntary system, $OW'EQ'$ dollars, must be substantially larger than the wage bill under the draft system, $OWCQ$ dollars.

Looking at this larger wage bill, the critics of the volunteer army argue that it is too expensive for the country. However, such an argument has some serious flaws in it. The low military wage forced upon the draftee seriously underrepresents the true cost of using him in the military services. As we have already noted, the true cost of inducting a young man into the military services is the value of what he would have produced as a civilian. The draftee is not only forced to serve in the military but also to pay a draft tax; he must bear the difference between the military pay and the true cost of having him in the army—the amount he could have earned in his civilian occupation. Under the volunteer system, the army pays the volunteer the wage he is willing to accept. The true cost of having him in the military is recognized by society and paid by all taxpayers, not by the draftees themselves. The main economic difference between the draft and voluntary systems is this: under the draft, the draftees shoulder the bulk of the cost; under the voluntary system, the taxpayers pay the total bill.

There are some factors that tend to favor the voluntary system. First, volunteers will tend to stay on longer. Thus, training (or turnover) cost may be reduced substantially. Second, the higher wage rate that has to be paid to volunteers will reduce the man/machine ratio in the military and will likely result in a better allocation of resources. Third, when volunteers are recruited and trained for the tasks for which they are suited, misallocation of resources (such as using a highly trained engineer on K.P. duty) will be reduced.

Now refer to Figure 9-7 and consider the effect of changing economic conditions on the price and quantity of volunteer military personnel. When the economy is booming, job opportunities in civilian life will be plentiful and civilian remunerations will be attractive. Thus, the supply curve of volunteers to the military will shift to the left and upward from S to S', causing the equilibrium price to rise and quantity to decrease. If there is a severe recession, on the other hand, the scarcity of civilian jobs will tend to shift the supply curve for military service to the right from S to S'', which will produce a lower equilibrium price and greater quantity. All such changes result in more efficient allocation of resources. The true cost of using a young man in the military is high in a prosperous period

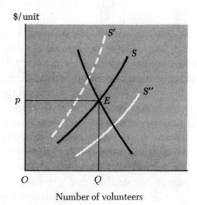

Figure 9-7 Impact of economic conditions on the military labor supply

because the man can produce more in civilian life. Similarly, when a recession lowers the productivity of the young man in civilian life, the pay needed to attract him into the military services would also be lowered.

Now, let us consider yet another objection to the volunteer army. What happens if an unpopular large-scale war develops? It is quite possible, under these circumstances, for the supply of volunteers to decrease greatly while the demand for military manpower increases substantially. Thus, we may conjecture that the demand and supply curves could look like the ones shown in Figure 9-8. The two curves fail to intersect, and there is no market solution to the military manpower requirement. In order to overcome this difficulty that may arise in an all-out war, the market solution must somehow be modified. For example, an adequate supply of wartime manpower may be assured by maintaining sufficient voluntary forces at all times or by lengthening the period of duty for which the volunteers must sign.

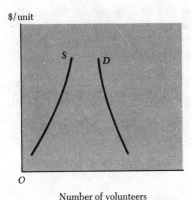

$/unit

O

Number of volunteers

Figure 9-8 Demand and supply for military manpower in a major war

APPENDIX 9

A. Determining the Optimal Input Combinations by the Method of the Lagrange Multiplier

The reader who is trained in calculus can readily obtain the results of section 9-2 by the method of the Lagrangian multiplier.

In order to maximize output subject to a given cost constraint, we form the following Lagrangian expression:

$$L = Q(a, b) - \lambda(p_a \cdot a + p_b \cdot b - C).$$

where a and b represent inputs, p_a and p_b show two input prices, and λ is an unknown constant.[3]

Partially differentiating this equation with respect to a, b, and λ and setting them equal to zero, we get

$$L_a = Q_a - \lambda p_a = 0$$
$$L_b = Q_b - \lambda p_b = 0$$
$$L_\lambda = -p_a \cdot a - p_b \cdot b + C = 0$$

(for notational simplicity, we use L_a, L_b, L_λ for $\partial L/\partial a$, $\partial L/\partial b$ and $\partial L/\partial \lambda$, respectively.)

From the first two equations, one obtains

$$Q_a/p_a = \lambda$$
$$Q_b/p_b = \lambda$$

Accordingly,

$$Q_a/p_a = Q_b/p_b = \lambda$$

[3]For a more detailed explanation of the Lagrangian expression, see Appendix 3B.

The economic interpretation of this equation says that the marginal physical product per dollar of input must be equal for all inputs. The equation can also be written as $p_a/Q_a = p_b/Q_b$, whose economic interpretation is the marginal cost of production.

The above equation can be written alternatively as:

$$Q_a/Q_b = p_a/p_b$$

In this form, it says that the numerical values of the slopes of the isoquant and the isocost line must be equal.

The Lagrangian expression for the minimization of the cost of production of a given output is

$$\text{Minimize } L = C(a, b) - \lambda[Q(a, b) - \bar{Q}]$$

which in our current context can be written as

$$L = p_a \cdot a + p_b \cdot b - \lambda[Q(a, b) - \bar{Q}]$$

The reader may wish to derive the mathematical conclusions obtained for the previous output-maximizing model for this cost-minimizing model.

B. Optimal Input Combinations: Kinked Isoquants

Suppose there are only a few production processes, and isoquants are, therefore, kinked as shown in Figure 9-9. The least expensive way to produce output $\bar{Q}$, given the input price ratio indicated by the isocost line CT, is to employ input combination E. At point E the isocost line touches the isoquant, but the slope of the isoquant is not defined. The optimal solution given by point E is a "corner tangency" solution.

In the continuous isoquant case, the equilibrium condition required the slopes of the budget line and the isoquant to be equal. In the case of few processes, *the equilibrium condition requires the isoquant to be steeper than the isocost line to the left of point E, and flatter than to the right of point E.*

Now consider the effect of changing input prices. Any proportionate change in both input prices—which does not affect the

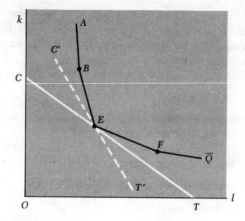

Figure 9-9 Optimal input combination with kinked isoquants

slope of the isocost line—will not alter the optimal input combination. The effect of input price changes that alter the slope of the isocost line, however, is quite different from that of the smooth isoquant case of section 9-2. Suppose an increase in the price of labor increase the slope of the isocost line as shown by $C'T'$ in Figure 9-9. Despite this change, the optimal solution still remains at point E.

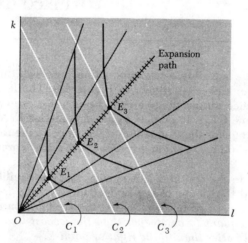

Figure 9-10 Expansion path with kinked isoquants

Unless the increase in the price of labor makes the new budget line steeper than the line segment *BE*, the optimal choice is not altered. Similarly, lowering the price of labor relative to that of capital will not change the input combination chosen unless the price change is large enough to make the budget line flatter than the isoquant segment *EF*. Clearly, *the producer will not change the choice of his production process unless the changes in input prices are large enough* to justify the shift.

When the slope of the isocost line coincides with that of the isoquant there is no unique equilibrium solution; all input combinations that are on the tangency segment are equally efficient.

Given a few-process production function pictured in Figure 9-10 and the assumed constancy of the input price ratio, the expansion path must be a straight line. The expansion of output is carried out by increasing input doses employed; only the absolute amounts of inputs used change without affecting the input ratio.

EXERCISES 9

Production Decisions and Costs

9-1 A professor who charges $30 an hour for his consulting work also spends about an hour per week cutting his own lawn. A neighborhood boy is willing to cut his lawn for $3.00 per week. Is the professor allocating his time inefficiently?

9-2 Keeping in mind that relevant cost is alternative or opportunity cost, estimate your cost of attending your college or university for a semester.

9-3 A staff member of a research organization who frequently travels estimated the cost of operating his business automobile as follows:

Depreciation	$800
Insurance	160
Gasoline and oil	470
Maintenance and repair	100
Garage, tools, and parking	50
Tax and license fee	60
Total	$1640

1. In your opinion, which of the above items are fixed costs?
2. Is there any private cost that should have been added to the above list to make it more complete?
3. Is there any additional social cost that must be considered as the cost of driving an automobile?

9-4 Assume that two inputs (labor and capital) are required to produce a product.

1. If the prices of both inputs double, how would this affect the optimal input combination? (Assume the pro-

duction is to be carried out anyway.)

2.   Suppose a change in supply condition causes the input price ratio p_l/p_k to decline. What is the impact of of this change on the optimal input combination selected under the following situations:

a.   If the production function is characterized by smooth isoquants?

b.   If there are only a few processes? (see Appendix 9B.)

9-5   A product can be produced by using either input a or b, and the firm's present output position indicates that:

$$MPP_a = 3, \ p_a = \$1, \ MPP_b = 6, \ p_b = \$4$$

Is the firm employing the cost-minimizing combinations of inputs a and b ? If not, what should the firm do?

9-6   Should an expansion path originate from the origin always? Why or why not?

CHAPTER TEN

SHORT - RUN AND LONG - RUN COSTS

In this chapter, we continue the discussion of costs started in the previous chapter. More specifically, we will examine short-run and long-run costs, the relationship between the short-run and long-run cost curves, and the notion of economies of size (or scale). Appendix 10 presents some additional short-run cost curves based on different sets of assumptions.

10-1 SHORT-RUN VERSUS LONG-RUN COSTS

In Chapter Seven, we introduced the concepts of short run and long run. There, we noted that the notion of time was merely incidental, and the distinction between the two analytical time periods was based on the existence or non-existence of a fixed input(s). *Short-run cost functions or curves describe costs when one or more inputs are fixed in quantity.* Let us assume that the plant capacity is the only input that cannot be varied readily. Then, the short run is the period in which the quantities of labor and materials can be varied at will but the size of the plant is fixed. The short-run costs, therefore, show how production cost changes as the rate of utilization of a given sized plant is varied.

The long-run cost functions or curves, on the other hand, describe costs when all inputs (including plant capacity) can be varied freely. The long run is a period in which the producer is free to choose from all technically feasible plant sizes, and to operate the chosen plant at any rate desired. For this reason, the long-run average cost curve is sometimes referred to as the *planning curve.* Because, at any given moment, a producer must operate a given size plant, which was constructed as the result of a long-run decision in the past, it may be said that actual production is always carried out in the short run.

10-2 SHORT-RUN COSTS: DEFINITIONS AND THEIR SCHEDULAR REPRESENTATION

In discussing short-run cost functions, economists usually omit the word, *short-run*. For instance, instead of referring to short-run total cost and short-run average cost, they simply talk of total cost and average cost. We will follow this practice except when short-run and long-run costs are being discussed together.

The total cost, TC, *of producing any output is defined as the minimum cost that must be incurred to produce that output.* The TC is the sum of the total *variable cost* (*which varies as output changes*) and the total *fixed cost* (*which is independent of the rate of output*). That is,

$$TC = TVC + TFC$$

Dividing this expression by the rate of output, q, we get the *average total cost*, ATC or simply, AC. (For ease of recognition, we shall henceforth use q to indicate the rate of output when there is only one product.)

$$ATC = \frac{TC}{q} = \frac{TVC}{q} + \frac{TFC}{q}$$
$$= AVC + AFC$$

where AVC and AFC show **average variable** and **average fixed** costs.

Marginal costs, MC, *show the increase in total cost* (*or total variable cost*) *per unit change in output.*[1] Thus,

$$MC = \Delta TC/\Delta q = \Delta TVC/\Delta q$$

Graphically, MC at any output rate shows the *slope* of the TC curve at that output rate.

---

[1]Since the total cost is the sum of total variable and total fixed costs and the total fixed cost cannot change by definition, an increase in total cost is identical to an increase in total variable cost. That is,

$$\Delta TC = \Delta TVC + \Delta TFC = \Delta TVC + 0 = \Delta TVC$$

In calculus notation,

$$MC = \frac{d(TC)}{dq} = \frac{d(TVC + TFC)}{dq} = \frac{d(TVC)}{dq}$$

Since MC shows the change in TC (per unit change in output) and TFC cannot change by definition, MC is not affected by the size of TFC. In general, *adding a constant to total quantity does not change the value of associated marginal quantity.* As an example, consider Figure 10-1, in which the graphs of two cost functions that differ by a constant sum, k, are shown. The two curves differ in heights only, their slopes (that is, their marginal costs) at any given level of output are identical, as indicated by parallel tangent lines.

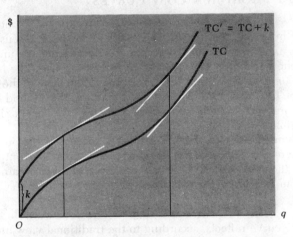

Figure 10-1 Fixed cost does not affect the slope of the TC curve

Table 10-1 shows a hypothetical short-run *cost schedule* that demonstrates the relationships among various cost concepts. The

Table 10-1   A Cost Schedule

(1) OUTPUT	(2) TC	(3) ATC	(4) AVC	(5) AFC	(6) MC
0	$256.00	—	—	—	$64.00
1	320.00	$320.00	$64.00	$256.00	20.00
2	340.00	( )	42.00	128.00	( )
3	355.00	118.33	33.00	85.33	13.00
4	368.00	92.00	28.00	64.00	13.00
5	( )	76.20	25.00	51.20	19.00
6	400.00	66.66	( )	42.66	31.00
7	431.00	61.57	25.00	36.57	49.00
8	480.00	60.00	28.00	( )	

TC of producing various outputs per unit of time (by applying various amounts of labor to a fixed quantity of capital) are shown in columns (1) and (2). Given this TC schedule, we can readily derive associated ATC, AVC, AFC, and MC column entries. The reader should fill out the blank spaces in the table to ascertain that he knows precisely how those cost figures are derived.

10-3 SHORT-RUN COST CURVES

In Figure 10-2a, we show a *conventional* TC curve that exhibits the properties usually assumed in textbook discussions of cost. It is a cubic curve that increases at a decreasing rate until point A is reached and then increases at an increasing rate. The height of the TC curve at any ouput level is equal to the sum of the vertical heights of TVC and TFC. Figure 10-2b contains the AC and MC curves that are qualitatively consistent with the TC curves shown in Figure 10-2a.

The minimum point on the MC curve, A', occurs at the output rate of q_1, where the TC curve has its point of inflection. The output rates at which the AVC and ATC curves are minimum are obtained from points B and C, where the rays from the origin touch the TVC and TC curves.

The AVC curve is U-shaped. The downward sloping portion of the curve reflects, according to the traditional view, the economies introduced by better utilization of the existing plant. But the AVC curve must eventually turn upward because (1) the MC curve must sooner or later turn upward due to the law of variable proportion, and (2) as soon as MC exceeds AVC, it is a mathematical necessity that the AVC curve turn upward.[2] The vertical distance, at any output rate, between the ATC and AVC curves shows AFC. The TFC, a constant sum, divided by a larger and larger output results in a smaller and smaller AFC; therefore, the vertical distance between ATC and AVC narrows with output. If the AFC curve is shown separately on its own, it will be a rectangular hyperbola, which approaches the quantity axis asymptotically as output increases.

10-4 THE RELATIONSHIP BETWEEN PRODUCT AND COST CURVES

The cost curves are derived by combining the technological information on production with the data on input prices.

[2]The relationships among total, average, and marginal products discussed in section 7-4 apply to any total, average, and marginal quantities, including various concepts of costs.

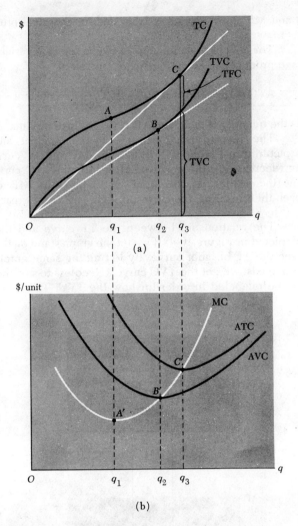

Figure 10-2   Relationships among various cost curves

Therefore, we can readily demonstrate, for the single-input case, that cost curves and product curves are inversely related. Assume that the input price remains constant. Then, the inverse relationship between the marginal cost and the marginal product is shown by the following equation.

$$MC = \Delta C / \Delta q = (p_l \cdot \Delta l)/\Delta q = p_l(\Delta l/\Delta q) = p_l \frac{1}{(\Delta q/\Delta l)}$$

$$= \text{constant} \cdot \frac{1}{MP_l}$$

217

where p_l and MP_l are the price of labor and the marginal product of labor.

The inverse relationship between average variable cost and average product can be similarly demonstrated.

$$AVC = (p_l \cdot l)/q = p_l(l/q) = p_l \cdot \frac{1}{(q/l)} = \text{constant} \cdot \frac{1}{AP_l}$$

where l is the quantity of labor and AP_l is the average product of labor.

The inverse relationship between product and cost curves is pictured in Figure 10-3. When the MP and AP curves are increasing (decreasing), the corresponding MC and AC curves are decreasing (increasing). At the input rate where the MP and AP curves reach their maxima, the corresponding cost curves reach their minima.

The relationship between the TP curve and the TVC curve is depicted in Figure 10-4. If we let the graph stand on the labor axis, we see the TP of labor curve. By letting the same graph stand on the output axis, we get the TVC curve. (Needless to say, the labor axis has to be relabeled in order to show the TVC: TVC = price of

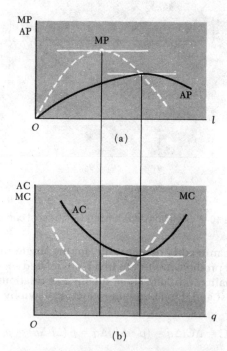

Figure 10-3 Relationship between the product and cost curves

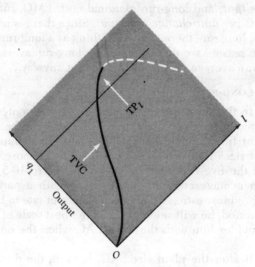

Figure 10-4   Relationship between TP and TVC

labor × quantity of labor.) Note the interesting relationship between the rates at which TP and TVC increase. When the TP is increasing at an *increasing* (decreasing) *rate*, the corresponding TVC increases at a *decreasing* (increasing) *rate*. Observe that when the TP starts to decline absolutely, the TC curve bends backward as shown by the dotted segment of the TVC curve. Since no producer will choose to incur higher cost to produce the same amount, say q_1, the negative segment of the TC curve must be discarded.

10-5 LONG-RUN COST CURVES

In the short run, there is some input(s) such as the plant capacity that cannot be varied at will. In the long run, there is no input constraint; thus, labor, raw materials, the size and number of plants, and the number of firms in the market can all vary. *Because the long-run cost is the cost when there is no limiting factor that tends to increase production cost, the long-run cost is always lower than (or at least as low as) the lowest short-run cost attainable.* We state this proposition in terms of total and average costs as follows:

$$\text{LTC}(q) \leq \text{STC}(q) \text{ and } \text{LAC}(q) \leq \text{SAC}(q) \text{ for all } q$$

where LTC and STC stand for the long- and short-run total costs and LAC and SAC show the long- and short-run average costs.

Various long-run costs are interpreted in the same manner as their counterparts in the short run. Thus, **LAC** *is simply* LTC *divided by output;* and long-run marginal cost, **LMC**, *shows the increase in* LTC *per unit change in output.* Since there is no input that is fixed in the long run, there is no such thing as a long-run fixed cost. For the same reason, we do not refer to a long-run average variable cost; a long-run average cost is a variable cost anyway.

LONG-RUN AVERAGE COST CURVE

In the short run the producer must be content with the best utilization of the given plant, but in the long run he can choose any size plant from among all feasible plant sizes. Suppose there are five plant sizes from which the producer can choose in the long run. Each of the five SAC curves shown in Figure 10-5 represents the short-run average cost curve associated with a particular size plant. If the producer estimates his desired output rate to be less than q_1 units per period, he will select SAC_1 as the best scale of plant since this plant provides him with the lowest AC when the output is less than q_1 units.

If after the plant size SAC_1 is built, the desired output turns out to be OA units per period, the firm must produce the output at the cost of AC dollars per unit. In the short run, the firm can only utilize the available plant in the most efficient manner. But when the time to replace the existing plant arrives, the firm will choose SAC_2, the plant size best suited to produce OA units per period.

If the rate of production is between q_1 and q_2, the best size is given by SAC_2. Similarly, the best sizes for the rates of production between q_2 and q_3, q_3 and q_4, and in excess of q_4 units are given by SAC_3, SAC_4, and SAC_5. If the expected output happens to be at the rate at which two SAC curves intersect (such as q_1 units per

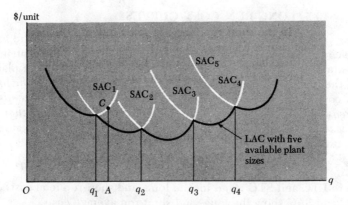

Figure 10-5 LAC curve with five plant sizes

period), either SAC_1 or SAC_2 will be just as good to the producer in terms of cost. Thus, some other consideration must enter the final choice between the two plant sizes.

That portion of each SAC curve that lies below any other SAC curves is shown in black. The entire zigzagged black curve, therefore, shows the lowest AC of producing each output when the firm is free to choose from the five available plant sizes. In other words, it shows the LAC curve with the five available plant sizes.

If the number of available plant sizes is greater, the LAC curve may look like the solid black portions of the SAC curves in Figure 10-6. If the plant sizes can be varied continuously, the LAC curve will be a smooth curve as shown by the white U-shaped curve.

In summary, the LAC curve shows the lowest AC of producing each output when all inputs can be varied freely. Because the LAC curve envelopes all SAC curves (that is, no SAC curve lies below the LAC), it is also referred to as the *envelope curve*. Another descriptive name given to the LAC curve is the *planning curve*; the producer can "plan" his production strategy referring to this curve.

LONG-RUN TOTAL COST CURVE

An alternative way of looking at the relationship between short-run and long-run cost curves is to examine the *long-run total cost, LTC, which shows the lowest TC of producing any output when the producer can freely vary all inputs.* By the very nature of the long-run planning period, the producer is free to choose the plant size that will produce the desired output at the lowest TC. Suppose that

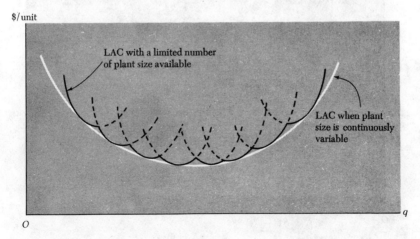

Figure 10-6   LAC curve with many plant sizes

only three plant sizes are feasible and that their TC curves are shown by STC_1, STC_2, and STC_3 in Figure 10-7. Given the current technology that limits the available plant sizes to the three STC curves shown, the cheapest way to produce any output less than q_1 is to build and use plant shown by STC_1. Similarly, the cost-minimizing production of the output between q_1 and q_2 units requires the construction and use of plant size STC_2. If the output is greater than q_2 units, the cost-minimizing plant size is STC_3. The portions of the STC curves that lie below any other STC curves (shown by solid black curves) show the lowest TC attainable in producing various outputs; thus, the solid black curve is the LTC curve, when there are three possible plant sizes.

If the plant size can be varied continuously, the LTC will be shown by the smooth white curve in Figure 10-7. For any level of output desired (such as those indicated by points A, B, and C), there is an STC curve tangent to the LTC curve. This particular STC curve shows the least-cost plant size required to produce the desired output.

Three hypothetical shapes of the LTC curve are shown in Figure 10-8. The LTC curve corresponding to the conventional U-shaped LAC is shown by LTC_1; like the conventional STC curve, this curve increases at a decreasing rate at first, but as production continues to expand it starts increasing at an increasing rate. The case in which LTC increases at a constant rate (and LAC is constant)

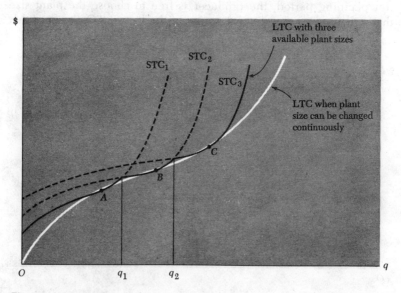

Figure 10-7 Long-run total cost curve

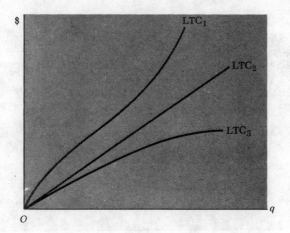

Figure 10-8 Shapes of long-run total cost curves

is shown by LTC_2. The case in which the rate of increase in LTC decreases (and LAC decreases) is shown by LTC_3. What specific form does an actual LTC curve take? This is an important question that must be settled by further empirical investigations.

10-6 THE RELATIONSHIP BETWEEN THE LONG-RUN AND SHORT-RUN AVERAGE AND MARGINAL COST CURVES

Given an LAC (or LTC) curve, we can readily derive the associated *long-run marginal cost*, LMC, *curve, which shows the extra cost incurred in producing one more unit of output when all inputs can be changed.* In Figure 10-9, the LAC and its LMC curve are shown together with three sets of SAC and SMC curves that represent different plant sizes. Referring to this figure, let us note the relationship between the long-run and short-run curves.

No SAC curve lies below the LAC curve. The LAC curve shows the minimum cost of producing each output when there is no input constraint at all; thus, the LAC at any output is lower than (or at least as low as) any SAC that is subject to the plant size constraint. Mathematically speaking, the LAC curve is the "envelope" of all SAC curves.

Given a continuous U-shaped LAC curve, only one SAC curve has its minimum point tangent to the LAC curve. The size of plant represented by this curve (SAC_2 in Figure 10-9) is referred to as the *optimal scale*. It is optimal only in the sense that this plant size is associated with the minimum LAC. Whether this plant size is

$/unit

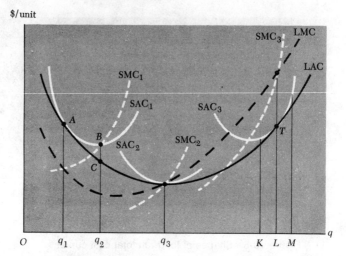

Figure 10-9   Relationship between long-run and short-run average and marginal cost curves

the profit-maximizing size *cannot* be known in the absence of information about the demand for the product.

The slopes of two curves are equal at the point of tangency between them. Thus, when the LAC curve is declining, all SAC curves have negative slopes where they are tangent to the LAC curve. Similarly, when the LAC curve is sloped positively, the slopes of all SAC curves must be positive where they are tangent to the LAC curve.

The cost-minimizing way to produce any output in the long run is to build a plant whose SAC curve is tangent to the LAC curve at the desired output. For instance, the best way to produce q_1 units per period in Figure 10-9 is to construct the SAC_1 plant and operate it at the unit cost of q_1A dollars. If after the SAC_1 size plant is built, the demand condition happens to dictate the production of q_2 units per period, then the producer will operate SAC_1 at the rate where its SAC is minimum. However, this is a short-run solution only. As soon as possible, he will build a new plant whose SAC curve is tangent to the LAC curve at point C. This new plant will produce q_2 units at q_2C dollars per unit, which is the minimum LAC attainable for q_2 units per period.

Note that the cost-minimizing long-run arrangement does not require that a given size plant be operated at its minimum point; rather it requires that a plant be operated where its SAC curve is tangent to the LAC curve. *When a given size plant is operated at the rate where its SAC is lowest, the plant is said to be operated at the optimal rate.* But it is optimal only in the sense of being operated at the lowest point on an SAC curve, *not* in the sense of attaining the minimum cost of producing that output in the long run.

When the LAC curve and an SAC curve are tangent, the LMC and the corresponding SMC curves intersect (that is, have the same value). This relationship between the long-run and short-run curves can be observed at the output rates of q_1, q_3, and L units per period in Figure 10-9. An intuitive explanation can be given. At output rate K, LAC is less than SAC, and therefore, LTC is less than STC. At output rate L, LAC = SAC and the corresponding LTC and STC are equal. Thus, when the output is increased from K to L, the increase in LTC (that is, LMC) must exceed the increase in STC (that is, SMC). Therefore, LMC is greater than SMC in the interval KL. Now consider the interval LM. As production is increased from L to M, the increase in LTC is smaller than the increase in STC. Thus, LMC must be less than SMC in this interval. Now, to the left of output L, at which the LAC and SAC curves are tangent, LMC > SMC; while LMC < SMC to the right of output L. Thus, it follows that LMC = SMC at output L, where the LAC and SAC curves are tangent.[3]

[3]Here is a mathematical proof. The tangency conditions between LAC and SAC at output $\bar{q}$ are given by:

$$\text{LAC}(\bar{q}) = \text{SAC}(\bar{q}) \tag{1}$$

and

$$\frac{d}{dq}\text{LAC}(q)\big|_{\bar{q}} = \frac{d}{dq}\text{SAC}(q)\big|_{\bar{q}} \tag{2}$$

We need to show that whenever the above conditions hold $\text{LMC}(\bar{q}) = \text{SMC}(\bar{q})$. Now,

$$\text{LMC}(q) = \frac{d}{dq}\text{LTC}(q) = \frac{d}{dq}\text{LAC}(q) \cdot q$$

$$= \text{LAC}(q) + q \cdot \frac{d}{dq}\text{LAC}(q) \tag{3}$$

Similarly,

$$\text{SMC}(q) = \frac{d}{dq}\text{STC}(q) = \text{SAC}(q) \cdot q$$

$$= \text{SAC}(q) + q \cdot \frac{d}{dq}\text{SAC}(q) \tag{4}$$

Now at $\bar{q}$ where the tangency condition is satisfied, the first members of the right-hand side in equations (3) and (4) are equal by equation (1) and the second members are equal by equation (2). Thus, the left-hand members of the equations (3) and (4) are equal, and $\text{LMC}(\bar{q}) = \text{SMC}(\bar{q})$ whenever LAC and SMC are tangent to each other.

10-7 ECONOMIES OF SIZE

Whether LAC decreases, increases, or remains constant as output is expanded is an important consideration in the study of cost. In economic literature, the relationship between output and LAC is generally discussed under the heading of the economies of scale or economies of size. Perhaps the term *economies of size* (or outlay) is more appropriate because all inputs need not increase in an equal proportion. However, we shall follow the prevailing convention in economics, and use the two terms *economies of scale* and *economies of size* interchangeably (remembering that the term *scale* is used loosely to mean size). *A firm is said to be subject to economies of size or scale when its LAC decreases as its output increases. Similarly, when LAC increases with output, the firm is said to be subject to diseconomies of size or scale.*

FACTORS CONTRIBUTING TO ECONOMIES OF SIZE

Economies of size or scale may arise from many diverse factors such as technological, financial, or institutional circumstances.

Increasing returns to scale. Recall that increasing returns to scale means a given percentage change in all inputs causes a greater percentage change in physical output. Given constant input prices, therefore, increasing returns to scale means that LAC will decline with output. The expansion path need not be a linear scale line. Thus, as the size of production budget is increased, production processes that use different capital/labor ratios may be used. In any case, the increase in physical returns per dollar of production outlay is an important source of economies of size.

Ease and economy of dealing with large quantities. A few factors that contribute to economies of size can be cited under this heading:

1. *Lower input prices.* A firm may obtain discounts for bulk purchases. The freight charge may be lower per unit of an input purchased. The economies may come from sources external to the firm. For instance, a general expansion in the industry may increase the demand for a particular resouce to such an extent that the suppliers can use more efficient methods of production and charge lower prices.

2. *Lower administrative cost per unit of output.* If the cost of administration does not increase in proportion to the size of the total production budget, the unit cost of administration must fall as production expands.

3. *Lower marketing cost.* The average cost of marketing tends to be lower when larger output is involved. The amounts of mar-

ket information secured and advertising coverage obtained tend
to increase more than in proportion to the increases in the
marketing buget.

4. *Lower cost of borrowing funds.* A larger firm is more apt to
have better access to borrowed funds and secure them at lower
rates.

Spreading of risks. As a firm's production increases,
the statistical law of large numbers works in its favor. The size of
inventory relative to the output can be reduced because the aggregate
behavior of a large number of customers (and/or suppliers) is more
predictable. Risks can be spread over different styles, products, and
locations.

The above discussion should make it clear that the factors that contribute to economies of size (that is, a decreasing LAC)
are diverse. The above discussion, however, fails to show the distinction between (a) economies that stem from being a single (or
only a few) buyers in a resource market, and (b) genuine economies
that stem from *improved* use of resources. The distinction is important for the efficiency question. While economies due to improved
use of resources represent an increase in economic efficiency, the
former may merely reflect the increased bargaining power of a larger
buyer(s).

ECONOMIES OF SIZE VERSUS RETURNS TO SCALE

The reader is also warned not to confuse *economies* of
size (or scale), which relate to LAC, with *returns* to scale, which relate
to the physical aspect of production. Economies of size refer to a
decreasing LAC, while increasing (decreasing) returns to scale describe more (less) than proportionate increase in output when all
inputs are increased in an equal proportion. For example, a decrease
in cost due to increasing returns to scale may be more than offset by
increases in input prices, and the firm may experience diseconomies
of size, that is, an increase in LAC.

THE SHAPE OF THE LONG-RUN AVERAGE COST CURVE

What is the most likely shape of the LAC curve? Many
economists agree that the LAC curve will decline at first with increasing output, but for high output there is very little agreement.[4]

[4]For example, see J. Johnston, *Statistical Cost Analysis* (New
York: McGraw-Hill, 1960), p. 24, and A. A. Walters, "Production and Cost
Functions: An Econometric Survey," *Econometrica*, January–April 1963,
pp. 40–41.

The usual argument for the inevitability of an eventually rising LAC curve is the diseconomies of size brought forward by the ever increasing size of management—the so-called pyramiding of management and associated inefficiency per dollar of outlay for top-level decision making. But it might also be argued that recent developments in computer technology and managerial techniques have made large managements relatively more efficient. Thus, further empirical evidence must be gathered before it can be determined whether the LAC curve, after its initial decline, will remain approximately constant or increase as output keeps on increasing.

10-8 EMPIRICAL COST CURVES

In the preceding pages of this chapter, we have discussed short-run and long-run costs based on the assumption of U-shaped AC (and cubic TC) curve. How well does this conventional hypothesis of U-shaped AC curve agree with various empirical findings? Let us answer this question by relying on A. A. Walters' survey article.[5]

Many cost studies have been made using time series, cross-section, engineering, and questionnaire data. The available empirical findings, however, fail to give any conclusive answer to the question we have posed. Let us see why.

Many cost studies have dealt with public utilities and railroads, probably due to the availability of data for regulated or nationalized business. These studies indicate that LAC in public utilities and railroads falls or remains constant, with the exception of the eastern railways in the United States. A few short-run cost studies of public utilities suggest that SAC also decreases down to capacity and that SMC is constant over the observed range. These findings, however, do not refute the shapes of the traditional cost curves: public utilities have always been considered an exception to the usual assumption of U-shaped cost curves.

More serious challenge to the credibility of the traditional U-shaped cost curve comes from the studies that found constant marginal cost in manufacturing industries. However, even here empirical findings are not unanimous. While quite a few studies found constant SMC and SAC curves that fail to rise, other studies found increasing SMC. Furthermore, A. A. Walters suspects that some researchers found constant SMC because nearly all of their statistical observations were for output levels far below the plant capacity. If so, the statistical findings will be valid only for below-capacity outputs. Clearly, the evidence accumulated in favor of the constant

[5]*Ibid.*, pp. 39–52.

SMC is not strong enough to discredit the hypothesis of U-shaped cost curves.

Studies of long-run costs in manufacturing were mostly questionnaire and engineering studies. These studies found L-shaped or generally declining LAC curves. However, economists place little weight on questionnaire studies because of their questionable methodology. The findings based on engineering studies are also defective because they concentrate only on production costs and ignore other costs such as administrative expenses. Dean and James, who studied LAC of shoe stores using cross-section data, found a U-shaped LAC curve but argued that it was mostly due to the inferior factors for which the firm paid the same prices. Obviously, the empirical evidence available is too meager to give any clear indication of the shape of LAC in manufacturing businesses.

In summary, the empirical findings indicate that public utilities and railways clearly experience increasing returns to size, that is, decreasing LAC. However, we know little about the shapes of LAC curves in manufacturing business. So far, we have had very few opportunities for collecting empirical data to refute directly the hypothesis of U-shaped cost curves. Thus, we do not have enough empirical findings with which to contradict the hypothesis of U-shaped cost curves.

The reader who is interested in documentations of the arguments paraphrased in this section and in more details of empirical cost studies should consult Walters' article cited in footnote 4.

APPENDIX 10

Some More Plausible
Short-Run Cost Curves

The conventional short-run cost curves examined in section 10-3 depend on a particular set of assumptions. Let us, therefore, conjecture some more possible shapes of cost curves that rest on different assumptions. For simplicity we will continue to assume that input prices do not change in all of the following models.

COST CURVES WHEN A MINIMUM
OUTLAY IS REQUIRED

Consider a production process in which a given size plant must be built to start production. Labor and (other variable inputs) needed can be purchased as needed in small units. The initial plant provided is large enough that it does not become a constraint in the relevant range of production. The nature of the production process involved is such that a certain minimum output must be produced if any is to be produced. The cost curves that represent these assumptions are shown in Figure 10-10.

Note that all cost curves are drawn only for a given range of output, in which the minimum output requirement is met and the plant capacity imposes no constraint. The TC curve is a straight line and the AVC and MC curves are given by an identical horizontal line. The AC curve will keep declining with output and approach the AVC = MC curve asymptotically. The economic significance of this model is to show that a certain minimum output must be produced before production can be undertaken and that in a wide range of output, production can proceed at a relatively constant AC.

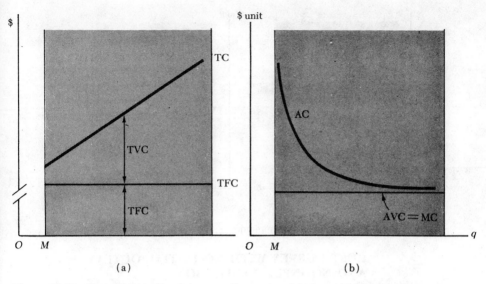

Figure 10-10   Cost curves with minimum outlay and no input constraint

COST CURVES WITH MINIMUM OUTLAY
AND AN INPUT CONSTRAINT

Let us now add to the assumptions of the above model the possibility of the plant capacity's becoming insufficient as output keeps increasing. Thus, in this model, the initial plant capacity is sufficient for a wide range of output; but after a certain point, the shortage of plant capacity becomes a bottleneck that increases the cost of production rapidly. The cost curves that reflect these assumptions are shown in Figure 10-11. The last segment of the TC curve increases at an increasing rate, reflecting the difficulty in production caused by the shortage of plant capacity. The AC curve is almost U-shaped. The downward segment is due to the existence of a fixed initial outlay; the nearly flat segment reflects the constancy of the AVC = MC curves coupled with the thinly spread initial outlay; the rising segment reflects the increasing MC and AVC due to the diminishing returns caused by the limitation of the plant space.

The cost curves are shown only for a certain range of output. The assumption involved is that a certain minimum output must be produced in order to carry out production efficiently and that there is a maximum ceiling on output due to the limited plant capacity.

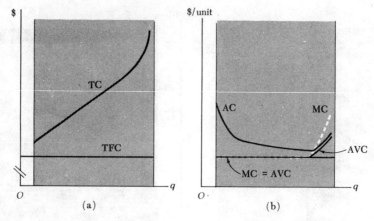

Figure 10-11 Cost curves with minimum outlay and an input constraint

COST CURVES WITH NO INITIAL OUTLAY AND NO INPUT LIMITATION

Consider a production process in which there is no initial outlay requirement and no input limitation. For instance, assume that the man-hours of fishermen's service and the machine-hours of fishing boats can be purchased as needed and that fishes are so plentiful that catches do not decline as fishing continues. Given these assumptions, the TC curve will be a straight line from the origin and the MC, AVC, and AC curves will be an identical horizontal line, as shown in Figure 10-12. The alert reader may have realized that this model does not really belong in this appendix, which discusses short-run cost curves. Since there is no input constraint, the model is really a long-run model. It is shown here only for the sake of comparison.

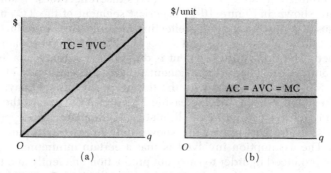

Figure 10-12 Cost curves with no initial outlay and no input constraint

EXERCISES 10

Short-Run and Long-Run Costs

10-1 Explain the difference between short-run and long-run cost curves.

10-2 In Chapter Seven, we examined the returns to variable proportions and returns to scale properties of production. With which property of production are short-run cost curves associated? Why?

10-3 Assuming that the input price remains the same, for the single input case, prove that MP and MC are inversely related.

10-4 Give precise definitions of LTC, LAC, and LMC.

10-5 Distinguish *economies* of size (or economies of scale in many conventional usages) from increasing *returns* to scale.

10-6 "The term *optimal scale* given to the short-run average cost curve having the lowest average cost of all plant sizes is misleading, since it has nothing to do with the profit-maximizing plant size. It will be less confusing if the so-called optimal scale is referred to as the least-cost size." Do you agree with this statement? Why or why not?

CHAPTER ELEVEN

THE FIRM
AND ALTERNATIVE
MARKET STRUCTURES

We are now ready to bring together some of the results obtained in previous chapters to study pricing and output decisions under various market structures. Chapter Three through Five explored how the utility-maximizing consumers determined their purchases of different goods and services. Demand curves of individual consumers furnish the basis from which both the firm's revenue functions and the market demand curve are derived. The theory of production and costs developed in Chapters Seven through Ten forms the basis for the cost and supply side of business operation. The purpose of Chapters Twelve through Sixteen is to bring together the demand and supply sides of business operations and to examine how pricing and output decisions of the firm are made under different market conditions.

The nature of optimal pricing and output decisions depends on the goal of the firm as well as on the economic environment or market structure in which the firm finds itself. Thus, we shall devote this chapter to examining the goal of the firm, the manner in which different market forms are classified, and the nature of revenue curves in different kinds of markets. Let us start with the discussion of the firm and its objective.

11-1 THE FIRM AND THE PROFIT-MAXIMIZATION HYPOTHESIS

The (business) firm is an entity that purchases various productive factors and transforms them into outputs that are sold.

The firm is the principal agent in the economic organization of market-centered economies like that of the United States. The firm must decide what business to enter, what plants and equipment to secure, how many units to produce, and at what price to sell. To say that the firm decides is a shorthand way of saying that the person(s) who control the firm decides.

In studying the pricing and output decisions of the business firm, economists usually rely on the *assumption of profit maximization.* That is, we assume that all benefits derived from the productive activities are reflected in total revenue received and that all costs incurred are reflected in total cost. *The difference between the total revenue and total cost is economic profit,* which, it is assumed, the firm attempts to maximize subject to the constraints imposed by consumer demand and production costs discussed in earlier chapters.

REALISM OF THE PROFIT-MAXIMIZATION HYPOTHESIS

Is the profit-maximization hypothesis *realistic?* Of course, not. When an individual owns a firm without managing it himself or when he owns and manages a firm himself, his primary motive must be to make money. But this is far from saying that his goal is to maximize profit. Instead of trying to maximize his profit, he may prefer to spend more time with his family, to spend longer hours at golf courses, to take longer vacations, to have a more attractive store, to have more congenial relations with his employees and customers, and so on. In analyzing the behaviors of the managers of large corporations, in which management and ownership are separated, the hypothesis of profit maximization seems even less realistic. Since corporate earnings do not directly accrue to the managers, they may lack strong motivations to maximize the firm's profit. Managers of large corporations may rather seek such other goals as growth in sales, expansion of the market share, attainment of technical sophistication, enhancing the security of their positions, attainment of more executive emoluments, acceptance of certain social responsibilities, and pursuit of a "satisfying" rather than the maximum profit. Corporations differ in resources possessed; technological sophistication; size; degree of competition, risk, and uncertainties faced; personalities of managers; and so on. Thus, different corporations may be guided by different sets of goals.

USEFULNESS OF THE PROFIT-MAXIMIZATION HYPOTHESIS

Is the assumption of profit maximization *useful* in microeconomic analysis? Definitely, yes. The profit-maximization hypothesis allows us to predict quite well the behaviors of business firms in the real world. It does not matter that few firms are maximizers in reality. What matters is that the behavioral assumption that treats firms as if they are maximizers allows us to predict their behaviors without too much difficulty and with reasonable accuracy. Very few people will dispute that the profit-maximization hypothesis is not only simple but also quite useful in predicting the price and output behaviors of business firms in response to changes in tax rates, wage rates, availabilities of resources, and so on. For example, the assumption of profit-maximizing firms allows us to predict the manner in which large oil companies will respond if their prices are controlled or if they are made subject to an excess profits tax.

FURTHER ARGUMENTS FOR THE PROFIT-MAXIMIZATION HYPOTHESIS

The economist relies on the profit-maximization hypothesis because it is useful in explaining and predicting business behavior. However, economic literature does contain some additional arguments in support of the hypothesis.

Profit motive is the *most pervasive force that governs the behavior of business firms.* In the case of small firms facing strong competition from others, they are forced to act as profit maximizers; they must do everything possible to increase sales and reduce costs in order to survive in their competitive environment. Large corporations seldom choose a course of action knowingly if it tends to reduce profit. Even large corporations must attain a certain minimum level of profit before they can entertain other goals. Witness the wide swings from prosperity to recession of the amounts of money corporations spend for socially oriented tasks. In prosperous times, corporations incur well-publicized expenditures for various charities, foundations, universities, cultural organizations, conservation efforts, environmental care, etc. But come recessions, you hear little about such concern for social responsibilities and more about their efforts to restore profitabilities.

The profit-maximization hypothesis is *simple*, and there are well-developed mathematical tools of analyzing maximization or minimization problems.

There does not exist an alternative hypothesis that can explain and predict business behavior better than the profit-maximization hypothesis. Profit maximization is the *single* best assumption available, and introduction of more "realistic" assumptions complicates the analysis considerably without adding much to the predictive power of the model.

In summary, we shall employ the assumption of profit maximization in most of the following chapters. We do so because profit maximization is the single best assumption available. It is simple, plausible, and yet provides a great deal of analytical insight into the firm's behavior. The relevance of the assumption of profit maximization in studying large corporations depends on the extent to which the actual forces that motivate the managers of large corporations diverge from the simple assumption of profit maximization.

11-2 PRICING OBJECTIVES IN LARGE CORPORATIONS: A DIGRESSION

Lest the reader be left with the erroneous notion that the economist refuses to recognize business goals other than profit maximization, let us digress for a while and examine pricing objectives mentioned by managers of large corporations.

Managers of large corporations are able to adjust their pricing policies to suit their goals. Pricing objectives of (the managers of) large corporations are difficult to ascertain, because objectives, unlike behavior, cannot be observed. Yet, objectives other than profit maximization are frequently said to be important in large corporations. Let us, therefore, examine the pricing objectives of large corporations, as *perceived* by their managers. Lanzillotti conducted lengthy interviews with officials of 20 large corporations hoping to ascertain the principal and collateral objectives that guide their pricing decisions.[1] His study showed that the most typical pricing objectives cited by corporate officials were:

1. To achieve a target rate of return on investment
2. To stabilize price and margin
3. To realize a target market share
4. To meet or prevent price competition

Target return pricing refers to formulating a price structure for various products in such a way as to yield a predetermined average corporate return in the long run. Prices of various products are determined by using the *cost-plus* or *standard-costing* approach. Costs (or standard costs) are calculated on the basis of normal production mix and standard volume — typically between 70 and 80 percent of capacity. Prices are established by adding, to such standard costs, margins, that are designed to produce the target profit rate on investment — typically stockholders' net worth and long-term debt. The target profit rate is perceived as a long-run goal, and the pricing procedure is designed to prevent cyclical or shorter-run changes in volume or product-mix from unduly influencing price.

In Lanzillotti's study, about one-half of the companies interviewed indicated that their pricing goals were to realize some

---

[1]This section, unless otherwise mentioned, is based on Robert F. Lanzillotti's "Pricing Objectives in Large Companies," *American Economic Review*, December 1958, pp. 921–940.

given returns. The average of the targets mentioned was 14 percent (after taxes); only one was below 10 percent; and the highest was 20 percent. Table 11-1 shows the target and actual rates of return for selected companies from Lanzillotti's study.

The difference between the target rates and actual rates, according to Lanzillotti, is due to three factors: (1) rising price levels, (2) generally prosperous nature of the time period covered, and (3) tendency to mention the minimum target figures as the target rates.

Stabilization of price was cited as an important secondary (or sometimes even primary) objective by companies like U.S. Steel, Alcoa, International Harvester, Johns-Manville, Du Pont, Union Carbide, and Kennecott. Firms feel that such prices maintained stable for a long period of time provide them with proper rewards, and that their customers prefer stable prices. They often feel that prices established by the cost-plus approach are "proper" prices.

The distinction between the goals of target rate of return on investment and stable prices based on the cost-plus approach is rather difficult to define. Cost-plus pricing seems definitely a step toward using a target rate of return as a guide in pricing policy.

Securing a target market share was, according to the Lanzillotti study, almost as important as securing a target rate of return in corporate managers' pricing decisions. Many corporations — which are giants in their fields — were careful to limit themselves; "they apparently did not wish to gobble up any market they entered, unless it was one which they had created, like nylon, asbestos pipe, aluminum screen wire, cable products, or some synthetic chemical."[2]

Table 11-1   Rates of Return on Investment for Selected
Large Corporations

COMPANY	TARGET RETURN ON INVESTMENT (AFTER TAXES)	ACTUAL RETURN ON INVESTMENT (AFTER TAXES, 1947–55)	
		Average	*Range*
Alcoa	10%	13.8%	7.8–18.7%
General Electric	20	21.4	18.4–26.6
General Motors	20	26.0	19.9–37.0
International Harvester	10	8.9	4.9–11.9
Sears Roebuck	10–15	5.4	1.6–10.7
U.S. Steel	8	10.3	7.6–14.8

Source: R. F. Lanzillotti, "Pricing Objectives in Large Companies," *American Economic Review*, December 1958, pp. 924–927.

[2]*Ibid*, p. 933.

A firm's use of target market share as a guide in pricing policy tended to vary from product to product. For products in which they enjoy a patent or innovative monopoly, they may set no limit to its market share. For products in which they face significant competition, they may strive for a certain maximum or minimum share of the market.

In connection with the objective of realizing a target market share, the reader may note W. J. Baumol's sales-maximization hypothesis. Essentially, he suggests that maximization of sales revenue subject to profit constraint may be a more likely goal of business than the traditional profit maximization.[3]

Matching competition may sometimes characterize the pricing policy of a firm. For instance, Lanzillotti writes: "In chemicals, Du Pont seems to apply a rule of thumb of adopting the going price in the markets for many standardized products where it never had or else had lost the leadership; for example, carbon tetrachloride, hydrogen peroxide, disodium phosphate, nitric acid, hydrochloric acid, and various rubber chemicals."[4] Market share psychology may significantly influence the policy of meeting competition. For instance, Esso Standard and Standard of Indiana modified their cost-plus prices in order to meet or forestall competition. There are cases in which companies are not simply meeting but preventing competition. For example, A & P, General Foods, and Standard of Indiana tended to localize price cuts to make it more difficult for new competition on its opening day or to discourage potential price cutters.

In the above paragraphs, we have examined what managers of large corporations considered to be their pricing objectives. Various objectives cited do suggest the importance of not ignoring variations among firms or industries in studying the behavior of large corporations. However, the assumption of profit maximization is not as unrealistic as the above list of goals might suggest. All those goals referred to may be summarized as a concern for profit in the present as well as in the future (or somewhat more technically for the discounted present value of the firm's return streams). But this is precisely what profit maximization is about.

11-3 MARKET STRUCTURES: ECONOMIC ENVIRONMENT IN WHICH THE FIRM OPERATES

The firm's price and output decisions are made in a given market. What, however, is a market? Economists use the term *market* in several different ways. Frequently, it is defined as a physical area

---

[3]For more detail, see section 15-7.
[4]Lanzillotti, *op. cit.*, p. 935.

within which the price of the commodity tends to be uniform. Alternatively, *a market can be viewed as the context within which voluntary exchanges among buyers and sellers take place.*[5]

There is no universal agreement among economists as to what is the best way to classify various market forms. Probably, the most widely used method is to classify alternative market structures on the basis of the *number* of sellers (and buyers) and the *homogeneity* or degree of differentiation of the product. Table 11-2 shows the taxonomy of market forms based on the number of firms and the nature of the product. The column headings show whether product is homogeneous or differentiated. *Products are said to be homogeneous if they are identical or indistinguishable. Products are said to be differentiated if buyers can distinguish them and attach different preferences.* The row headings show the number of sellers in the market.

A market is said to be perfectly competitive or simply competitive when there are numerous sellers (and buyers) and the product is homogeneous. When there is only one seller in the market, we have a monopoly. The taxonomy of market forms treats monopoly as having a homogeneous product, because there is no other firm in the market that can supply similar goods. However, it is more important to realize that a monopolist sells a product for which there is no close substitute. Otherwise, the market context in which buyers and sellers interact will contain several sellers of differentiated products; a clear violation of the definition of monopoly! *When a few large firms supply the bulk of the market output, the market is said to be an oligopoly.* Depending on whether the products are homogeneous or differentiated, we have a pure or differentiated oligopoly. *Monopolistic competition is the market in which many (relatively small) sellers deal in slightly differentiated products.*

There are many variants of the above models. *If there is only one buyer (instead of one seller), we have a monopsony. The market in which only two sellers (rather than a few sellers) exist is called a duopoly.* The market in which there are only a few buyers is

Table 11-2 Market Classifications

NUMBER OF FIRMS	NATURE OF PRODUCT	
	Homogeneous	*Differentiated*
Many	Perfect competition	Monopolistic competition
Few	Pure oligopoly	Differentiated oligopoly
One	Monopoly	(Not applicable)

[5]Kelvin Lancaster, *Introduction to Microeconomics*, 2d ed. (Chicago: Rand McNally, 1974), p. 45.

THE FIRM AND ALTERNATIVE MARKET STRUCTURES

named oligopsony. The market in which a single seller faces a single buyer is referred to as a bilateral monopoly.

The size of a market and the nature of the production function (and the shape of the long-run average cost curve) have important bearing on the number of firms that will emerge in the market. If the total output demanded in the market can be produced by a single firm operating in the decreasing segment of its LAC curve, a *natural monopoly* (such as an electric utility) develops. If there is a substantial size or scale economy, and only a few firms can supply all output demanded in the market, an oligopolistic market develops. If there is little size economy, and it takes many firms to supply the market output, monopolistic or perfect competition develops.

In this section we have simply identified different market structures. A more complete discussion of each market model is offered in the following sections.

11-4 PERFECT COMPETITION

The market in which there are many buyers and sellers and the product is homogeneous is called perfect competition. The real world approximations to this theoretical model of competition are found in the markets for various agricultural products. A (perfectly) competitive market possesses the following characteristics.

Large number of sellers and buyers. There are numerous sellers and buyers in the market, each of whom is small relative to the market. Since no seller or buyer is large enough to affect the market price, they *take the market price as a given parameter beyond their control*, and try to sell and buy as much as they wish at that price. In this sense, the economic agents in perfectly competitive markets are the *price-takers* and quantity-adjusters. No buyer or seller worries about the influence of his action on others, nor does he worry about the influence of any other's action on him: each buyer or seller, taken by himself, is too small a part of the market to have any appreciable influence on others. Since there is no rivalry among buyers and sellers, competition in this market is said to be *impersonal.*

Homogeneous product. Perfect competitors deal with a homogeneous product. That is, the commodity traded is an identical good with no features to differentiate it from goods supplied by other firms in the market. Thus, buyers are unconcerned about the source of the good; no single seller's product is preferred to that of any other seller. Furthermore, sellers do not care to whom they sell; they have no preference among the many buyers that exist in the market.

Absence of collusion or artificial restraint. All economic agents in perfect competition act independently, and there is no collusion among sellers or buyers. Furthermore, no government restraints are placed on price, output, entry, and similar factors.

Perfect mobility of resources. All resources must possess perfect mobility. This means that workers can move from one job to another and from one region to another. It means that firms may expand or contract their plants, or enter or leave a market as they choose. It implies that no one monopolizes resources and that the owners of natural and man-made resources are free to channel them into uses that yield higher returns.

Perfect knowledge. All buyers and sellers in the market possess perfect knowledge. Both buyers and sellers know the nature of the product and the prevailing market price. Thus, no buyer will offer a price higher than the prevailing one; and no seller will sell at a price lower than the prevailing price. Accordingly, a single price for the product (or resource) must prevail in the market.

Sometimes, the concept of *pure competition* is distinguished from that of perfect competition. The difference is a matter of degree. The model of pure competition relaxes the last two requirements and assumes less than perfect mobility and knowledge. The first three requirements are common to both models. In this book, we shall use the terms, *perfect competition, pure competition,* and *competition* interchangeably.

The reader is warned not to be trapped by the day-to-day connotation of the word *perfect.* Perfect competition is simply a kind of market in which many sellers and buyers deal in a homogeneous product. It is not implied, for instance, that there is a greater amount of competition in this market than in others.

11-5 PURE MONOPOLY

Pure monopoly, or simply, monopoly (from Greek *mono* for one and *polein* for sell) is a market structure in which there is a single seller of a good with no close substitute. Good examples are public utilities such as electric, water, and telephone companies.

Since the monopolist is the only seller in the market, the demand curve facing him is the market demand curve itself. Being the sole supplier of a good without close substitutes, the monopolist has substantial control over the price he charges. He may lower the price and increase the quantity sold, or he may limit his output to raise the price. Thus, a monopolist is a *price-maker* or *price-searcher* who is in search of the price-quantity combination that will maximize his profit. However, even a monopolist cannot set both his price and his quantity; given a single-valued demand function, selecting a price necessarily implies choosing the accompanying quantity.

Since the monopolist is, by definition, a single seller with no close substitutes, the cross elasticities of demand between the monopolist's product and the other related goods are rather low.

The monopolist, therefore, believes that his action will have little effect on others, and vice versa.

The monopolist has no other seller in the market that directly competes with him. However, he does face some important indirect and/or potential competition. For instance, the monopolist has to *compete for consumer dollars.* Purchasing power can be expended on a multitude of commodities, and the monopolist must fight for his share. Promotional advertising such as "Discover the comfort of total electric living" and "Live dependably with gas" represents the monopolist's effort to obtain a greater share of the consumer dollars. Publicly regulated monopolists such as telephone and electric companies must consider the effects of their policy decisions on *public opinion.* The substantial effort expended on public relations advertising is a good testimony for such a concern. A firm that is a monopolist in one market context *may not be a monopolist in another context.* For instance, even if a firm has a monopoly on copper, it may face substantial competition from aluminum and other metals. A grocer who is a monopolist in a rural town may still have to consider the competition from large supermarkets in nearby cities. The monopolist cannot ignore the *threat of potential new entry* into the market. The attempt to maximize profit may invite a potential competitor into the market and jeopardize his monopoly position.

11-6 OLIGOPOLY

The market that is dominated by a few sellers who clearly recognize their mutual interdependence is called oligopoly (from Greek *oligi* for few and *polein* for sell). *If the firm in oligopoly produces a homogeneous product* (such as steel, cement, lumber, and plate glass), *the market structure is called a pure (or homogeneous) oligopoly.* When the product is differentiated (as in automobiles and cigarettes), *the industry is referred to as a differentiated oligopoly.*

What distinguishes oligopoly from other market structures is the behavioral characteristics of the firms; they clearly *recognize their mutual interdependence.* Each firm recognizes that a major policy change on its part tends to provoke reactions from its competitors. Thus, an oligopolist who contemplates changing his price, product, and/or sales policies must take into account his competitors' reactions, which may have significant effects on himself. For instance, an automobile producer planning to introduce a subcompact car or a detergent manufacturer about to invoke a major advertising campaign must carefully consider the possible counterstrategies of his competitors and their effects on his position in the market.

Few people will dispute the fact that large corporations dominate the American economic scene and that many markets are oligopolistic. Automobiles, steel, aluminum, cigarettes, and electrical equipment are prime examples of oligopolies in which large corporations play dominant roles. However, oligopolists need not be corporate giants. Two or three druggists who are located in a small town or gas stations that occupy opposite corners of an intersection are also oligopolists. What is important is not the size, but the recognition of their interdependence among the firms. It may also be noted that the total number of firms in the market need not be small. For instance, there were 599 firms in the industrial category, "Soap and detergents" in 1967.[6] But the four largest firms in this category produced 70 percent of the total value of shipments. Thus, this market is a perfectly good example of oligopoly—a market in which a few firms recognizing their mutual interdependence dominate the scene.

The variety of interdependence that can exist among oligopolists and the difficulty of guessing competitors' strategies or counterstrategies create a great deal of *uncertainty* in oligopoly. For instance, the shape and position of an oligopolist's demand curve depend not only on his own product and promotion policy but also on his competitors' price, product, and advertising strategies.

Competition in a purely competitive market is impersonal: each firm seeks to maximize its own profit without paying any attention to its competitors. Competition in oligopoly, however, is characterized by personal *rivalries* among firms that recognize their mutual interdependence. A multitude of strategies and counterstrategies among oligopolists are possible. They may engage in cutthroat competiton, or take "live and let live" attitudes, or reach a partial agreement, or collude to attain a common goal. When products are differentiated, nonprice competition in the form of product differentiation and sales promotion also become important policy variables.

11-7 MONOPOLISTIC COMPETITION

The market in which a large number of firms sell slightly differentiated products is called monopolistic competition. Approximations of monopolistic competition may be found in the markets for clothing, cosmetics, service stations, beauty salons, and so on, in large cities.

Because each monopolistic competitor's product is slightly differentiated from those of others, each has a slight control over its price, unlike the perfect competitor, who has no control whatsoever over its price. That is, each monopolistic competitor can influence its sales volume by charging different prices. Because their products are slightly differentiated, monopolistic competitors can

[6]See Table 15-1 on p. 325.

also adjust the degree of product differentiation and the amount of sales promotion in their search for maximum profits.

Since there are a large number of firms, the behavioral assumptions involved in the model of monopolistic competition are very much like those of perfect competition. Each firm recognizes itself as only one of many in the market and perceives no influence of its actions on other firms. Thus, competition is impersonal, and rivalry in the day-to-day sense of the word does not exist among the firms. The impact of one firm's action is so thinly spread over all other firms in the market that no single firm is affected perceptibly.

As in the case of perfect competition, there are no barriers to entry and there is no collusive action among monopolistically competitive firms.

11-8 REVENUE CURVES FACING A FIRM

Depending on whether a firm has any ability to influence the price at which it sells, the revenue curves facing a firm can be classified into two groups. First, we will examine the revenue curves facing a perfectly competitive firm, which has no influence whatever on the price at which it sells its product.

TOTAL, AVERAGE, AND MARGINAL REVENUE CURVES FACING A COMPETITIVE FIRM

The market price is a given datum for a perfectly competitive firm. Its total revenue, TR, therefore, is given by the price of the good—which is a constant—times the units sold, pq. The TR curve is a straight line from the origin, as shown by Figure 11-1. The increase in TR is proportional to the increase in output or sales volume; thus, the slope of the TR curve is constant.

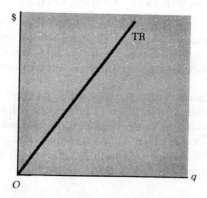

Figure 11-1 A competitive firm's TR curve

Since a competitive firm can sell any output it cares to offer for sale at the given market price, its price or average revenue, AR, per unit of output sold is constant. Any additional output can be sold at the given market price; thus, the marginal revenue, MR, is also equal to the price. Accordingly, in perfect competition,

$$MR = AR = \text{market price}$$

The AR and MR curve for a competitive firm is shown in Figure 11-2.

TR, AR, AND MR CURVES FACING AN IMPERFECTLY COMPETITIVE FIRM

The demand curve facing an imperfectly competitive firm—a firm in monopoly, oligopoly, or monopolistic competition—slopes downward to the right, indicating that the firm has some control over price. Needless to say, the demand curve facing a monopolist has a greater negative slope than that of a monopolistic competitor, whose product is only slightly differentiated from those of the others. The important thing in our current context is that the demand curve facing an imperfect competitor is negatively sloped. Since the price must be lowered to sell a larger output, the TR curve of an imperfect competitor is concave downward as shown in Figure 11-3a. The AR curve, whether it be linear or curvilinear, slopes downward to the right. Whenever the AR curve has a negative slope, the MR is less than the AR. This statement holds true whenever the output is greater than zero (or one in discrete case). If AR curve is linear as shown in Figure 11-3b, the numerical slope of the MR curve is twice as steep as that of the AR curve. TR increases as sales increase as long as MR is positive, and reaches its maximum when MR is zero. Recall from section 6-11 that the price elasticity of demand is elastic,

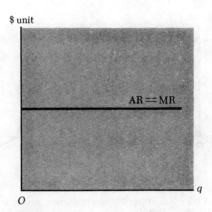

$ unit

AR $=$ MR

q

O

Figure 11-2   A competitive firm's AR and MR curves

unitary, or inelastic according as MR is positive, zero, or negative. Since a profit-maximizing firm will never operate where its MR is negative, it follows that an imperfect competitor will never willingly operate where its price elasticity of demand is inelastic. Thus, only the portions of the curves to the left of the vertical dotted line in Figure 11-3a and b are relevant to a profit-maximizing imperfect competitor.

The main purpose of this chapter has been to introduce some preliminary concepts and relationships needed to develop the theories of price and output determination in alternative market situations. Thus, we shall not attempt to apply the tools introduced in this chapter at this point. Applications will be introduced after we discuss the models of price and output determination in various market structures in the following chapters.

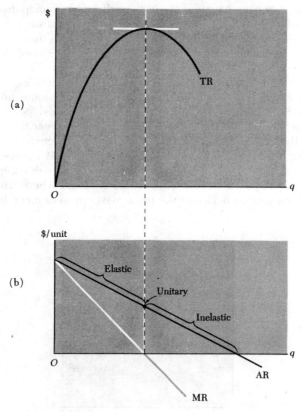

Figure 11-3 An imperfect competitor's revenue curves; (a) the TR curve, (b) the AR and MR curves

EXERCISES 11

The Firm
and Alternative Market Structure

11-1 What is perfect competition? Is there more "competition" in perfect competition than in oligopoly?

11-2 What is monopoly? What do you think is the most important cause of monopoly in the United States? (Later compare your answer with that given in Section 14-1.)

11-3 Give the best example you can of monopolistic competition, and justify your selection.

11-4 Firms may be dichotomized as price-takers and price-searchers. Classify the firms in perfect competition, monopoly, oligopoly, and monopolistic competition either as price-takers or as price-searchers, and justify your classification.

11-5 Suppose the AR function of a firm is given by $p = 200 - 2q$. Find the MR and TR functions of this firm. Will the graph of the TR function be linear or curvilinear? Why?

11-6 Explain why a monopolist will never willingly operate in the output range in which the demand for its product is inelastic.

CHAPTER TWELVE

PRICE AND OUTPUT UNDER PERFECT COMPETITION

We are now ready to study the determination of price and output under various market situations. In this and the next chapter, we shall examine the perfectly competitive case. The main tasks facing us in this chapter are to introduce the concept of the market period, study the nature of pricing decisions in the market period, and examine pricing decisions in the short run.

Traditionally, perfect competition has been the first market model to be examined. There are several reasons for this. First, the perfectly competitive model is perhaps the simplest model, which serves as a convenient starting point. Second, the perfectly competitive model, despite its simplicity and abstractness, can provide rather useful explanations and predictions. Third, the model serves as the standard against which various imperfectly competitive models — all models that are not perfectly competitive — can be compared.

12-1 PERFECT COMPETITION: A RECAPITULATION

Let us briefly recapitulate the nature of perfect competition, or simply, competition, discussed in detail in section 11-4. Perfect competition is the market structure in which a *large number* of buyers and sellers of a *homogeneous* product act independently to maximize their satisfaction or profit. The market price of the good is determined by the interaction of the total market demand and the total market supply. Since the product is homogeneous and all buyers and sellers are well informed, a uniform price prevails in the market. This market price is taken as a given datum by an individual buyer or seller who, taken by himself, can exert *no perceptible influence on price.* What one buyer or seller does is inconsequential to another buyer or seller. In this sense, perfectly competitive markets are characterized by *impersonal competition.*

· 12-2 THE MARKET PERIOD

In discussing production and cost in sections 7-3 and 10-1, we defined the economic time periods of the short run and the long run. The short run is the time period during which the rate of output can be varied only through a change in the usage of variable factors. Thus, the short run is characterized by the existence of some fixed input(s). The long run is the time period in which all inputs are variable. There is no such thing as a fixed input or fixed cost in the long run.

Another concept of economic time period we must introduce now is *the market period or the very short run, in which output cannot vary.* Each firm has a fixed stock of the commodity on hand, and the total stock in the market — which is the aggregate of all individual firms' stocks — is also fixed. Examples of stock or supply fixed for a certain period of time are abundant; they include the number of the outstanding shares of International Business Machine (IBM), the number of hotel rooms available in a given town on a given day, the number of seats available for a concert, the number of physicians in a town, the amount of inventory of a particular good in a particular town, and so on. Agricultural crops already harvested are frequently cited examples of fixed stocks in perfectly competitive markets.

The analysis of price in the market period differs substantially depending on whether the good is perishable or not. *A good is perishable if it cannot be stored until the next market period.* The good may physically deteriorate, or it may become obsolete or out of fashion, or the cost of storing it may be excessive relative to its value.

12-3 PRICING OF PERISHABLE GOODS IN THE MARKET PERIOD

Suppose the good involved is a perishable one. Each firm possesses a certain amount of the perishable good, and knows that its action does not influence the market price. Then, the profit-maximizing strategy of each firm would be to sell its entire stock of the perishable good for whatever price it can command.

A firm's supply of the perishable good in the market period is equal to its entire stock; it is willing to sell its entire holdings for whatever price it can get. The graphic representation of an individual firm's supply of the perishable good is a vertical line, which represents the size of its stock. Because each firm's supply curve is a vertical line, the market supply curve obtained by aggregating the individual supply curves must also be a vertical line. The vertical line SS' in Figure 12-1 is the market supply curve, and shows the size of the total stock available in the market; regardless of the price, the quantity of the perishable good offered for sale in the market period is absolutely fixed.

As already explained in Chapter Two, the shape and position of the market demand curve depends on such variables as the price of the good, prices of related goods, and income and taste of consumers. The intersection of the downward-sloping demand curve, DD', with the vertical supply curve, SS', determines the equilibrium price, $\$p$, for the perishable good.

ALLOCATIVE FUNCTION OF PRICE
IN THE MARKET PERIOD

Note that the price mechanism here performs an important function of allocating available stock, OS. If price were lower than $\$p$ in Figure 12-1, the quantity demanded would be larger than the available stock and there would be a shortage: for example, AB units at the price of $\$p_1$ per unit. If price were any higher, say, $\$p_2$, there would be a surplus, GH, and some sellers would be left with unsold spoiling goods. At the equilibrium price of $\$p$ per unit, all buyers who are willing to pay the price can get the commodity, and no surplus or shortage will exist. It should be emphasized that the

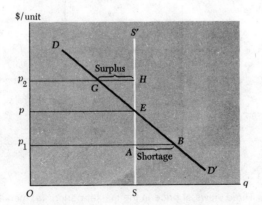

Figure 12-1   Price determination in the market
period: perishable good

words *shortage* and *surplus* have meaning only at a specified price. Thus, a good is, by definition, scarce even when a surplus exists.

THREE VIEWS OF DEMAND AND SUPPLY
FOR A PERISHABLE GOOD

The three parts of Figure 12-2 show demand and supply curves (for a perishable good in the market period) as seen from three different points of view: (1) for the entire market, (2) by an individual buyer, and (3) by an individual seller. Figure 12-2a shows that when the market supply is perfectly inelastic, as shown by the vertical line, SS', the market demand alone determines the level of price. If demand is larger, as indicated by D_2, the price will go up to p_2. A lower demand, such as D_1, will cause the price to drop to p_1. Supply, by definition of the market period, is fixed and cannot be affected by changes in demand. Thus, the price of a perishable good in the market period is independent of its cost of production.

Figure 12-2b shows the demand and supply curves for an individual buyer in the market. Assume that the equilibrium market price is $\$p$. A single buyer, being an insignificant part of the total market, can buy all he wants at the going market price, $\$p$. Thus, the supply curve for an individual buyer is a horizontal line. The intersection of this horizontal supply curve with the downward-sloping individual demand curve gives the equilibrium quantity of b units for the buyer.

Now shift your attention to Figure 12-2c, which shows the demand and supply curves for an individual seller. A single seller

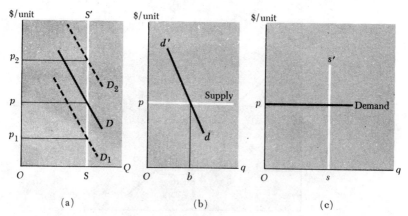

Figure 12-2 Three views of price in the market period; (a) market demand and supply, (b) individual buyer's demand and supply, (c) individual seller's demand and supply

in a perfectly competitive market can sell all he wishes at the going price. Thus, the demand curve facing the seller is a horizontal line. His supply curve is a vertical line reflecting the fixed stock available to him.

Observe that the vertical scales in the three graphs are identical. The horizontal axes of the three graphs, however, are not comparable. Obviously, a given distance in Figure 12-2a, which shows the total market, represents many times those of Figures 12-2b and c, which show a single buyer or seller. There is no reason why the horizontal scales in b or c should be the same.

12-4   PRICING OF NONPERISHABLE GOODS IN THE MARKET PERIOD

When a good is storable, it would be unwise to assume that the sellers will dump it on the market for whatever price it will command. If the price is high the seller will tend to offer a large portion of the stock for sale, and if the price is low he will tend to hold a large portion of the stock until the next period. Thus, the supply curve of a storable good in the market period is positively sloped (and is no longer equal to the vertical line indicating the available stock). This positively sloped supply curve, however, will have a vertical segment, as shown in Figure 12-3a. The vertical segment represents the total stock available in the market period. The size of the stock, therefore, serves merely as a limiting factor. Given the market demand and supply curves of a storable good in the market period shown in Figure 12-3a, the equilibrium price is $\$p$ and the quantity exchanged is Q. At $\$p$ per unit, the sellers choose to sell Q and hold QS.

RESERVATION DEMAND

In Figure 12-3b, the situation is reexamined from a slightly different and often useful angle. *The functional relationship between quantities the owners want to hold (or reserve for themselves) and prices of the good is called the reservation demand.* The quantities the owners want to reserve for themselves are simply the difference between the total stock in the market and the quantities offered for sale at various prices. Thus,

Reservation demand = stock − supply

In Figure 12-3a, the reservation demand is shown by the horizontal distances between the supply curve S_0JS' and the vertical line SS' that shows the size of the total stock. For instance, at prices equal to or greater than SJ dollars, sellers want to hold none; at $p = \$SB$, they want to hold AB units; and at $p = \$SC$, they will

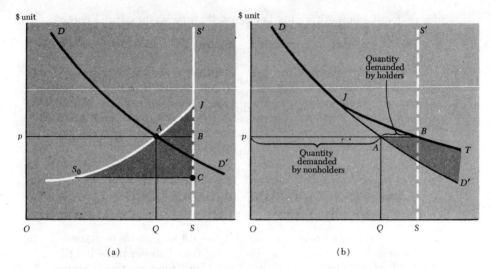

Figure 12-3 Price and quantity exchanged in the market period: storable good

hold S_0C units. By adding the reservation demand of the holders to the demand of the buyers, the total or combined market demand curve DJT in Figure 12-3b is obtained. Any point on this combined demand curve (such as point B) shows the sum of the quantity demanded by nonholders (pA units) and the quantity demanded by holders (AB units). The intersection of the curve DJT with the vertical line SS' indicating the available stock in the market period determines the equilibrium price, $\$p$, and output, Q units.

The formal results obtained from Figure 12-3b are identical to those of Figure 12-3a. However, the concept of reservation demand eloquently demonstrates the importance of the role of the owners' own demand for the commodity in the formation of the equilibrium market price. For example, consider how the price of General Motors (GM) shares is determined. Even though a large number of GM shares is outstanding, only a very small fraction of the shares is demanded by the buyers in the various stock exchanges on any given day. Given this low level of demand, why would the price of GM shares not drop more drastically? Because there is a huge reservation demand on the part of GM shareholders. The quantity demanded by the holders plus the quantity demanded by the nonholders equal the total number of outstanding shares at the price quoted for the stock in the market. The market price of the stock, therefore, is a true equilibrium price. Similar analysis explains the prices of houses in a community, used cars, rare books and coins, and storable agricultural commodities.

12-5 THE FIRM'S OUTPUT DECISION IN THE SHORT RUN

Let's now examine how the firm selects its profit-maximizing output in the short run. The interaction of the market demand and supply functions (or curves) determines the equilibrium market price and output. Given the market price, individual firms in a perfectly competitive market can sell any quantity they wish at the going market price. In the short run, as already noted, a firm can change its rate of output but is incapable of changing some factors such as its plant size. The number of firms in the market is also fixed since the time period is not long enough to allow any entry into or departure from the market. The decision problem facing a competitive profit-maximizing firm in the short run, thus, is choosing the optimal rate of output using the existing plant.[1] We shall examine the nature of the profit-maximizing output selection by using (1) the total curves approach and (2) the marginal and average curves approach.

OPTIMAL OUTPUT DECISION: TOTAL CURVES APPROACH

The market price is a given datum for a perfectly competitive firm, and its total revenue curve is a straight line. By definition, profit is the difference between the total revenue, TR, and the total cost, TC. Given the TR and TC curves of the firm, the profit-maximizing output is found where the *vertical distance* between the TR and TC curves is greatest. In Figure 12-4, the profit-maximizing output is q units per period. Moving either to the right or to the left will reduce the amount of profit earned by the firm. The firm thus has no incentive to change its output, and the equilibrium is a stable one. Note that at the equilibrium output, the marginal cost (given by the slope of the tangent line to TC) is equal to the marginal revenue (which is the slope of the TR curve). In the next section, we will show that the equality of MR and MC is a necessary prerequisite for profit-maximizing output selection. That the equality of MR and MC does not guarantee profit maximization is depicted at the output of L units per period: here MR = MC, but TC is greater than TR and the loss (not profit) is maximized. Shortly, we will discuss the conditions needed to guarantee the selection of profit-maximizing output. For the moment, however, let us move on to the graphic analysis using the marginal and average curves.

---

[1]The term *plant* is used in a generic sense to represent all fixed inputs. Equipment as well as skilled personnel (the supply of which cannot readily be increased) are included in the concept of plant, all of which are fixed in the short run.

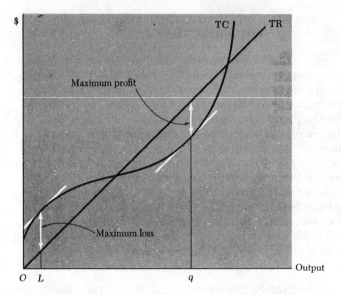

Figure 12-4 Determination of profit-maximizing output in the short run: total curves

12-6 OPTIMAL OUTPUT DECISION IN THE SHORT RUN: MARGINAL CURVES APPROACH

A firm in perfect competition can sell all it wishes without affecting the market price. Thus, the demand or average revenue, AR, curve facing an individual firm is a horizontal line at the height of the market price. For a perfect competitor, his AR or demand curve is also his marginal revenue, MR, curve. Since all output is sold at the same price, the extra revenue obtained by an extra unit of sale is equal to the market price; thus, MR = p = AR. Figure 12-5 shows the MR (which is also demand and AR) curve of a firm together with its marginal cost, MC, curve. This graph depicts the essence of the *marginal analysis* – the economist's favorite tool of optimization, in which additional gains and additional costs are weighted against each other.

THE MARGINAL ANALYSIS

Any output decision that increases the TR more than the TC must increase profit. Now MR shows the additional revenue obtained by selling one more unit of output, and MC shows the additional cost of producing one more unit of output. In order to determine whether a profit-maximizing firm should expand, retain, or reduce its current rate of production, all it needs to do is to compare

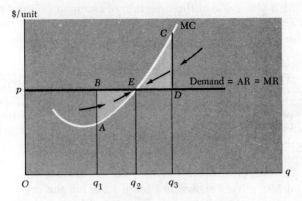

Figure 12-5 The MR = MC principle

its MR and MC curves. That is, the profit-maximizing firm should:

$$\left\{ \begin{array}{l} \text{Increase} \\ \text{Maintain} \\ \text{Reduce} \end{array} \right\} \quad \text{its output according as} \quad \left\{ \begin{array}{l} \text{MR} > \text{MC} \\ \text{MR} = \text{MC} \\ \text{MR} < \text{MC} \end{array} \right\}$$

In terms of Figure 12-5, if the current output is less than q_2 per period, MR > MC and the output must be expanded as indicates by the arrows pointing to the right. Similarly, if the current output is greater than q_2, MR < MC and the output must be reduced. Thus the profit-maximizing equilibrium output is q_2, at which MR = MC as indicated by point E.

Suppose in Figure 12-5, the output is increased from q_1 to q_2, by how much will the firm's profit change? The easiest way to answer this kind of question is to concentrate on the changes in TR and TC. By definition, the *change in profit* $\Delta\pi$ is:

$$\Delta\pi = \Delta\text{TR} - \Delta\text{TC}$$

As the output is increased from q_1 to q_2 TR increases by q_1BEq_2 dollars (price times the change in output, or the area under the MR curve between q_1 and q_2), and TC increases by q_1AEq_2 dollars (area under the MC curve between q_1 and q_2). Accordingly, the increase in profit is ABE dollars. In symbols,

$$\Delta\pi = \Delta\text{TR} - \Delta\text{TC} = q_1BEq_2 - q_1AEq_2 = ABE$$

Similarly, the increase in profit as the output is reduced from q_3 to q_2 units per period is ECD dollars. Note that the convenient way to find the "change" in profit is to concentrate on the MR and MC curves. Also observe that the direction of change in output is important. In Figure 12-5, if the output is increased from q_2 to q_3, the change in profit is negative ECD dollars (that is, profit will decrease by ECD).

SHORT-RUN OUTPUT DECISIONS

Given the average and marginal cost curves (or functions) and the price at which the good can be sold in the market, how should the competitive firm determine its profit-maximizing output in the short run? We can answer this question in two parts. First, we should ask whether the firm should produce at all or not. Second, if the firm should produce, what then is the optimal output?

Suppose the firm's cost curves are shown by the AC, AVC, and MC curves shown in Figure 12-6, but the price—which is not shown in the graph for our current problem—is lower than the minimum AVC indicated by the height of point S in Figure 12-6. Then, there is no output at which TR can be as large as total variable cost, TVC. If the firm decides to produce any output under the circumstances, it will incur a loss due to operation in addition to the fixed cost, which the firm cannot avoid in the short run. Clearly, the profit-maximizing output strategy is to *produce none* (that is, shut down) *when the price is lower than the minimum* AVC.

Now assume that price is equal to or greater than the minimum AVC, and the profit-maximizing output strategy requires the production of some output. Let us examine the output decision involved by referring to Figure 12-6. Assume that the price is $\$p$ per unit. Thus, the horizontal line labeled Demand = AR = MR shows the

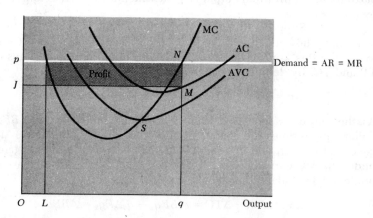

Figure 12-6 Output decision in the short run: marginal and average curves

firm's demand, average and marginal revenue curve. Let the AC, AVC, and MC curves show the firm's costs. Given these revenue and cost curves, the output that maximizes the firm's profit is q, where MR = MC. At this output level, the firm earns profit of MN dollars per unit, and the total profit received is equal to the area $JpNM$. If the output is expanded to the right of q, MC exceeds MR and the profit will be reduced. If the output is reduced from q to the left, the resulting reduction in TR is greater than the reduction in TC and total profit will be reduced. Clearly, if the firm is to produce at all, *the maximum profit is attained at q units per period, where* MR = MC.

NECESSARY CONDITIONS AND SUFFICIENT CONDITIONS

Note that MR = MC also at the output of L units per period. This output rate, however, shows the profit-minimizing or loss-maximizing output. Obviously, the equality of MR and MC— which is necessary for profit maximizing nonzero output selection —is not sufficient to guarantee it. *The requirement that the profit-maximizing firm, if it is to produce at all, must produce where its* MR = MC *is called the necessary condition for profit maximizing output selection.* It is a prerequisite for profit-maximizing output; but it cannot assure profit maximization. The MR of a perfectly competitive firm is always equal to its price. Thus, the necessary condition for profit maximization for a perfectly competitive firm that produces is frequently stated as p = MC rather than MR = MC.

The conditions that can guarantee the selection of the profit-maximizing output for a firm that produces are twofold: (1) *the equality of* MR *and* MC and (2) *the slope of the* MC *curve greater than the slope of the* MR *curve.* These conditions are called the *sufficient conditions* for profit maximizing nonzero output selection. Assuming that the firm decides to produce, producing where MR=MC and the slope of MC > the slope of MR assures profit maximization.[2]

In Figure 12-6, the sufficient conditions are satisfied at output q, which is the profit-maximizing output. At output L, MR = MC but the slope of MC (which is negative) is smaller than the slope of MR = p (which is zero): the sufficient conditions are not satisfied, and L is not the profit-maximizing output. (L is the profit-minimizing output because the sufficient conditions of profit minimization are MR = MC and the slope of MC that is smaller than that of MR.)

[2]See Appendix 12 for "necessary," "sufficient," and "necessary and sufficient" conditions.

12-7 THE SUPPLY CURVE OF A COMPETITIVE FIRM

Now let us shift our attention to Figure 12-7a and examine how the supply curve of a competitive firm is derived. This can readily be accomplished by changing the market price and observing how the firm adjusts its quantity supplied. If the price given to the firm by the market is $\$p_1$, the firm supplies q_3 units. As long as price is higher than the minimum average cost, the firm will supply the output given by MR = MC and earn some profit. What happens if the price drops to $\$p_2$ – one which is lower than the AC, but is still equal to or higher than the minimum AVC? When the price is lower than AC, the strategy of the firm is to minimize its loss. If the firm closes down, its loss is equal to the total fixed cost, $EABD$ in Figure 12-7a. This loss can be reduced, however, by operating where MR = MC and producing q_2 units. When q_2 units are produced, the firm's TR, Op_2Cq_2, exceeds its total variable cost, $OEDq_2$, by the area labeled loss reduction, Ep_2CD. This excess of revenue over variable cost gained by producing q_2 units offsets a part of the loss due to the fixed cost. The unavoidable minimum loss in Figure 12-7a is p_2ABC, and this can be attained only if the firm produces where MR = MC. Thus, we conclude that *a profit-maximizing* (or loss-minimizing) *firm produces where* MR = MC *when price is lower than* AC *but is still higher than* AVC.

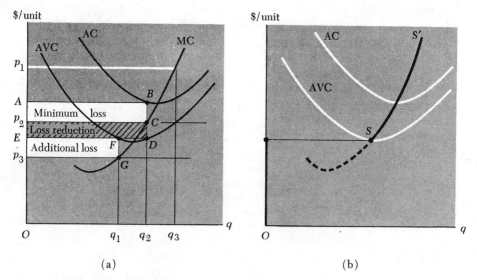

(a)   (b)

Figure 12-7 Derivation of the competitive supply curve

If the price is equal to the minimum AVC, what should the firm do? As far as the amount of loss incurred is concerned, this is a borderline case in which it does not make any difference whether the firm operates or closes down. However, we will assume that in this borderline situation, the firm continues to operate. This assumption is plausible for several reasons: (1) a higher valuation is given to a going concern than to a closed firm, (2) more prestige is attached to the owner or manager of a going concern than to that of a firm that has ceased to operate, (3) by keeping the operation going, the firm will not lose competent personnel.

If price is lower than the minimum AVC, the firm should shut down its operation. Since price cannot even cover AVC, continuing the operation will only increase the size of loss. For instance, in Figure 12-7a, if the firm follows the MR = MC rule blindly when the price is p_3, its loss will be increased by the area p_3EFG. (A firm may operate even in this situation if it expects to make substantial profit in later periods and if keeping the operation going currently is essential for the future operation of the firm.)

In summary, a competitive firm should produce the output given by MR = MC whenever the price is equal to or greater than the minimum AVC. When the price is lower than the minimum AVC, the profit-maximizing output is zero. *Thus, the portion of the MC curve on or above the AVC curve shows the supply curve of the perfectly competitive firm.* Figure 12-7b shows the supply curve of the competitive firm by solid black curves. The black heavy line segment on the price axis shows that the quantity offered for sale is zero at prices lower than the minimum AVC.

12-8 THE DECISION RULE FOR A COMPETITIVE FIRM IN THE SHORT RUN

We have seen that the competitive firm maximizes its profit in the short run by producing, if it produces at all, where MR = MC and where the slope of the MC curve is steeper than that of the MR curve. These conditions (the sufficient conditions) for profit maximization guarantee the maximum profit if the firm is to produce at all. We have also shown that no output is the best output when the price is lower than the minimum AVC. Clearly, a complete decision rule must incorporate the case in which $q > 0$ as well as that in which $q = 0$. *The necessary and sufficient conditions for the attainment of the profit-maximizing output in the short run are*:

1. Whenever $p \geqslant$ minimum AVC, produce where MR = MC and the slope of the MC curve is greater than that of the MR curve.

2. When $p <$ minimum AVC, produce zero output, that is, shut down the operation.[3]

When these conditions hold, profit maximization is guaranteed; and when profit is maximized, these conditions must hold. When two events A and B are so related that A implies B and B implies A, they are said to satisfy the "necessary and sufficient" conditions.[4]

12-9 THE INDUSTRY OR MARKET SUPPLY CURVE IN THE SHORT RUN

In discussing the price and output decisions of a firm in the short run, we have so far assumed that market demand and supply curves are given. In Chapter Six, we saw how the market demand curve is derived. Let us now examine how the market supply curve is derived from the supply curves of individual firms in the market.

An *industry is defined by many economists as a collection of firms producing a homogeneous product*.[5] Thus, firms in a perfectly competitive market taken together form an industry, and the *market or aggregate supply curve* for competitive firms is frequently referred to as the *industry supply curve*. Similarly, terms such as *market demand* and *industry demand* may be used interchangeably in perfect competition.

The *market* or *industry supply curve portrays the functional relationship between the prices of a good and various quantities offered for sale by all firms in the market*. Thus, as the first approximation, we claim that the market supply curve is obtained by *summing individual firms' supply curves*. Suppose the market contains n identical firms with the supply curve shown in Figure 12-8a. Then the total quantity offered for sale in the market at any given price, must be

---

[3]Since MR $= p$ in perfect competition, the above decision rule can be restated by substituting p for MR. For perfect competition, it is immaterial whether we talk of MR $=$ MC or $p =$ MC, or whether we talk of the slope of the MR curve or that of the price line.

[4]See Appendix 12 for more details.

[5]There is no generally accepted definition of an industry. Often an *industry* is *defined more broadly as a set of firms that produce close substitutes* (that is, goods with high positive cross elasticities of demand). A broader definition such as this becomes necessary if we are to talk about imperfectly competitive markets with differentiated products such as automobile and bicycle industries. However, the terms *close* and *high* are ill-defined, and the concept of an industry becomes elusive. In practice, the economist defines an industry to suit his own problem at hand. For instance, he may study the housing industry, the mobile home industry, or the office space leasing industry in a particular city, ignoring self-owned and occupied office spaces.

n times as large as the quantity offered by a single firm. The market supply curve is shown in Figure 12-8b with the market output axis compressed. The market output, Q, when the price is p dollars is, by construction, n times the single firm's output, q.

The statement that the competitive market supply curve is the horizontal summation of individual firms' supply curves was called the first approximation. The guarded statement was necessitated because it was true only if industry-wide changes in output did not affect resource prices. Let us, therefore, introduce the case in which industry-wide expansion raises resource prices, and examine how this increase in resource prices affects the derivation of the market supply curve.

In Figure 12-9a the curve mc_1 shows the marginal cost of the representative single firm when the market output is at a given level. If this firm is the only firm that is changing output, it moves along the mc_1 curve. If the price of the product is \$$A$, then the firm produces q_1 units. Assuming there are n identical firms in the market, the quantity supplied in the market is $Q_1 = nq_1$. Now suppose the price of the product increases to \$$B$ and all the firms in the market respond by increasing their output. When the output is increased industry-wide, the firm cannot move along its mc_1 curve. The industry-wide expansion in output raises resource prices and the mc_1 curve of the firm is pushed upward to mc_2. Thus, each firm increases its output to q_2 (not to BB'' units on the original mc_1 curve), and the market output increases to Q_2 units. Similarly, the increase in the price of the product to \$$C$ induces an industry-wide expansion of output that shifts the cost curve to mc_3. Individual firms, thus, produce q_3 units

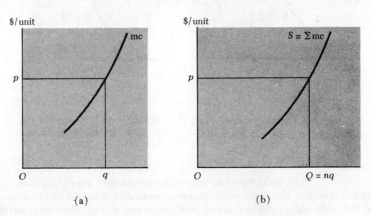

(a) (b)

Figure 12-8 Industry supply curve as the horizontal summation of individual firms' supply curves; (a) a firm's supply curve, (b) the industry supply curve

and the market output is n times this output, $Q_3 = nq_3$. Connecting points A', B', and C', we obtain the curve ss'. This curve, then, is the short-run supply curve of the firm when industry-wide changes in output increase resource prices. The curves mc_1, mc_2, and mc_3, on the other hand, are the short-run supply curves of the firm when only a single firm is changing its output. *When industry-wide changes in output affect resource prices, the industry or market supply curve is obtained as the horizontal summation of the individual firms' ss' curves*—the curves that reflect the industry-wide changes in output and the corresponding changes in resource prices.

In summary, when there are changes in resource prices associated with industry-wide changes in output, the short-run market supply curve is *not* the sum of the marginal cost curves of individual firms drawn from the assumption of constant factor prices and production functions.[6] Rather, the industry supply curve is obtained by the horizontal summation of the ss' curves that take into consideration the changing factor prices (and/or production functions).

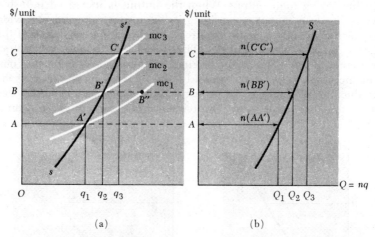

Figure 12-9 Industry supply curve when industry-wide changes in output affect resource prices; (a) a firm's supply curve, (b) the industry supply curve

[6]An industry-wide change in output may alter the production coefficients. For instance, many pumps operated simultaneously in a given oil field may reduce the amount of oil flow per pump. The effect is to shift the cost curves upward, and can be analyzed in the same manner as the cost increase caused by increasing factor prices.

APPENDIX 12

Necessary Conditions, Sufficient Conditions, and Necessary and Sufficient Conditions

DEFINITIONS

Necessary, sufficient, and *necessary and sufficient* conditions are mathematical terms that are distinguished as follows.

If A is a necessary condition of B, A is implied by B $(A \Leftarrow B)$. That is, if B holds, then A must be true. For example, womanhood (A) is a necessary condition of motherhood (B). Thus, motherhood implies womanhood, and being a woman is a prerequisite of being a mother.

If A is a sufficient condition of B, A implies B $(A \Rightarrow B)$. That is, whenever condition A is satisfied, B holds. However, B may also hold true in the absence of A. For example, the Fourth of July is a sufficient condition for a holiday in the U.S. But a holiday does not have to be the Fourth of July, and other occasions give holidays to the American people.

A necessary and sufficient condition is one in which the relationship between A and B holds in both ways mentioned above. That is, A implies B and B implies A $(A \Leftrightarrow B)$. For example, let A and B be the first day of the week and Sunday. Then, $A \Rightarrow B$ and $B \Rightarrow A$. The necessary and sufficient condition is complete; the first day of the week includes all Sundays and nothing else. As another example, consider the correspondence between numerical and letter grades. Suppose the grade of A is assigned to numerical grades of 90 or more. Then, A implies numerical scores of 90 percent or more, and 90 percent or more numerical scores implies A. Note again, that A includes all numerical scores that are 90 or more and no other score.

THE COMPETITIVE FIRM'S
PROFIT-MAXIMIZING
OUTPUT DETERMINATION

As an economic application of necessary conditions and sufficient conditions, let us consider the profit-maximizing output decision of a competitive firm. The profit function of a competitive firm is given by

$$\pi(q) = pq - C(q)$$

where p, q, and $C(q)$ stand for price, output, and total cost.

The *necessary condition* (assuming that $q \neq 0$) for profit maximization is obtained by setting the first derivative of the profit function equal to zero.

$$\frac{d\pi}{dq} = p - C'(q) = 0$$

and

$$p = C'(q)$$

Thus, the necessary condition is $p = \mathrm{MR} = \mathrm{MC}$. This condition is frequently referred to as the *first-order condition*.

To satisfy the sufficient condition for profit maximization, in addition to $\mathrm{MR} = \mathrm{MC}$, the second derivative of the profit function must also be negative. (This latter requirement is frequently referred to as the *second-order condition*.)

$$\frac{d^2\pi}{dq^2} = \frac{dp}{dq} - C''(q) < 0$$

and

$$\frac{dp}{dq} < C''(Q)$$

The sufficient conditions, therefore, require that (1) $\mathrm{MR} = \mathrm{MC}$ and (2) the slope of the price ($\mathrm{AR} = \mathrm{MR}$) line be less than the slope of the MC curve. It is assumed that $q \neq 0$.

For the necessary and sufficient conditions, see section 12-8.

EXERCISES 12

Price and Output under Perfect Competition

12-1 Suppose that (a) the stock of a good available is 300 units, (b) the supply curve of the good in the relevant range is given by $p = 20 + 1/5q$, and (c) the demand curve for the good is given by $p = 100 - .2q$.

1. Derive the equation that shows the reservation demand for the above good.
2. Obtain the combined demand curve of the buyers and sellers.
3. Determine the equilibrium price.

12-2 From the information given by the curves shown in the following figure, determine what is the maximum profit that

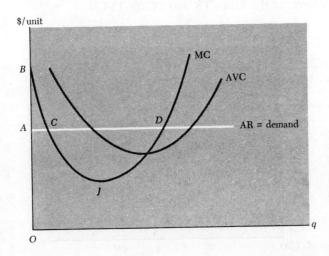

can be earned. Assume that there is no fixed cost. (You are not allowed to draw in any additional lines.)

12-3 Assume a perfectly competitive industry in which there are 100 firms each having an identical scale plant. The demand and supply curves for the industry are given by:

Demand: $Q = 20,000 - 10\ p$

Supply: $Q = \frac{1}{9}(10\ p - 3,000)$

1. Determine the equilibrium price and output for the industry.
2. Obtain the marginal cost curve of an individual firm. (Hint: Remember that the industry supply curve is obtained by summing the marginal cost curves of 100 firms.)
3. Determine the profit-maximizing output for an individual firm.

12-4 Assume that you are a teaching assistant who has just discussed the price and output decision of a competitive firm using the following diagram. One of the students in the class objects to your statement that q° is the optimal output, and claims that q_1 (the output at which the average cost is lowest) is the best choice as clearly shown from the visual impression of the profits received at the two output levels. He asserts that area $GBEF$ is clearly larger than the area $ABCD$. Prove to your students, the visual impression not withstanding, that area $GBEF <$ area $ABCD$.

12-5 According to the decision rule for profit maximization in the short run, the competitive firm should shut down if the market price is lower than the firm's minimum AVC. Restate this rule in terms of the firm's TR and TC (or TVC).

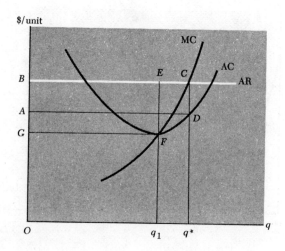

CHAPTER THIRTEEN

PRICE AND OUTPUT UNDER PERFECT COMPETITION-CONTINUED

In this chapter, we continue the study of price and output in perfect competition. The main tasks facing us are the examination of pricing decisions in the long run, the efficiency of competitive market solutions, and the effect of an industry-wide change in output on input prices. Some examples and applications conclude the chapter.

13-1 THE LONG-RUN ADJUSTMENT

The short run was, by definition, a period in which only the rate of operation could be changed. The change in market output in the short run, thus, comes from the change in the rate of operation of the existing plants. In the long run, however, two additional sources of change in output come in to make the industry supply curve considerably more elastic. The firms can adjust their plant sizes, and new firms may enter and the existing firms may leave the industry. In reality, the long-run adjustment process is characterized by simultaneous adjustments in the number of firms and the size of plants as well as the rate of operation. However, for the sake of analytical simplicity, we will (1) study the manner in which a firm adjusts its plant size and rate of operation, assuming that the market price remains constant, and then (2) analyze how the entry and exit of firms bring about the genuine long-run equilibrium for all firms in the industry.

13-2 THE LONG-RUN ADJUSTMENT DESIRED BY A SINGLE FIRM

Suppose the price established by the intersection of the market demand and supply curve is p dollars per unit in Figure 13-1,

271

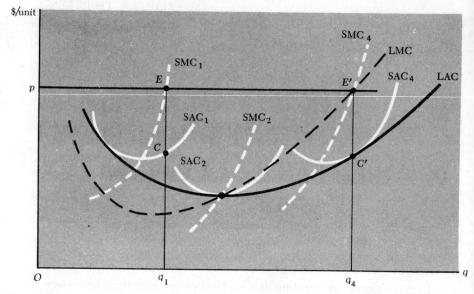

Figure 13-1 Long-run adjustment sought by a single firm

and the firm's current plant size is represented by SAC_1 (and SMC_1). Assume, for simplicity, that all firms in the industry have identical cost curves; thus, the cost curves shown in Figure 13-1 are those of the "representative" firm.

By definition, a perfectly competitive firm considers the market price as a given datum and perceives itself as having no perceptible influence on the market price. Given the market price, p, and its relevant cost curves, SAC_1 and SMC_1, the profit-maximizing combination for the firm in the short run is shown by point E, at which $SMC_1 = p$. The firm will produce q_1 units per period and will reap substantial economic profit.

The firm, however, will not be content with operating the SAC_1 plant. Given the market price, p, which the firm takes as a given datum, and the LMC and LAC curves, the profit-maximizing output in the long run is clearly q_4, where $LMC = p$. The plant size that can produce this output at the lowest average cost is SAC_4. Thus, the firm wishes to build plant SAC_4 and operate it at the rate of q_4 units per period. If these plans materialize, the firm's SMC_4 and LMC curves would intersect the price line at E'. Since $LMC = SMC_4 = price$, the firm would not be able to improve its profit position any further. The firm would be earning a substantial profit per period.

In summary, the single competitive firm, which assumes the market price would remain constant, wishes to maximize his long-run profit by building the SAC_4 plant and operating it at the rate of q_4 units per period. Note that the most profitable plant size is not necessarily the so-called optimum scale, which generally is defined as the size that gives the minimum average cost in the long run (SAC_2 in Figure 13-1).

13-3 LONG-RUN ADJUSTMENT FOR ALL FIRMS IN THE INDUSTRY

E' in Figure 13-1 shows the long-run equilibrium position for the representative firm that would be attainable were it not for the entry of other firms, which would lower the market price. The lucrative position, E', of Figure 13-1, however, is an unattainable dream. The dream is shattered by the ease with which other firms can enter the industry and lower the market price.

Let us examine the details by referring to Figure 13-2a, which shows the market demand and supply curves and Figure 13-2b, which reproduces Figure 13-1 in a simplified form. Suppose the market demand and supply curves are given by D and S_1. The equilibrium price is then p_1, and the firm maximizes its long-run profit by selecting combination E' in Figure 13-2b. The firm in this industry earns a substantial economic profit. However, the existence of such a lucrative return will attract new firms into this perfectly competitive industry—which, by definition, has no barriers to entry. Suppose such

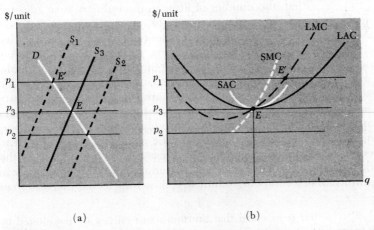

Figure 13-2 Long-run equilibrium in perfect competition; (a) the market demand and supply, (b) a single firm's position

a large number of firms were attracted into the industry that the short-run supply curve of the industry shifts to S_2, and the price of the commodity drops to p_2. With the price of p_2, there is no output at which the firm can recover its cost,[1] and the existing firms in the industry will suffer losses. Some firms thus will leave the industry, and cause the industry supply curve to shift to the left and the price to move upward.

Whenever the price exceeds the minimum LAC, there will be a tendency for new firms to enter and lower the price. On the other hand, whenever the price is lower than the minimum LAC, there will be a tendency for firms to leave the industry and make the price move up. Thus, *the industry can be in long-run equilibrium only if the price is equal to the minimum LAC*. In terms of Figure 13-2*a*, the number of firms in the industry in long-run equilibrium must be so adjusted that the industry supply curve is S_3 and the price is p_3 dollars per unit. The firm produces q^* units per period (Figure 13-2*b*), and neither earns an economic profit nor incurs an economic loss. Because there is no economic profit to be earned in the industry, there is no temptation for outsiders to enter the industry. Since every firm is recovering its alternative costs—the highest return factors can earn in all other employments—there is no inducement for the firms to leave the industry.

13-4 THE EFFICIENCY OF COMPETITIVE LONG-RUN EQUILIBRIUM

The long-run equilibrium of a perfectly competitive industry—in which price equals LAC, LMC, SAC, and SMC—possesses some important efficiency properties.

First, the number of firms in the industry is so adjusted that the price of the product is equal to the minimum average cost (LAC = SAC). By assumption, profit potentials in various competitive industries are known to resource owners, and resources move freely among alternative employment seeking the highest returns available. If the price of the product is greater than the minimum LAC, and resources can earn in this industry more than what they can earn elsewhere, more resources will flow into this industry. On the other hand, if price is lower than the minimum LAC and the resources employed in this industry fail to earn the maximum returns they can receive in alternative employments, resources will flow out of the industry. The equality of price and the minimum LAC in the long-run equilibrium of a competitive industry, therefore, means that *resources*

---

[1] It is assumed that the firm's cost curves are not altered by the entry and exit of firms. The cases in which resource prices are affected by the entry and exit of firms will be examined in section 13-6.

are efficiently employed in the perfectly competitive configuration of an economy. All resources are earning their alternative costs, the maximum they can receive in their alternative employments.

Second, the output is produced at the *lowest possible cost.* Each firm produces its output at the lowest point on its LAC curve, which shows the minimum costs of producing various output when all inputs can be freely varied. (In terms of the SAC curve, each firm operates at the lowest point on the lowest SAC curve, that is, it operates the optimal size plant at the optimal rate.) Furthermore, the buyers can secure the product at the price that is equal to this minimum LAC.

Third, under certain simplifying assumptions, the competitive long-run equilibrium *maximizes the social gain.* The price buyers are willing to pay for the product may be taken as showing the value (marginal utility) of the commodity to the society. The LMC — which shows the additional cost that must be incurred by the representative firm in producing another unit of the product — may be used as an indicator of the marginal social cost. If these assumptions are reasonable, it follows that production of the good should be increased as long as the price (the marginal social benefit) exceeds the LMC (the marginal social cost). Thus, the competitive long-run equilibrium in which the price of the product is equal to the LMC satisfies the efficiency requirement suggested by the marginal analysis, marginal social gain = marginal social cost. This conclusion must be modified if the operation of the industry creates *external economies or diseconomies, that is, if there are benefits or harms to the society that are not reflected in the price charged or the cost incurred by the firms in the industry.*[2]

It is because of such efficiency properties in the long-run equilibrium that the perfectly competitive model is frequently used as the standard against which various market models are compared. However, saying that perfect competition has certain desirable properties is not the same as asserting that all industries should be perfectly competitive. For example, if the individual firms' minimum LAC outputs are large relative to the total market demand, as in public utilities or the plate glass industry, perfect competition may be a rather inefficient arrangement.

The situation described by the competitive equilibrium in the long run should not be construed as the state of the industry to be reached at any specific time. Rather, it should be conceived as the situation toward which the firms in the industry will move in the long run, if no further changes in demand and supply conditions

---

[2]Detailed discussion of the economic efficiency of the competitive model will be found in Chapter 19.

interrupt such an adjustment process. In the real world, where additional changes occur constantly, new adjustment processes will start long before the old adjustment process produces the long-run equilibrium position.[3]

13-5 THE IDENTITY OF THE MINIMUM LAC FOR ALL FIRMS

We have shown that in the long-run competitive equilibrium, firms produce at the minimum average cost possible and price is equal to this minimum cost. Nonexistence of profit or loss characterizes the long-run equilibrium in perfect competition. Since there is a single price in the industry, the above statements can be true only if every firm in the industry has an identical minimum LAC. Type and quality of resources owned, production techniques adopted, and management available are likely to differ among different firms in the industry. Then, how can all firms in an industry end up with an identical minimum LAC? The answer is provided by the competitive bidding furnished by the price mechanism. A firm's short-run cost advantage must be due to the possession of either reproducible or nonreproducible factors. In the long run, the cost advantage due to reproducible factors will be eliminated as competitors replace their inferior factors with superior ones. The advantage attributable to nonreproducible factors will dissipate in the form of higher explicit or implicit wages, rent, and/or interest. For instance, if the advantage is due to the good fortune of having hired a very competent manager at a salary below his alternative cost, the wage of this manager will tend to be bid up by the competitive process. Unless the firm pays the manager a salary commensurate with his capabilities, another firm will bid him away. If the advantage is due to the superior organizing ability of the owner, the owner must raise the alternative cost of using himself in his own business. Thus, any cost advantage that may exist will, in the long run, disappear as implicit or explicit factor payments, and all firms in the industry will end up with an identical minimum LAC.

13-6 CONSTANT, INCREASING AND DECREASING COST INDUSTRIES

Depending on whether resource prices are unaffected, bid up, or bid down as an industry-wide expansion in output takes place in the long run, we have constant, increasing, or decreasing cost industries.

[3]H. T. Koplin, *Microeconomic Analysis* (New York: Harper & Row, 1971), p. 130.

CONSTANT COST INDUSTRY

In analyzing the long-run adjustment of the industry in the previous section, we assumed that perfect mobility exists and that the position of the long-run cost curves is not affected by the entry or exit of the firms and corresponding changes in the industry output. This assumption implies that the prices of the resources used in the industry remain constant whether output is substantially increased or decreased. *An industry in which the resource prices are independent of the rate of usage is referred to as a constant cost industry.*

In Figure 13-3, the industry demand and supply curves are given by D and S, and the firm is in long-run equilibrium with its LAC and SAC equal to the price, established by the intersection of D and S. Now suppose demand increases to D'. In the short run, the industry supply can be increased only along its short-run supply curve S. The new short-run equilibrium price determined by the intersection of S and D' is p_2. The representative firm increases its output to q_2, where its SMC equals the new, higher market price.

The large economic profit enjoyed by the firms in the industry, however, attracts more firms into the industry. As more firms enter the industry, the usage of resources by the industry increases. However, this industry being a constant cost industry, the resource prices do not change; and the cost of production to the existing firms as well as the new firms remains at the previous level. Thus, a representative firm's cost curves are not altered at all. When

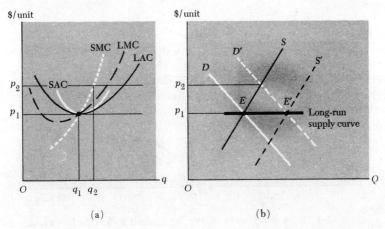

Figure 13-3   Constant cost industry; (a) the firm's cost curves, (b) the industry supply curve

the supply curve is shifted to S' by the entry of new firms, the industry will again be in long-run equilibrium. The new price is equal to the old LAC and SMC. Connecting the original industry equilibrium point E with the new equilibrium point E', the horizontal long-run industry supply curve is obtained. *A constant cost industry, thus, has a horizontal long-run industry supply curve, and the prices of resources remain constant as the industry output changes.*

INCREASING COST INDUSTRY

Now let us assume that the elasticity of supply of resources is less than perfect, and, therefore, that the entry and exit of firms influence resource prices. *When the prices of resources used in an industry vary directly with the rate of industry output, we have an increasing cost industry.* That is, in an increasing cost industry, the cost curves of the firm will be shifted upward as the expansion of the industry output bids up the prices of resources used by the industry. In Figure 13-4b the original long-run equilibrium for the industry is given by point E. The firm's equilibrium position is given by point A in Figure 13-4a. Suppose again that an increase in demand shifts the demand curve to D', and raises the short-run industry price to p_2. The representative firm in the industry enjoys economic profit, and this profit attracts new firms into the industry. As the industry output expands, prices of resources are bid up and the cost curves of the firm are shifted upward from LAC_1 to LAC_2. When the supply curve is shifted to S' by the new entry, the long-run equilibrium is restored again. Note, however, the price is now higher and the new cost curve

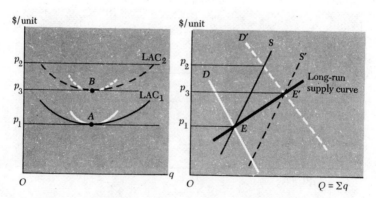

Figure 13-4 Increasing cost industry; (a) upward shift in the firm's LAC, (b) positively sloped industry supply curve

LAC_2 of the firm is tangent to this higher price. The long-run supply curve secured by connecting the original and new equilibrium points E and E' has a positive slope. *An increasing cost industry, therefore, has a positively sloped long-run industry supply curve, and the prices of resources increase as the industry output expands.*

DECREASING COST INDUSTRY

A decreasing cost industry has a negatively sloped long-run industry supply curve, and the prices of resources decrease as the industry output increases. Thus, an increasing industry output is accompanied by a downward shift in the LAC curve. Decreasing cost is difficult to visualize in the context of pure competition. The case in which substantial external economies exist may cause the phenomenon of decreasing cost. As an example, consider the cost of pumping water out of a coal mine. As the mining industry expands and more nearby mines pump out water, the amounts of water seepage into individual mines decrease; and the costs of pumping out water for individual mines will tend to decrease.

Needless to say, the more important cases are the constant and increasing cost industries. Whether an industry will be a constant or increasing cost industry depends on whether the industry's usage of resources is an insignificant or an important part of the total demand for the resources. For instance, the pencil industry can increase its output substantially without affecting the price of lumber. Similarly, the needle industry's output can hardly affect the price of steel. However, the automobile industry is not likely to be able to expand its output substantially without affecting the prices of, say, steel and tires. The supply elasticities of resources are also important: highly elastic supply coefficients will allow large increases in the quantities supplied without increasing the resource prices significantly.

RETURNS, ECONOMIES, AND INCREASING (OR CONSTANT) COSTS

This may be a good time for the reader to clarify the meanings of (1) constant or increasing cost industry, (2) constant or decreasing returns to size or scale, and (3) economies or diseconomies of size or scale. The first, the increasing or constant cost industry, is determined solely by the impact of industry output on resource prices. The second, the question of returns to size or scale, describes the technical relationship between output and the doses of inputs. The third, the economies or diseconomies of size or scale, describes whether the LAC curve is downward-sloping or upward-sloping.

13-7 LONG-RUN ADJUSTMENT IN AGRICULTURE:
An Application

The model of perfect competition, in which a homogeneous product is produced by many different firms and auctioned off in a well-informed market, is an entity rather difficult to observe in the real world. Agriculture is frequently cited as the largest single industry that provides a close approximation to perfect competition.

Consider the characteristics of agriculture. First, there are a *large number of farmers*, none of whom is large enough to affect market prices perceptibly. Second, farm products are graded into standardized *homogeneous products* (No. 3 yellow corn, etc.). Brand names are seldom found, and individual producers rarely advertise in attempts to increase their demands. Third, entry into agriculture is relatively easy. Capital requirements are small compared with those of many other industries. Farm operators can readily learn and adopt new methods of growing crops and raising livestock. Fourth, *prices of many agricultural products are established by auctioning processes* in such a well-organized market as the Chicago Board of Trade. The interactions of many bids and offers in free markets determine the market prices. The prices change frequently within a day, and are quoted in cents and often in fractions of a cent, suggesting that small changes in demand and supply affect prices.

Since agriculture conforms sufficiently well to the model of perfect competition, it would be interesting to see whether the long-run adjustment process observed in this industry agrees with the result suggested by the theoretical model of sections 13-2 and 13-3.

The agricultural sector of the United States includes many farmers who barely manage to subsist from their farming operations. The marked difference in the per capita income in the United States and the per capita income of the American farm population shown in Table 13-1 confirms the discrepancy in per capita productivity between the farm and nonfarm population. Note that per capita income for the farm population fell far short of the U.S. per capita income for every single year shown in the table. Furthermore, very substantial proportions of the income of the farm population were derived from nonfarm sources. For instance, the farm population derived between 47 to 48 percent of their income from nonfarm sources in years 1970, 1971, and 1972. The American farmers' per capita income, which has been far below that of the U.S. population in general, suggests that many farmers may have been incurring economic losses, in the sense that their earnings fall below their alternative costs — what their labor and other resources could have earned in alternative employments.

Table 13-1   Per Capita Income of Farm Population and Population in General in the United States, 1950–72 (in dollars)

ITEM	1950	1955	1960	1965	1970	1971	1972
Farm Population							
From all sources	844	922	1,195	1,908	2,913	3,095	3,536
From farm sources	612	597	737	1,096	1,554	1,612	1,879
From nonfarm sources	272	325	458	812	1,359	1,483	1,657
Population in general	1,501	1,881	2,219	2,773	3,935	4,160	4,481

Source: *Statistical Abstract of the United States*, 1973, pp. 322, 595.

Given the above situation, according to the long-run adjustment process suggested by the model of perfect competition, the number of farms must be reduced by the exit of farmers, particularly small, marginal ones. How well does the prediction of this theoretical model agree with what actually took place in American agriculture? Table 13-2 shows that the theoretical model's prediction agrees rather well with the empirical evidence. The number of farms has steadily declined from 5.6 million in 1950 to 2.8 million in 1973, while the average acres per farm has increased from 213 to 385 in the same period. Many smaller farmers have dropped out of farming operations, and the average size of a farm has increased substantially. Increase in the number of larger farms reflects the changing agricultural technology that makes mechanized large-scale farming more efficient. As a matter of fact, the number of farms with 1,000 acres or more has increased from 121 thousand in 1950 to 151

Table 13-2   Number of Farmers and Average Acreage in the United States, 1950–73

ITEM	1950	1955	1960	1965	1970	1971	1972	1973°
Farms (in thousands)	5,648	4,654	3,963	3,356	2,954	2,909	2,870	2,831
Average acres per farm	213	258	297	340	373	377	381	385

°Preliminary
Source: *Statistical Abstract of the United States*, 1973, p. 585.

thousand in 1969. In 1969, these large farms owned 54.4 percent of all farm land and 29.3 percent of all crop land harvested.[4]

The market forces of competition have thus performed, though slowly and somewhat capriciously, the important function of making the agricultural sector more efficient by reducing the number of small, marginal farmers, and increasing the number of more efficient, larger farmers. The transfer of marginal farmers from agriculture to other sectors of the economy in which they can earn more income, needless to say, is an improvement in efficiency. The increase in the average size of the remaining farms, which reduces the average cost of producing agricultural products, also is an improvement in efficiency.

13-8 SOME MORE APPLICATIONS OF COMPETITIVE MODELS

The competitive model can be applied to many specific parts of agriculture, such as the cattle industry. For instance, suppose that the market demand and supply for cattle is such that the cattle price is high and cattlemen find themselves receiving substantial economic profits. Enticed by such lucrative profits, many cattlemen increase the size of their herds, expand their ranches, and some new ranches open up. As the supply of cattle increases, the price of cattle is brought down. If the new price is such that many ranchers find it unattractive, some will start reducing their herds and others leave the cattle business entirely. Thus, there is a continuous tendency for the supply of cattle to adjust to the so-called long-run equilibrium position in which price equals the alternative cost of production.

The competitive model may even be applied to certain manufacturing industries. For example, the cotton textile industry has been cited as the manufacturing industry approximating perfect competition. The principal product of this industry, gray print cloth, is well standardized and graded according to its weight and closeness of weave. No brand names or advertising effort differentiate the product of one mill from that of the others. There are a large number of mills, and entrance into the industry is relatively easy.

During the period of 1924–26, the cotton textile industry suffered from substantial excess capacity and rates of return much lower than those that prevailed in other manufacturing industries. How did the firms in this industry respond to the situation? Precisely in the way the competitive model would predict. A steady exit of

[4]*Statistical Abstract of the United States,* 1973, p. 587.

marginal mills ensued: the total number of spindles in place fell from a peak of 38 million in 1925 to 27 million in 1938.[5]

13-9 MARGINALISM IN PRACTICE: THE CASE OF CONTINENTAL AIR LINES

A very important tool of analysis introduced in this chapter, which will appear repeatedly throughout the book, is marginal analysis. The case described here is adapted from a *Business Week* article and illustrates a practical application of marginal analysis.[6]

Continental Air Lines, Inc., during 1962, filled only half the available seats on its Boeing 707 jet flights, a record some 15 percentage points worse than the national average. Instead of eliminating a few runs in order to raise the average load considerably, Continental bolsters its corporate profits by deliberately running extra flights that aren't expected to do more than return their out-of-pocket costs — plus a little profit. Such marginal flights are an integral part of the overall operating philosophy that has brought small, Denver-based Continental — tenth among the 11 trunk carriers — through the bumpy postwar period with only one unprofitable year.

This philosophy leans heavily on marginal analysis. Put most simply, marginalists maintain that a company should undertake any activity that adds more to revenues than it does to costs — and not limit itself to those activities whose returns equal average or "fully allocated" costs.

The approach, of course, can be applied to virtually any business, not just to air transportation. It can be used in consumer finance, for instance, where the question may be whether to make more loans — including more bad loans — if this will increase net profit. Similarly, in advertising, the decision may rest on how much extra business a dollar's worth of additional advertising will bring in, rather than pegging the advertising budget to a percentage of sales — and, in insurance, where setting high interest rates to discourage policy loans may actually damage profits by causing policyholders to borrow elsewhere.

The job of determining "true" marginal costs may be highly complex, time-wasting, and too expensive. But even a rough

[5]Lloyd G. Reynolds, "Competition in the Cotton-Textile Industry: A Case Study," in Walter Adams and Leland E. Traywick (eds.), *Readings in Economics,* (New York: Macmillan, 1948).
[6]"Airline Takes the Marginal Route," *Business Week*, April 20, 1963, pp. 111–113. Reprinted by special permission.

application of marginal principles may come closer to the right answer for business decision-makers than an analysis based on precise average cost data.

Proving that this is so demands economists who can break the crust of corporate habits and show concretely why the typical manager's response — that nobody ever made a profit without meeting all costs — is misleading and can reduce profits. To be sure, the whole business cannot make a profit unless average costs are met; but covering average costs should not determine whether any particular activity should be undertaken. For this would unduly restrict corporate decisions, and cause managements to forgo opportunities for extra gains.

The nature of marginal analysis is readily summarized by the following illustration:

Marginal analysis in a nutshell

Problem: Shall Continental run an extra daily flight from City X to City Y?

The facts: Fully allocated costs of this flight $4,500
Out-of-pocket costs of this flight $2,000
Flight should gross $3,100

Decision: Run the flight. It will add $1,100 to net profit because it will add $3,100 to revenues and only $2,000 to cost. Overhead and other costs, totaling $2,500 ($4,500 minus $2,000) would be incurred whether the flight is run or not. Therefore, fully allocated or "average" cost of $4,500 are not relevant to this business decision. It's the out-of-pocket or "marginal" costs that count.

Continental's approach to scheduling is this: it considers that the bulk of its scheduled flights will have to return at least their fully allocated costs. Overhead, depreciation, insurance are very real expenses and must be covered. The out-of-pocket approach comes into play only after the line's basic schedule had been set. Then Continental goes a step further to see if adding more flights will contribute to the corporate net. Similarly, if it is thinking of dropping a flight with a disappointing record, Continental puts it under the marginal microscope: "If your revenues are going to be more than your out-of-pocket costs, you should keep the flight on."

By "out-of-pocket costs" Continental means just that: the actual dollars that Continental has to pay out to run a flight. It gets the figure not by applying hypothetical equations but by circulating a proposed schedule to every operating department concerned and finding out just what extra expenses it will entail. If a ground crew already on duty can service the plane, the flight isn't charged a penny of their salary expense. There may even be some costs eliminated in running the flight; they won't need men to roll the plane to a hangar, for instance, if it flies on to another stop.

Most of these extra flights, of course, are run at off-beat hours, mainly late at night. At times, though, Continental discovers that the hours aren't so unpopular after all. A pair of night coach flights on the Houston–San Antonio–El Paso–Phoenix–Los Angeles leg, added on a marginal basis, have turned out to be so successful that they are now more than covering fully allocated costs.

Continental's data handling system produces weekly reports on each flight, with revenues measured against both out-of-pocket and fully allocated costs. Continental uses these to give each flight a careful analysis at least once a quarter. But those added on a marginal basis get the fine-tooth-comb treatment monthly.

EXERCISES 13

Price and Output under Perfect Competition – Continued

13-1 Explain why the economic profit becomes zero for competitive firms in the long-run equilibrium, and elaborate on why competitive firms will be in equilibrium when they are making no economic profit.

13-2 In Figure 13-5, which shows the LAC and LMC curves, draw in the three sets of SAC and SMC curves that can produce the levels of output marked off by the vertical dotted lines most efficiently.

13-3 Many restaurants in large cities sell their lunch-hour meals at prices that are said not to be able to cover the full cost. Are these restaurants applying marginal analysis in their luncheon menu pricing? Discuss.

13-4 It is claimed that resources are ideally allocated in the long run in a perfectly competitive industry.

    1. In what sense is the competitive resource allocation ideal?
    2. What are the assumptions (or qualifications) necessary in claiming that the perfectly competitive industry allocates resources optimally?

13-5 The following is quoted from a price theory textbook: "Assume that all firms in a perfectly competitive industry have identical LAC curves. The typical firm's LAC curve then is also the LAC curve of the industry." Do you agree with this statement: Why or why not?

13-6 "The term *perfect* or *pure competition* is undesirable because it tends to make students believe that competition is more perfect or pure in this market than in other forms of markets. Other terms such as the *price-takers' market* and *atomistic competition* are preferable because they describe the nature of competition that prevails in the market without the possibility of misleading students." Comment.

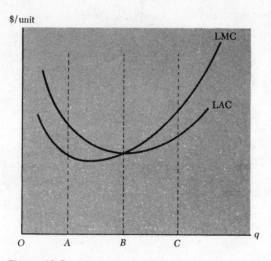

Figure 13-5

Figure 10

CHAPTER FOURTEEN

PRICE AND OUTPUT UNDER PURE MONOPOLY

In Chapters Twelve and Thirteen, we examined the model of perfect competition—an extreme case in which numerous sellers and buyers dealing with a homogeneous product behave as price-takers and quantity-adjusters. In this chapter, we will examine the other extreme model, pure monopoly or simply, monopoly. The first five sections will discuss the basic model of monopoly; the remainder of the chapter will introduce somewhat more complex or applied models, such as multiplant or multimarket monopolist, price discrimination, and the effect of taxation on monopoly price and output decisions.

14-1 BASES OF MONOPOLY: BARRIERS TO ENTRY ·

What causes monopolies? A monopoly is an industry in which there is a single seller. The fact that there is only one seller suggests that there must be some important barriers to entry. It is traditional for microeconomics texts to discuss the subject of barriers to entry in connection with the study of oligopoly—an industry in which there are a few sellers only. We will, however, make a brief note of the major barriers to entry that can contribute to the formation and continuation of a monopoly. First, *legal restrictions* due to patents and government franchises may be the most important causes of monopoly. Second, a single firm may control the *supply of key raw materials*. Some of the well-known examples are bauxite; nickel, diamonds, sulfur, and radium. Third, the industry may be a so-called *natural monopoly*—an industry in which the efficient size of plant is large relative to the size of the market, and the monopolist's LAC declines throughout the relevant range of output. Prime examples of natural monopolies are public utilities. A more detailed discussion of the barriers to entry will be given in Chapter Fifteen, where oligopoly is analyzed.

14-2 PRICE AND OUTPUT DECISIONS IN THE SHORT RUN

The model of monopoly that explains the price and output decisions of the monopolist in the short run is very much like that of the perfectly competitive model of Chapter Twelve. The difference between the two models arises from the fact that the monopolist's demand curve has a negative slope while the perfect competitor's demand curve is horizontal.[1]

Throughout this chapter, we shall, for simplicity, assume that a monopolist purchases his inputs in a competitive resource market; he can buy all needed resources without affecting their prices. The cost curves of the perfectly competitive model in the previous chapter, therefore, will be equally applicable in this chapter. The cases in which the resource market is imperfect and the monopolist's rate of purchase affects resource prices will be analyzed in Chapter Seventeen, which deals with employment of resources.

TOTAL CURVES APPROACH

As in the case of the competitive model, we can again present the profit-maximizing output decision rule in two parts. First, ask whether there is any output level at which the total revenue, TR, exceeds the total variable cost, TVC. *If TR is less than TVC at all output levels, the profit-maximizing strategy is to shut down*, and absorb the loss due to the total fixed cost, TFC, which cannot be avoided in the short run. Any attempt to produce will result in a greater loss since the TR from any such operation will fall short of the TVC that must be incurred for the operation. Second, *if there are output levels at which the TR exceeds the TVC, produce where the vertical distance between the TR and TC is at maximum*. (Since TC and TVC differ by the TFC alone, the vertical distance between TR and TVC will also be at maximum at the profit-maximizing output.)

Figure 14-1 shows the TR, TC, and TVC curves of a monopolist. The TR curve is concave downward, reflecting the monopolist's demand curve, which has a negative slope. Since there is a range of output in which TR exceeds TVC, the profit-maximizing output strategy is to produce Q° units per period, where the vertical

[1]This section confines itself to a single-plant monopolist. Multiplant monopoly model is given in section 14-6.

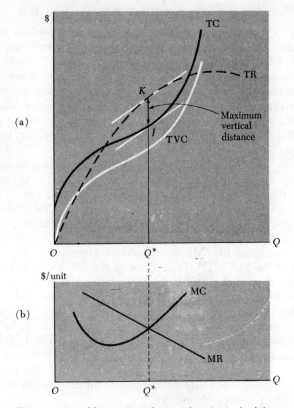

Figure 14-1 Monopoly price and output decision;
(a) total curves, (b) marginal curves

distance, *JK*, between the TR and TC curves is greatest. Note that, at the profit-maximizing output, the TR and TC curves have the same slope; that is, the MR equals the MC, as shown in Figure 14-1*b*. Furthermore, at Q^* the slope of the MC curve is steeper than the slope of the MR curve. Clearly, the monopolist should produce, if he produces at all, where MR = MC and the slope of MC exceeds that of the MR (the *sufficient conditions* for profit maximizing nonzero output selection).[2]

[2]Mathematically the profit function to be maximized is

$$\pi(q) = R(q) - C(q)$$

Differentiating this profit function with respect to *q* and setting it equal to zero, we have the necessary condition for profit maximization:

AVERAGE AND MARGINAL CURVES APPROACH

Again, the decision rule for the selection of profit-maximizing output and price for the monopolist may be given in two parts. First, does the AR curve lie above the AVC curve in some output range? If not, the best strategy in the short run is to shut down and incur the loss due to the fixed cost, which cannot be avoided in the short run. If there is an output range in which the AR curve is located above the AVC curve, the profit-maximizing output is where MR = MC and the slope of the MC curve is greater than that of the MR curve.

The monopolist's AR and MR curves as well as his MC and AC (or ATC) curves are shown in Figure 14-2. There are outputs at which the AR curve lies above the AC (the AVC curve, which is lower than the AC by the AFC, is not shown to avoid cluttering the graph), and the optimal strategy is to produce Q^* units per period. The output of Q^* units per period satisfies the sufficient conditions for profit maximization: MR = MC and the slope of the MC is greater than that of the MR at Q^*. (The slope of the MC curve at Q^* is positive, while that of the MR curve is negative.) Now the monopolist must decide the price at which the output is to be sold. Since the monopolist is assumed to seek the maximum profit, he sets the price at \$$P$ per unit—the maximum price per unit at which he can sell the profit-maximizing output, Q^*. The profit per unit is BA dollars and the total profit received by the monopolist is π dollars per period.

The *necessary and sufficient conditions* for the monopolist to maximize his profit in the short run are analogous to those given for the perfect competitor:

1. If AR = p < AVC for all possible output levels, shut down (produce zero unit).
2. If AR ⩾ AVC in an output range, produce where MR = MC and the slope of the MC curve is greater than that of the MR curve.

$$\pi'(q) = R'(q) - C'(q) = 0$$

and

$$R'(q) = C'(q)$$

The necessary condition, therefore, requires that MR = MC.

The sufficient condition for profit maximization is given by

$$\pi''(q) = R''(q) - C''(q) < 0$$
$$R''(q) < C''(q)$$

That is, the slope of MR is less than that of MC.

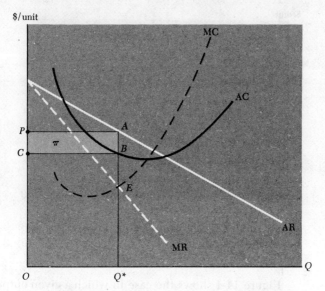

Figure 14-2 Monopoly price and output decision: marginal and average curves

14-3 NOTE ON THE NONEXISTENCE OF THE MONOPOLY SUPPLY CURVE

The monopolist's MC curve above its AVC curve is *not* his supply curve. Point *E* in Figure 14-2, at which the MR and MC curves intersect, shows the profit-maximizing quantity to be produced. However, in order to find the profit-maximizing price, we must move vertically until point *A* on the AR curve is reached. Thus, depending on the shape and location of the demand curve, the profit-maximizing output will be sold at different prices. Because there is no one-to-one correspondence between price and quantity, it is impossible to talk of a monopolist's supply curve.

The lack of a unique relationship between the price charged by a monopolist and his quantity supplied (and the corresponding ambiguity in the concept of supply for the monopolist) can be readily seen by referring to Figures 14-3 and 14-4. Figure 14-3 shows the case in which a given supply price is associated with two distinct output rates. Given the monopolist's MC, the optimum output is Q_1 or Q_2 units per period depending on whether the demand curve is given by D_1 or D_2.

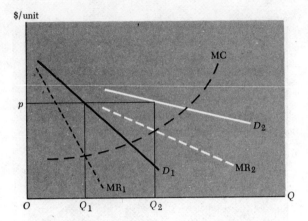

Figure 14-3 A single monopoly price associated with two distinct outputs

Figure 14-4 shows the case in which a given output rate is associated with two different prices. MR equals MC at the output of q^* units per period. But the monopolist's supply price will be p_1 or p_2 depending on whether the relevant demand condition is described by the demand curve D_1 or D_2.

Figures 14-3 and 14-4 clearly show that there is no unique one-to-one relationship between price and quantity supplied by a monopolist. Thus, we conclude that the concept of supply is not well defined for a monopolist (or more generally, for any imperfect competitor).

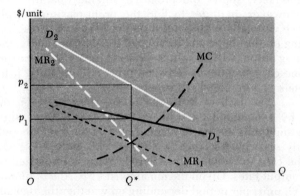

Figure 14-4 A single monopoly output associated with two distinct prices

14-4   LONG-RUN PRICE AND OUTPUT DECISIONS

In the short run, the monopolist's decision problem is to maximize his profit subject to the given size plant, already built and operating. In the long run, the monopolist must, first of all, decide whether he should be in business or not. If the demand and cost conditions are such that long-run average cost, LAC, cannot be covered, the monopolist will abandon his business. Assuming that the monopolist decides to stay in business, the second decision facing him is choosing the most profitable size of plant and operating it at the most profitable rate. In this section, we will deal with the long-run equilibrium of a monopolist who has only one plant. Section 14-6 will analyze the case of a monopolist with multiple plants.

Figure 14-5 shows the long-run average and marginal cost curves of a monopolist together with his average and marginal revenue curves. Given these curves, the profit-maximizing output of the monopolist in the long run is Q_l at which his LMC curve intersects his MR curve. In order to produce this output at the lowest LAC possible, the monopolist builds the plant indicated by SAC* in Figure 14-5. The minimum SAC and LAC at which the monopolist can produce Q_l units is Q_lC dollars per unit. The price at which the monopolist can sell his output is p_l dollars per unit. Thus, his profit is π_l dollars per period. Given the revenue and cost curves, there is no way the monopolist can improve his profit position: thus, he is in a long-run equilibrium.

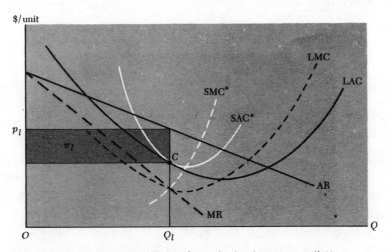

Figure 14-5   Long-run equilibrium for a single-plant monopolist

In summary, the **necessary and sufficient conditions** for the long-run profit maximization are:

1. If AR < LAC for all possible outputs, abandon the business.
2. If AR ≥ LAC for some range of output, produce where LMC = MR and the slope of the LMC curve is greater than that of the MR curve.

In the long-run equilibrium, a perfectly competitive firm receives zero economic profit because the ease of entry and exit eliminates any profit or loss in the industry. A monopolist, however, *may* enjoy his profit even in the long run because it is difficult for other firms to enter the market and break up the monopoly. Whether a monopolist's profit will actually be positive or zero depends on his revenue and cost conditions. Needless to say, a negative profit is inconsistent with a long-run equilibrium position.

14-5 COMPETITION VERSUS MONOPOLY: A COMPARISON

The monopolist's long-run equilibrium position is reproduced in Figure 14-6, which is a simplified version of Figure 14-5. Note that the monopolist's price is higher than his average or marginal cost, that his output is smaller than the minimum cost output Q_m, and that he may reap profit even in the long run. The monopolist's long-run equilibrium price and output are, therefore, quite a contrast to the perfectly competitive long-run equilibrium, in which price is equal to the lowest average cost and marginal cost, and profit is nonexistent.

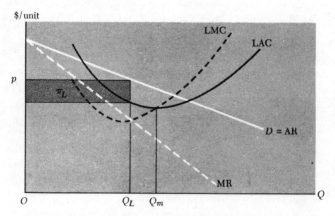

Figure 14-6 Competitive versus monopoly price and output

Comparing the long-run equilibrium of the monopolist with that of a perfect competitor, many writers cast the monopolist as a villain who contrives to create scarcity and keep the price high in order to reap a large profit. He is accused of misallocating scarce resources by not employing enough resources in the monopolized industry, thereby forcing resources to seek employment in less productive areas. Such accusations directed against the monopolist, however, are valid only if the cost conditions are assumed to be identical under monopoly and under industry-wide changes in output in perfect competition. Since cost conditions are likely to differ under the two different market structures, the comparison of monopoly output and price with those of perfect competition is rather hazardous. It is thus necessary to make specific assumptions regarding the nature of cost conditions before we can proceed to compare monopoly with perfect competition.

CONSTANT RETURNS TO SIZE

Suppose that the production condition of an industry is characterized by constant returns to size or scale. Also assume that the industry is a constant cost industry, that is, resource prices remain constant as industry output changes.[3] Then the average and marginal costs of production (within the relevant range) are constant and the same for the monopolist and for the perfectly competitive industry. Such cost conditions and the market demand curve are depicted in Figure 14-7. The perfectly competitive industry produces the output at which its LAC and LMC equal the price; thus, the competitive output is Q_c and price is p_c. On the other hand, the monopolist produces where his LMC equals his MR; thus his output and price are Q_m and p_m. Figure 14-7 shows that, *when the constant returns to size prevails* and resource prices remain the same, the following comparisons of monopoly versus perfect competition will hold true:

$$Q_m < Q_c$$
$$p_m > p_c$$
$$\pi_m > \pi_c = 0$$

where π, Q, and p show profit, output, and price, and the subscripts m and c identify monopoly and competitive industry.

Social welfare effects of competition versus monopoly. Using the constant cost model, we can also show that perfect competi-

[3]This simplifies our analysis. Furthermore, the changes in resource prices that affect the monopolist and the competitive producers alike are not important in comparing the two market structures.

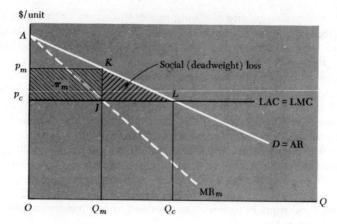

Figure 14-7 Monopoly versus perfect competition: constant returns to size

tion maximizes social welfare, and that monopoly creates a social loss. For simplicity, assume that there are no *externalities—benefits or costs to the society that do not enter into the private revenue and cost calculations*—and, therefore, private benefits and costs are equal to social benefits and costs. Now, the industry demand curve shows prices the consumers are willing to pay for various quantities. Since the consumer will not purchase the last unit at the prevailing price unless he thinks the benefit received from the good is equal to the price he has to pay, the price of the good may be taken as the indicator of the marginal social benefit of the good. The marginal cost curve (which, by assumption, is the same for both the monopolist and the perfectly competitive industry) shows the additional cost of producing an extra unit of output. Since there are no externalities, this marginal cost curve may be construed as indicating the marginal social cost. The output that maximizes the social welfare, then, is the competitive industry output, Q_c, where the marginal social benefit is equal to the marginal social cost.

Effects on consumers' surplus of competition and monopoly. Under competition, the total benefit or gain to the society is equal to $OALQ_c$ in Figure 14-7. (This is so because the total social gain is equal to the area under the $D = AR$ curve, which indicates the marginal social benefit.) The total social cost of producing the competitive output is equal to Op_cLQ_c—the area under the MC curve, which indicates the marginal social cost. *The excess of the total social gain over the total social cost is shown by the triangle* ALp_c, *and is referred to as consumers' surplus under perfect competition.*[4]

Now assume that the industry is reorganized as a monopoly. The monopoly output, price, and profit will be Q_m, p_m, and π_m dollars, respectively. What happens to consumers' surplus that existed under competition when the industry is transformed into a monopoly? As shown in Figure 14-7, the original competitive consumers' surplus is now divided into three parts: (1) the new, smaller consumers' surplus under monopoly, AKp_m, (2) the monopoly profit, π_m, and (3) the triangle JKL, which goes neither to the consumers nor to the monopolist. *The triangle* JKL, *therefore, represents the social waste due to the monopoly arrangement, and is referred to as the welfare triangle, deadweight loss, social loss, waste of monopoly, and so on.*

INCREASING RETURNS TO SIZE

Let us now consider the industry in which indivisibilities are important and significant economies of size (or scale) exist. As in the previous case, resource prices are assumed to remain constant. In such an industry, the monopolist who can take advantage of large-scale production can produce the product at an average cost much lower than that of perfectly competitive firms, which must operate small-size plants. In Figures 14-8a and b, the industry demand curve —which is the same in the two graphs— is shown by the $AR = D$ curve. The long-run average and marginal cost curves, LAC and LMC, for the competitive arrangement in Figure 14-8a are shown by the same horizontal curve: more output can be produced without affecting costs by more small firms entering the market. The monopolist's LAC curve is U-shaped and declines in the relevant range, indicating the economies of size advantage available to the monopolist. Given the industry demand and cost conditions depicted in Figures 14-8a and b, the industry output and price under the

---

[4]The notion of *consumer's surplus* was introduced by Alfred Marshall. He noted that the price a consumer pays for a commodity is generally much lower than what he would be willing to pay rather than go without it. The satisfaction a consumer derives from the purchase of a commodity thus generally exceeds that which he sacrifices in paying its price. Marshall named this surplus of satisfaction derived by the consumer the "consumer's surplus." (Suppose Figure 14-7 shows the demand curve of a consumer. Then, the consumer who purchases Q_c units of the good derives $OALQ_c$ dollars worth of satisfaction, but pays only Op_cLQ_c dollars: the excess of the satisfaction derived by the consumer over what he pays, ALp_c dollars, is the consumer's surplus). See Marshall's *Principles of Economics*, 8th ed. (New York: Macmillan, 1941), pp. 124–128, 811.

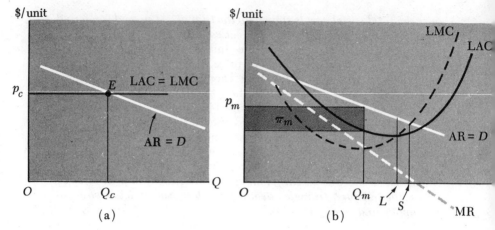

Figure 14-8 Monopoly versus competition: increasing returns to size; (a) under competition, (b) und monopoly

competitive arrangement are given by point E, where the AR ($=D$) curve intersects the LAC = LMC curve. The competitive industry price and output are p_c and Q_c. If the industry is organized as a monopoly, the monopolist will produce where his MR equals his LMC and his price and output will be p_m and Q_m.

As can be seen from Figure 14-8*b*, the monopolist's output is smaller than his lowest cost output, OL, and the social welfare–maximizing output, OS; his price is higher than LAC and LMC; and his profit is π_m dollars. However, in this case, the monopolist's output is greater than the competitive industry output; and the monopoly price is lower than the competitive market price. *When there are significant economies of size* (and the market demand is large enough to justify a large-scale production), the relevant comparisons between monopoly and competition may be as follows:

$$Q_m > Q_c$$
$$p_m < p_c$$
$$\pi_m > \pi_c = 0$$

The monopolist here appears to be a hero rather than a villain.

DECREASING RETURNS TO SIZE

The reader may ponder over the case in which there is decreasing returns to size and the monopolist's cost of production using a large plant is substantially higher than the cost of competitive firms that have smaller-size plants. Is this case a likely one? The next

300

section examines the monopolist coping with the case of decreasing returns to size by building many plants of the optimal size.

14-6 MULTIPLANT MONOPOLIST

Many large firms operate more than one plant. When the monopolist has *two plants* to produce the output that he sells in a *single market*, how does he determine the profit-maximizing allocation of production between two plants?[5] Answers to this question differ depending on the economic time period involved. We will, therefore, examine the short-run decision problem first.

SHORT-RUN PRICE AND OUTPUT DECISIONS

The curves labeled MC_a and MC_b in Figure 14-9 show the marginal costs of two plants A and B, while the MC_t curve represents the horizontal summation of MC_a and MC_b. The MC_t curve shows the firm's marginal cost when it uses either plant A or plant B, whichever has a lower marginal cost. By equating its MR and MC_t, the monopolist determines his profit-maximizing output and price, Q_t and p. In order to produce Q_t units at the least possible cost, the monopolist allocates production between the two plants in such a way as *to equalize the marginal cost of production in both plants.*[6] This can be easily done graphically by extending the horizontal line *CE* in Figure 14-9c all the way to the left. Dropping the perpendicular lines to the quantity axis from the points where the horizontal line intersects MC_a and MC_b, we obtain the quantities to be allocated to plants A and B, Q_a and Q_b. Since the MC_t curve is the horizontal summation of MC_a and MC_b, it is clear that $Q_t = Q_a + Q_b$. Also note that our graphical technique assures that the marginal costs at plants A and B are equal when their outputs are Q_a and Q_b units, respectively.

To sum up, the profit-maximizing multiplant monopolist allocates the production of his output between two plants in such a way as to *equalize the marginal costs in the two plants.*

LONG-RUN PRICE AND OUTPUT DECISIONS

If the optimal (the minimum LAC) plant size is small relative to the total market demand, the monopolist will expand his output by increasing the number of plants that are of the optimal size. Let us see why.

[5]This analysis can be readily extended into a model of n plants.

[6]Unless this condition is attained, the monopolist can always reduce his cost of production by shifting the production of some units from the high MC plant to the low MC plant.

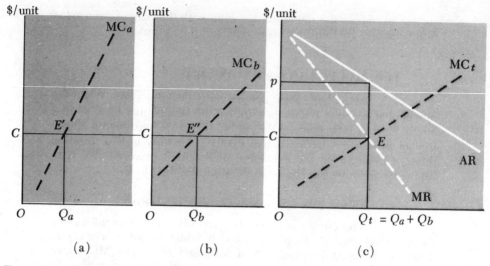

Figure 14-9 Monopolist with two plants and one market; (a) plant A, (b) plant B, (c) the firm

The LAC curve in Figure 14-10a shows the minimum AC that must be incurred in producing various output if the monopolist were to rely on a single plant that produces the desired output at the least cost. The minimum average cost attainable shown by SAC* is C dollars per unit. Assume that the size of the minimum-cost plant SAC* is small relative to the market. Under such a circumstance, the monopolist's cost of production will be minimized if he produces the desired output by constructing as many optimal-size plants as required. By duplicating the minimum-cost plant, the multiplant monopolist can supply a larger output without incurring any higher average cost of production. Thus, the LAC and LMC curve relevant to the multiplant monopolist is shown by a horizontal line going through point C in Figure 14-10b.[7] By equating his MR and his LMC the monopolist decides to produce Q units per period of time. The monopolist then constructs as many optimal-size plants as necessary to produce his total output. The figure assumes that it takes n plants to produce his total output; thus, Q = nq.

[7]The LAC curve in Figure 14-10a is relevant if the monopolist attempts to increase his output by varying his plant size. Since the monopolist expands his output by duplicating the optimal size plant, the relevant LAC curve for the multiplant monopolist is the flat LAC curve in Figure 14-10b.

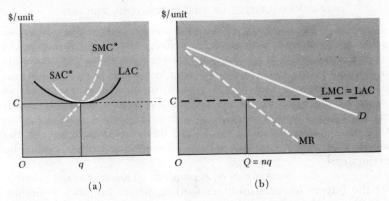

Figure 14-10 The long-run monopoly equilibrium with *n* identical plants; (a) the cost curves for a single plant, (b) the LAC = LMC curve with *n* minimum-cost plants

If increasing the number of plants causes the prices of resources to be bid up, the LMC curve of a multiplant monopolist will have a positive slope, and the SAC* curve will shift upwards as the number of plants is increased. If the output increases by less than the output of a single optimal-size plant, then the monopolist will have to operate one or more plants at more than the optimal rate, or build a new plant and use it at less than the optimal rate. This will make his LMC (as well as LAC) somewhat higher than *C* dollars per unit.

14-7 PRICE DISCRIMINATION

Price discrimination is said to exist when an identical good is sold at different prices. For example, identical sunglasses may be sold at $4 in popular department stores, and at $10 at airport terminals. More broadly, price discrimination also includes "the sale of two or more similar goods at prices which are in different ratios to marginal cost."[8] Good examples are the standard and deluxe models. A deluxe dishwasher with fancy trimmings and minor additional features usually sells at prices substantially higher than the standard model. Thus, the ratio of the deluxe model price to its marginal cost is higher than that of the standard model price to its marginal cost. *Thus, we define price discrimination as selling an identical good at different prices or selling two or more similar goods at prices that are in different ratios to marginal costs.*

[8]George J. Stigler, *The Theory of Price*, 3d ed. (New York: Macmillan, 1966), p. 209.

PREREQUISITES OF DISCRIMINATORY PRICING

The seller must have a monopoly power. The purpose of price discrimination is to increase profit by charging different prices to different buyers or by charging different prices for different units purchased by the same buyer. In order to be able to charge different prices to different individuals, groups, or for different amounts of usage by the same buyer, the seller must have a monopoly power (as we assume in this chapter), or a group of sellers must engage in tacit or explicit collusion regarding their price policies. In the absence of such concerted action, price discrimination cannot be maintained.

The market can be separated. That is, it is not possible for the buyers to resell in other markets where the price is higher. Some examples of market separation are domestic versus foreign markets, medical care for a rich versus for a poor person, and electric supply for home versus for business.

The elasticities of demand in different markets must be different. The purpose of price discrimination is to increase the total revenue by charging relatively higher (lower) price in the market in which demand is relatively inelastic (elastic) at around the price prevailing in the market.[9] Thus, if the price elasticity coefficients of demand in different markets were the same, there would be no need for any price discrimination.

FIRST-DEGREE OR PERFECT PRICE DISCRIMINATION

There are different kinds of price discrimination. *The discriminatory pricing that attempts to take away the entire consumer's surplus is called first-degree or perfect price discrimination. The form of price discrimination that attempts to siphon off a part of a consumer's surplus is called second-degree price discrimination.*[10] *The designation of third-degree price discrimination is attached to intermarket price discrimination in which different prices are charged in well-separated markets, but within each market, a uniform price prevails for all buyers.* Let us start with first-degree price discrimination.

The model of *first-degree or perfect price discrimination* assumes a monopolist who knows the demand curves of each of his customers and who attempts to extract the maximum amount possible from each customer. Thus, the monopolist charges each consumer the maximum sum he is willing to pay rather than go

[9] For a detailed discussion on this point, see footnote 11.

[10] These names were originally coined by the British economist, A. C. Pigou. See *The Economics of Welfare*, 4th ed. (New York: Macmillan, 1938), pp. 278–279.

without the commodity; that is, he attempts to take away the entire
consumer's surplus.

In Figure 14-11, in the absence of price discrimination,
the consumer could have purchased q units of the good for $OPBq$
dollars. Since the demand curve shows the prices the consumer
would be willing to pay for various quantities indicated, the area
under the $D = AR$ curve, $OABq$, can be taken as the indicator of the
total benefits received by the consumer when he purchases q units
of the good. The difference between this benefit and the money expenditure incurred by the consumer, $OPBq$, is the Marshallian consumer's surplus; and is shown by the triangle PAB in Figure 14-11.
The monopolist who practices first-degree price discrimination wants
the consumer to pay not only $OPBq$ dollars but also PAB dollars
(which corresponds to the consumer's surplus). Thus, he makes an
all-or-nothing offer of $OABq$ dollars for q units.

Clearly, first-degree price discrimination is the limiting
case: the monopolist charges different prices to each of his customers
in his attempt to extract the maximum possible sum from each of his
buyers. Needless to say, such discriminatory pricing is not possible
unless customers are few in number and can be well separated, as
in the case of a physician with a few rich patients or a management
consultant with a few corporate clients. Nevertheless, the model
of first-degree price discrimination does shed an important analytical
insight into many discriminatory pricing practices. For instance,
it explains why medical doctors may charge higher fees to the rich
than to ordinary people; and why lawyer's fees are related to the
amount of money involved in the case rather than the amount of work
involved. Such a phenomenon as the existence of a monthly golf card
along with daily golf fees also reflects the golf course owners' attempts
to extract more money from their customers.

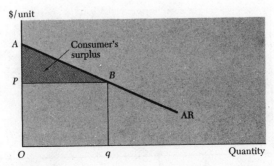

Figure 14-11 First-degree price discrimination

SECOND-DEGREE PRICE DISCRIMINATION

In order to increase his total revenue and profit, a monopolist may charge different prices for different size purchases, as in the cases of rates charged by electric and gas utilities. This pricing practice is known as *second-degree price discrimination*. A monopolist practicing second-degree price discrimination attempts to siphon off a part (rather than the entire amount) of the consumer's surplus. Let us see how this is accomplished. Suppose the monopolist has a large number of customers as in the case of a utility, and a typical consumer's demand curve is as shown in Figure 14-12. In practicing second-degree price discrimination, the monopolist charges p_3 dollars per unit for the first A units of purchase, p_2 dollars per unit for the purchase falling between A and B units, and p_1 dollars per unit for the purchase exceeding B units. Suppose the consumer uses C units per period of time, then, the monopolist's revenue will be only Op_1JC dollars if he does not engage in any price discrimination. However, by practicing second-degree price discrimination, the monopolist can increase his total revenue by the shaded rectangles. Even though the consumer cannot keep the entire consumer's surplus of p_1LJ dollars, he does enjoy the consumer's surplus represented by the three triangles. Second-degree price discrimination, thus, falls somewhere between first-degree discrimination (which eliminates consumers' surpluses completely) and the next section's third-degree discrimination (which charges a different but single price in each of the separate markets and thus does not take away any consumer's surplus).

THIRD-DEGREE PRICE DISCRIMINATION

A monopolist may sell his good at different prices in different markets, but keep the price uniform within each separate market. This discriminatory pricing practice is referred to as *third-*

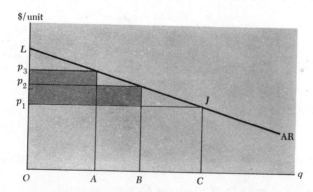

Figure 14-12 Second-degree price discrimination

degree price discrimination. Let us examine this case by assuming that the monopolist produces his product in a *central plant* and sells it in *two separate markets.* How can the monopolist decide the optimal total output, the quantities to be sold in each market, and the prices to be charged in each market? This question can be answered referring to the set of graphs in Figure 14-13. The demand and MR curves facing the firm in market I and market II are shown in parts *a* and *b*, and the combined marginal revenue, MR_t, curve of the firm together with its MC curve is shown in part *c*. The MR_t curve is obtained by summing the MR curves in market I and II horizontally, and shows the additional revenue the firm can secure by selling an additional unit of output either in market I or market II, whichever has a higher MR.

In order to maximize his profit, the monopolist must produce Q_t units per period of time—the rate of output at which his MR_t is equal to his MC. The monopolist must now allocate this output between market I and II in such a way as to equalize the marginal revenues in the two markets. In order to accomplish this we extend a horizontal line going through point E all the way to the left and let it intersect MR_1 and MR_2 at points E_1 and E_2. These two points immediately establish the profit-maximizing quantities to be sold in markets I and II; Q_1 and Q_2 units. Since the MR_t curve is obtained as the summation of MR_1 and MR_2, it necessarily follows that $Q_t = Q_1 + Q_2$. Since MR_1 equals MR_2, the monopolist cannot increase his total revenue by any reallocation of the output between the two markets.

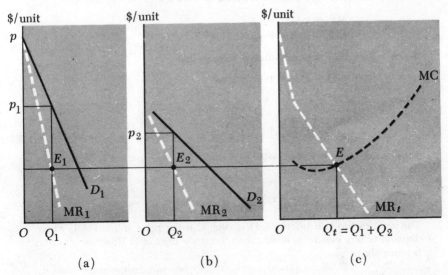

Figure 14-13 Third-degree price discrimination; (*a*) market I, (*b*) market II, (*c*) the firm

The prices charged in the two markets are p_1 dollars in market I and p_2 dollars in market II, as can be readily seen from the demand curves in the two markets. The price charged in market I is higher than the price in market II. To maximize his profit, the monopolist must charge a higher price in the market in which demand is relatively inelastic in the relevant range, and a lower price in the market in which demand is relatively elastic in the relevant range.[11]

The reader must have noticed the similarity in the analysis of the above one-plant two-market model with that of the multiplant model discussed in section 14-6. The two models are analyzed by slightly different applications of an identical technique.[12]

Examples of third-degree price discrimination abound. The third-degree price discrimination explains why admissions to a theater are so different for adults and children, even though each person occupies a seat regardless of his age. Different prices charged for members and nonmembers, in foreign markets and the domestic market, for male and female customers, and so on, are all examples of third-degree price discrimination.

14-8 PRICE DISCRIMINATION AS MEANS OF SURVIVAL: An Application

We have seen that a monopolist can increase his total revenue by practicing price discrimination. Thus, it is possible that a

[11]Consider the following equations, which show the relationship between MR, price, and elasticity for each of the two markets.

$$MR_1 = p_1(1 + 1/\eta_1)$$
$$MR_2 = p_2(1 + 1/\eta_2)$$

Since $MR_1 = MR_2$ in equilibrium it follows that

$$p_1(1 + 1/\eta_1) = p_2(1 + 1/\eta_2)$$

Thus,

$$\frac{p_1}{p_2} = \frac{(1 + 1/\eta_2)}{(1 + 1/\eta_1)}$$

Suppose demand is more elastic in market II than in market I; for example, η_2 is -4 and η_1 is -2. Then,

$$\frac{p_1}{p_2} = \frac{(1 - 1/4)}{(1 - 1/2)} = \frac{0.75}{0.50} = \frac{3}{2}$$

The ratio of the two prices (3/2) is such that the price in market I, where demand is less elastic, is higher than the price in market II, where demand is more elastic.

[12]This analytical similarity is even more clearly revealed by the mathematical treatment of the two models given in Appendix 14.

monopolist who cannot survive without price discrimination may recover all of his costs or may even make an economic profit if he can practice price discrimination. As a matter of fact, railroads' justification for their discriminatory rates for different goods rests precisely on such an argument.

In Figure 14-14, the curves D_1 and D_2 represent the demand curves facing the monopolist in two separate markets. The horizontal summation of the two demand curves yields the kinked demand curve, ABC. Note that the total demand curve ABC lies below the AC curve at all levels of output. If the monopolist must charge a single price in both markets, there is no way he can recover his entire cost. By charging different prices in the two markets, however, the monopolist may be able to survive and prosper. Suppose the monopolist, using the procedure shown in determining optimum outputs and prices for third-degree price discrimination,[13] sells Q_1 units at p_1 dollars per unit in market I, and Q_2 units at p_2 dollars per unit in market II. The graph shows that the average price per unit for the entire amount of output sold in the two markets, p_t dollars per unit, is higher than the average cost of production for the entire output, $Q_t = Q_1 + Q_2$. The monopolist, who would have been out of business had he charged a single price, is now receiving an economic profit.[14]

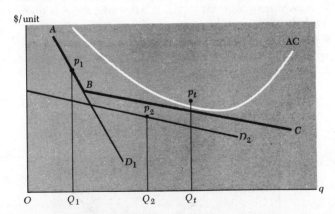

Figure 14-14 Price discrimination as a means of survival

[13]To avoid cluttering the graph, various MR curves and the MC curve are omitted from the graph. The reader should consult section 14-7 for the mechanics of third-degree price discrimination.

[14]The numerical figures used in constructing this graph are $p_1 = \$40$, $q_1 = 15$, $p_2 = \$25$, and $q_2 = 40$. Thus, the average price for the entire output is: $p_t = [(\$40 \times 15) + (\$25 \times 40)] \div 55 = \$29.09$. The average cost of producing 55 units in Figure 14-14 is lower than the average price of $29.09.

An interesting consequence of the above analysis is the possibility that those who pay the higher price under price discrimination might be paying a price lower than that which would have prevailed in the absence of price discrimination. Natural gas may be such an example. Prices paid by households for natural gas are higher than interruptible industrial rates. Suppose a uniform price is to be charged to all users, and the price paid by industrial users go up substantially. If this increase in price causes a large reduction in the amount of natural gas sold for industrial purposes, the natural gas industry may not be able to take advantage of the economies of size accruing to the industry, and the price paid by the household users may even become higher than those that prevailed under the discriminatory scheme.

14-9 REGULATION OF PUBLIC UTILITIES:
An Application

The rates charged by public utilities such as telephone, gas, and electric companies are generally regulated by a public regulatory agency. Consider the following simplified version of the regulatory problems involved. In Figure 14-15, given the revenue and cost curves, the price desired by the monopolist is p_1 dollars per unit. *However, most public utility commissions are said to establish their rates in such a way that* AR = AC. If AR = AC, there is no monopoly profit and the firm merely receives the normal or "fair" returns. In Figure 14-15, the regulated rate is p_2 dollars per unit. Note that this

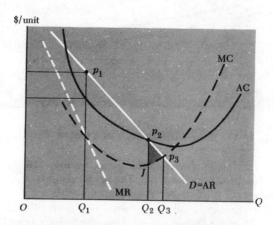

Figure 14-15 Monopoly versus regulated prices

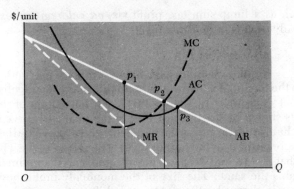

Figure 14-16   Regulated prices: another case

regulated rate forces the monopolist to lower his price and increase his output.

Assuming that the social marginal gain and the social marginal cost may be represented by the AR and MC curves, *some economists argue that the regulated rate should be p_3 dollars per unit, where the AR curve intersects the MC curve.* The increase in the net social gain brought forward by this decrease in price and increase in output is shown by the shaded area Jp_2p_3. However, in Figure 14-15, the monopolist would incur a loss at the price of p_3 dollars per unit, since this price is lower than the monopolist's average cost. This loss, in turn, would necessitate a subsidy. Since additional taxes must be collected to finance this subsidy, the effect on the resource allocation of such taxes must be considered. It is possible that this effect may greatly offset the social gain due to the AR = MC pricing. Furthermore, AR = MC pricing in Figure 14-15 means that the users of a particular good are subsidized by the society in general. Is this desirable for the society? The question cannot be answered without making a value judgment regarding the relative deservingness of the utility users and nonusers.

As an exercise the reader should examine Figure 14-16, and decide what is the best regulatory price. Is there any additional problem that arises from your choice?

14-10   THE EFFECTS OF VARIOUS TAXES ON MONOPOLY PRICE AND OUTPUT:
An Application

As applications of the model of monopoly let us examine the effects on monopoly output and price of some specific forms of taxes such as a lump-sum tax, profit tax, *ad valorem* tax, excise tax, and subsidy (that is, a negative tax).[15]

A LUMP-SUM TAX

Suppose a *lump-sum tax* of t dollars per period is imposed on the monopolist. How would this affect the monopolist's price and output decisions? In Figure 14-17, the imposition of the lump-sum tax is shown by the upward shift of the total cost curve from TC to TC': a lump-sum tax raises the height of the TC curve by the amount of the tax, regardless of the output level. The slopes of the TR and TC curves (that is, MR and MC) are not affected, and the optimal output, Q^*, remains the same. The size of the monopoly profit, however, is reduced as is shown by the downward shift in the profit curve from π to π'. In summary, the effect of a lump-sum tax is merely to reduce the monopoly profit without affecting his pricing and output decisions.

A PROFIT TAX

Suppose a tax of r percent per period is imposed on the monopoly profit. How would such a tax affect the monopolist's pricing

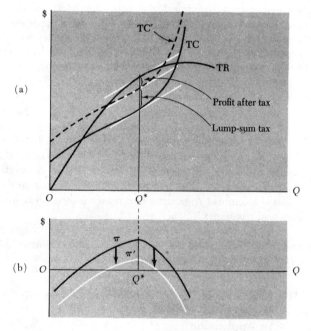

Figure 14-17 Effect of a lump-sum tax; (a) upward shift of the TC curve, (b) downward shift of the profit curve

[15]For a mathematical treatment, see Appendix 14.

and output decsions? In order to simplify our analysis, let us assume that the monopolist cannot shift such a tax at all and, therefore, the incidence of the tax is entirely on himself. Given this assumption, the monopolist who wants to maximize his after-tax profit will also maximize his pre-tax profit. Whatever profit the monopolist makes, he gets to keep $(1-r)$ times the profit. Clearly, the larger the pre-tax profit, the larger is the after-tax profit.

AN EXCISE TAX OF t DOLLARS PER UNIT

Suppose the *excise tax* of t dollars per unit is imposed on a monopolist's product. How would this affect the monopoly price and output. As shown in Figure 14-18, the imposition of an excise tax can be shown either as a downward shift in the MR curve or as an upward shift in the MC curve.[16] Either graphic method will give an identical result. An excise tax shifts the MR or MC curve and, therefore, affects the monopolist's price and output. Given the usual shapes of the revenue and cost curves (that is, a downward-sloping AR and an upward-sloping MC), the effect of an excise tax is to raise the price and reduce the output. Thus, an excise tax tends to reduce the resources flowing into the production of the taxed commodity and divert them to some other uses.

AN AD VALOREM TAX

While the excise tax is a constant sum per unit of output, *the ad valorem tax is a constant percentage of the commodity price.* Diagrammatically, this tax is represented by a shift of the demand

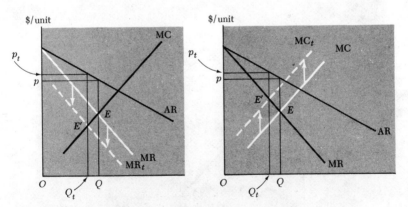

Figure 14-18   Two ways of showing the effect of an excise tax; (a) downward shift of the MR curve, (b) upward shift of the MC curve

[16]For detail, see the mathematics of an excise tax given in Appendix 14.

curve as shown in Figure 14-19. For simplicity, let us assume a linear demand function and a 50 percent *ad valorem* tax. The imposition of this tax shifts the monopoly demand curve from D to D_t: the vertical distance from the quantity axis to D_t is 50 percent of the distance to the original D, regardless of the output level. The marginal revenue curve corresponding to D_t is MR_t, which shows the additional after-tax revenue the monopolist can secure from an extra unit of sale. The equality of this MR_t and MC gives the monopoly output Q_t and the monopoly price p_t. The effect of an *ad valorem* tax is, therefore, to reduce the output and raise price. (The reader is advised to draw in the MR curve corresponding to the original D, determine the pre-tax monopoly price and output, and confirm the preceding statement regarding the effect of the *ad valorem* tax on the monopoly price and output.)

A SUBSIDY: A NEGATIVE TAX

Since *a subsidy is merely a negative tax*, no new analysis is required. If the subsidy is s dollars per unit, its effect can be studied by the technique used in analyzing the effect of the excise tax. The per-unit subsidy can be represented either as an upward shift of the MR curve or as a downward shift of the MC curve.

If the subsidy is a fixed fraction of price, its effect can be studied by the technique employed in analyzing an *ad valorem* tax. Given a linear demand curve, such a subsidy will be represented by a clockwise pivoting of the demand curve around the point at which the demand curve intersects the quantity axis.

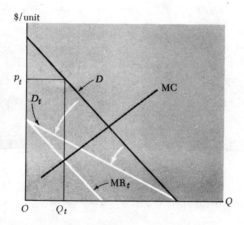

Figure 14-19 Effect of an *ad valorem* tax

APPENDIX 14

Mathematical Notes

In the text, we have offered graphical analysis of the multiplant monopolist, third-degree price discrimination, and the effects of various taxes. In this appendix, we treat the same subjects using elementary calculus. Many readers with a little calculus may find this mathematical approach easier.

MULTIPLANT MONOPOLIST

The profit function of a monopolist with a central market and two plants can be written as:

$$\pi(q) = R(q) - C_1(q_1) - C_2(q_2)$$

where $q = q_1 + q_2$. To find the maximum of this function we differentiate it partially with respect to q_1 and q_2, and set the results equal to zero.

$$\frac{\partial \pi(q)}{\partial q_1} = R'(q) \frac{\partial q}{\partial q_1} - C_1'(q_1) = 0$$

$$R'(q) = C_1'(q_1) \qquad \left[\because \frac{\partial q}{\partial q_1} = \frac{\partial(q_1 + q_2)}{\partial q_1} = 1 \right]$$

$$\frac{\partial \pi(q)}{\partial q_2} = R'(q) \frac{\partial q}{\partial q_2} - C_2'(q_2) = 0$$

$$R'(q) = C_2'(q_2) \qquad \left[\because \frac{\partial q}{\partial q_2} = \frac{\partial(q_1 + q_2)}{\partial q_2} = 1 \right]$$

Thus,

$$R'(q) = C_1'(q_1) = C_2'(q_2)$$

The last equation shows that the necessary condition for profit maximization for the two-plant monopolist is to equate his marginal revenue with his marginal costs in plant 1 and plant 2.

The second-order condition for profit maximization is given by:

$$\frac{\partial^2 \pi}{\partial q_1^2} = R''(q) - C_1''(q_1) < 0$$

$$\frac{\partial^2 \pi}{\partial q_2^2} = R''(q) - C_2''(q_2) < 0$$

The sufficient conditions for profit mazimization, therefore, require that (1) $MR = MC_1 = MC_2$ and (2) the slopes of the MC curves of both plant 1 and plant 2 be greater than that of their MR curve.

THIRD-DEGREE PRICE DISCRIMINATION

The mathematical analysis of the third-degree price discrimination model is entirely analogous to that of the multiplant monopoly model. Let the profit function of the monopolist with two markets and a central plant be given by

$$\pi(q) = R_1(q_1) + R_2(q_2) - C(q_1 + q_2)$$

Differentiating partially the above expression with respect to q_1 and q_2 and setting them equal to zero, we have

$$\frac{\partial \pi(q)}{\partial q_1} = R_1'(q_1) - C'(q_1 + q_2) = 0$$

$$R_1'(q_1) = C'(q_1 + q_2)$$

$$\frac{\partial \pi(q)}{\partial q_2} = R_2'(q_2) - C'(q_1 + q_2) = 0$$

$$R_2'(q_2) = C'(q_1 + q_2)$$

$$\therefore R_1'(q_1) = R_2'(q_2) = C'(q_1 + q_2)$$

The last equation shows that the necessary condition for profit maximization is given by $MR_1 = MR_2 = MC_t$. The reader who has difficulty in establishing the second-order condition that requires the slopes of MR_1 and MR_2 to be smaller than that of MC_t should consult the mathematics of the multiplant model.

A LUMP-SUM TAX

When a lump-sum tax of t dollars is levied, the monopolist's profit function is given by

$$\pi(q) = R(q) - C(q) - t$$

The necessary condition for profit maximization is

$$\frac{d\pi(q)}{dq} = R'(q) - C'(q) = 0$$

and

$$R'(q) = C'(q)$$

The MR = MC rule is not affected by the lump-sum tax, a constant that vanishes during the differentiation process.

A PROFIT TAX

The monopolist's after-tax profit function is given by

$$\pi(q) = (1 - r)[R(q) - C(q)], \, 0 < r < 1$$

where r is the profit tax rate. The output that maximizes the after-tax profit is given by

$$\frac{d\pi(q)}{dq} = (1 - r)R'(q) - (1 - r)C'(q) = 0$$

Thus,

$$R'(q) = C'(q), \text{ since } (1 - r) \neq 0$$

The profit tax does not change the MR = MC decision rule.

AN EXCISE TAX

When there is an excise tax of t dollars per unit, the monopolist's profit function is given by

$$\pi(q) = R(q) - C(q) - tq$$

The first-order condition for the profit maximization is

$$\frac{d\pi(q)}{dq} = R'(q) - C'(q) - t = 0$$

Therefore,

$$R'(q) - t = C'(q) \text{ or } R'(q) = C'(q) + t$$

Clearly, the MR = MC rule must be modified to reflect the existence of the excise tax. Furthermore, the two alternative expressions in the last equations make it clear that an excise tax may be treated either as lowering the MR or as raising the MC.

AN AD VALOREM TAX

The monopoly profit function, when there is an *ad valorem* tax of r percent, is given by

$$\pi(q) = (1 - r)R(q) - C(q),\ 0 < r < 1$$

The profit maximizing output is

$$\frac{d\pi(q)}{dq} = (1 - r)R'(q) - C'(q) = 0$$

and

$$(1 - r)R'(q) = C'(q)$$

The monopolist determines his optimal price-quantity combination by equating his MC with his after-tax MR, that is, the portion of MR he is allowed to retain.

A SUBSIDY OF s DOLLARS PER UNIT

Given an s dollar per unit subsidy, the monopolist's profit function is given by

$$\pi(q) = R(q) + sq - C(q)$$
$$\pi'(q) = R'(q) + s - C'(q) = 0$$
$$R'(q) + s = C'(q) \text{ or } R'(q) = C'(q) - s$$

Thus, the monopolist equates his marginal cost to the sum of the marginal revenue and the subsidy per unit.

A SUBSIDY OF r PERCENT ON THE VALUE OF SALE

Given an r percent subsidy on the value of sale, the monopolist's profit function is given by

$$\pi(q) = (1 + r)R(q) - C(q)$$
$$\pi'(q) = (1 + r)R'(q) - C'(q) = 0$$
$$(1 + r)R'(q) = C'(q)$$

Thus, the monopolist equates his marginal cost to his marginal receipt including the r percent subsidy on the value of sale.

EXERCISES 14

Price and Output under Pure Monopoly

14-1 Consider a florist who is selling Mother's Day corsages. It is getting late in the afternoon of the day before Mother's Day. The florist estimates the demand for his corsages for the rest of the day as follows:

Price	$3.00	$2.50	$2.00	$1.50	$1.00	$.50
Quantity	30	50	70	100	200	300

1. Assume that the corsages are specially designed for Mother's Day and cannot be used for any other purpose, that the florist paid $1.25 for each corsage, and that he has 300 corsages on hand. Given these assumptions, what price and quantity should the florist choose in order to maximize his profit?
2. Does your answer to (1) suggest any generalization about the role of a *sunk cost* (cost that has already been incurred) in making decisions in the market period or the very short run?

14-2 The following table shows a portion of a revenue and cost schedule for a monopolist.

Output	Price	Total revenue	Total cost	Marginal revenue	Marginal cost
. . .	. . .	. . .	. . .	. . .	. . .
3	$114	$342	$355	$74	($)
4	104	416	368	54	13
5	94	470	381	( )	19
6	84	504	400	14	31
7	74	518	431		

319

1. Fill in the missing blanks of the above table.
2. In perfect competition, price is always equal to marginal revenue. Why is marginal revenue always less than price in an imperfectly competitive market?
3. What are the two possible ways to determine the profit-maximizing output, given the above table?
4. What is the maximum profit that can be secured?

14-3 A monopolist's marginal revenue and marginal cost are given by the following equations:

$$MR = 40 - q$$
$$MC = 50 - 2q, \quad q \leqslant 25$$

1. What is the profit-maximizing output? Why?
2. Graph the MR and MC functions and check whether your algebraic solution in (1) is reasonable.
3. Give the sufficient conditions for profit maximization (for the usual interior solution as opposed to the corner or border solution you had in the current problem.)
4. Restate the MR = MC rule (the necessary condition) to take care of the discrete cases or corner solution cases in which the MR = MC rule must be slightly modified.
5. Assuming that there is no fixed cost, what is the maximum profit the monopolist can earn?
6. If the monopolist's fixed cost is $200, would it change his short-run profit-maximizing output? Why or why not?
7. If the monopolist's MR function was given by $MR = 30 - q$, what is his profit-maximizing output? Why?

14-4 Given linear revenue and cost curves, prove that the long-run equilibrium output of a perfectly competitive industry is twice that of a monopolist.

14-5 The cost and revenues curves of a public utility company are given in Figure 14-20.

1. What are the profit-maximizing output and price for the monopolist?
2. What is the price that will make the monopolist break even?
3. Now consider the cost and benefit to society of expanding the monopoly output from Q_2 to Q_3.

   a. Which area shows the additional cost to society?
   b. Which area shows the additional benefit to the society?

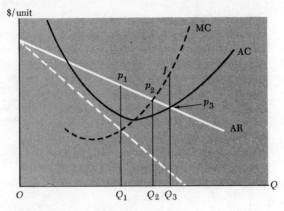

$/unit

Figure 14-20

c. Which area, therefore, shows the net loss to society?

d. State explicitly the assumptions you have relied on in answering the above three questions.

4. If you are the regulator of this public utility, where would you set the price? Why?

14-6 The following table shows the weekly advertising rates charged by a small college newspaper.

Price per column Inch	Size of advertisement (column inches)
$1.00	under 15
.90	16 to 20
.85	21 to 25
.80	26 to 30
.75	31 or more

1. Define precisely what is meant by price discrimination?

2. Is the above advertising rate schedule an example of price discrimination? Why or why not?

CHAPTER FIFTEEN

INDUSTRIAL CONCENTRATION AND OLIGOPOLY

We now leave the extreme worlds of perfect competition on one hand and monopoly on the other, and enter the imperfectly competitive world of oligopoly and monopolistic competition.

Oligopoly is the market structure in which a few sellers who clearly recognize their mutual interdependence produce the bulk of the market output. The diversity of interrelationships that exist among oligopolistic firms makes it extremely difficult to construct a general theory of oligopoly. As a matter of fact, there is as yet no such thing as a general theory of oligopoly. The literature of oligopoly to date consists of various models that analyze some specific aspects of oligopolistic behavior, such as price leadership, collusion, market sharing, and price rigidity. Our study of oligopoly in this chapter must also proceed in terms of more or less isolated models. But before we start examining specific oligopoly models, let us obtain an overall view of (1) industrial concentration in the American economy, which reveals the oligopolistic structure of many markets, and (2) various barriers to entry, which contribute to the continuing existence of oligopoly or monopoly.

15-1 THE MEANING OF INDUSTRY

In discussing oligopoly, it is difficult to avoid using the term *industry*: we talk of the automobile, cigarette, and·cereal industries. Modern economists frequently use the word *industry* with reference to an oligopoly (or even monopolistic competition) because the term *industry* is often defined not only as a set of firms producing a homogeneous product (the traditional narrow definition) but also as *a set of firms producing close substitutes* (more general definition required for empirical works). For empirical works (in which we are frequently faced with differentiated goods), we have little choice but to adopt the latter definition and interpret the meaning of the word *close* to suit research problems at hand. Thus, an industry may be defined very broadly for one purpose, and defined rather narrowly for another. In practice, many empirical workers rely on the Census Bureau's *Standard Industrial Classification*, SIC, which classifies industries at various levels of aggregation. The largest SIC category is the two-digit level, which produces between 10 and 99 industries. The three-digit category gives classification between 100 and 999, and the four-digit classification allows industry divisions ranging from 1,000 to 9,999.[1] For example, the four-digit classification gives such industrial categories as primary aluminum, flat glass, and motor vehicles, shown in Table 15-1.

15-2 CONCENTRATION RATIOS

One of the most frequently used measures of industrial concentration is the so-called four-firm (or eight-firm) concentration ratio. *A four-firm concentration ratio shows the percentage of the total, say, sales provided by the four largest firms in the industry.* Similarly, an eight-firm concentration ratio reveals the market share (the percentage of the total) provided by the eight largest firms. The yardstick used to measure concentration ratios or market shares may be sales, employment, value of shipments, or assets. The most frequently used concentration ratios are based on shipment figures. The Census Bureau's recent study reported the concentration ratios (based on value of shipments) for U.S. manufacturing industries in 1967, a few of which are reproduced in Table 15-1. This table clearly demonstrates the importance of large firms in many America industries. In the flat glass industry, the four largest firms supplied 94 percent of the value of shipment in 1967, while the eight largest firms supplied 98 percent of the total value of shipment. Aluminum, motor vehicles, cereals, cigarettes, etc., also represent industries with rather high concentration ratios. On the other hand, dresses and costume jewelry show low concentration ratios indicating the importance of design and style differences in those industries.

A more comprehensive view of industrial concentration is provided by Table 15-2, which shows frequency distributions of four-firm concentration ratios compiled from *1967 Census of Manufactures.* According to this frequency distribution, the largest four

[1]For detail, see *Standard Industrial Classification* (Washington, D.C.: U.S. Government Printing Office, Bureau of the Budget, 1945).

Table 15-1 Concentration in Selected Industries, 1967

INDUSTRY	Value of Shipments Made by (percent)		Number of Firms in Industry
	4 Firms	8 Firms	
Primary aluminum	(D)	100	10
Flat glass	94	98	39
Motor vehicles	92	98	107
Cereal preparations	88	97	30
Cigarettes	81	100	8
Petroleum & coal products	82	92	38
Sewing machines	81	92	83
Tire and inner tubes	70	78	119
Soap and detergents	70	78	599
Aircraft	69	89	91
Radio and TV receiving sets	49	69	303
Bread, cake and related products	26	38	3,445
Costume jewelry	22	31	763
Women's & Misses' dresses	7	9	5,008

(D) Withheld to avoid disclosing figures for individual companies.
Source: *1967 Census of Manufactures*, Vol. 1, Sec. 9

firms had 30 percent or more of the market shares in about 61 percent of the manufacturing industries. In approximately 6.4 percent of the manufacturing industries, the concentration ratios were 80 percent

Table 15-2 Distribution of Manufacturing Value of Shipments by Four-Firm Concentration Ratio, 1967

CONCENTRATION RATIO (PERCENT ACCOUNTED FOR BY FOUR FIRMS)	Number of Industries	Percent of Total	Cumulative Percentage
Under 20 percent	66	17.0%	100.0
20–29	86	22.1	83.0
30–39	70	18.0	60.9
40–49	49	12.6	42.9
50–59	37	9.5	30.3
60–69	34	8.7	20.8
70–79	22	5.7	12.1
80–89	16	4.1	6.4
90 or more	9	2.3	2.3
TOTAL	389	100.0	

Source: *1967 Census of Manufactures*, Vol. 1, Sec. 9.

or more. The median concentration ratio was 36.6 percent. The table does show that large firms predominate many markets in the American economy. But at the same time, it shows that concentration ratios vary widely from industry to industry, and there are industries in which no large firms possess dominating influences.

Clearly there are substantial variations in concentration ratios among different industries. Do the performances of the industries in which concentration ratios are high differ substantially from those with low concentration ratios? Efforts have been made to answer such a question.[2] For instance, Bain found a significant difference between profit rates in industries with eight-firm concentration ratios of above 70 percent and profit rates in industries having lower concentration ratios. Stigler also found a relationship, though a weak one, between concentration and profitability when the four-firm concentration ratios exceeded 80 percent. David Schwartzman distinguished industries in which the four-firm concentration ratios in terms of employment were 50 percent or more from other industries in which the ratios were less than 50 percent. He found a significantly higher ratio of price to average variable cost, and estimated the effect of higher concentration on price was at 8.3 percent of average variable cost.

What is happening to concentration ratios through time? Obviously, different industries undergo different changes. For instance, the Aluminum Company of America monopolized aluminum until World War II, but the industry is now an oligopoly with such competitors as Kaiser and Reynolds. On the other hand, concentration has increased substantially in retailing with the growth of retail chains, discount stores, and supermarkets. According to a study based on the Census Bureau data, the four-firm concentration ratios increased, remained more or less unchanged, and declined in 21 percent, 37.7 percent, and 22 percent, respectively, of the American manufacturing industries between 1947 and 1958.[3] Thus, many changes in industrial concentration seemed to have canceled each other out, and left concentration in 1947 and 1958 just about equal. Richard Low summarizes the present state of our knowledge of the trend in concentration by saying, "either concentration has declined

[2]This summary is based on James W. McKie, "Market Structure and Function: Performance versus Behavior," in J. W. Markham and G. F. Papanek (eds.), *Industrial Organization and Economic Development: In Honor of E. S. Mason* (Boston: Houghton Mifflin, 1970), pp. 3–25.

[3]Morris A. Adelman, "Monopoly and Concentration: Comparisons in Time and Space," in Richard E. Low (ed.) *The Economics of Antitrust* (Englewood Cliffs, N.J.: Prentice-Hall, 1968), p. 50. This is quoted in Richard E. Low, *Modern Economic Organization* (Homewood, Ill.: Irwin, 1970) p. 100.

over time or it has remained relatively constant, probably with some minor cycles along the way."[4]

Though concentration ratios provide useful concise measures of industrial concentration, their limitations must be noted.[5]

1. Industries listed in the Census Bureau's *Standard Industrial Classification* are loose constellations. Not all products in them actually compete, and sometimes products in different industrial classifications may compete with each other, for example, wool yarn and synthetic fibers.
2. Imports are not included. Imports may be an important source of competition in many industries, for example, chemicals, cameras, radios, typewriters, television sets, and clocks and watches.
3. The ratio describes concentration at the national markets but says nothing about regional or local markets. "In the case of bread, a Congressional committee reported the top four companies had 20 percent of sales nationally, but in 23 states their sales exceeded 50 percent, and in particular cities the level of concentration ran still higher."[6]
4. Concentration ratios provide no information on the relative distribution of firms at the top. For example, industry A and B both have a four-firm concentration of 80 percent. But in A, each of the four firms may hold approximately similar market shares; while in B, the top firm may have 50 percent and the remaining three firms divide 30 percent. The competitive characters of industries A and B, needless to say, differ significantly.
5. One must go beyond the four-firm concentration ratio. For instance, studies show that where the industry share held by the second four firms more closely approximates that of the first four, competition will be keener and profit margins of leading firms lower.
6. The significance of a given concentration ratio varies depending on whether the industry is growing or decaying. Since a growing market usually offers opportunities for new firms to enter, and reduce the leader's market share, concentration that persists in such an industry would be of more concern.

[4]*Ibid.*, p. 102.

[5]William N. Leonard, *Business Size, Market Power, and Public Policy* (New York: Crowell, 1969), pp. 59–60.

[6]Daniel B. Suits, *Principles of Economics* (New York: Harper Row, 1970), p. 359.

Concentration ratios are quite valuable measures in helping us place where a given industry belongs in the continuum of the market structures from perfect competition to monopoly, *provided* we recognize the limitations involved and refuse to be guided blindly by the simplistic appearance of numerical figures.

15-3 BARRIERS TO ENTRY

The ease or difficulty with which a new firm can enter a market is an important determinant of market structure. Monopoly or oligopoly can persist only if there are some barriers to the rate of entry. Furthermore, the actual or potential entry of new firms influences price, product, and promotion strategies of the existing firms. Thus, barriers to entry is an important topic in economics. However, what constitute important barriers to entry is a difficult question for which economists have no common answers: definitive answers must await more empirical investigations. Among the barriers to entry cited frequently in economic literature are economies of large-scale production, patents and franchises, control of key resources, product differentiation, large financial requirements, secrecy, and charging prices not high enough to attract a major new entrant into the market.

ECONOMIES OF SIZE

In section 11-3, we noted that the nature of the production function and the accompanying cost curves compared with the size of the market has an important bearing on the nature of the market structure. Let us now see how economies of size become a barrier to entry. In Figure 15-1, the curves labeled D, $\frac{1}{2}D$, and $\frac{1}{3}D$ represent the total, one-half, and one-third of the market demand. Suppose the long-run average cost curve of the firm in this industry (and that of any prospective entrant) is represented by LAC. Given the market demand, D, and the LAC curve, it is clear that only one firm can operate in this industry. If there were two firms, assuming that they share the market equally, both will lose. Thus, the economies of size and the nature of demand that exist in this industry preclude an additional entrant.

If the relevant LAC curve of the firm is LAC′, two or three firms could have profitably shared the market; since the LAC′ curve intersects the $\frac{1}{2}D$ and $\frac{1}{3}D$ curves. Similarly, if the market demand curve were to lie substantially to the right and above, more firms could have profitably entered even if the cost curve is shown by LAC.

Economies of size are important barriers to entry in public utilities such as electricity, gas, water, and telephone. On the other hand, in many manufacturing industries they may constitute a rather

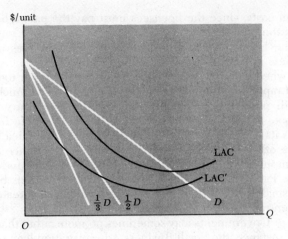

Figure 15-1   Shape and position of LAC relative to the market demand as an entry barrier

unimportant barrier to entry. For instance, J. S. Bain showed that the optimal plant size is usually a rather small fraction of the total market demand.[7]

GOVERNMENT AND ENTRY BARRIERS

Governments can influence entry conditions through franchises, patents, subsidies, and import quotas. *Franchises — privileges to do something otherwise legally prohibited, such as the right to operate a bank or a radio station* — are important barriers in various utilities such as electricity, gas, water, and telephone. They are also important barriers in such areas as radio and television, banking, transportation (airlines, truck and bus lines, and taxi), funeral homes, and some professions.

Patent is the exclusive right to a process or product granted to an inventor for a period of 17 years. It gives the inventor the right to exclude others from his discovery or to license them on his own terms. Patents, needless to say, are intended to promote inventions by rewarding the inventors. A patent on a new product may lead to monopoly or oligopoly. Aluminum, rayon, and ethyl gasoline were among such examples. More frequently, patents on new products create differentiated products. Patents on new processes affect

[7]"Economies of Scale, Concentration, and Entry," *American Economic Review*, pp. 15–39. March 1954.

production costs, since the licensees must pay the patent holder for the use of the processes.

Economists still disagree among themselves as to the effectiveness of patents in preventing new entries. Some economists question whether the 17-year lifetime of a patent is not too long in the age of rapid technological changes; they feel that a much shorter period will provide a sufficient inducement, reduce entry barriers, and promote faster economic growth. Another debatable feature of a patent is its exclusive nature. Many economists argue that the right to exclude others should be eliminated from patent, since royalties under compulsory licensing should provide sufficient inducement or reward. Patent harrassment may also become a serious barrier to entry for small firms: large firms holding patents can threaten small potential entrants with costly legal suits.[8]

Governments may sometimes promote rather than hinder entry. For instance, the Small Business Administration loan programs promoted the entry of small business firms into markets. It is well known that the federal government established Kaiser and Reynolds in primary aluminum by selling them government-built aluminum plants for less than their original cost. Governments have also helped many new entrants in various professions through their fellowships and research grants.

CONTROL OF KEY RESOURCES

Key resource(s) needed for a product may be controlled by the established firm. If the prospective new entrant cannot obtain the input or any suitable substitute for it, he is effectively excluded from the market. Alcoa had such a position with regard to bauxite. Other well-known examples in which control of inputs poses as the major barrier to entry include diamonds, nitrates, nickel, and sulfur.

The discovery of new domestic or foreign sources for the key resource involved may lead to new entry. For instance, the sulfur industry saw a major new entry as the Mexican sulfur was developed.

Again, how important the role of key raw materials is in preventing entry is debatable. Scientific progress may turn formerly uneconomical inputs into usable substitutes, a better substitute product may be developed using other inputs, synthetic inputs may be developed, and so on.

PRODUCT DIFFERENTIATION

We have already mentioned the possibility of patenting a new product design. Thus, the control of superior product design by the existing firms through patents may deter the entry of new firms

[8]See Richard E. Low, *Modern Economic Organization*, p. 199, and the references cited therein.

into the market. Similarly, the established brand names and reputations of quality and service associated with them may make it difficult for a newcomer to enter the market and establish himself. The newcomer must overcome consumer attachment to established brands, and obtaining a large sum of financial resources needed for such an endeavor may be more difficult and expensive for a newcomer than for the established firms.

In his classic study of entry, J. S. Bain noted that product differentiation was a major entry barrier in such consumer-goods industries as gasoline, cigarettes, distilled liquor, fountain pens, and automobiles. He estimated that a new entrant's product had to sell from 10 to 25 percent less than that of a well-established brand in order to overcome the brand advantage.[9]

Again the empirical importance of product differentiation as an entry barrier is unsettled. For one thing, product differentiation is hard to quantify. There are even cases in which product differentiation may facilitate entry. For instance, a slightly improved or differentiated product may be able to capture a previously ignored submarket, such as teenagers' magazines, men's cologne, college packs, and MBA (Master of Business Administration) magazines.

LARGE FINANCIAL REQUIREMENTS

A prospective new entrant may be barred from an industry because it requires a large financial resource, which a newcomer finds it difficult to secure. Borrowing a large sum of money is rather difficult for a newcomer and often is much more expensive than it is for a firm with a long-established history of successful operation. Equity financing is also difficult or costly for a newcomer who is not well known in the capital market. Frequently, automobile and cigarette industries are cited as examples of the industries in which large financial requirements prevent new entrants.

Again it is not clear how important the financial requirement barrier to entry may be. The development of large conglomerate firms—which are engaged in business activities in many different industries—may significantly lower the financial requirement barrier to entry. Frequently, a large conglomerate firm may be able to acquire large financial resources needed at a cost comparable to the "ins" of the industry it plans to enter.

SECRECY

An inventor of a new product or process may decide to keep his invention secret rather than having it patented. If he is successful in preserving the secrecy, and therefore, in preventing (or

[9]*Barriers to New Competition* (Cambridge, Mass.: Harvard University Press, 1956), pp. 127–129.

retarding the rate of) entry, his rate of return may be higher than the case in which he shared his invention with others and received royalties. Ingredients for Coca-Cola are cited as an example of such secrecy. Again, the status of secrecy as a barrier to entry is subject to question. The reader, for instance, will find no difficulty in citing strong competition Coca-Cola faces from other close substitutes.

LIMIT PRICING

An industry in which the rate of return is substantially higher than in other industries obviously invites prospective entries. Thus, established firms in an industry may keep their prices (and accordingly, their rate of profits) relatively low with the hope of hiding the profitability of the industry and staving off prospective new entrants. *Limit pricing refers to this practice of charging a price lower than the profit-maximizing one in an attempt to discourage new entries. The limit price refers to the maximum price the established firms believe they can charge without inducing a significant entry.*

It sounds reasonable that existing firms should take the threat of entry into consideration in establishing their prices. However, the questions of how widespread is the practice of limit pricing and how important it is in discouraging entry are still unsettled.

The factors contributing to entry barriers are closely related to those contributing to industrial concentrations. Just as efforts were made to relate the performance of an industry to the level of concentration, efforts have been made to relate the performance of an industry (such as the rate of returns) to the difficulty of entry. For instance, a recent study by H. M. Mann shows that the average rates of profit in industries with very high barriers to entry (nickel, sulphur, ethical drugs, flat glass, automobile, cigarettes, and liquor) were, on the average, substantially higher than in industries with moderate to low or substantial barriers.[10]

In the preceding two sections, we have examined industrial concentrations that show the empirical significance of oligopoly, and entry barriers that tend to perpetuate oligopoly and monopoly. It is now time for us to move on to the study of some specific oligopoly models.

15-4 PRICE LEADERSHIP

Oligopolists are keenly aware of their mutual interdependence. An oligopolist's pricing decision must, therefore, take into account likely reactions of his rivals and how they may affect his

[10]"A Note on Barriers to Entry and Long-Run Profitability," *The Antitrust Bulletin*, Winter 1969, pp. 845–849.

profit. A careless pricing decision may lead to cut-throat price competition, which lowers everyone's profit. One way to avoid such price competition and establish a price acceptable to all oligopolists in the market is to rely on the price leadership (or followership) arrangement, in which firms in the market follow the prices set by the leader. There are two major variants of price leadership, the dominant firm model and the barometric firm model.

THE DOMINANT FIRM MODEL

The assumptions of the *dominant firm model* are as follows: (1) The industry consists of one dominant firm and many small firms. (2) The dominant firm sets the market price and allows the small firms to sell all they wish at this price. The dominant firm's market share is given by what is left. (3) Small firms, realizing their subordinate positions, behave as if they are perfect competitors. They sell quantities at which their marginal costs equal the price set by the dominant firm.

Given the above behavioral assumptions, the market demand curve, the supply curves of the small firms, and the marginal cost curve of the dominant firm, a simple graphic model that produces a determinate solution can be easily constructed. In Figure 15-2, let *DD'* show the industry demand curve. The supply curve of all small firms is labeled Σmc since it is obtained by summing horizontally the marginal cost curves of each firm. By assumption, small firms can sell all they wish at the price set by the dominant firm, and the dominant

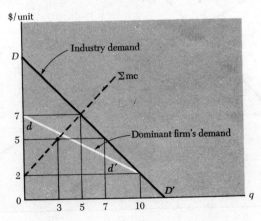

Figure 15-2 Derivation of the dominant firm's demand curve

firm takes the rest. Thus, the dominant firm's quantity demanded, q_d, is given by:

$$q_d = \begin{pmatrix} \text{total quantity} \\ \text{demanded} \\ \text{in the market} \end{pmatrix} - \begin{pmatrix} \text{quantity supplied} \\ \text{by all} \\ \text{small firms} \end{pmatrix}$$

If the price is $7, the small firms supply 5 units and the dominant firm's q_d is zero. At the price of $5, small firms supply 3 units and the dominant firm's q_d is 4 units. If the price is as low as $2, small firms cease to supply any, and the dominant firm's q_d is 10 units – the total quantity demanded in the market. The dominant firm's demand curve, $dd'D'$, shows the locus of price-quantity relationships obtained in the above manner; it is attained by substracting horizontally the Σmc curve from the market demand curve, DD'.

Now we are ready to explain how the dominant firm selects the price that is most profitable to itself. In Figure 15-3, DD', $dd'D'$, and Σmc curves show the market demand, the dominant firm's demand, and the small firms' combined supply, respectively. The

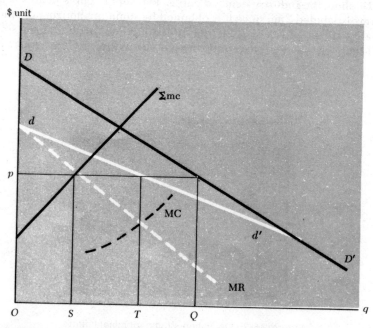

Figure 15-3 Price leadership by the dominant firm

dominant firm's marginal revenue curve that corresponds to its demand curve is labeled MR. The marginal cost curve of the dominant firm is labeled MC. Given these revenue and cost curves, the profit-maximizing output and price for the dominant firm are T units and p dollars. At this price set by the dominant firm, the small firms are willing to sell S units. By the very constuction of the graph, S units are equal to TQ units, and the sum of the quantities sold by the dominant and small firms (T plus S units) is equal to the total quantity demanded in the market, Q units, at the price of p dollars per unit.

The reader may have noticed that the neat determinate solution of the dominant firm model is obtained by assuming away the oligopolistic interdependence. Since small firms are assumed to be completely subservient and behave like perfect competitors, the single dominant firm has no rivals whose strategies and counter-strategies will influence its profitability. However, some variants of the current model can be constucted. For instance, there may be a few major firms and a number of small firms in the industry. The dominant firms as a group may then establish the price at which they will allow all small firms to sell whatever they wish. Or the model may be modified to allow differences in product quality, and a pattern of prices reflecting the differences in quality may be introduced. Sometimes, the small firms as a group in the above illustrations are said to form the *competitive fringe* of the industry.

THE BAROMETRIC FIRM MODEL

Another form of price leadership is barometric price leadership, in which a firm initiates well-publicized price changes that are generally followed by other firms in the industry. The price leader need not be the largest firm. For example, "International Paper was for a long period the price leader in newsprint although it produced less than one-seventh of the output, and it was succeeded in this role by Great Northern, a small firm."[11] The price change announced by the leader serves as a "barometer" that reflects the changing demand and supply conditions in the market. The barometric price leader does not act to impose its decisions on others but rather indicates price changes that seem desirable in the market. Unless the price leader sets the price that reflects, with reasonable accuracy, the demand and supply conditions in the industry, it is not likely to continue its role as the barometric leader.

According to a recent study, price leadership in large-scale industry has developed from the earlier experience of cut-throat

[11]George J. Stigler, "The Kinky Oligopoly Demand Curve and Rigid Prices," in G. J. Stigler and K. E. Boulding (eds.), *Readings in Price Theory* (Homewood, Ill.: Irwin, 1952), p. 431.

competition and accompanying violent fluctuations in price and earnings. Price leadership helps avoid such experience by introducing well-publicized systematic price changes that reflect the changing market conditions.[12]

SIGNIFICANCE OF PRICE LEADERSHIP

Price leadership has been observed quite frequently in many American industries. For instance, Kaplan, Dirlam, and Lanzillotti cite the following firms, which frequently played the role of price leader: U.S. Steel, Esso Standard (gasoline), A & P (retail grocery).[13] The same study cites Goodyear Tire and Rubber, National Steel, Kroger (retail grocery), and Gulf Oil (gasoline) as price followers.[14] In the case of aluminum, the same study reveals that the role of price leadership frequently shifted among Alcoa, Reynolds, and Kaiser.[15]

According to Kaplan, Dirlam, and Lanzillotti, corporate managers justified their price leadership arrangements on such grounds as price stability, customers' perference for stable prices, and selected prices being consistent with oligopolists' profit goals at more or less normal capacities.[16]

15-5 CARTELS

When there are a few important firms in the industry that recognize their mutual interdependence, there is a strong temptation to collude in order to lessen competition, lessen uncertainty, lessen new entry, and increase profit. The form of collusion may range all the way from mere "gentlemen's agreement" to explicit collusion spelling out various details.

A *cartel is a collusive arrangement among firms designed to limit competition.* Since the passage of the Sherman Antitrust Act (1890), cartels have been illegal in the United States. Before then, collusive arrangements that fixed prices were quite common in many U.S. industries. Even since the passage of the Sherman Act, not a few illegal collusive agreements among firms have been detected. In many European countries and Japan, a cartel is legal and a rather common arrangement. Though open or secret collusive agreements provide the best examples of cartels, we may consider as cartels such

---

[12]A. D. H. Kaplan, J. B. Dirlam, and R. F. Lanzillotti, *Pricing in Big Business* (Washington, D.C.: Brookings Institutions, 1958), pp. 269–272.
[13]*Ibid.*, Part I.
[14]*Ibid.*, pp. 201–207.
[15]*Ibid.*, p. 32.
[16]*Ibid.*, pp. 271–272.

diverse groups as trade associations, labor unions, professional groups, and agricultural cooperatives.

The two most important means of reducing competition available to a cartel are price fixing and establishment of production and marketing quotas.

PRICE FIXING BY A CARTEL

Suppose a group of firms joins in a cartel in order to reduce price competition and maximize *their joint profit*. Assuming that the product is a homogeneous good, what is the price that maximizes the total cartel profit? The answer to this question is quite simple. In Figure 15-4, the market demand and marginal revenue curve facing the cartel are labeled AR and MR. If we assume that input prices are not affected by the industry output rate, the industry's MC curve is obtained by horizontally summing all firms' MC curves. The curve thus attained is labeled "cartel's MC." By equating the cartel's MR and MC, the profit-maximizing price and output for the cartel, p° and Q°, are readily established.[17] Basically this is a simple monopoly solution, since the firms colluding as a cartel are acting to maximize their joint profits.

The above analysis hides the real difficulty involved in the solution, which is the problem of distributing the total profit

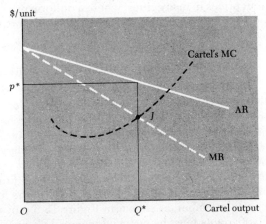

Figure 15-4   Joint profit maximization by a cartel

[17]This solution implies that the total output is allocated among member firms in such a way that each produces the quantity at which its MC equals the cartel MR which is $Q^{\circ}J$ dollars in Figure 15-4. See section 14-6.

among cartel members. If each firm produced the output at which its marginal cost equals the cartel marginal revenue, and were allowed to keep all profit it generates, the low-cost firm would end up with the bulk of profit. This solution is clearly not acceptable to high-cost firms. No simple solution to the problem of distributing profit among cartel members exists; the actual distribution among cartel members depends on their relative bargaining powers, influenced by such diverse factors as production costs, financial strengths, consumer attachment to each producer's brand, and each firm's ability to inflict damages to others by refusing to join the cartel.

Cartel price fixing may take the so-called *loose* form, in which member firms are allowed to sell all they can at the price established by the cartel management. Under this arrangement, firms may compete in terms of services, advertising, etc., but not in terms of price. Note that the Retail Price Maintenance, or *Fair Trade* Law established a loose cartel. In states where this law was effective, retailers could not sell the covered merchandise at prices lower than the manufacturers' suggested retail prices.[18] Thus, firms competed in terms of services, guarantees, advertising, and easier credit. In other cases, a loose cartel may impose restrictions on some nonprice competition. For instance, the Code of Ethics of the Certified Public Accountants prohibits its members from advertising themselves or submitting a competitive bid for a job. Lawyers and physicians also have similar arrangements.

Cartel price-fixing arrangements may be *formal,* as in the case of haircut prices in many cities, where a uniform price is charged; or it may be *informal,* as in the case of medical doctors who charge similar prices for office visits.

SALES QUOTA ESTABLISHMENT BY A CARTEL

In its effort to avoid the rigors of competition, a cartel may establish a sales quota for each of its members. Consider a competitive industry in which there are n firms that sell a homogeneous product and have an identical cost curve. As shown in Figure 15-5, each of the n firms is supplying q units where its marginal cost is equal to the price established by the market, p dollars per unit. The total industry output is n times q units. Now let the n firms combine in a cartel in which each is given an equal share of the total market, q units per cartel member, as shown in Figure 15-6. Any change in a cartel member's quota must be matched by equal changes in all other members' quotas; that is, any output change will be an industry-wide change that affects price. Thus, a cartel member, unlike the perfectly competitive firm, perceives its demand curve as sloping downward

[18] In many states, however, the law was not effectively enforced.

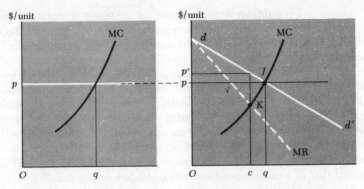

Figure 15-5 Price and output of a competitive firm

Figure 15-6 Price and output of a cartel member

to the right. Given the downward-sloping demand curve, *dd'* in Figure 15-6, the profit-maximizing output for the representative cartel member is *c* units where its MR equals its MC. His price must be raised to *p'*. Therefore, the cartel establishes each member's quota as *c* units and sets the price at *p'* dollars per unit. The immediate effect of forming a cartel, thus, is to reduce the industry output from *nq* to *nc* units and raise the price and profit of its members.

The above simplistic model of establishing quotas, however, does not apply in most real cases: the products may be differentiated, various firms' cost curves may differ substantially, and when there are a large number of firms an agreement may be hard, if not impossible, to come by. Indeed, there is yet no deterministic solution to the problem of establishing quotas among member firms. The final agreement that can be reached depends largely on such factors as various member firms' relative positions in the cartel and their bargaining power and skill. Some of the bases on which quotas among firms are established include recorded *sales volumes* in the past, the estimated *production capacities,* and *geographical areas.* Complications, however, abound. Past sales volumes can differ substantially depending on the base period chosen. Cartel members may overexpand their capacities in order to increase their quotas. Geographical division of the domestic or world market is feasible only if there is a very small number of large firms in the cartel.

THE TRANSIENCE OF CARTELS

Unless a cartel is sanctioned legally, the life of a cartel is likely to be unstable and transient for a multitude of reasons, some of which are given below.

Free-riding firms. There is a strong temptation for a firm to stay out of a cartel. Let us refer to Figure 15-7 and see how a firm may reap a greater profit than a cartel member by staying out of the cartel arrangement.

Suppose there are a large number of firms in a cartel. A firm that refuses to join the cartel reasons that, since it is a rather unimportant part of the total industry, it can sell whatever it wishes at the going price set by the cartel. In Figure 15-7, the price and output of a cartel member are shown by p and C units. A firm that decides to "free ride" the cartel arrangement, however, can sell F units (where its MC equals the cartel price p), and its total profit will exceed that of a cartel member by the shaded area, JKL.

Since free-riders get more profit, there is a strong temptation to become free-riders. But too many free-riders will destroy the cartel. Clearly, a cartel is difficult to form and maintain if there are a large number of firms. If there are only a few firms, no firm can be a free-rider with impunity.

New Entrants. Firms that can enter a cartelized industry without joining the cartel can enjoy the advantage accruing to the free-riding firm discussed above. This being the case, a cartel will be very short-lived in an industry for which there are no significant entry barriers.

Chiselers. There is a strong temptation for a cartel member to give a secret price concession or to violate the quota agreement. For example, consider a cartel member who gives a secret price concession to a few of its customers. In Figure 15-8, the firm is originally selling C units at the cartel price of p dollars per unit. Now the firm that has a secret price concession in mind visualizes the

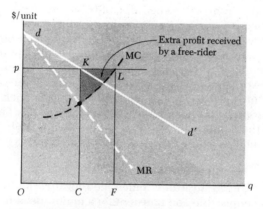

Figure 15-7 A free-riding firm

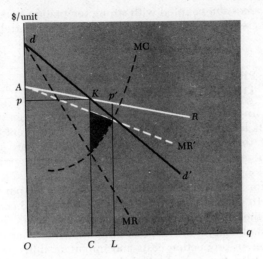

Figure 15-8 Secret price concession by a cartel member

demand facing its product (when it alone offers a secret price cut to a few of its customers) to be given by the gray line *AR* going through point *K*. Comparing his newly perceived MR curve, *MR'*, and his MC curve, the firm sees the possibility of increasing its profit by the shaded area. If this firm were to succeed in lowering its price secretly to *Lp'* dollars per unit, its sales would expand to *L* units per period and its profit would increase by the shaded area per period. However, such secret price concession does not go long unnoticed. As the number of chiselers increases, the cartel agreement breaks down.

OBSTACLES TO THE FORMATION OF CARTELS

While there is a strong incentive for oligopolists to collude, there are also some important obstacles that make it difficult to collude in a cartel. As already noted, in the United States, the *Sherman Antitrust Act* forms an important legal barrier to a cartel. Thus, an attempt to lower the rigors of competition takes a form such as price leadership rather than an explicit collusion, which is illegal. Other things being equal, *the larger the number* of firms, the more difficult it is to form and maintain a cartel; consensus is harder to come by and policing difficulty increases rapidly with increasing membership. A successful cartel, unless legally sanctioned, usually requires an industry in which there are only a few firms. *Differences in products* as well as *differences in costs* also make it difficult to reach an agreement that is acceptable to all firms involved. The advent of a *recession* coupled with strong temptation to deviate from the cartel agreement tends to break down many cartels during a recession.

15-6 PRICE RIGIDITY IN OLIGOPOLY: THE KINKED DEMAND CURVE MODEL

In the preceding section we have seen that cartel arrangements tend to be short-lived; there is a persistent temptation to undercut the price and increase the market share and profit. However, there are instances in which some oligopoly prices remain stable for a long period of time. For instance, from 1926 to 1938, the price of sulfur "remained absolutely stationary at $18 per ton except for 2 years. In one of those years the price varied by 3 cents per ton from $18; in the other year it varied by 2 cents per ton."[19] This stability in price existed despite the fact that the period was characterized by many changes in production costs and important shifts in demand.[20]

Paul Sweezy's kinked demand curve model[21] attempts to explain why such price stability or rigidity may exist. Note that Sweezy wants to explain *why price and output stay where they are* and not how price and output are established at a particular level.

In Figure 15-9, two demand curves facing an oligopolist are shown. Assume that the current market price is given by the height of point *P*. *DD'* shows what happens to price and output when the oligopolist's price is matched by all other oligopolists in the industry. The flatter curve, *dd'*, shows what happens to price and output when the oligopolist's price changes are not matched by other oligopolists. The *dd'* curve is flatter than *DD'* since a price reduction by the oligopolist alone expands his sale at the expense of other oligopolists. Similarly the oligopolist will find some of his customers shifting to others if he is the only one who is raising the price.

Now let us introduce Sweezy's crucial behavioral assumption. He assumes that *other oligopolists will match a reduction in price* in order to protect their market share, *but will ignore an increase in price*, which poses no threat to their market shares. The demand curve that reflects this assumption is given by the kinked

[19]Marshall R. Colberg, William C. Bradford, and Richard M. Alt, *Business Economics: Principles and Cases*, rev. ed. (Homewood, Ill.: Irwin, 1957), p. 276. This is quoted in Kalman J. Cohen and Richard M. Cyert, *Theory of the Firm: Resource Allocation in a Market Economy* (Englewood Cliffs, N.J.: Prentice-Hall, 1965), p. 250.

[20]Cohen and Cyert, *Ibid.*

[21]Paul M. Sweezy, "Demand under Conditions of Oligopoly," *Journal of Political Economy*, Vol. 47, 1939, pp. 568–573. This is reprinted in Stigler and Boulding, *op. cit.*, pp. 404–409.

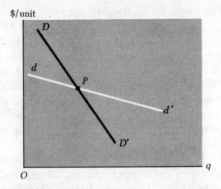

Figure 15-9 Two demand curves facing an oligopolist

(sharply bent) demand curve, *dPD'* in Figure 15-10. The marginal revenue curve corresponding to this kinked demand curve is composed of two discontinuous dotted line segments. Now *assume* that the prevailing price in the market is $p, that is, the height of the kink on *dPD'*. If the oligopolist's marginal cost is given by the curve labeled MC, then the most profitable output and price clearly occur

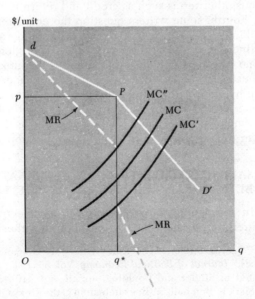

Figure 15-10 Sweezy's kinked demand curve model

at the point of the kink. Since the MR curve is discontinuous at q^*, we cannot assert the optimality in terms of MR = MC. However, a little marginal analysis makes it clear that the profit-maximizing output is q^*: any deviation from q^* reduces profit. Now note the important fact that even though cost may change substantially as represented by MC' or MC", the optimal output does not change. The best price still remains at the height of the kink. A substantial change in demand may result only in a parallel horizontal shift in the demand curves, causing each firm's output to expand but the price to remain rigid at the level of the kink.

Sweezy's model shows how the oligopolist's view regarding his competitors' reactions to price changes might importantly affect his pricing behavior. The way oligopolists perceive the nature of their mutual interdependence is reflected in their pricing behavior.

There are several important criticisms against the kinked demand curve model. First, the model fails to explain why the oligopoly price is set at the level of the kink; rather, it is an *ex post facto* rationalization. Second, Sweezy's behavioral assumption is subject to question. Why not assume, for instance, that the rivals will match price increases as well as price decreases?[22] Third, the price rigidity reflected in the published lists tends to overexaggerate the inflexibility of price. The actual prices charged customers may fluctuate substantially even when the published lists remain unaltered. Various other terms such as credit and return privileges may also change. Fourth, some writers question the empirical relevance of Sweezy's kinked demand curve model. After studying nineteen oligopolistic industries during the years 1929–37, Stigler concluded that there is no empirical evidence that supports the kinked demand curve hypothesis. He argues that frequent price changes observed contradict the hypothesis that oligopolists believe in the existence of a kink.[23] Primeaux and Bomball examined electric utilities that are operated as a monopoly and those that are operated as duopoly, and found a greater price stability in monopoly than in duopoly.[24]

15-7 SALES MAXIMIZATION: AN ALTERNATIVE BEHAVIORAL ASSUMPTION OF THE FIRM

In discussing non-profit-maximizing objectives in section 11-2, we referred to the sales maximization hypothesis. Now we

[22]George Stigler, "The Kinky Oligopoly Demand Curve and and Rigid Prices," *Journal of Political Economy,* Vol. 55, 1947, pp. 432–449. This is reprinted in Stigler and Boulding, *op. cit.,* pp. 410–439. Walter J. Primeaux and Mark R. Bomball, "A Reexamination of the Kinky Oligopoly Demand Curve," *Journal of Political Economy,* July–August 1974, pp. 851–863.
[23]*Ibid.*
[24]*Ibid.*

are in a position to examine this hypothesis and compare it with the profit-maximizing hypothesis. *In essence, William Baumol's sales-maximization hypothesis suggests that the maximization of sales revenue subject to a profit constraint may be a more likely goal of large business firms than the assumption of profit maximization.*[25]

SALES MAXIMIZATION WITHOUT PROFIT CONSTRAINT

Let us refer to Figure 15-11, and examine the nature of the sales-maximization model. Given the TR and TC curves shown in part *a*, the profit-maximizing output is q_π where the firm's MR equals MC, as shown by the parallel lines tangent to the TR and TC curves. Let us now examine the sales-maximizing firm's output selection, assuming that it is not subject to any other constraint (such as the need to maintain a minimum level of profit). The sales-maximizer produces the output that will maximize its TR or total sales receipts. Thus, it produces q_s units per period, where its MR = 0 and its TR is at maximum.

Figure 15-11*b* shows the total profit curve. Note that the sales-maximizer's profit is smaller than the profit-maximizer's. The sales-maximizer seeks the largest sales revenue even at the expense of some profit. Also note that the sales-maximizer's output is larger than the profit-maximizer's. This is necessarily so because the sales-maximizer expands his output until his MR reaches 0 but the profit maximizer stops where MR = MC > 0. (MC must be always positive since efficient production implies that it costs more to produce more.)

SALES MAXIMIZATION SUBJECT TO PROFIT CONSTRAINT

It is plausible that a sales-maximizing firm may have to maintain a certain minimal level of profit to keep its stockholders happy, etc. Let us now examine the effect of introducing such a constraint on the sales-maximizing model. In Figure 15-12, q_π is the profit-maximizing output, and q_s is assumed to be the output at which the TR is maximum. If there were no profit constraint, the sales-maximizer would produce q_s units per period. Let us, however, assume that the minimum profit level the firm must maintain is $A per period. The height of the white line AA' indicates this profit constraint. In order to maximize his TR subject to this profit constraint, the sales-maximizer now produces AA' units per period. The TR keeps increasing until q_s units per period is produced, but the profit constraint forces the sales-maximizer to stop at AA' units. Similarly, if the profit constraint is shown by the height of line BB' in Figure 15-12, the sales-maximizing output will be BB' units per period.

[25]See William J. Baumol, *Business Behavior, Value and Growth*, rev. ed. (New York: Harcourt, Brace & World, 1967); and for a brief description of his, *Economic Theory and Operations Analysis*, 3d ed. (Englewood Cliffs, N.J.: Prentice-Hall, 1972), pp. 325–327.

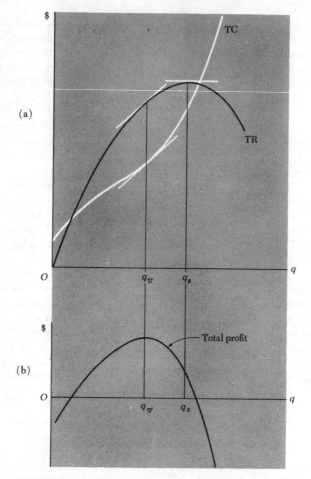

Figure 15-11 Profit versus sales maximization; (a) total revenue and cost curves, (b) total profit curve

Note that the sales-maximizing output under a profit constraint is still larger than the profit-maximizing output. The case in which the profit constraint equals the maximum profit attainable is the limiting situation in which q_π and sales-maximizing output subject to the profit constraint are equal. If the profit constraint is lower than the profit associated with the sales-maximizing output, q_s, as indicated by the dotted line II', the constraint is redundant. The sales-maximizer would not want to produce more than q_s units per period anyway.

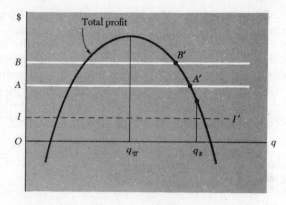

Figure 15-12 Sales maximization subject to a profit constraint

FIXED COST AND THE SALES-MAXIMIZER'S PRICE AND OUTPUT

In discussing competitive and monopoly models, we have seen that a fixed cost does not influence the short-run profit-maximizing price and output decisions. Thus, a sunk or fixed cost is irrelevant for short-run profit-maximizing decisions. However, a fixed cost does affect the short-run price and output decisions of a sales-maximizer. Referring to Figure 15-13, let us see why. Let the

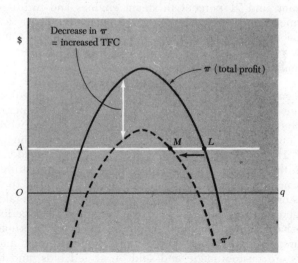

Figure 15-13 Effect of an increased fixed cost on sales-maximizing output

current profit curve for the sales-maximizer be shown by π, and his sales-maximizing output subject to the profit constraint of $A per period by AL units per period. Suppose an increase in the firm's fixed cost (say, due to an imposition of a lump-sum tax) lowers the sales-maximizer's profit curve to π'. Observe that the sales-maximizing output subject to the profit constraint is now reduced to AM units per period. Since the sales-maximizer is selling a smaller output, he must find a higher price at which to sell his sales-maximizing output.

We have too much material on oligopoly to cover in a single chapter. So let us defer additional analytical materials to the next chapter, and look at some applications.

15-8 ELECTRICAL EQUIPMENT INDUSTRY IN THE 1950s: A Case Study in Oligopoly Behavior

In highly concentrated industries, there develops a cohesive tendency among firms. Recognizing their strong interdependence, they tend to establish mutually acceptable price, differentiation, and selling practices. However, in some highly concentrated industries, such a cohesive tendency may fail to develop due to some important structural variations peculiar to the industries. A good example is the electrical equipment industry in the 1950s.

The electrical equipment industry is a highly concentrated one. The four-firm concentration ratios in 1963 were 93 percent, 76 percent, and 71 percent in steam engines and turbines, power transformers, and circuit breakers, respectively. There were only three major producers in turbines and only four or five in transformers and heavy-duty switch gears in the 1950s, in which the well-known electrical conspiracies took place.

Since barriers to entry were high and the market was highly concentrated, one would have expected a tight oligopolistic discipline — effective tacit collusion with results approximating maximum joint profits. If the price leadership arrangement were to take place, General Electric, the largest overall seller, would be the logical leader.[26] However, neither tacit collusion nor price leadership took place in the industry. Instead, there have been alternating periods of overt market-sharing arrangement and price warfare. In 1961, executives of heavy electrical equipment producers — General Electric, Westinghouse, and others — were found guilty of price-fixing and market-sharing arrangements carried out in secret meetings around the country in the 1950s. Large generators, turbines, and circuit breakers are custom-made and sold on sealed bids, and the firms

[26]McKie, *op. cit.*, pp. 12–13.

agreed in advance on who was to be the successful bidder and the price at which bids were to be entered. Periodically, such a cartel arrangement broke down, and price warfare ensued. Each time, however, the collusion was reestablished until the dramatic event of the conspiracy trials.[27]

What are the structural variations peculiar to the electrical equipment industry that led it to override the cohesive tendency of highly concentrated oligopoly and to resort to alternating overt collusion and price warfare?

Nature of demand. Heavy electrical equipment is custom-made and is of high monetary value. Furthermore, orders for such equipment are placed intermittently. A supplier who fails to obtain a particular contract, might have to wait several years for a chance at another bid, keeping his plants operating well below capacity. Thus, there were heavy pressures applied to electrical equipment divisions to secure bids in any way possible. The divisions responded by alternating between overt price-fixing and market-sharing arrangements and drastic price cutting. The observed alternations between overt collusion and price warfare show the inherently unstable nature of the practices found in this industry in the 1950s.

Nature of products. Large turbines, generators, and circuit breakers are custom-made. When a product is well standardized, as in cigarettes and soft drinks, a tacit agreement in price is fairly easy to attain, since price is visible to everyone and firms' practices can be policed readily. However, when products are made to order, it is practically impossible to have tacit price and/or output arrangements that can be effectively policed. Thus, agreements among firms tend to take illegal overt form. This was the case at least until the electrical conspiracy came to the surface.

Cost structure. Firms in the electrical equipment industry have large investments in fixed plant and equipment. Thus, the cyclical downturns and intermittent nature of demand posed a serious excess-capacity problem. This excess capacity in turn generated the desire to collude to share the market or to engage in price cutting, since marginal costs were far below prices when there were large idle capacities.

The case of the electrical equipment industry illustrates the difficulty of generalizing about oligopoly behavior. Many oligopolistic markets have their own peculiar structural variations, and oligopoly behavior in these markets cannot readily be explained by any general theory.

[27]*Ibid.* Also see "The Incredible Electrical Conspiracy," *Fortune,* April and May 1961, and G. L. Bach, *Economics,* 7th ed. (Englewood Cliffs, N.J.: Prentice-Hall, 1974), pp. 367–368.

15-9 THE ORGANIZATION OF PETROLEUM EXPORTING COUNTRIES: AN INTERNATIONAL CARTEL

Let us now turn our attention to an international cartel that has enjoyed an enormous sucess in recent years.

A HISTORICAL SKETCH

The Organization of Petroleum Exporting Countries, OPEC, was formed in 1960 by Iran, Iraq, Kuwait, Saudi Arabia, and Venezuela, in response to unilateral reductions in the posted prices of crude oil by the multinational petroleum companies in 1959 and 1960. During the 1960s membership of OPEC grew to eleven with the entry of Abu Dhabi, Algeria, Indonesia, Libya, Quatar, and Nigeria. The OPEC members account for some 85 to 90 percent of the world's crude oil export. The OPEC's declared goals are to raise the member governments' revenue (taxes and royalties) from crude oil production and to gain control over exploration and production from the major oil companies.

The formation of the OPEC cartel made the oil companies partly restore the price cuts. However, the OPEC failed to function as a cohesive cartel during the 1960s, and remained relatively impotent due to the worldwide surplus of oil and its inability to act in unison. The downward movement of crude oil price that began in 1957, according to M. A. Adelman, continued through Spring 1970, with only occasional and temporary reversals.[28]

The Great Oil Crisis of 1971 surprised the Western world. After the Suez Canal was closed in 1967, tanker rates soared and oil companies turned to oil sources closer to their major markets: thus, they stepped up the Libyan production rapidly. With the passage of the next few years, Europe became dangerously dependent upon Libya for over 30 percent of its oil.[29]

In May 1970, the Libyan government forced production cutbacks for most of the companies operating there in order to force them to agree to higher taxes. Almost simultaneously, another event seriously pinched European oil. On May 3, 1970, a French work crew damaged the 750-mile Trans-Arabian Pipeline that crosses Jordan and Syria en route to the Lebanese port of Sidon. For eight-and-a-half months the Syrians permitted no repair work, which meant that nearly half a million barrels of oil a day were denied to Europe.

[28]*The World Petroleum Market* (Baltimore, Md.: Johns Hopkins University Press, 1972), p. 191.
[29]Gurney Breckenfeld, "How the Arabs Changed the Oil Business," *Fortune*, August 1971, p. 113 ff.

The companies producing in Libya quickly agreed to a tax increase that was only a fraction of the price increase. The Persian Gulf producing countries then demanded and gained the same increase. Whereupon, Libya, which had not rescinded the production cutbacks, demanded a further increase, and the Persian Gulf countries followed suit. The Tehran-Tripoli Agreements of early 1971 were the final results of the negotiations. The agreements were to increase the per barrel price of oil by approximately 50 percent over 1969 as of mid-1971, and by about 75 and 100 percent as of 1975 and 1980.[30] Payments to the governments in the Persian Gulf, Libya, and Venezuela in 1969 were $6.7 billion. The payments envisaged for years 1971, 1975, and 1980 in view of the Tehran-Tripoli Agreements were $12.4 billion, $22.0 billion, and $41.2 billion.[31]

The OPEC countries have been meeting frequently to reevaluate their strategies and to renegotiate the terms with the oil companies. For instance, they were able to negotiate a revision of the 1971 agreements after the devaluation of the dollar in 1972, and to dictate a huge increase in oil price in December, 1973. In early 1975, the OPEC is reported to be inclined to keep the oil price at the current level (with appropriate adjustment for changes in price level).[32]

THE ACCOMPLISHMENTS AND STRENGTH OF OPEC

There is little argument that the oil crisis of 1971 was real and that the OPEC cartel was genuinely successful in raising prices and increasing revenues to the member governments, particularly during the years 1973 and 1974. The petroleum exporting countries never before had such a degree of control over the world petroleum market.

Historically, producer cartels have not endured. Competition within and outside the ranks has led to the dissolution of cartels. However, the OPEC has some uncommon strengths that explain its success story. First, relatively few producer governments control a large part of the world oil reserves and account for some 85 to 90 percent of world trade in oil. Second, the key countries, notably, Saudi Arabia, Kuwait, Libya, and Abu Dhabi, have large reserves and little need for current foreign exchange earnings. Thus, they can afford to take a long-run look and cut back production to prevent oversupply of oil in the world market. Third, oil is a commodity for which there is no good substitute, at least in the short run. Some estimates of the short-run price elasticity of demand for oil puts it at around −0.15. Thus, a price increase can increase the total revenues of the

---

[30]Adelman, *op. cit.*, p. 251.
[31]*Ibid.*, p. 252.
[32]*The Economist*, February 1, 1975.

OPEC members substantially. Fourth, the solidarity of the OPEC members has been enhanced by the cartel's successes, particularly, in 1973 and 1974, in increasing its revenues, moving toward increased government participation, and using oil as a political weapon.

FACTORS AFFECTING THE FUTURE OF OPEC

Has the dramatic turnaround of 1971 marked the beginning of a new era in the world petroleum market? Can the OPEC, which has discovered the strength in concerted actions, maintain the oil price at its current high level or even raise it further? To answer this question, we must examine the factors affecting the demand and supply sides of the world oil market.

On the demand side, we noted that the short-run elasticity of demand for oil is rather low. However, like the demand for any other good, the long-run price elasticity of demand for oil will be much larger than its short-run counterpart. Consuming countries will have much better chances of finding substitutes for oil and ways to reduce the use of oil.

In examining the supply side of the world petroleum market, we must, first of all, note the very wide margin that exists between the price of oil and its cost of production. In the Persian Gulf region in 1968, for instance, the cost of production per barrel of oil was between 10 and 20 cents, while the realized crude oil price was $1.83 per barrel.[33] Because production cost is such a small fraction of the total revenue from crude oil production, there is a strong temptation to increase production and sell even at secret cut-rate prices, especially when a rival may enjoy it if you do not.

The potential supply of highly profitable oil will be increased substantially by more explorations and added production capacities of the OPEC member countries. Some studies estimate the OPEC to be faced with over 30 percent excess capacities by 1980 if the oil price remains at the level of 1974 (estimated at $9.60 per barrel by the World Bank).[34] The OPEC will be faced with the difficult task of allocating production cutbacks of this magnitude. among its members, who differ in their oil reserves, population density, the current versus future needs for oil revenues, and military and political ambitions. For instance, countries such as Iran, Venezuela, Iraq, Algeria, Indonesia, and Nigeria—with large populations and ambitious development plans—want more current revenues. While Saudi Arabia, Kuwait, Libya, and Abu Dhabi—which have small popula-

[33]Adelman, *op. cit.*, pp. 76–77.
[34]Hollis B. Chenery, "Restructuring the World Economy," *Foreign Affairs*, January 1975, pp. 242–263.

tions, large oil reserves, and limited abilities to absorb development projects—are more interested in maintaining the world petroleum price over the years to come.[35]

Also not to be forgotten on the supply side is the possibility of substantial increase in non-OPEC oil production from such sources as the North Sea and Alaskan fields.

The long-term cost of non-OPEC sources of energy, according to Chenery, is estimated to be the equivalent of $7.00 to $8.00 per barrel (in 1974 prices) in the Persian Gulf.[36] Thus, if the oil price stays at the 1974 level of $9.60 per barrel or higher, the development of other energy sources such as nuclear and solar energy, oil shale, tar sands, and coal are sure to be encouraged. In the long run, the price of the OPEC oil cannot stay above that of the non-OPEC sources of energy.

Already in 1974 and 1975, excess capacities are reported to have developed: Saudi Arabia, Kuwait, Libya, and Abu Dhabi, for instance, were producing at far below their capacities in early 1975.[37] Some price shadings, easier credit terms, etc., were observed; and some cartel members who need more current revenues are said to be tempted to step up production.[38]

OPEC: AN ENDURING OR ANOTHER TRANSIENT CARTEL?

Can the OPEC countries maintain their cohesiveness and sustain the price of oil at the level of 1974, or at least, at the level of the cost of alternative energy supplies in the long run? Can it do it despite the strong temptation among its members to increase production and despite likely increases in non-OPEC oil and alternative energy supplies? The answer lies in the OPEC's ability to establish and enforce production quotas among its members, who differ in their oil reserves, political and military ambitions, and current and future economic needs. The OPEC's task is a formidable one because there are too many ways to chisel. Behind high f.o.b. prices may lie lower tanker rates and generous credit terms. Producer countries may finance a refinery at low cost to the buyers or make low-cost loans. There may be buy-back deals, barter deals, and exchanges of crude in one part of the world for crude in another part. "The world oil cartel of the 1930s was eroded by this kind of competition."[39] Will the new one in the 1970s?

[35]*Ibid.*
[36]*Ibid.*
[37]*Newsweek*, March 3, 1975, p. 57.
[38]*Ibid.*
[39]Adelman, *op. cit.*, p. 258.

EXERCISES 15

Industrial Concentration and Oligopoly

15-1 What is a concentration ratio? Discuss the advantages and disadvantages associated with this concept.

15-2 Joe S. Bain argues that "in at least half or more of all such industries the leading firms are in a significant degree larger than necessary for the attainment of efficiency in production and distribution. Seller concentration is, in a corresponding sense, unnecessarily high." (*Industrial Organization*, 2d Ed., New York: Wiley, 1968, p. 199.) Discuss the economic implications of such findings.

15-3 Discuss the role of a firm's fixed cost in its price and output decision in the short run for (1) a profit-maximizer and (2) a sales-maximizer.

15-4 Let a dominant price leadership model be specified by the following:

Industry demand: $Q = 250 - \frac{1}{2}p$

Total quantity supplied by small firms: $q = -180 + 9p$

Dominant firm's marginal cost: $MC = 1q$

Given this model, determine (*a*) the dominant firm's profit-maximizing output, (*b*) its price, and the total industry output.

15-5 Consider a cartel that produces a homogeneous product while cost conditions among member firms differ. In order to minimize the production cost, how should this cartel allocate production among its members?

15-6 Suppose the cartel cited in the preceding problem faces markets that can be easily separated and in which the elasticities of demand are different. Show how the cartel may establish the price and output that maximizes the joint cartel profit.

15-7   Consider the following figure, in which, we may say somewhat loosely, there are three output levels at which MR=MC.

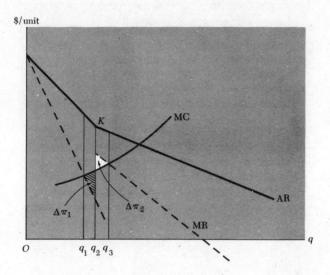

1.   Assume in the above figure that the going market price is given by point K. Then, what is the behavioral assumption implicit in the shape of the demand curve?
2.   The MR = MC rule fails to give a determinate optimal solution. In order to determine the optimal output, we must compare the relative sizes of $\Delta\pi_1$ and $\Delta\pi_2$. Why?
3.   Complete the following table.

Suppose	*then, the profit- maximizing output is*
$\Delta\pi_1 > \Delta\pi_2$	_____
$\Delta\pi_1 = \Delta\pi_2$	_____or_____
$\Delta\pi_1 < \Delta\pi_2$	_____

CHAPTER SIXTEEN

FURTHER TOPICS IN OLIGOPOLY AND MONOPOLISTIC COMPETITION

In this chapter we will complete the discussion of oligopoly started in Chapter Fifteen, and then move to the subject of monopolistic competition. Appendix 16 presents the theory of games approach to oligopoly. The unfinished topics in oligopoly to be taken up in this chapter are product variation and sales promotion and the evaluation of oligopoly.

16-1 NONPRICE COMPETITION: PRODUCT VARIATION AND SALES PROMOTION

The recognition of mutual interdependence among oligopolists tends to make them avoid competition in terms of price. Therefore, oligopoly provides a fertile ground for product variation and sales promotion activities. Oligopolists may believe that product variation and/or sales promotion tend to affect their competitors less and, accordingly, to evoke less direct reactions. Furthermore, copying well-excuted advertising or emulating a successful product variation is much more difficult than matching a price reduction; it may take a considerable length of time or it may be impossible to emulate a unique new design.

PRODUCT DIFFERENTIATION

*A product is **differentiated** if any significant basis exists for distinguishing the goods (or services) of one seller from those of* *another.*[1] Differentiation may be based on certain *physical characteristics of the product* itself, such as patented features, trade marks, design, color, or style. It may also exist with respect to *conditions surrounding its sale,* such as the convenience of store location, prompt service, and courteousness.

When products are differentiated, the volume of sales depends not only on price but also upon the skill with which the good is differentiated from others and made to appeal to a particular group of buyers.[2]

How much should the firm spend on product differentiation in order to maximize its profit? Our familiar marginal analysis suggests that any activity should be carried out to the point where the marginal revenue of the activity is equal to the marginal cost of the activity. Thus, the monopolistic competitor must increase his product differentiation as long as the marginal revenue of differentiation, MR(d), exceeds the marginal cost of differentiation, MC(d). The profit-maximizing degree of differentiation is attained when MR(d) = MC(d).[3] For example, consider a resort motel that competes with many other motels and hotels in an area. It may attempt to increase its profit by refurnishing its rooms and offering additional services. As long as such remodeling increases its total revenue by a sum greater than the change in total cost due to the renovation, it pays for the motel to undertake the refurnishing. The marginal analysis suggests that the profit-maximizing degree of remodeling is attained when the marginal revenue from remodeling is equal to the marginal cost of remodeling.

SELLING COSTS

While production costs include all expenses incurred in providing and transporting a good or service to the buyer, *selling*

[1]Edward H. Chamberlin, *The Theory of Monopolistic Competition,* 6th ed. (Cambridge, Mass.: Harvard University Press, 1948), p. 56.

[2]*Ibid.,* pp. 71–72.

[3]Mathematically, profit is now the function of output (or price) and product differentiation. Thus,

$$\pi(q,d) = R(q,d) - C(q,d)$$

The first-order conditions for profit maximization are:

$$\frac{\partial \pi}{\partial q} = \frac{\partial R}{\partial q} - \frac{\partial C}{\partial q} = 0$$

$$\frac{\partial \pi}{\partial d} = \frac{\partial R}{\partial d} - \frac{\partial C}{\partial d} = 0$$

The second equation says that for profit maximization MR(d) must be equated with MC(d).

costs include all expenses incurred in order to increase the demand for the good or service. Examples of selling costs are advertising in its many forms, free samples, and sweepstakes. Successful advertising, for instance, will increase the demand for the product and shift the demand curve rightward and upward. Advertising may provide information to buyers. Or it may manipulate buyers' motivations and knowledge, without providing any genuine information, and succeed in increasing demand. Perhaps, repeated display of a brand name falls in this category.

What is the optimal selling cost or advertising strategy for an oligopolist? Again, the marginal analysis suggests that the profit-maximizing outlay in advertising is attained when the marginal revenue of advertising, $MR(a)$, is equal to the marginal cost of advertising, $MC(a)$. As long as an additional dollar spent on advertising increases the total revenue by more than a dollar, it pays to advertise. If $MR(a)$ is smaller than $MC(a)$, the firm is clearly overspending on advertising.

Oligopolists' activities in introducing new varieties or new advertising campaigns will be affected significantly by the likely reactions of their rivals. Introduction of a new product may be forestalled if the oligopolist thinks that competitors can successfully emulate it and the earnings from the existing lines will materially decline due to such wholesale introduction of new varieties. An oligopolist may abstain from a vigorous advertising campaign lest he evoke equally or even more energetic advertising from competitors, since such competitive advertising may not increase total industry sales while the advertising costs for all involved soar.

An oligopolist's profit potential depends on price as well as nonprice variables. Thus, he must examine not only price but product variety and selling expenses. Since a change in any of these variables affects the effectiveness of other variables, the optimal price, product variety, and selling expense must be simultaneously determined.

16-2 SOME OBSERVATIONS ON THE EFFECTS OF OLIGOPOLY

Since there is no such thing as the general theory of oligopoly, no general evaluation of oligopoly is possible. Yet, certain observations on the effects of the oligopolistic market structure can be made.

PRICE, OUTPUT, AND PROFIT

How do oligoply price, output, and profit compare with those of perfect competitors? For simplicity, let us assume (1) that the total industry demand remains the same whether the market is organized perfectly competitively or oligopolistically, and (2) that there are no significant economies or diseconomies of size, that is, long-run average costs are the same for perfect competitors and oligopolists. Given these assumptions, the competitive industry supply curve can be represented by the LAC = LMC line in Figure 16-1. Assume that the D curve shows the industry demand. Then the competitive long-run equilibrium solution is shown by point C where the AR and LAC = LMC curves intersect. Thus competitive price and output are p_c dollars and Q_c units.

To facilitate comparison, assume that oligopolists form a perfect cartel and seek joint profit-maximizing price and output. Then, the oligopoly profit-maximizing solution is shown by point J, and its equilibrium price and output are p_o dollars and Q_o units. Clearly, the oligopoly *price is higher and output smaller* than the competitive counterparts. Now assume that oligopolists act individually (without any tacit or overt collusion) to maximize their profits. Since an oligopolist's demand curve slopes downward to the right, his profit-maximizing output, at which LMC = MR, must be smaller than the LMC = AR output, and his price (= AR) must be higher than his MR = LMC = LAC.

Thus, given the assumptions of the same market demand and the same constant long-run cost, the basic criticisms against monopoly—the twin evils of too small output and too high price—apply equally well to oligopoly. Oligopolists stop their output at the level where their MR = MC lest they spoil the market. However, consumers' desire for more oligopoly output is clearly indicated by their willingness to pay a price that is higher than oligopolists' mar-

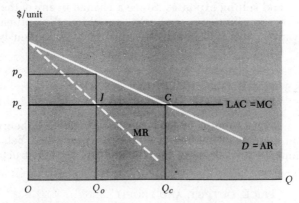

Figure 16-1 Competitive versus oligopoly price and output

ginal costs. Ideally, resources from other areas of the economy should flow into oligopoly, and increase oligopoly output and reduce its price. But barriers to entry prevent such inflow of resources; the result is too small output in oligopoly and too much resources in other areas.

As long as some barriers to entry prevent the inflow of new firms, oligopolists *may earn profit even in the long run.* If entry is rather difficult and the slopes of oligopoly demand curves are steep, oligopoly prices may be substantially higher than the competitve ones and oligopolists may reap large profits. As entry barriers are reduced and as the demand curves flatten, the excesses of oligopoly prices over those of perfect competitors will become smaller.

Do not forget that the above comparisons rest on two rather crucial assumptions. First, the market demand is assumed to be the same whether the market is organized as an oligopoly or perfect competition. If oligopolists' sales promotions and/or product variations increase the market demand substantially, it may even be conceivable for the oligopoly output to be larger and its price to be lower than those of the competitively organized industry. Second, it was assumed that the oligopolistic firms could be broken up into many smaller firms that can exert little influence on market prices. However, it is quite likely that the industry thus reorganized may contain too many firms with plants far smaller than the optimal (minimum-cost) size and the average cost of production as well as price may soar.

PRODUCT DIFFERENTIATION AND SALES PROMOTION

There is the continuing, unresolved controversy over the welfare effect of the *product differentiation* and *selling expenditures* that are so important in oligopoly. The existence of a large number of varieties in design, color, size, packaging, etc., increases the scope of choices available to the consumer. Quite frequently consumers welcome such varieties and are willing to pay for them. But many consumers as well as economists wonder whether the additional satisfaction generated by various product differerentiating measures is worth its cost — satisfaction that could have been generated by using resources to produce other things. Do we waste too much resources in annual automobile model changes? Changing clothing styles help sell more clothes and increase Gross National Product; but do they really increase our welfare or satisfaction? What about the people who own expensive clothes that have become obsolete by style changes? Sales promotions are important in oligopolistic market structure. The television networks seem to find little difficulty in finding advertisers who are willing to pay high prices for TV advertisements. How much of such advertising really increases the total industry demand, and therefore, its output? How much of such advertising expenditures is just for intra-industry competition aimed at the expansion or retention of advertisers' market shares? In summary, product differentiation and sales promotion are important policy variables in oligopoly; yet the effects of such activities are difficult to ascertain in unambiguous ways.

RESEARCH AND DEVELOPMENT

Economic efficiency of oligopoly price, output, product differentiation, and sales promotion are at best dubious. But oligopolists score rather well in their *research and development* (R & D) activities that promote economic growth. A monopolist, being the single seller in the market, may lack strong pressure or motivation to spend a large amount of resources on R & D. Perfect competitors and monopolistic competitors are generally too small to have financial and/or technological capabilities to engage in R & D activites. Most research and innovation produced by private corporations, therefore, come from large and not-so-large oligopolists.[4] Oligopolists face important competition in their industry, and there is a strong incentive to come up with new or better products and/or methods of production.

16-3 MONOPOLISTIC COMPETITION

Chamberlin developed his model of monopolistic competition by combining the behavioral characteristics of perfect competition with differentiated products.[5] Thus, in monopolistic competition, there is a large number of firms, none of which is large enough to have any appreciable impact on the market price. Entry into (and exit from) the market is relatively easy. Many firms with slightly differentiated and readily substitutable products can enter the market with little difficulty. Since each firm's product is slightly differentiated from those of others, the demand curve facing a firm slopes downward to the right. The demand for a monopolistically competitive firm's product, however, is rather elastic, since there are many good substitutes.

As we noted in section 16-1, differentiation can take many diverse forms: it may be in the physical characteristics of the good, the circumstances in which the good is sold, or may simply be imaginary. It is worth noting that geographical location is a sufficient basis for differentiation. Neighborhood convenience stores are differentiated in terms of location. Consumers prefer nearby stores even though the merchandise sold and the circumstances in which they are retailed are very much alike.

---

[4]A substantial number of innovations comes from the efforts of individuals at universities and government organizations.

[5]Edward H. Chamberlin, *op. cit.* The first edition was published in 1933.

The mechanics of analyzing the optimal price and output decision in the short run for a monopolistically competitive firm is essentially identical to that of a pure monopoly model. Given the cost and revenue curves shown in Figure 16-2, the short-run profit-maximizing output is given by q^* and the maximum price that can be charged for this output is p^* dollars per unit. Depending on the relative positions of revenue and cost curves, a monopolistically competitive firm may make a profit, incur a loss, or just break even. The firm depicted in Figure 16-2 is receiving an economic profit.[6]

LONG-RUN EQUILIBRIUM IN MONOPOLISTIC COMPETITION

The happy state of affairs depicted in Figure 16-2, however, cannot persist in the long run. Since monopolistic competition is the market structure in which entry is easy, the existence of lucrative profit shown in Figure 16-2 attracts new firms. Such entry of new

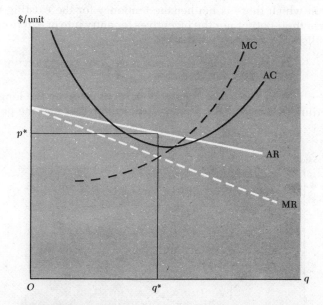

Figure 16-2 Short-run price and output decision in monopolistic competition

[6]This summarizes the relevant aspect of Chamberlin's short-run analysis. His presentation includes many details that are ignored here as unimportant in understanding observed behavior in the real world. Those interested in details should consult Chamberlin's original work, cited in footnote 1.

firms in turn will reduce the share of the total market available to existing firms and shift their demand curve to the left. (Needless to say, exit of firms will shift remaining monopolistic competitors' demand curves to the right.) The long-run equilibrium position for a monopolistic competitor is shown in Figure 16-3. In the long-run equilibrium the monopolistic competitor's d = AR curve must be tangent to his LAC curve. When the LAC curve is tangent to his demand curve, his LMC curve must intersect his MR curve. Since MR = LMC at the output of q^*, any movement away from q^* in either direction will reduce his profit (or in the case of Figure 16-3, make him incur a loss). Thus, the monopolistic competitor has no incentive to change his output. Since point E depicts the situation in which there is zero economic profit, there is no incentive for other firms to enter the market. Because zero economic profit means that firms in the market are recovering their alternative costs (the maximum sum their resources can earn elsewhere), there is no incentive for the firms to leave the market. Thus, point E does describe the long-run equilibrium, in which there is neither the tendency for the existing firms to change their output nor the incentives for entry into or exit from the monopolistically competitive market.

COMPARISON OF MONOPOLISTIC AND COMPETITIVE LONG-RUN EQUILIBRIUM

With the aid of Figure 16-4, let us compare the long-run equilibrium positions of the monopolistic competitor and the perfect

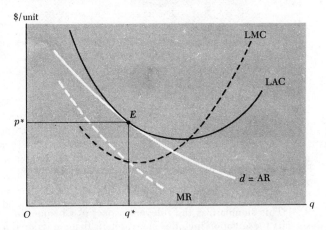

Figure 16-3 Long-run equilibrium in monopolistic competition

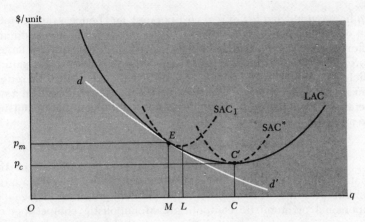

Figure 16-4 Comparison of monopolistic competition with perfect competition

competitor. The long-run equilibrium position of the monopolistic competitor is at E, where his demand curve is tangent to his LAC. From Chapter Thirteen, we know that the long-run equilibrium price and output of a perfect competitor is shown by point C', where LAC is at its minimum. Comparing point E with point C', we note that *price is higher and output is smaller* under monopolistic competition than under perfect competition. That is, $p_m > p_c$ and $q_m < q_c$. This conclusion is a mathematical necessity, since a downward-sloping demand curve must be tangent to the LAC curve to the left of its minimum point, where its slope is zero.

Like perfect competitors, monopolistic competitors *receive zero economic profit* in the long-run equilibrium. The ease with which resources can flow into the market reduces each firm's market share and its profit dissipates into thin air.

Chronic *existence of excess capacity* typifies monopolistic competitors in the long-run equilibrium. *Excess capacity is defined as the difference between the minimum LAC output (that is attained by building the optimal-size plant and operating it optimally) and the actual long-run equilibrium output.* In Figure 16-4, the excess capacity is shown by $MC = OC - OM$. This total excess capacity can be considered as composed of two parts: (1) LC shows excess capacity due to building too small a plant, and (2) ML shows excess capacity due to underutilization of the plant built.

The existence of excess capacity "suggests that the same total output, if produced by a smaller number of more sizable firms can be provided at a lower real cost per unit, and hence a smaller total use of society's scarce resources."[7] If the number of firms producing differentiated goods can be reduced, each firm can become larger, more efficient, and prices will become lower. However, this gain in efficiency and lowering of prices must be weighed against the reduction in product varieties. Whether such a change will result in a net social gain is a matter of value judgment that lies completely outside the analysis.

MONOPOLISTIC COMPETITION: AN EVALUATION

We have presented an elementary summary of the Chamberlinian model of monopolistic competition, in which a large number of firms with slightly differentiated products engages in impersonal or atomistic competition. Monopolistic competitors do not recognize any interdependence among their price, product differentiation, and selling cost decisions, since they consider themselves to be an unimportant part of the total market. Entry into the market is easy.

How important is the model of monopolistic competition as a tool of analysis in economics? Economists answer this question differently depending on their view of the empirical relevance of the monopolistically competitive model. Those who believe that retail groceries, clothing stores, shoe stores, barbershops, service stations, and so on are reasonably well described by monopolistic competition treat the Chamberlinian model as a significant contribution to economic theory. On the other hand, there are economists who believe that monopolistic competition is an empirically empty model, because it is difficult to find a market that fits the assumptions of monopolistic competition. They argue that when a product is homogeneous, as in wheat and lumber, the competitive model is more appropriate, and that what often appears to be a good candidate for a monopolistically competitive case "nearly always turns out to be oligopoly—both in structure and in most behavioral characteristics."[8] They believe that markets in which product differentiation is quite effective and brand preferences are strong (such as automobiles, cigarettes, and detergents) are best analyzed by oligopoly models.

However, Edward Chamberlin's work as a whole commands high respect within the economic profession. Most contempo-

[7]William J. Baumol, "Monopolistic Competition and Welfare Economics," *American Economic Review, Papers and Proceedings*, May 1964, p. 50. Also see K. J. Cohen and R. M. Cyert, *Theory of the Firm* (Englewood Cliffs, N.J.: Prentice-Hall, 1965), pp. 221–226.

[8]Jesse W. Markham, "Monopolistic Competition after Thirty Years," *American Economic Review, Papers and Proceedings*, May 1964, p. 53.

rary economists will agree that Chamberlin contributed significantly to the enrichment of economic theory by filling in the missing gap between perfect competition and monopoly, by suggesting the importance of empirical measurement, by explicitly introducing product differentiation and selling costs as economic variables, and by contributing to the analysis of oligopoly. The fact that the American Economic Association presented a special program entitled "Monopolistic Competition after Thirty Years" during its 1963 annual meeting is a signal tribute to Chamberlin's work.

16-4 PRODUCT DIFFERENTIATION IN CONSUMER-GOODS VERSUS PRODUCER-GOODS INDUSTRIES: An Application

How important is product differentiation in the various sectors and industries of the American economy? Although systematic data based on measurements are unavailable, some judgments about the apparent incidence of product differentiation in the principal sectors of business activity may be made.[9] For instance, we note that, by and large, product differentiation tends to be *more important in consumer-goods industries* than in producer-goods industries.

Producer-buyers are generally well informed about the qualities and properties of the goods they buy, and are thus less susceptible to persuasive appeals of sellers. In addition, numerous producer goods are standardized raw materials, for which there is little opportunity for product differentiation. For example, in agriculture, forestry, fishery, and mining, product differentiation is generally of negligible importance. Product differentiation is also negligible in manufacturing industries making producer goods; it is difficult to differentiate standardized (or built-to-specifications) products procured by expert buyers. Basic industrial raw materials such as steel, copper, cement, and industrial chemicals, for example, clearly come under this heading. But in the case of producer goods for which the provision of services by the manufacturer is an important element of the transaction, and of producer goods that are large and complex devices, product differentiation may become as important as it is in consumer-goods categories. This would be true, for example, of large, complex farm machinery and of business office machines.

Product differentiation is important among many manufacturers and processors who produce consumer goods. The consumer-buyers of these goods often tend to be poorly informed, and are frequently susceptible to persuasive advertising. Goods like

[9]Materials in this section are adapted from Joe S. Bain's *Industrial Organizations*, 2d ed. (New York: Wiley, 1968), pp. 235–238.

cigarettes, soap, and liquor are strongly differentiated through advertising appeals; goods like autos and electrical appliances evidence differentiation resting on product design and on the consumer's dependence on the seller's reputation; goods like gasoline and tires display a differentiation that rests in considerable part on the character of the manufacturer's distributive and service facilities.

By contrast, product differentiation is relatively unimportant in basic "necessity" consumer goods such as food, clothing, and household supplies. These are relatively simple in character and function, and the housewife (as principal consumer-buyer) purchases them frequently. In the industries producing fresh and processed meats, groceries of most sorts, children's shoes and clothing, and the like, effective product differentiation has generally remained negligible.

The intensity and basis of product differentiation among individual industries vary greatly. Bain considered such evidences of product differentiation as product design, quality or reputation, advertising, and service to customers, and ranked the industries as having "great," "slight," or "negligible" product differentiation. Included among the industries with "great" product differentiation were cigarettes, distilled liquor, automobiles, farm machinery and tractors, high-priced fountain pens, and typewriters.[10]

16-5 CAN ADVERTISING CHANGE SEASONAL PATTERNS IN DEMAND?: An Application

Advertising is an important marketing tool in oligopoly or monopolistic competition. It is used to influence consumer preferences among different brands and products in a particular time period. Advertising may also be used to re-allocate resources over time. Let us examine the case of January white sales, and see how this selling practice redistributes the sales of towels and linens through various months.[11]

Important seasonal variations exist in the utilization of department store capacities. The two periods during which physical facilities and capacities are particularly underutilized are after Christmas and the summer periods. If demand for some group of goods can be increased during these slack periods, the marginal cost of providing these goods will be much smaller than in other periods; no additional cost needs to be incurred to secure more personnel and physical facilities. White goods—towels and linens—are ideal choices for this role because of their even usage throughout the year. The

[10]*Ibid.*, pp. 238–240.

[11]Julian L. Simon, *Issues in the Economics of Advertising* (Urbana, Ill.: University of Illinois Press, 1970), pp. 207–217.

question is whether advertising can produce the desired change in the seasonal patterns of the white goods sale.

Table 16-1 shows the percentages of annual advertising expenditures incurred in January and February together with the percentages of total sales accounted for by household goods for selected years between 1947 and 1963. An examination of 1947 and 1948 data makes it clear that the advertising expenditures for towels and linens were high in January compared with February (and the rest of the months). High promotional expenditures incurred for the January white sale produce higher sales in January: while sales in February were lower than the yearly averages (except in 1947), sales in January were substantially larger than the annual averages. Advertising thus seems to have succeeded in altering the seasonal patterns of white good sales. Now, compare the years 1947–48 with 1962–63. The January white sale advertising expenditures increased significantly between the two periods. The increased advertising outlays are accompanied by substantial increases in white good sales during January, whereas low advertising February months were associated with very poor sales figures. Thus, "it seems safe to conclude that exogenous changes in the advertising pattern affected the pattern of seasonal sales of household textiles."[12]

The experience of August white sales — which is a post—World War II phenomenon, unlike the January white sale, which goes back to 1900 — also supports the above findings. According to the index

Table 16-1   Advertising and Sales for Towels and Linens

YEAR	PERCENTAGE OF YEARLY ADVERTISING FOR TOWELS AND LINENS IN EACH MONTH		PERCENTAGE OF TOTAL STORE SALES ACCOUNTED FOR BY HOUSEHOLD GOODS		
	January	*February*	*Annual Average*	*January*	*February*
1947	12.0	6.0	3.2	4.6	3.4
1948	12.8	5.7	3.2	5.5	2.8
.	.	.	.	.	.
.	.	.	.	.	.
1962	19.0	—	3.0	6.4	2.6
1963	19.2	—	3.0	6.9	2.6

Source: Julian R. Simon, *Issues in Economics of Advertising* (Urbana, Ill.: University of Illinois Press, 1970), pp. 207–217.

[12]*Ibid.*, p. 216.

of household textile sales, January and August sales of various categories of white goods rose far more than other categories of goods between 1947–49 (the base year) and 1965—even though their annual shares remained the same or declined slightly.

A shift in sales to low-capacity months in which the marginal cost of sales is low is a definite improvement in economic efficiency, and, therefore, is a valid example of the use of advertising for social betterment.[13]

[13]The critical reader may have noticed a difficulty contained in the Simon study. Since January white sale advertising informs more people of lower prices, the effect of increase in sales that comes from lower prices cannot be separated from that of advertising. Thus, the increased sales in January and August reflect the combined effect of advertising and lower prices, not that of advertising alone.

APPENDIX 16

The Theory of Games

One of the important developments in economic theory in the 1940s was the publication of von Neumann and Morgenstern's *Theory of Games and Economic Behavior*.[14] In this volume the authors extended the game theory and applied it to the study of economic behavior. Many economists were excited about this new development and wished that it would lead to the construction of a general theory of oligopoly. A vast literature on game theory developed since von Neumann and Morgenstern's original work, and game theory has been applied in such areas of economics as oligopoly theory, bargaining theory, and general equilibrium theory. However, the great expectations of the earlier years have gradually subsided, and most economists today think that game theory models are more useful in analyzing specific business problems than in constructing a general theory of oligopoly. Nevertheless, game theory models are important additions to the economist's box of tools. A simple game theory model reveals the nature of interdependent oligopolistic decision processes better than any other oligopoly model available.

The theory of games is a rather complicated mathematical discipline, a thorough exposition of which goes beyond the scope of our study. Thus, we will simply introduce some of the terminology of game theory and examine the process of making interdependent decisions with the aid of very elementary games.

GAME THEORY TERMINOLOGY

The theory of games analyzes optimal behavior of participants in "games of strategy," in which each strives for his maximum gain and the outcome depends not only on his actions but also on those

[14]John von Neumann and Oscar Morgenstern, 2d ed. (Princeton, N.J.: Princeton University Press, 1947).

of other participants.[15] In such games of strategy or interdependent decision-making processes, interests of participants (or players) may conflict or coincide. There may be uncertainty for each player because other players' actions may not be known with certainty.[16]

Games are described by specifying unambiguous *rules of the game* (as in chess). The theory assumes that each player is completely informed about the payoffs or outcomes of alternative strategies. A strategy is a complete specification of how a participant will play under all contingencies, represented by choices of all other players and of nature. The payments made by all players may add up to zero, as in poker, in which gains of some are exactly balanced by losses of others. Such games are called *zero-sum games.* Other games are of *constant-sum* or *variable-sum* variety. Any constant-sum game can be made a zero-sum game by the addition or subtraction of a constant. Depending on the number of players in the game, games are classified as *two-person games,* three person games, etc. If a player selects a particular strategy (such as strategy A or strategy B), he chooses a *pure strategy;* if he uses a chance mechanism selected by himself to make this selection, he chooses a *mixed or statistical strategy.*

TWO-PERSON ZERO-SUM GAMES

The simplest game is a two-person, zero-sum game, in which players A and B each have a finite number of strategies and make their choices unknown to each other. The nature of such a game can be explained referring to the payoff matrix of Table 16-2.[17] Let A_i represent pure strategies available to player A, and B_i, those available to player B. The interactions of rows and columns show *the payoffs to player A from player B.* Player A wishes to choose the largest of the payoffs shown; player B attempts to select the smallest (since the table shows his losses and A's gains).

The most desirable payoff to A is 8; B's is −10. A could obtain 8 if he chooses A_1, and B selects B_1. However, A's choice of A_1 matched by B's selection of B_3 will inflict on A a loss of 10 (that is, payoff of −10). Since A assumes that B will do his best to minimize A's payoff no matter what strategy A chooses, the minimum payoff associated with each of A's strategies is vital. The minimum payoffs for each row (A's strategies) are shown in the last column, labeled "row minima." These entries show the worst that could happen to A for each of his possible strategies. As the best defensive strategy, A seeks the maxi-

[15]Oscar Morgenstern, in the *International Encyclopedia of Social Sciences* (New York: Macmillan and Free Press, 1968) Vol. 6, p. 62.
[16]*Ibid.*
[17]This table is from Morgenstern, *op. cit.*, p. 64.

Table 16-2   Payoff Matrix for a Two-Person
Zero-Sum Game (payments
to A from B)

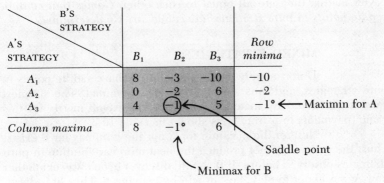

A'S STRATEGY \\ B'S STRATEGY	B_1	B_2	B_3	*Row minima*	
A_1	8	−3	−10	−10	
A_2	0	−2	6	−2	
A_3	4	⊝−1◄	5	−1*◄——Maximin for A	
Column maxima	8	−1*	6		

Saddle point

Minimax for B

mum of the row minima, or the *maximin*, which is the starred entry −1
(strategy A_3) of the payoff matrix. Conversely, player B knows that, no
matter what strategy he chooses, player A will select the strategy that
maximizes A's gain. Thus, player B wants to minimize the column
maxima, that is, he seeks the *minimax* solution, which is also −1
(strategy B_2). *When players act in this manner, we say that each player
is using minimax strategy—that is, each player selects the strategy
that minimizes his maximum loss.* A's maximin solution equals B's
minimax solution in our payoff table; the point at which maximin
equals minimax is called a *saddle point*—the circled entry in the
payoff matrix.[18]
    When the saddle point solution is reached, neither A nor
B has any incentive to change strategy. Given A_3, B's move away

[18]The name comes from the fact that in the following picture
of a saddle, point S is the minimum for the movement along the direction of
the solid arrow; but it is the maximum for the movement along the dotted
arrow.

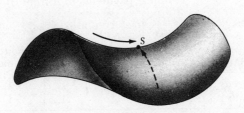

Figure 16-5   Saddle point

from the circled saddle point to either left or right will increase his loss. Similarly, given B_2, A's movement away from the saddle point will reduce his payoff. If there is more than one saddle point in the payoff matrix, they are all equal to each other. *Games that contain saddle points in pure strategies are called strictly determined.*

MIXED STRATEGIES

Unfortunately most games do not have saddle points in pure strategies, and thus are *not strictly determined*. The simplest case is illustrated by matching pennies. The payoff matrix for this game (payments to A from B) is shown in Table 16-3.

Neither the maximin for A nor the minimax for B exists. Thus, the game does not produce the neat minimax solution in pure strategies observed before. If B should discover in one way or another how A was about to play, he can win by copying A. Thus, it is disadvantageous for either player to show any preference for heads or tails or to display a regularity (such as alternate showing of head or tail). How can A prevent B from discovering his next move? The best A can do is to randomize his selection by, say, tossing the coin before showing it. This assures that heads and tails will in the long run appear with equal frequencies (no preference), and without any regularities. What A does is to select heads or tails with probability of 1/2. He himself does not know which strategy he will select. He selects a mixture of possible strategies with probabilities specified by himself (1/2 in this case).

What is the payoff for A if he plays by tossing coins? This can be determined easily as follows:

B's strategy	Expected payoff of A
Heads	$1/2(1) + 1/2(-1) = 0$
Tails	$1/2(-1) + 1/2(1) = 0$

Table 16-3   Payoff Matrix for Matching
Pennies (payments to A from B)

A'S STRATEGY \ B'S STRATEGY	Heads	Tails	Row minima
Heads	1	−1	−1
Tails	−1	1	−1
Column maxima	1	1	

If B plays heads, A will win 1 with probability of 1/2 (when he plays heads) and lose 1 with probability of 1/2 (when he plays tails). Thus, A's expected payoff when B plays heads is $1/2(1) + 1/2(-1) = 0$. Similarly, the expected payoff when B plays tails is 0. Since in matching pennies no preference or regularity should be shown, players should choose heads or tails with equal probability. The expected payoff of the game is zero.

The selection of optimal mixed strategy, however, is not always so simple. Let there be a premium on matching heads over matching tails as shown in the payoff matrix of Table 16-4.

Table 16-4   Payoff Matrix with Premium on
Matching Heads over Tails
(payments to A from B)

A'S STRATEGY \ B'S STRATEGY	Heads	Tails	Row minima
Heads	2	−1	−1
Tails	−1	1	−1
Column maxima	2	1	

In this game A stands to gain. But how can A realize this gain? If A chooses heads and B chooses heads, A gains 2. However, expecting this possibility B may choose tails and A may end up with loss of 1. A, in turn, realizes this possibility and shows tails, and so on. Obviously, there is no pure strategy solution and a mixed strategy is called for. What are the optimal mixed strategies to be chosen by players? That is, what should be the probabilities with which heads or tails should appear in the mixture of strategies? We shall show that the best mixed strategy of A is to choose heads with probability of 0.4.

The expected payoff to A from B when A shows heads with the probability of p and tails with the probability of $1 - p$ are as follows:

B's strategy	Expected payoffs to A
Heads	$p(2) + (1 - p)(-1) = 3p - 1$
Tails	$p(-1) + (1 - p)(1) = 1 - 2p$

Expected payoffs to A when B shows heads are $3p - 1$, which clearly increases as the value of p increases. Expected payoffs when B shows tails, however, are given by $1 - 2p$, and decreases as p increases. It can be shown that A's optimal (maximin) solution is obtained by equating the expected payoff when B shows heads to that when B shows tails.[19] Thus, the optimal mixed strategy is obtained by letting:

$$3p - 1 = 1 - 2p$$
$$p = 0.4$$

The optimal mixed strategy for A is to choose heads with the probability of 0.4 and tails with the probability of 0.6. And the expected payoff of the game is (by substituting $p = 0.4$ into $3p - 1$ or $1 - 2p$):

$$3(0.4) - 1 = 0.2 \text{ or } 1 - 2(0.4) = 0.2$$

Player A can expect to win 0.2 penny per game in the long run.

Von Neumann proved that all two-person zero-sum games can be made strictly determined by introducing mixed strategies. The strategic decision involved is the specification of the randomization device and the assignment of proper probabilities to each of the available pure strategies.

SOME DIFFICULTIES INVOLVED IN GAME THEORY

Our illustrations so far have been in terms of two-person zero-sum games. However, most games applicable to business and economic situations are of nonzero-sum varieties. For instance, in a typical market transaction, both the buyer and the seller gain. Two giants in an oligopolistic industry may collude and increase the profits of both firms. In a cut-throat warfare, every firm involved can lose. As we consider games in which more than two players are involved and as we introduce the possibilities of collusion among the players, games get complex rapidly, and results with any predictive value are hard to come by.

The minimax strategies, the heart of Von Neumann and Morgenstern's theory, are perfect from a defensive point of view. However, a theory of true offensive strategies requires new ideas and has not yet been developed.[20]

Many economists criticize the minimax strategy as being unduly pessimistic. It assumes that the opponent always succeeds in choosing the strategy that is most damaging. It doesn't allow a player to take advantage of the situation in which the opponent may not choose such a strategy. Some suspect that a businessman may try

---

[19]For simple graphic solution, see Henri Theil, *et al.*, *Operations Research and Quantitative Economics* (New York: McGraw-Hill, 1965), pp. 146–148.

[20]Morgenstern, *op. cit.*, p. 65.

to maximize his gains assuming very favorable reactions on the part of his competitors as well as of nature.

PIG FARMERS: A NONCONSTANT-SUM GAME WITH MORE PLAYERS

Some of the complications that arise when there are more than two persons or when the game is not zero-sum can be illustrated by the following example.[21] Consider the nonzero-sum game for a pig breeder A. His problem is how many pigs to breed each year. Suppose that in addition to A there are 1,000 other pig breeders, all faced with the same problem. It would seem to be a 1,001-person game, but by combining all others under the one name "colleagues," pig breeder A can consider it as a game between himself on the one hand and his colleagues collectively on the other.

Suppose now that all pig breeders can produce either 10 or 25 pigs. If all breeders produce 10 pigs, there will be few pigs on the market that year, and each will bring in a good price of $400. Since the costs of breeding are $250, each pig clears a profit of $150 for his breeder. Hence, A gains $10 \times 150 = \$1,500$. Each and every one of his colleagues also earns a $1,500 profit. If A decides now to start producing 25 pigs, while all his colleagues continue to breed only 10, there will be 15 more pigs on the market. This will not perceptibly influence the price, and thus A gains $25 \times 150 = \$3,750$. What happens, however, if every breeder produces his capacity of 25 pigs? Then, there will be a large supply, and the market price will fall sharply to $275. This leaves a profit of $25 for each pig and of $25 \times 25 = \$625$ for each farmer. If A in this situation were to produce only 10 pigs, his profit would drop to $10 \times 25 = \$250$.

Thus, A has two possibilities, which we shall indicate by $A10$ and $A25$. His profit depends upon what his colleagues do. For convenience we assume that either all colleagues produce 10 or they all produce 25 pigs. These two possibilities will be indicated by $C10$ and $C25$. The payoff matrix, which gives the yearly profit for each farmer, is shown in Table 16-5.

From this scheme, A concludes immediately that he should produce as many pigs as possible. Whatever his colleagues do he is better off producing 25 rather than 10 pigs. He will make a profit of $3,750 instead of $1,500 if his colleagues produce only 10 pigs each, and a profit of $625 instead of $250 if all others produce up to capacity. In short, $A25$ *dominates* $A10$.

[21]Quoted from Henri Theil, *et al., Operations Research and Quantitative Economics* (New York: McGraw-Hill, 1965), pp. 152–153. The author expresses his thanks to the publisher for the permission to quote from this work.

Table 16-5

A'S STRATEGY	OTHER'S STRATEGY	
	C10	C25
A10	A, $1,500 C, $1,500	A, $250 C, $625
A25	A, $3,750 C, $1,500	A, $625 C, $625

But now the tragedy. Each and every one of the individual pig breeders can make a similar payoff matrix. Each can consider the 1,000 others collectively as colleagues, and each will, just like A, decide to produce a lot of pigs. So they will each make a profit of $625 a year. If they agreed to produce only a few pigs, however, they would all make a profit of $1,500. The decision that is correct for each individual farmer is collectively wrong. This simple game shows one of the reasons why many people think that occasionally the government should interfere in the market of agricultural products, and in practice nearly every government does.

In conclusion, let us devote a few words to games for more than two persons. One of the complications that can arise is that it may be profitable for a number of players to form a combination or cartel. Then a new game results, with fewer participants and a modified payoff matrix. In fact, even when there are only two players, cartels cannot wholly be excluded. Two airlines competing on the same route can (and as a rule do) make some rules to mitigate the competition. Sometimes, especially in Europe, they even start working together on a specific route. Admittedly, if it is a zero-sum game, they cannot both profit from combining, but as a matter of established fact, many games are not zero-sum.

EXERCISES 16

Further Topics in Oligopoly and Monopolistic Competition

16-1 The cigarette industry was forbidden to advertise on TV as of January 1972.

    1. How would this affect the sales and profit of the industry?

    2. Would you say that TV cigarette advertising tended to increase the industry demand or that it merely redistributed a given demand among different brands?

16-2 The following are often cited as examples of monopolistic competition:

    a. retail clothing stores in large cities
    b. gasoline service stations in large cities
    c. the furniture industry

    1. Which of the above is the best example of Chamberlinian monopolistic competition? Why?

    2. Which of the above is the least satisfactory example of Chamberlin's monopolistic competition? Why?

16-3 Some large cities occasionally experience the so-called gasoline price war. Does Chamberlin's large-group model apply here? Which, if any, of the Chamberlinian assumptions is violated in this case?

16-4 It is well known that the basic chemical or pharmaceutical ingredients of various brands of *aspirin* are identical. Yet, one can find in most U.S. towns a well-known, nationally advertised brand selling at three or four times as high a price as that of an unadvertised brand. How can you explain this phenomenon?

16-5 "Resale price maintenance,* if effective and accompanied by ease of entry, is likely to produce excess capacities in affected industries." Comment.
(*The law that prohibits selling covered merchandise at prices below manufacturers' suggested retail prices)

16-6 "Advertising enables us to have free radio and TV and inexpensive newspapers and magazines." Do you agree with this quotation? Are radio and TV free, or to quote a popular question, "Is there such a thing as a free lunch?"

The remaining exercises are for those who studied the appendix.

16-7 Given the following payoff (from B to A) matrix:

A'S STRATEGY \ B'S STRATEGY	B_1	B_2	B_3	*Row minima*
A_1	20	6	3	_____
A_2	15	8	10	_____
A_3	0	3	7	_____
Column maxima	___	___	___	

1. Fill in the row minima and column maxima entries in the above table.
2. Is the game strictly determined? That is, does it have a saddle point? _____
3. What is the minimax solution to this game? _____
4. What is the value of this game to player A? _____.

16-8 The following payoff matrix (from B to A) is reproduced from Table 16-4 of the text.

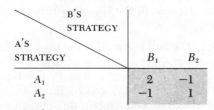

A'S STRATEGY \ B'S STRATEGY	B_1	B_2
A_1	2	−1
A_2	−1	1

1. What is B's optimal strategy? _____
2. What is B's expected payoff (or the value of the game to B)?
3. Is B's value of the game consistent with A's value of the game shown in the text?

16-9 Examine the following payoff matrix (to A from B):

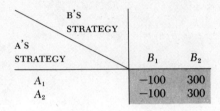

1. What is the nature of firm A's dependence on firm B?
2. What is the nature of firm B's dependence on firm A?
3. In examining B's strategies, we note that B_1 is dominated by B_2. What do we mean by "dominated"?

CHAPTER SEVENTEEN

PRICING AND EMPLOYMENT OF RESOURCES

In the preceding chapters, the discussion of production and cost was succeeded by several chapters on pricing and output decisions under various market structures. We are now ready to discuss the factors that affect the demand and supply of productive resources (inputs, or factors) the firm must have in order to produce its outputs.[1] In this chapter, we shall be concerned primarily with the determination of factor prices and the theory of demand for productive factors. Initially, our analysis proceeds under the assumption of perfectly competitive product and factor markets. The case of imperfectly competitive product and/or factor markets is introduced toward the end of the chapter. The chapter-end applications examine such controversial topics as the "equal pay for equal work" argument and the minimum-wage law. Additional topics in pricing and employment of resources are introduced in Chapter Eighteen.

Though our primary concern in this chapter is the theory of demand for productive resources, it must be remembered that the study of pricing and employment of factors is also vital in understanding income distribution (which largely determines one's ability to command goods and services in the marketplace). Individuals' incomes in a market economy like ours are determined largely by the quantities of resources they can offer for sale and the prices they command. Those with talents, skills, property, etc., that are in short supply and are sought after by many can command high

[1]Terms such as *resources, productive resources, factors, factors of production, inputs,* and *productive inputs* are used interchangeably in most economic writings. We shall also follow these conventions.

prices for such objects. People who have few objects that are marketable receive little income, and their abilities to command goods and services in the market are limited.

17-1 DETERMINATION OF FACTOR PRICE

The price of a productive factor such as labor in a competitive market is determined, like that of a good in the commodity market, by the interaction of demand and supply for the factor. In Figure 17-1, the industry demand curve, D, is obtained by summing individual firms' demand curves for the factor. Similarly, the industry supply curve, S, is constructed by summing individual factor owners' supply curves.

Lest we confuse the factor market discussion with that of a commodity market, we shall use v to represent the quantity of an input and w to represent its price. Given the demand and supply curves pictured in Figure 17-1, the equilibrium price and quantity for the factor are w^* dollars per unit and v^* units per period. The demand and supply analysis of the commodity market applies just as well to the factor market. If the price of the factor is higher than w^*, there will be a surplus, or unemployment, of the factor; if the price is lower than the equilibrium price, there will be a shortage of the factor.

THE NATURE OF DEMAND AND SUPPLY FOR A FACTOR

The forces affecting demand and supply in the factor market may be quite different from those in the commodity market.

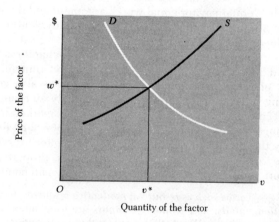

Figure 17-1 Demand and supply in the factor market

For instance, we shall show in the following section that the demand for a factor is a *derived demand; that is, the demand for such productive factors as labor and capital goods is derived from the demand for final goods that are produced by using the productive services.* Thus, a change in the demand for a final good will change the demand for the factors used in producing the product. A change in production technology is likely to create different patterns of demand for productive factors. A change in the availability and/or price of a substitute or complementary factor will change the demand for the related factor.

The *supply of a factor* may be affected by quite different forces from those affecting the commodity supply. For instance, the location of a labor supply curve is greatly influenced by such institutional factors as labor unions, laws relating to child and woman labor, general and vocational education, G.I. Bills, the AMA's position toward medical school enrollment, etc. However, the market labor supply curve will be positively sloped because higher wages must, in general, be offered to entice more labor service into the market. The supply of land (as a location or overall area) is completely inelastic. However, the supply of land for a specific purpose (such as growing wheat) is positively sloped, showing that if wheat cultivation is more profitable, the wheat acreage will be increased at the expense of acreage devoted to some other uses not as remunerative. The supply curve of *intermediate inputs—goods that are produced by firms to be used in further production by other firms—*will be positively sloped, since such goods are commodities produced by firms. In summary, despite some peculiarities attached to the supply of factors, the market supply curve of labor, land for a specific use, or an intermediate good will be positively sloped.

The traditional microeconomic approach to the study of the factor market is to assume that the price of a factor is already established by the competitive forces in the market, and to examine how the firm selects the optimal quantity of the factor to be purchased at the given price. We shall also follow this convention in starting our discussion of the factor market.

17-2 EMPLOYMENT OF A FACTOR UNDER PERFECT COMPETITION

Our purpose in this section is to show how the firm selects its profit-maximizing quantity of an input under a specific set of assumptions. We assume the following:

1. *Perfect competition prevails both in the product market and in the factor market.* Thus, the firm can sell all its output at the going market price. Similarly the competitive wage rate is

already established by the market, and the firm adjusts its employment of a factor given this wage rate.

2. There is only *one variable factor* (such as a specific kind of labor), and the quantities of other cooperating inputs are fixed. This assumption will be relaxed later.

THE VALUE OF MARGINAL PRODUCT AND THE OPTIMAL INPUT DECISION

Given the above assumptions, how does the firm determine the optimal quantity of, say, labor to be employed? Fortunately, we need not start from scratch to answer this question. The marginal analysis with which we analyzed consumer behavior and the various product markets is just as useful in examining the factor market. The marginal analysis suggests that if the additional revenue you can obtain by hiring a man (using him in production, and selling the product) is greater than the wage you have to pay him, you should hire him. *The additional revenue brought in by an additional unit of an input, $\Delta TR/\Delta v$, is called the marginal revenue product, MRP, of that input.*[2] *In the special case in which the product market is perfectly competitive, it is referred to as the value of the marginal product, VMP.* Since ΔTR in a perfectly competitive commodity market is equal to Δq times the price of the commodity, p, we have:

$$VMP = \frac{\Delta TR}{\Delta v} = \frac{p \cdot \Delta q}{\Delta v} = p \cdot MPP$$

The VMP of an input is equal to the product of the price of the good produced and the marginal physical product of the input.

Using the concept of VMP, we can now state the optimal input decision rule for a firm that operates in perfectly competitive commodity and factor markets. If the VMP of an input is greater than (equal to, less than) its price, then increase (maintain, reduce) the usage of the input. Needless to say, the quantity of input refers to the rate of flow, for example, 1,000 man-hours per week. Using v to show the quantity of an input to be employed and W for the input price, we may summarize the decision rule by the following shorthand notation:

$$VMP = W : \begin{matrix} > & : v \nearrow \\ & : v \rightarrow \\ < & : v \searrow \end{matrix}$$

A NUMERICAL EXAMPLE OF OPTIMAL INPUT DECISIONS

Let us consider a numerical example referring to the hypothetical data given in Table 17-1. Column (1) shows the amount

[2]Also known as the *marginal value product* and *marginal net revenue product*.

Table 17-1 Value of Marginal Product and
a Competitive Firm's Employment Decision

(1)	(2)	(3)		(4)	(5)
		VALUE OF			OPTIMAL DIRECTION OF CHANGE
	MARGINAL	MARGINAL		PRICE	IN
QUANTITY	PHYSICAL	PRODUCT		OF	INPUT
OF	PRODUCT	(VMP)		INPUT	USAGE
INPUT	(MPP)	= \$5 × MPP			
1	10	\$50	>	\$25	Increase
2	9	45	>	25	Increase
3	8	40	>	25	Increase
4	7	35	>	25	Increase
5	6	30	>	25	Increase
6	5	25	=	25	Do not change (equilibrium)
7	3	15	<	25	Decrease

of an input (say, labor) used per unit of time (say, week). Column (2) shows the marginal (physical) product of the input.[3] Assuming that the produced good sells at \$5 per unit, the VMP entries in column (3) are obtained by multiplying the MPP's in column (2) by \$5. Column (4) indicates that the going price of the input (say, the wage rate) is \$25 per week. Comparing the size of VMP and the wage rate in columns (3) and (4), it is clear that the firm should hire more labor if VMP is greater than the wage rate. Similarly, if VMP is less than the wage rate, the firm should reduce its use of labor. Thus, *the equilibrium rate of employment is attained where VMP is equal to the wage rate.*

---

[3]The reader may wish to review Table 7-1 on p. 165, in which the marginal product of labor is derived from the total product schedule and the three stages of production are marked off. In section 7-6, it was shown that the producer will choose to operate only in Stage II. For our current purpose, it is important to note that the marginal product of labor (MP_l) *declines* but remains positive in Stage II. Thus, only the declining portion of the MPP schedule is shown in Table 17-1.

A GRAPHIC ANALYSIS OF OPTIMAL INPUT DECISIONS

Let us now consider a graphic analysis of the employment of a factor. A marginal physical product, MPP, curve is given in Figure 17-2a. Given an MPP curve, the VMP curve is obtained simply by multiplying MPP by the price at which the product sells. Figure 17-2b, in which the vertical axis shows VMP (the dollar value of MPP), contains three possible VMP curves — VMP depends not only on MPP but also on the market price of the product, p. If the price of the product produced and sold is $2, the VMP curve is much steeper than if the price is only $1 or $.50.

The VMP curve must eventually slope downward to the right. This follows from the law of diminishing returns by which MPP must eventually decline. Therefore, VMP, which is the product of the fixed price of the good and MPP, must eventually decline. Furthermore, we have shown in section 7-6 that the producer will choose to

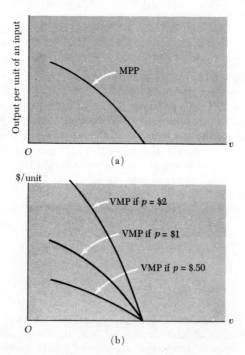

Figure 17-2 The relationship between MPP and VMP curves; (a) marginal physical product curve, (b) value of marginal physical product curves

operate only in Stage II, in which MPP declines but remains positive. Thus, only the declining segment of the VMP curve is relevant for optimal input decisions.

In Figure 17-3, a VMP curve and the value of average product, VAP, curve that corresponds to this VMP curve are shown. Suppose the price of the input is W per unit, then the profit-maximizing rate (quantity per unit of time) of employment is v^*, where the VMP curve intersects the horizontal line WE — whose height shows the price of the input. The total variable cost of hiring the input is $OWEv^*$, and *the total revenue product — the total revenue generated by Ov^* units of the variable input — is $OJKv^*$*. The shaded area, $WJKE$, represents *the excess of the revenue over the variable factor cost and is referred to as the gross (or residual) profit*. Out of this gross profit, the firm must pay for the fixed factors (say, capital and land), and what remains will be the (pure) economic profit.

17-3 A COMPETITIVE FIRM'S FACTOR DEMAND CURVE

We have seen that a competitive, or price-taker, firm will adjust its employment of an input in such a way that the VMP of an input equals its price. In Figure 17-4, if the wage rate is B per week, the firm will purchase BB' units of labor per week. Similarly, if the going wage rate is $C, D, E,$ or F dollars, the amount of the input demanded by the firm will be $CC', DD', EE',$ or FF' units, respectively. If the wage rate is higher than the maximum value of average product,

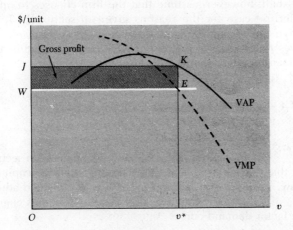

Figure 17-3 A competitive firm's optimal input decision

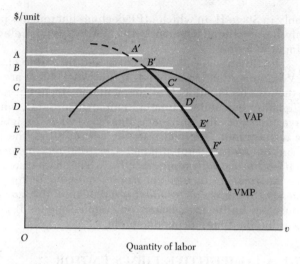

Figure 17-4   Demand curve for a factor

VAP, the firm will not hire any labor. For instance, if the wage rate is $A and the firm hires AA' units of labor (the amount at which VMP = the wage rate), the total variable cost will exceed the total revenue product; and the firm will incur an avoidable loss.[4] The case in which the wage rate is equal to VAP is a borderline situation: the gross profit is zero whether the firm hires BB' units or shuts down the operation. We shall, however, assume that the firm chooses to operate in this borderline case for the reasons given in section 12-7. Thus, a competitive firm's factor demand curve is given by the *portion of the* VMP *curve that lies on or below the* VAP *curve.* In Figure 17-4, the factor demand curve is shown by a heavier solid curve.

17-4 FACTOR DEMAND CURVE WHEN COOPERATING INPUT(S) CAN BE CHANGED

The derivation of the factor demand curve in section 17-3 assumed that the quantities of other inputs, such as capital, were fixed. Now, we relax the assumption, allow the desired adjustment in the use of cooperating factor(s), and observe how this change will affect the factor demand curve.

[4]Unlike the fixed cost that cannot be avoided in the short run, the labor cost is a variable cost that can be avoided even in the short run.

A reduction in the market wage rate will induce the firm to hire a larger amount of labor. As more labor is used in the production process, the firm will increase the use of the cooperating factor, capital. This increase in capital cooperating with labor, in turn, increases the MPP of labor, and shifts the VMP curve of labor upward and rightward. In Figure 17-5, if the wage rate is $W and the VMP of labor is shown by the curve labeled VMP, the equilibrium input combination is given by point E. The firm hires v units of labor. Now, as the wage rate drops to $W', the firm hires more labor and increases the amount of the cooperating factor, capital. Since there is additional capital with which to work, the productivity of labor increases and the appropriate VMP curve is now given by VMP'. The new equilibrium is at E', where the current wage rate line, W'E', crosses the VMP' curve. Drawing a freehand curve through points E and E', we secure *the factor demand curve for labor, when the amount of capital is changeable.* This demand curve is flatter than the VMP curve.

17-5   THE INDUSTRY FACTOR DEMAND CURVE

We have seen how the competitive individual firm's demand curve for an input is obtained from its VMP curve, or its modification when the usage of cooperating factor(s) can be varied. As in the case of the market demand curve for a commodity, the *industry factor* demand curve is obtained by summing individual firms' factor demand curves. But there is an important additional consideration that affects the shape of an individual firm's factor demand curve when all firms in the industry are hiring greater amounts of an input and

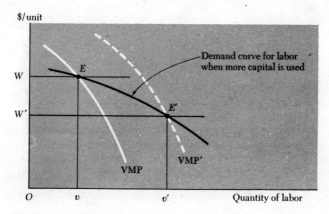

Figure 17-5 Demand curve for a factor when cooperating factor can be changed

expanding the industry output. Suppose the price of an input declines and all firms in the industry hire more of the input and increase their outputs. The ensuing increase in the industry output, of necessity, depresses the price of the good; this decrease in the commodity price, in turn, lowers the VMP curve downward. In Figure 17-6, the original equilibrium position of the firm is given by point E, where its factor demand curve d_1 (which is the VMP of labor curve) intersects the wage rate line WE. As the input price is reduced from $W to W', however, there is an industry-wide increase in the usage of the input, which increases the industry output and reduces the commodity price. The reduction in the commodity price *shifts* the firm's factor demand curve—via its effect on VMP—downward to d_2. Thus, the effect of the decline in the wage rate from $W to W', when there is an industry-wide increase in the use of labor, is to increase the individual firm's usage from WE to $W'E'$ per period—not to $W'J$. Connecting the successive equilibrium points with a freehand curve, the factor demand curve dd' is obtained. The industry factor demand curve is obtained as the sum of all such dd' curves.

17-6 SHIFTS IN A FACTOR DEMAND CURVE

In the preceding section, we have seen that a VMP curve may shift when the amount of cooperating input(s) is changed. The following are brief descriptions of the factors that tend to shift a VMP curve.

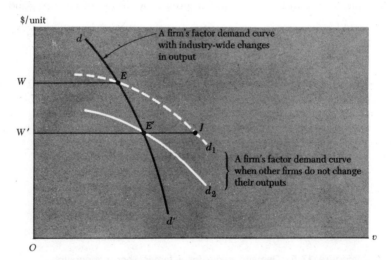

Figure 17-6 Factor demand curve with industry-wide changes in output

1. *Technological progress.* An improved technology will increase MPP of an input and shift the VMP curve upward.
2. *Amount and quality of cooperating factor.* If a greater amount or the same amount of a better-quality cooperating factor is used, the productivity of an input will increase and the VMP curve will shift upward.
3. *Price of the commodity.* If changing market demand and supply conditions raise the price of the commodity produced by an input, the input's VMP curve shifts upward.
4. *Miscellaneous.* Any other factors that affect the price of the commodity produced or the marginal physical product of the input will affect the position of the VMP curve. For example, a repeal of the excise tax on the good produced by an input may increase the net after-tax price received by the producer, and shift the VMP curve upward. Similarly, an increase in the price of a cooperating factor tends to reduce the demand for an input.

17-7 DETERMINANTS OF ELASTICITY OF DEMAND FOR A FACTOR

What determines the elasticity of demand for an input? First, like the elasticity of demand for a commodity, the most important determinant of the elasticity of demand for a factor is the *availability of a substitute,* in this case, an input (or technological) substitute(s). If a firm depends on electricity as its source of power, and if there is no alternative source of power supply, the firm's price elasticity of demand for electricity has to be very inelastic. Second, the *price elasticity of demand for the product* (produced by using a particular input) has important bearing on the elasticity of demand for the input. If a little change in the input price that is passed forward to the product price causes a relatively large change in the sale of the product, the quantity of this input used will also be affected substantially. Thus, the more elastic is the demand for the product, the more elastic is the demand for the factor input. Third, *time* is an important determinant of the factor elasticity of demand. Given a longer time, demand for an input will be more elastic.

17-8 THE RELATIONSHIP BETWEEN INPUT AND OUTPUT DECISIONS

A decision to produce *x* units of output implies a decision to employ the optimal combination of inputs needed to produce the output. The equivalence of the competitive firm's output and employment decisions, therefore, can be readily demonstrated for the single-input case. The optimal output decision for a competitive firm requires that it equate its commodity price to its marginal cost of producing that good. The marginal cost for a competitive firm (assuming labor to be the only variable input) is equal to the wage rate, W, times the amount of additional labor used, ΔL, for each additional unit of output. Thus, we may write

$$MC = \frac{\Delta TC}{\Delta Q} = \frac{W \cdot \Delta L}{\Delta Q} = W(\Delta L/\Delta Q) \qquad (17\text{-}1)$$

The equilibrium condition in the product market, thus, requires

$$p = W(\Delta L/\Delta Q) \qquad (17\text{-}2)$$

The equilibrium condition in the input market for a competitive firm is given by

$$W = VMP = p(\Delta Q/\Delta L) \qquad (17\text{-}3)$$

The equilibrium condition for the input market given by (17-3), however, can be rearranged to make it exactly the same as (17-2), which gives the equilibrium condition for the product market. Clearly, the optimal input decision and the optimal output decision are identical.

17-9 FACTOR DEMAND AND INPUT DECISION UNDER IMPERFECT COMPETITION

Let us now abandon the assumption of the perfectly competitive commodity and factor markets, and consider a more general case.

MARGINAL REVENUE PRODUCT, MARGINAL RESOURCE COST, AND OPTIMAL INPUT DECISION

What is the additional revenue brought in by an additional unit of an input when competition is imperfect? When competition is imperfect, the firm's product price declines as its output increases. Therefore, the relevant *marginal revenue product*, MRP, is obtained by multiplying the MPP and the marginal revenue, MR, which declines as output increases. Thus,

$$MRP = MR \cdot MPP$$

The reader may note that the VMP is merely a special case of MRP; if the commodity market is perfect, price is equal to marginal revenue, and therefore,

$$MRP = MR(MPP) = p(MPP) = VMP$$

When the factor market is competitive, the employer can buy all the input he needs at the going market price. When the

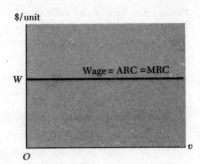

Figure 17-7 Resource costs in a competitive factor market

factor market is imperfectly competitive, a large employer tends to bid up the market price of the input he purchases. Thus *the cost of an additional unit of input, the marginal resource cost,* MRC,[5] will be larger than the input price. In Figure 17-7, for a firm in a competitive factor market, the going wage rate is equal to the marginal and average resource costs. The case of an imperfectly competitive factor market is shown in Figure 17-8. As the rate of input usage increases, the factor price is bid up; thus, the wage rate line, or the average resource cost curve, ARC, has a positive slope. The marginal resource cost, MRC, curve corresponding to the ARC curve is shown by a dotted line, and must lie above ARC.

The marginal decision rule applied to the employment of an input when the commodity and input markets are both imperfectly competitive, therefore, requires the comparison of the marginal revenue product and the marginal resource cost. In order to maximize

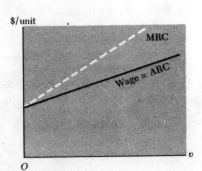

Figure 17-8 Resource costs in an imperfect market

[5]Such terms as *marginal factor cost, marginal resource cost, marginal input cost,* and *marginal expense of input* are used interchangeably in economic literature.

profit, the firm must increase (decrease, not change) the usage of an input according as its MRP is greater than (less than, equal to) its MRC. In terms of the shorthand notation used in section 17-2:

$$
\text{MRP} = \text{MRC} : \begin{cases} > & : v \nearrow \\ & : v \rightarrow \\ < & : v \searrow \end{cases}
$$

A GRAPHIC ANALYSIS

In Figure 17-9, various factor cost and revenue product curves are shown for a firm that faces imperfect competition in both commodity and factor markets. The MRP curve must eventually slope downward to the right for two reasons. First, as in the case of VMP, MRP (which is the product of MR and MPP) declines due to the law of diminishing returns. Second, unlike the case of VMP, MRP must decline because MR decreases as more output produced by greater quantities of input comes to the market.

The selection of the profit-maximizing input usage, given the revenue and cost curves in Figure 17-9, is rather obvious. *The profit-maximizing solution is indicated by point E, where* MRP *curve intersects the* MRC *curve.* Thus the firm will employ v^* units of input and pay v^*L dollars per unit—the lowest price the factor suppliers are willing to accept for v^* units (as indicated by the ARC curve). The firm will receive the gross (or residual) profit of *WJKL* dollars. As indicated in Section 17-2, the firm pays for other productive

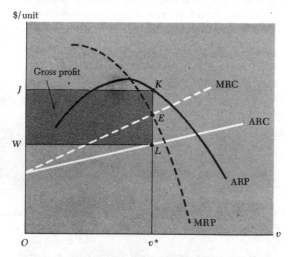

Figure 17-9 Optimal input decision when both the factor and product markets are imperfect

factors out of this gross profit and what is left becomes the economic profit.

THE MRP CURVE IS NOT NECESSARILY THE DEMAND CURVE

Depending on whether the factor market is perfectly competitive or imperfectly competitive, the MRP curve may or may not be the demand curve for an input. *When the factor market is imperfect* and the MRC and ARC diverge, *the MRP is not the demand curve* for an input. Point E in Figure 17-9 gives the optimal quantity, v^*, but not the price paid to the input; the price must be obtained from the ARC curve. Therefore, the MRP curve fails to show the price-quantity locus that defines a demand curve.

When the input market is competitive, however, the MRP curve is the demand curve for an input. In Figure 17-10, we assume an imperfectly competitive product market; thus, we label the revenue productivity curve MRP, not VMP as we would if we assumed a perfectly competitive product market. Various possible wage rate lines are, however, shown by horizontal lines: the firm buys in a competitive factor market, and the factor price is not affected by the amount this firm purchases. The optimal employment decisions (equating MRP and the wage rate) under the given conditions will require the firm to employ AA', BB', CC', or DD' units according to whether the wage rate is A, B, C, or D dollars. Clearly, the MRP curve

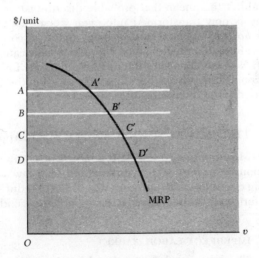

Figure 17-10 Factor demand curve with competitive factor market and imperfect product market

on which points A', B', C', and D' are located shows the locus of price-quantity relationships that identifies the firm's demand curve for the input.

17-10 EQUAL PAY FOR EQUAL WORK: An Application

The competitive market solution to the remuneration of a worker is to pay him according to his value of marginal productivity. Thus, paying equally all those workers whose values of marginal product are equal makes sense. Since in many occupations we find that women and minority groups are paid less than white males performing similar tasks, the appeal for "equal pay for equal work" is frequently heard. One basic difficulty involved in translating this motto into operation is the ambiguity of the term, equal work. How do we know that the two workers perform equal work? Suppose a male and a female accountant are hired by a public accounting firm; do they necessarily have the same productivity? Wouldn't the net productivity—after allowing for the training costs, probable number of years for which the employee may remain with the firm, etc.— differ substantially for the two workers? If they do differ, wouldn't paying the same salary for the two workers violate the principle of so-called equal pay for equal work? Suppose the productivity of a male accountant is higher(??) than that of a female accountant, and that the employer is legally required to pay the same salary to both, wouldn't the employer decline to employ the female employee? Of course! Wouldn't this mean that probable discrimination in the form of lower pay is now transformed into even worse discrimination in the form of no employment and no pay? Again, of course. It is no wonder, therefore, that (male) labor unions have advocated such laws.

No one objects to the ideal of equal pay for equal work. The operational difficulty of this slogan comes from the difficult task of measuring the productivities of each worker.

17-11 THE LEGAL MINIMUM WAGE: An Application

Minimum-wage legislation has its origin in our concern for the economic welfare of the workers toiling at low wages under poor working conditions. Its purpose was to stop or reduce the exploitation of unfortunate workers, and to raise their wages and purchasing power.

IMPERFECT LABOR MARKET

The labor market visualized by the supporters of minimum-wage laws may be described by Figure 17-11. The factor market is imperfect, and the employers are assumed to be wage-setters.

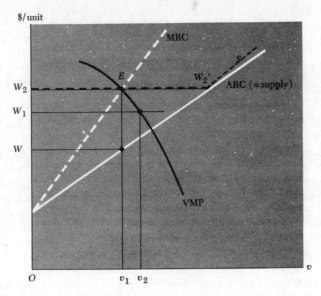

Figure 17-11   Legal minimum wage: imperfect factor market

Thus, the labor supply curve to the employer slopes upward, and the marginal resource cost curve lies above the average resource cost curve. For simplicity, we assume a competitive product market, and draw a VMP curve of labor. Given the VMP curve and the MRC and ARC curves, the profit-maximizing employer hires v_1 units of labor (where MRC = VMP) and pays the wage rate of W dollars per unit. The wage rate being paid, $\$W$, is clearly lower than the value of the marginal product of labor, $\$W_2$; in that sense, labor may be said to be "exploited".

Suppose the minimum wage is legislated to be W_2 dollars. This minimum wage changes the supply curve to $W_2 W_2' S$; the wage cannot be lower than the horizontal line $W_2 W_2'$, but in order to hire workers in excess of $W_2 W_2'$ units, higher wages indicated by the supply (ARC) curve must be paid. When the supply curve is flat (as in the $W_2 W_2'$ segment), it is both ARC and MRC curves; thus, $W_2 W_2'$ curve is also MRC for the employer subject to the minimum wage coverage. The profit-maximizing solution where MRC = VMP is given by point E. The employer employs v_1 units (same as before the minimum-wage legislation), but now pays the wage that is equal to the value of marginal product. There is no exploitation.

If the minimum wage were set somewhere between W and W_2 dollars, say, at W_1, the effect would be to increse employment from v_1 to v_2 units and also raise the wage rate from W to W_1 dollars. Thus, if the employers had wage-setting powers and were paying wages lower than VMP, the minimum-wage legislation could increase the wage rate, and may even increase employment as well.

COMPETITIVE LABOR MARKET

Many writers suspect that few employers of unskilled workers, for whom the minimum wage law is intended, have enough power to set the wage on their own. Thus, they believe that a competitive factor market model may be a closer approximation to the unskilled labor market. The effect of a minimum-wage law when the factor market is competitive is shown in Figure 17-12. The equilibrium wage rate and employment before the minimum wage law is shown by point E, where the VMP curve intersects the horizontal wage rate line WW'. When the minimum wage is set at $\$W_1$, the new equilibrium is established at E'. The effect of the minimum-wage requirement is to raise the wage rate to those who remain employed; but a high price is paid, namely, the reduction in employment of v_2v_1 units. What good can the high minimum wage do to a worker who cannot find employment? Furthermore, some unemployed workers will seek their jobs in fields that are not covered by the minimum-wage law, and depress the wage rates in those areas. It is because of such unintended adverse effects on employment and wage rates that an economist referred to the minimum-wage law as the "most anti-Negro law on our statute books — in its effect, not its intent."

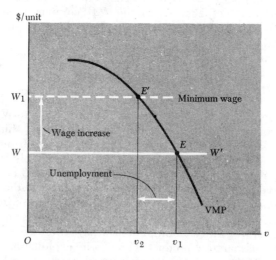

Figure 17-12 Legal minimum wage: competitive factor market

The federal minimum wage law can be considered as a spatial application of the equal-pay-for-equal-work argument. It may be argued that the workers in the South and North who do similar work be paid similar wages; and, therefore, that the wage rates in the South be raised to the Northern levels by a federal minimum wage law. The impact of such legislation will not be felt directly in the North, where the wage rates are already above the minimum, but the wage rates and employment in the South will be affected significantly. It will create unemployment in the South and/or slow down the movement of Northern industries to the South seeking that profit associated with lower wage costs. Can this be why the major supporters of minimum-wage laws are Northern legislators, unions, and industries?

EXERCISES 17

Pricing and Employment of Resources

17-1 Examine the following table, which shows the production function of a firm, and answer the questions below.

Number of variable input	Total output	Marginal physical product	Value of marginal product	Average physical product	Value of average product
10	1600	150	$750	160	$800
11	1750	100	500	159.2	795.5
12	1850	( )	( )	154.2	770.8
13	1930	( )	( )	148.5	( )
14	2000	( )	( )	142.9	( )
15	2050			136.7	( )

1. Assume that the price of the product is $5 per unit, and fill in the missing blanks in the above table.
2. From the information provided in the table, complete the following demand schedule for the input.

Input price	$750	500	400	350	300
Quantity demanded					

3. State concisely the rule for employing the profit-maximizing quantity of input when the data is discontinuous, as in the above table.

4. Suppose the "number of variable input" column above in problem (1) read 110, 111, 112, . . . , 115; would it change your demand schedule in problem (2)? Explain.

17-2 The following table shows the production function of a firm.

Output When Labor and Machines
Are Both Variables

UNITS OF LABOR \ UNITS OF MACHINES	11	12	13
10	120	180	220
11	130	195	240
12	136	205	255
13	140	213	265

1. Assuming that the firm sells its product competitively at $2 per unit, compute the VMP's of labor when labor is combined with 11, 12, 13 units of machines, respectively.

UNITS OF LABOR	VMP OF LABOR WHEN COMBINED WITH		
	11 machines	*12 machines*	*13 machines*
11	_____	_____	_____
12	_____	_____	_____
13	_____	_____	_____

2. Plot the three VMP curves on graph paper.

17-3 Suppose the pricing and output decision of an oligopolist is adequately explained by Sweezy's kinked demand curve model. What then is the implication for the elasticity of demand for the factors needed to produce the product?

17-4 Determine the profit-maximizing quantity of labor, l, to be employed given the following data:

$$\text{MPP}_l = 100 - 5l, \ p_l = \$5, \text{ and } p_x = \$10,$$

where MPP_l, p_l, and p_x stand for the marginal product of labor, price of labor, and the price of the commodity produced.

17-5 With the aid of some simple graphs, explain under what situations you would expect the imposition of a legal minimum wage to:

1. Have no effect on wages and employment. (Cite at least two possible examples.)
2. Increase the wage rate as well as the magnitude of unemployment.
3. Increase the wage rate and the amount of employment.
4. Increase the wage rate without reducing the amount of employment.
5. In the economic scene of the U.S., which of the above is the most likely case? Why?

17-6 Suppose a congressman advocates raising the legal minimum-wage rate so that the wages received by Black workers increase.

1. What is the impact of the higher minimum wage on the total wages received by the Black workers as a whole? Why?
2. Would discriminatory hiring practices be increased or decreased by the higher minimum wage? Why?

17-7 Many legislators' first concern may be the interest of their own constituents. Why is it then that the support for the minimum-wage law (which raises the wage rates in the South above its current rates but does not affect the wages in the North, which are already above the minimum) comes primarily from Northern legislators?

CHAPTER EIGHTEEN

ADDITIONAL TOPICS ON PRICING AND EMPLOYMENT OF RESOURCES

In this chapter we continue the discussion of pricing and employment of resources started in Chapter Seventeen by introducing such additional topics as economic rent, quasi-rent, wage differentials, substitution and income effects of an input price change, and bilateral monopoly. Applications dealing with labor union goals and policies and the single-tax proposal conclude the chapter.

18-1 ECONOMIC RENT

In its day-to-day usage, the term *rent* or *rental* refers to the price paid for the use of a good such as a house, an automobile, a television set, or a plot of land. However, rent means a very special thing in economic literature. *Economic rent is the payment to a factor over and above what is necessary to keep the factor in its current use.* In other words, economic rent is a payment to a factor in excess of its alternative cost, and practically any factor (not just land) may receive an economic rent.

Let us examine the nature of economic rent by referring to Figure 18-1, in which the industry demand and supply curves for a factor are shown. Given the demand and supply curves, the equilibrium price and quantity of the input are W dollars and v units. The total factor payment is OWEv dollars. Now we must ask whether the entire amount of payment, OWEv dollars, is needed to keep v units of the factor in the industry. Since each point on the supply curve shows the marginal cost of offering an additional unit of the factor, the payment needed to keep v units of the factor in the industry is

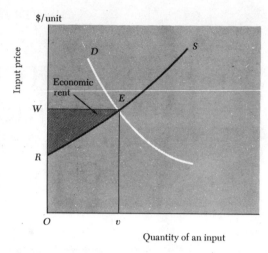

Figure 18-1 Economic rent

shown by the area *OREv*. Therefore, *the shaded area RWE* — the difference between the total factor payment, *OWEv*, and the payment necessary to keep *v* units in the industry, *OREv* — *shows the economic rent* accruing to the factor employed in this industry.[1]

Note that any factor whose supply is less than perfectly elastic receives an economic rent. In general, the steeper the supply curve of a factor, the larger is its economic rent. If the supply of a factor is perfectly inelastic, its supply curve is vertical and the entire amount of payment to the factor is economic rent. Indeed, the term *economic rent* owes its origin to the fact that land is the classic example of a fixed resource. On the other hand, if the supply of a factor is perfectly elastic, its supply curve is horizontal and the factor payment contains no economic rent.

The simplest and most obvious example of economic rent is payment to a factor whose supply is completely fixed. For example, consider a commercial lot located at a particular place. The supply curve of such a plot of land is shown by a vertical line *FS* in Figure 18-2; the amount of land offered for sale is fixed (*F* acres) regardless of the price offered for the plot. When the supply of a

[1] Alfred Marshall called this economic rent the "producer's surplus"; the area *RWE* represents the return to the factor in excess of its alternative cost and is in the nature of a surplus. See his *Principles of Economics*, 8th ed. (New York: Macmillan, 1949), p. 811.

The reader will note the similarity between this concept of producer's surplus and that of the consumer's surplus encountered in section 14-5.

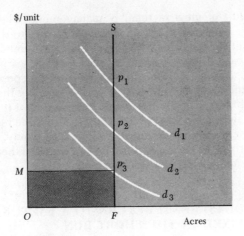

Figure 18-2 Pure economic rent

factor is completely inelastic, its price is determined by the level of demand alone. In Figure 18-2, the price will be p_1, p_2, or p_3 depending on whether the demand curve for the plot is d_1, d_2, or d_3.

Suppose there is only one use for the plot of land, and the demand curve for the plot is d_3. Then the total payment to the landowner must be OMp_3F dollars — OF acres times OM dollars per acre. How much of this payment is economic rent? The answer is the entire amount! Since the land cannot be removed from its current location and there is no alternative use for the land, nothing has to be paid to retain it in its current use. The entire amount of payment is in excess of the factor's alternative cost, and is, therefore, an economic rent. *Return to a factor whose supply is completely fixed is often referred to as a pure economic rent.*

The entire return to a factor whose supply is completely inelastic is economic rent, a surplus whose size depends only on the demand for the factor. Whether such surplus happens to be large or small has no effect on the availability of the fixed factor. It is clear, therefore, that reducing or taxing away the payment to the fixed resource does not affect the allocation of that resource.

In discussing the example of the plot of land, we have assumed that there is only one use for the land and concluded that the entire amount of payment to the landlord was economic rent. However, it is important to note that *the concept of economic rent is relative:* whether a payment to a factor is rent or alternative cost depends on whether we are considering the matter from the point of view of an individual firm, an industry, or the whole economy. Consider a quarterback who receives $200,000 per annum from team N.

From the point of view of team N management, what it pays the quarterback is economic cost; unless it pays the quarterback $200,000 per annum, other teams will bid him away. Assume now that the quarterback can, if he is unable to play football, earn $15,000 per annum as an insurance salesman. Then, from the point of view of the football industry, the alternative cost of keeping the man in that industry is $15,000, and the difference (between what it actually pays him and the alternative cost) of $185,000 is economic rent. Similarly, from the point of view of the entire American economy, any payment to the quarterback in excess of what he can make in the best alternative foreign employment is economic rent.

18-2 QUASI-RENT: RETURN TO A FACTOR FIXED IN THE SHORT RUN

Actual day-to-day operation of a firm is carried out in the short run. In order to produce a commodity, for instance, a firm must have a given plant and equipment to which it adds variable inputs to produce the desired commodity. In order to secure the service of a variable input, the firm must pay the input the price equal to its alternative cost. Since the supply of a fixed input to a firm in the short run is, by definition, fixed, the fixed input receives only what is left after paying the variable factor its alternative cost. Thus, the return to a fixed factor is in excess of what is necessary to keep the fixed factor in its current employment, and, therefore, is in the nature of an economic rent. The supply of a fixed input, however, is fixed only in the short run. Returns to a fixed input are not economic rent in the long run because it would not be replaced unless it can earn, in its current employment, the sum equal to its alternative cost. *Thus, short-run returns to a fixed input are often called a quasi-rent.*

In terms of Figure 18-3, in which the short-run cost curves are shown, the total revenue associated with the profit-maximizing output, q^*, is $OBEq^*$ dollars. Out of this total revenue, the firm must pay the variable factors their alternative cost, $OACq^*$ dollars. What remains after paying the variable input, $ABEC$ dollars, is quasi-rent. That is,

$$\text{Quasi-rent} = TR - TVC$$

Quasi-rent can be divided into two parts, the fixed cost and pure economic profit. The return that would have been earned if the fixed factors were utilized in their best alternative employment gives rise to the sum of the total fixed cost. The quasi-rent minus the total fixed cost is the (pure) economic profit. That is,

$$\text{Economic profit} = \text{Quasi-rent} - TFC$$
$$= TR - TVC - TFC = TR - TC$$

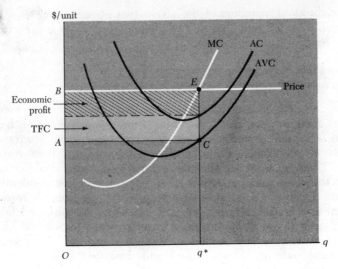

$/unit

MC   AC

AVC

B

E

Price

Economic
profit

TFC

A

C

O   *q**   *q*

Figure 18-3   Quasi-rent = TR − TVC

This equation clearly shows that our definition is consistent with
the notion of economic profit we have used throughout this book.
If the fixed cost exceeds the quasi-rent, needless to say, the pure
economic profit is negative, and the producer incurs a pure eco-
monic loss.

GROSS PROFIT AND QUASI-RENT

In section 17-2, the difference between the total revenue
product and the total resource cost was defined as the gross (or
residual) profit. What is the relationship between this gross profit
and quasi-rent? Let us answer this question by assuming a simple
competitive model in which one variable input (labor) is combined
with a fixed input (capital). *The total revenue product of labor is
equal to the number of units produced by labor multiplied by the
commodity price.* Since there is only one variable input, this total
revenue product must be equal to the total revenue of the firm; thus,
TRP = TR. The total cost of hiring the variable input (*total resource
cost*, TRC) is the total labor cost, which is the firm's total variable
cost; thus TRC = TVC. Now, we know that

Gross profit = TRP − TRC

and

Quasi-rent = TR − TVC

409

The right-hand members of the above two equations are equal because TRP = TR and TRC = TVC. Thus, *gross profit is identical to quasi-rent!*

18-3 NONHOMOGENEOUS INPUTS AND WAGE DIFFERENTIALS

In Chapter Seventeen, we analyzed the employment of factors assuming implicitly that there were two homogeneous factors called labor and capital. However, the real world is characterized by thousands of different kinds of labor, not by a single homogeneous labor. Thus, we must say something about how wages are determined when there are many groups of labor that are only partial substitutes for one another. An example of only partially substitutable inputs is skilled and unskilled labor. Skilled labor can do unskilled labor's work; and if the skilled labor's wage is attractive enough, some unskilled laborers may transform themselves into skilled workers by additional training. Thus, skilled and unskilled labor groups are partial substitutes for each other.

WAGE DIFFERENTIALS BETWEEN THE SKILLED AND UNSKILLED

When there are many different kinds of labor that are only partially substitutable, there naturally follows a multitude of wage differentials among various labor groups. Consider a simplified case in which only two groupings of labor, skilled and unskilled, are recognized. Also, assume that the total supply of labor is completely inelastic; that is, they are willing to work for whatever competitive wage they can command. In Figure 18-4a, the supply of unskilled labor is represented by a vertical line UU'. Though the skilled labor market offers a more attractive wage, the unskilled workers do not possess the necessary technical skill to enter the skilled market. Thus, they are willing to work in the unskilled labor market for whatever wage they can get. The market demand for the unskilled labor (derived by a sort of summation of individual firms' marginal revenue product curves as explained in section 17-5) is given by D_u. The equilibrium wage rate established by the intersection of supply and demand is $\$W_u$.

In Figure 18-4b, the supply curve of the skilled labor is represented by the solid half-line SS'. Note that the dotted line segment is not a part of the supply curve. If the wage rate in the skilled market is lower than the unskilled wage rate, W_u, the skilled worker will move out of the skilled group and join the unskilled labor market, where he can receive W_u dollars per unit of time. Thus, the prevailing wage rate in the unskilled market provides the floor to the skilled wage rate. The line segment OW_u is the trivial portion of the skilled labor supply curve, which shows that no skilled worker will

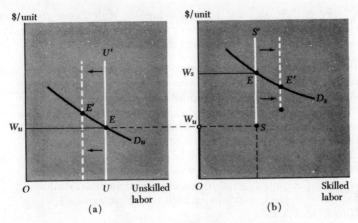

Figure 18-4 Wage differentials; (a) unskilled group, (b) skilled group

be willing to work at wage rates below $\$W_u$. The intersection of the market demand for the skilled labor, D_s, and the supply curve, SS', establishes the skilled wage rate at the level of $\$W_s$. The wage differential between the skilled and unskilled labor groups is $\$W_uW_s$ per unit.

The wage differential between the skilled and unskilled may widen or narrow. If the higher wage in the skilled group encourages some unskilled workers to be trained and enter the skilled labor market, the wage differential will narrow. The dotted vertical lines drawn in Figures 18-4a and b show a reduced supply of the unskilled labor raising the unskilled wage, and the increased supply in the skilled labor lowering the skilled wage. Labor union apprenticeship rules and the medical profession's insistence on holding down the enrollments in medical schools illustrate the restrictions placed on entry in their attempt to maintain or increase wage differentials. On the other hand, increased efforts in technical education and more scholarships and loans provided in some professional schools tend to increase the supply of technicians and professionals. Other things being equal, such programs tend to narrow wage differentials or prevent them from becoming wider.

COMPENSATING AND NONCOMPENSATING DIFFERENTIALS

Various wage differentials may be classified as being either of a compensating or a noncompensating type.[2] *Compensating*

[2]Paul Samuelson uses the terms *equalizing* and *nonequalizing differences*. See his *Economics*, 9th ed. (New York: McGraw-Hill, 1973), pp. 579–580.

411

wage differentials account for nonmonetary differences that exist among different jobs. For example, any of the following will tend to require a payment of a higher wage differential:

Unpleasantness and/or inconvenience, as in overtime work, night shifts, and work on Christmas day; risky occupations, such as race car driving and piloting airplanes; longer hours involved, as in practicing medicine; irregularity of employment, as in construction work and athletic coaching; short working life, as in boxing and playing football; low social prestige attached to the occupation, such as being a mortician; higher cost of training required, as in various medical specialties; work that requires living in remote areas, such as Alaska and foreign countries; and jobs in high living-cost areas, such as Hawaii and Alaska.

While the compensating type of wage differentials do explain some of the reasons for the existence of a wide variety of wage differentials, there are numerous wage differentials that must be explained in terms of noncompensating differentials. *Noncompensating wage differentials are those that are due to inherited and acquired differences in the quality of labor as well as those caused by imperfections in the labor market.* For instance, not many people are born with the biological traits necessary to become a successful heavyweight boxer, and still fewer get an opportunity to develop their latent talents to become a heavyweight champion. Similarly, good quarterbacks or plastic surgeons command high wage differentials over other people because most people are blessed neither with the biological traits required nor with the means and opportunities to develop themselves into quarterbacks or surgeons. Thus, the supply of quarterbacks or surgeons (relative to the demand for them) remains small, and they continue to command high wage differentials. Biological and acquired quality differences among people are the major reasons why there are so many different kinds of labor and so many different wage rates. Since the qualities of labor are different, labor groups compete with each other only partially. For instance, welders and auto mechanics, electricians and bricklayers, economists and mathematicians, and so on, are only partially substitutable for each other; accordingly, substantial wage differentials between such groups may persist for a long period of time.

Noncompensating wage differentials may also be caused by market imperfections. Lack of the knowledge of job opportunities may cause wage differentials to exist among different jobs and locations. Immobility of labor may cause chronic unemployment and low wages in depressed areas. Labor unions, minimum-wage requirements, and discrimination against minorities, may also explain many wage differentials.

18-4   LEAST-COST INPUT DECISIONS:
TWO OR MORE INPUTS

The sizes of wage differentials for different groups of labor will be determined by the demand and supply conditions in different markets. As the wage rate in each labor market is established by the supply and demand in that market, there will develop an equilibrium pattern of wages (and wage differentials).

Given the equilibrium pattern of wage rates, how should a profit-maximizing producer allocate his production budget among different grades of labor? Let us answer this question for the simple case of skilled and unskilled labor groups. From section 17-2, we know that the producer should hire each grade of labor in such a way that its value of marginal product is equal to its wage rate. That is,

$$\text{VMP}_u = w_u$$

and

$$\text{VMP}_s = w_s$$

where the subscripts u and s identify the unskilled and skilled labor groups. Combining the above two equations, we can obtain the following equation:

$$\frac{\text{VMP}_u}{w_u} = \frac{\text{VMP}_s}{w_s}$$

This equation says that a profit-maximizing producer should hire unskilled and skilled labor in such a proportion that the VMP per dollar spent on the unskilled labor is precisely equal to the VMP per dollar spent on the skilled labor.

From section 17-9, we know that the general expressions (which apply to perfect as well as imperfect markets) for the value of marginal product and input price are the marginal revenue product and the marginal resource cost, MRP and MRC. Therefore, generally speaking, a profit-maximizing producer must hire various inputs in such a way as to satisfy the following equilibrium condition:

$$\frac{\text{MRP}_1}{\text{MRC}_1} = \frac{\text{MRP}_2}{\text{MRC}_2} = \cdots = \frac{\text{MRP}_n}{\text{MRC}_n}$$

18-5   THE SUBSTITUTION AND OUTPUT EFFECTS
OF AN INPUT PRICE CHANGE

The impact of an input price change on the quantity of that input purchased can be decomposed into two analytically distinct effects, the substitution and output effects. Consider a simple model in which the price of capital, k, remains the same and that of labor, l, declines. Let the original equilibrium position in Figure

18-5a be given by E_1. As the price of labor, p_l, is lowered relative to the price of capital, p_k, the optimal input combination required to produce the same output, q_1, shifts to E_2, where the new p_l/p_k ratio is equal to the marginal rate of technical substitution, MRTS.

The new least-cost combination, E_2, produces the same output as before by employing more of now relatively cheaper labor and less of now relatively more expensive capital. Thus, it must now cost less to produce an additional unit of the good; that is, the new input combination must be associated with a lower marginal cost, MC. Such a decrease in MC is represented in Figure 18-5b by a shift of the curve from MC to MC'. Now, given the price of the good—which is assumed to remain at $\$p$ per unit, the profit-maximizing output increases to q_2 units. Going back to Figure 18-5a, the increased output is indicated by isoquant q_2. The least-cost combination to produce this output is given by E_3—where isoquant q_2 is tangent to the isocost line, and the MRTS is equal to the p_l/p_k ratio. Note that the total amount of increase in labor employed is $l_3 - l_1$, and that this total effect can be decomposed into the substitution effect, $l_2 - l_1$, and the output effect $l_3 - l_2$. Thus,

$$\text{Total effect} = \text{substitution effect} + \text{output effect}$$
$$(l_3 - l_1) \qquad\qquad (l_2 - l_1) \qquad\qquad (l_3 - l_2)$$

The reader must undoubtedly have noticed the similarity of the above analysis to that of the substitution and income effects of a change in the price of a good. The substitution effect is entirely

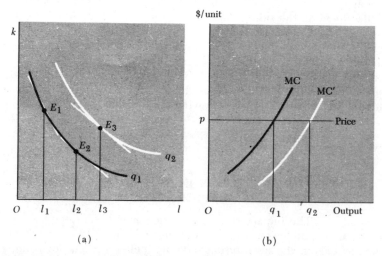

Figure 18-5 Substitution and output effects of an input price change

analogous. However, the output effect is different from the income effect of the consumer's case. While the consumer is subject to a budget constraint, a business firm is not, and, therefore, can increase its production budget if the demand for its good justifies additional output.[3]

18-6   BILATERAL MONOPOLY

Bilateral monopoly arises when a single seller (monopolist) faces a single buyer (monopsonist). Real world examples of bilateral monopoly are few, with the exception of perhaps the labor market in a small town. For instance, the relationship between the single uranium mining company and the uranium miners' union in a remote town will be an example of a bilateral monopoly.

The solution to a bilateral monopoly is said to be "indeterminate." In Figure 18-6, the single buyer's demand curve is labeled D_b. This curve is the marginal revenue product curve of the factor being demanded. If we assume that the monopsonist believes that the price of the factor is determined by forces beyond his control (or what is the same thing, if the monopsonist is assumed to behave as if he were buying in a perfectly competitive factor market), the marginal revenue productivity curve of the factor can be taken as the monopsonist's demand curve for the factor.[4] From the single seller's point of view, however, the buyer's demand curve for the input, D_b, represents his average revenue curve. Thus, we can give the curve an alternate label, AR_s—the seller's average revenue curve. The marginal revenue curve to the seller, MR_s, that corresponds to this

[3]If the reader extends the isocost lines going through E_1 and E_3 leftward they will cut the k axis at the same height, indicating that the production budget has been held constant in the illustration.

Suppose the reduction in the price of labor has shifted MC' curve of Figure 18-5b further to the right and the q_2 isoquant in part a must be located further away from the origin. The isocost line tangent to this new q_2 isoquant and parallel to the isocost line going through E_2 must cut the q_k axis at the higher point, indicating that the production budget has been increased. Thus, the movement from E_2 to E_3—which is now on the new isoquant—and the accompanying change in the amount of labor used will now include the effect of an increased purchase in labor due to an increased production budget. This increased purchase—which is in addition to the output effect measured with the given production budget—may be called the "increased (or decreased) outlay" effect. C. E. Ferguson calls this the profit-maximizing effect. See his *Mircoeconomic Theory*, 4th ed. (Homewood, Ill.: Irwin, 1975), p. 374.

[4]Note that the MRP curve is not the demand curve for an input when the input market is imperfectly competitive. (See section 17-9).

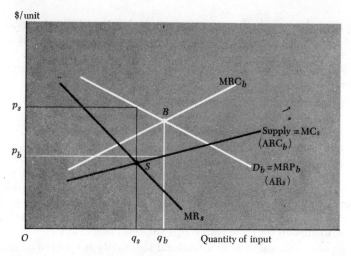

Figure 18-6 Bilateral monopoly

AR_s curve can readily be obtained using the familiar graphical technique.

The curve labeled "Supply = MC_s" shows the seller's marginal cost curve. As noted in section 14-3, a monopolist does not have a supply curve. But, if it is assumed that the monopolist behaves as if his price were determined by forces outside his control (that is, if he behaves as if he were a perfectly competitive seller), then the MC_s curve may be considered his supply curve. Now from the single buyer's point of view, the seller's supply curve shows his average cost of resource. Thus, we give the curve an alternate designation, ARC_b—the average resource cost to the buyer. The curve marginal to this ARC_b is labeled MRC_b—the marginal resource cost.

Given the cost and revenue curves shown in Figure 18-6, the monopsonist's (or the single buyer's) profit-maximizing decision is indicated by point B, where his white demand or marginal revenue product curve intersects his white marginal cost curve. Thus, the monopsonist will desire to hire q_b units at the price of p_b dollars per unit—the minimum price that must be offered in order to secure q_b units.

The monopolist (or the single seller), however, has a quite different idea regarding his profit-maximizing quantity and price. His optimal selection is indicated by point S, where his black marginal cost curve, MC_s, intersects his black marginal revenue, MR_s, curve. He wishes to sell q_s units at the price of p_s dollars per unit—the maximum price indicated by the buyer's demand or MRP curve.

The price desired by the monopsonist shows the lower limit of the price, which could be realized only if he could force the monopolist to act as if he were a perfect competitor. Similarly, the price wished for by the monopolist shows the upper limit, which could be attained only if the monopsonist were forced to behave as a perfect competitor. Since the wishful thinkings of the monopsonist and the monopolist cannot materialize in a bilateral monoply model, the actual price and quantity that will prevail are said to be "indeterminate."

The word *indeterminate* in economic literature means that the economic analysis taken by itself cannot produce a determinate solution. The determination of actual price and quantity depends on the bargaining powers of the parties involved. The major determinants of a bilateral monopolist's bargaining power are perhaps his ability to inflict damages to his opponent and his ability to withstand damages inflicted on him by his opponent. Thus, such factors as the possibility of a strike or lock-out, the financial condition of the union or the company, the popularity of the union leadership among the rank and file or of the corporate leaders among the board members may all play important roles in determining the bargaining powers of the parties involved.

18-7   UNION GOALS AND WAGE POLICIES:
An Application

We have just seen that a bilateral monopoly model of wage negotiation produces an indeterminate result. As simple applications of the tools acquired in studying the bilateral monopoly, let us consider the cases in which only one of the parties involved is imperfectly competitive.

MONOPSONIST VERSUS COMPETITIVE LABOR SUPPLY

The case in which a monopsonist confronts competitively supplied labor is shown in Figure 18-7. The curve labeled S is the competitive labor supply curve, and the curve labeled MRC shows the marginal resource cost of labor to the monopsonist. The MRP curve shows the marginal revenue product of labor to the monopsonist. Given these curves, the monopsonist's profit-maximizing solution is indicated by point B; he hires L units of labor per period at the wage rate of W dollars per unit.

Note that, in this case, the wage rate is lower than the marginal revenue product of labor.

COMPETITIVE BUYER VERSUS MONOPOLY UNION

Let us now consider a case in which a single large union that monopolizes the labor supply faces buyers who behave competi-

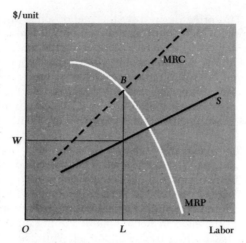

Figure 18-7 Monopsonist versus competitive labor supply

tively. In Figure 18-8, the MC curve shows the marginal cost to the union of supplying labor. The competitive demand curve for labor (which is the horizontal summation of individual buyers' demand curves) is shown by the curve labeled D. Given this demand or average revenue curve, the union's marginal revenue curve is the MR_s curve.

Depending on its objective, the union has a few alternatives from which to choose:

The maximization of the gains to the union as a whole. In order to attain the maximum gains for the union as a whole, the union would seek the level of employment at which its MC_s curve intersects its marginal revenue, MR_s, curve. Thus, it sets the wage rate at AG dollars per period and offers A units of labor per period.

The maximization of total wage receipts. If the union wants to maximize the size of the total wage received, it must seek the rate of employment at which its marginal revenue, MR_s, is zero. Thus, union policy would seek B units of employment per period and BR dollars of wage rate.

The maximization of employment. In order to attain the goal of securing maximum employment for union members, the union must seek the rate of employment at which its MC curve intersects the demand curve for labor; this solution is shown by point N. The union policy will seek C units of employment per period and CN dollars of wage rate. If the wage rate were higher than CN, there would be unemployed union members. On the other hand, if the wage

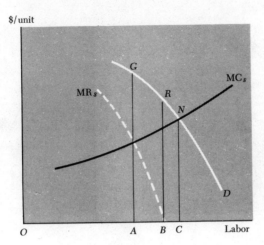

Figure 18-8   Competitive buyer versus monopoly union

rate were lower than *CN*, the quantity of labor supplied would fall short of the quantity demanded.

UNIONIZATION OF A COMPETITIVE LABOR MARKET

Suppose the wage and employment rates are competitively determined, as shown in Figure 18-9a. The curve labeled *S* shows the competitively supplied labor, and the *D* curve represents the competitive firms' total demand for labor. The equilibrium wage rate is $W and the equilibrium rate of employment per period is *N* units. Figure 18-9b shows the picture of an individual firm. Given the market wage rate of $W, the optimal combination for the firm is indicated by point *B*, where its VMP curve intersects the wage line *WB*. It hires *n* units per period and pays the wage rate equal to the labor's value of marginal product.

Now let the labor market be unionized. What can the union do for its members? It may survey the market demand and supply curves and decide to make no change. (Note that point *E* in Figure 18-9a corresponds to the maximum employment combination *N* of Figure 18-8). However, it is doubtful that a newly organized union that has monopoly power of labor supply will decide to maintain the status quo of pre-union days. Therefore, let us suppose that the union decides to seek a higher wage rate indicated by $W'. (This wage rate may be the gain-maximizing, or revenue-maximizing variety of the previous example, or some other compromise solution of wage and employment rates.) From the demand and supply curves

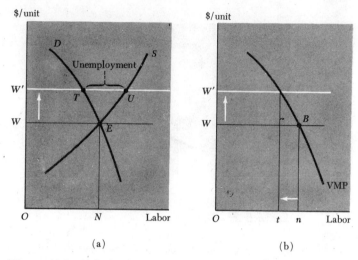

Figure 18-9 Unionization of a competitive labor market; (a) the industry, (b) the firm

of Figure 18-9a, it is clear that the union could secure such an increase in wage only at the expense of TU units of unemployment.[5]

When the competitive wage rate is already being paid, the union cannot attain a higher wage rate without sacrificing the number employed. However, this is not to say that the union cannot do any good for its members. For instance, if the demand for labor is inelastic at the existing wage, the union's ability to secure a higher wage rate will increase the total wage receipts by the employed and unemployed union members. The union may conceivably develop a redistributive scheme that increases the amount of wage received by each union member.

18-8 HENRY GEORGE'S SINGLE-TAX PROPOSAL: An Application

In his famous book *Progress and Poverty* (1879), Henry George proposed to substitute a single tax on land rent for the numerous other taxes by which public revenues were then raised. Henry George was a self-taught economist who understood the economic effects of taxes and framed his proposal in such a manner as to cause

[5]As shown in Figure 18-9b, the representative firm reduces its employment of labor by tn units. Thus, TU = n(tn), if there are n buyers in the market.

the minimum injury to the efficiency of the private enterprise economy.[6] He emphasized that the single tax on land rent—unlike numerous other taxes that hampered the production and exchange processes—did not affect the allocation of resources at all. Thus, he argued that substituting the single tax for all other taxes would promote the growth of production and exchange at rates heretofore undreamed of. Let us examine Henry George's argument that the single tax on rent has no harmful economic effect.

In Figure 18-10, the amount of a particular land available is shown by the vertical line *SS'* and the demand curve for this land in its most remunerative use is indicated by the *D* = AR curve. In the absence of any governmental interference, the equilibrium price is *A* dollars per unit and the total revenue of the landowner is *OAES* dollars per period. Suppose a 50 percent tax on all land income is introduced. Would the supply of land change? No. The land was being used in its most productive use, and the new land tax applies to all uses of land. Thus, the use that was most profitable before the tax still remains the most profitable one. Would the demand curve for the land change? Again, no. Since the productivity of the land does not change, the derived demand curve for the land (that is, the *D* = AR curve) does not change. Thus, the equilibrium market price still remains at *A* dollars per unit. The amount of land used for the particular purpose still remains the same. Clearly, the land tax has

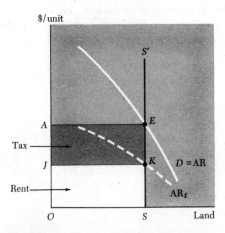

Figure 18-10 Incidence of the tax on rent

---

[6]J. A. Schumpeter, *History of Economic Analysis*, (New York: Oxford University Press, 1955), p. 865.

not affected the manner in which the land is utilized. The landowner, however, must now turn over half of his total rent receipts to the government. The *incidence (or final resting place)* of the tax on rent is completely on the landowner. Graphically, this situation is shown by the downward shift of the demand curve to the AR_t curve. This AR_t curve shows the amount of rent (per unit of land) the landowner can retain after paying the land rent tax. The landowner receives *OAES* dollars from the tenant, but is able to keep only *OJKS* dollars. The public revenue from the rent tax is *JAEK* dollars.

The important thing to note is that a tax levied on a completely inelastically supplied good is absorbed entirely by the supplier. Furthermore, such a tax does not distort the allocation of land usage, because it affects neither the supply of nor the demand for the land.[7]

Henry George's single-tax proposal as a panacea for the ills of taxation has many serious weaknesses. He grossly overestimated the revenue-producing ability of a tax on land. The single tax on land alone, even if it had a confiscatory rate, would not come near to meeting the revenue requirements of modern governments. The landowners who purchased their land while land prices were much lower are hard to separate from those who purchased their land more recently at much higher prices. Even if the value judgment regarding the desirability of taxing unearned rent income is accepted—not all agree that unearned income should be taxed more heavily—it is difficult to separate the value of land due to the original purchase price from that due to improvement. However, Henry George's argument that a tax on a perfectly inelastically supplied good cannot distort the allocation of resources is unassailable.

[7]This conclusion is true only if a uniform rate of tax is imposed on all uses of land. If the tax is imposed on some selected uses only, or if the tax rates differ from one use to another, the tax will distort the allocation of resources.

APPENDIX 18

The Elasticity of Substitution
and Distributive Shares

Given input prices and technological constraints, an entrepreneur chooses the input ratio (l/k) that will minimize his production cost. As input prices change, the entrepreneur will substitute a cheaper input for more of an expensive one, and the l/k ratio will change. A rather useful gadget in the economist's box of tools will be an instrument that measures the extent to which the optimal l/k ratio will change given a change in the input price ratio, p_l/p_k. The elasticity of substitution, σ — which was devised by J. R. Hicks[8] — measures the responsiveness in the optimal input ratio to a change in input price ratio, and is defined as follows:[9]

$$\sigma = \frac{\text{relative change in } (k/l)}{\text{relative change in } (p_l/p_k)}$$

$$= \frac{d(k/l)}{k/l} \div \frac{d(p_l/p_k)}{p_l/p_k}$$

Note that the numerator has a k/l ratio while the denominator has a p_l/p_k ratio. When there is a relative increase in p_l/p_k, the entrepreneur who finds labor relatively more expensive than capital will substitute k for l and cause the k/l ratio to increase. Thus, the

[8] *The Theory of Wages* (New York: Macmillan, 1932), p. 117.

[9] There is a different way of expressing σ. In equilibrium, an isoquant is tangent to the isocost line. Thus,

$$-p_l/p_k = -MP_l/MP_k = MRTS$$

Substituting MRTS for p_l/p_k, we can define, as Hicks did, the elasticity of substitution as:

$$\sigma = \frac{d(k/l)}{k/l} \div \frac{d(MRTS)}{MRTS}$$

direction of substitution is clear and the sign of σ is always positive (unless $\sigma = 0$). The value of σ ranges from zero to infinity. $\sigma = 0$ implies a fixed proportion production process and $\sigma = \infty$, identical inputs. In general, the larger the value of σ, the greater is the substitutability between the inputs involved.

Just as we classified price elasticity into three categories, σ may be classified as follows:

$\sigma < 1$: inelastic

$\sigma = 1$: unitary

$\sigma > 1$: elastic

There is an important relationship between the categories in which σ falls and distributive shares of factors. Consider a two-factor model in which the total income, y, is the sum of labor's share $(p_l \cdot l)$, and capitals's share $(p_k \cdot k)$. That is,

$$y = p_l \cdot l + p_k \cdot k. \tag{18-2}$$

Then, the relative shares of labor and capital are given by $(p_l \cdot l)/y$ and $(p_k \cdot k)/y$, and the ratio of labor's share to that of capital is

$$l^\circ / k^\circ = \frac{p_l \cdot l}{p_k \cdot k} = \frac{p_l/p_k}{k/l} \tag{18-3}$$

With the aid of equation 18-3, we can readily examine the effect of a change in the p_l/p_k ratio on labor's share relative to that of capital. Suppose $\sigma < 1$. Then a given percentage change in p_l/p_k is accompanied by a smaller percentage change in the k/l ratio, and the ratio, l° / k°, increases. For an example, let us assume $\sigma = 1/2$. Then a 20 percent increase in p_l/p_k is accompanied by a 10 percent increase in the k/l ratio. Therefore,

$$l^\circ / k^\circ = \frac{1.2(p_l/p_k)}{1.1(k/l)}$$

Clearly, if $\sigma < 1$, labor's share relative to that of capital increases following an increase in the price of labor relative to that of capital. This must be so since $\sigma < 1$ implies that a given percentage change in the p_l/p_k ratio does not invoke as large a percentage change in the k/l ratio due to the difficulty in substituting k for l.

Since analogous reasoning applies when $\sigma = 1$ or $\sigma > 1$, the relationship between the elasticity of substitution and the relative distributive shares may be stated as follows:

An increase in the p_l/p_k ratio will cause labor's distributive share, relative to capital's share, to

$$\left. \begin{array}{l} \text{increase} \\ \text{remain the same} \\ \text{decrease} \end{array} \right\} \quad \text{according as} \quad \left\{ \begin{array}{l} \sigma < 1 \\ \sigma = 1 \\ \sigma > 1 \end{array} \right.$$

EXERCISES 18

Additional Topics
on Pricing and Employment
of Resources

18-1 The following tables show the production function, the demand schedule for the good, and the demand schedule for the input (labor).

I. Production Function				II. Demand for Good		III. Demand for Labor	
QUANTITY OF LABOR	TP	TRP	MRP	QUANTITY	PRICE	PRICE OF LABOR	QUANTITY OF LABOR
1	24	___		24	$1.00	$16	___
2	45	___	___	45	.90	10	___
3	60	___	___	60	.80	7	___
4	70	___	___	70	.70	5	___
5	78	___	___	78	.60	4	___
6	83	___		83	.50		

1. Show that $MRP_l = MR \cdot MPP_l = \dfrac{\Delta TR}{\Delta l}$.

2. Fill in the TRP column, combining the information on TP and the demand schedule for the good. The TRP is the total revenue brought in by the total amount of input employed.

3. Fill in the MRP column.

4. Complete the demand schedule for labor input. (Assume that the input market is perfectly competitive.)

18-2 Assume a production process in which either input a or b may be used to produce the desired output. The present production and cost conditions involved are as follows:

$$MPP_a = 4, \ MPP_b = 10, \ p_a = \$2, \ \text{and} \ p_b = \$8.$$

1. In order to minimize the cost of producing the current level of output per period, what should the firm do?
2. Should the firm employ only one input? Why or why not?
3. If the price of the good produced ($p_x = MR$) is $1 per unit (and the input market is competitive as indicated by constants p_a and p_b), what should the firm do in order to maximize its profit?
4. If the price of the good ($p_x = MR$) is 50 cents, what should the firm do to maximize its profit?
5. Suppose the production and cost data were as follows:

$$MPP_a = 4, \ MPP_b = 10, \ p_a = \$2, \ \text{and} \ p_b = \$5$$

If the firm is at its profit-maximizing equilibrium at the current rate of production, what must be its MR?

18-3 "Economic rents to factors are surpluses, not necessary to induce the supply of their services. If they are taxed away, the allocation of the factors will not be affected." Do you agree? Why or why not?

18-4 Answer the following questions related to a legal rent ceiling.

1. Under what circumstances would you expect the introduction of a legal rent ceiling to:

    a. Have no effect on the price and quantity of rental housing?

    b. Create a lower rent and a shortage? Elaborate on the meaning of the term, shortage.

2. Is rent return to the owners of rental housing units a quasi-rent? Explain.
3. How would the rent receipts be affected by the introduction of the rent ceilings?
4. Speculate on the long-run effect of a legal rent ceiling on the supply of rental housing. Make your assumption(s) specific.

18-5 A labor union may raise the wages of its members in three ways: (a) by restricting the labor supply, (b) by enforcing wage rates higher than the current rates (for example, the minimum wage), and (c) by increasing the demand for labor. Discuss how a union may increase the demand for its members' labor supply.

CHAPTER NINETEEN

GENERAL EQUILIBRIUM AND WELFARE ECONOMICS

Throughout the preceding chapters, we have employed the technique of partial equilibrium analysis to study various parts of the economy. In this chapter we explicitly recognize the interdependence of various parts of the economy, and devote the first two sections to an introductory examination of the idea of general equilibrium. In sections 19-3 through 19-7 we study simple welfare economics: we will introduce the welfare criterion known as the Pareto optimality condition, examine how perfect competition fares under this criterion, and survey some additional criteria of welfare judgment. Input-output analysis and cost-benefit analysis are introduced as applications toward the end of the chapter.

19-1 INTERDEPENDENCE IN THE ECONOMY

Our studies in the preceding chapters have been partial equilibrium analyses that rested on *ceteris paribus* assumptions. We have studied profit- or utility-maximizing behavior and decisions in each segment of the economy *as if* they were independent of the other segments of the economy. For instance, we have studied:

Households in their role as consumers who allocate their income among various goods and services so as to maximize their utility subject to their income constraints. Incomes of the consumers—which depend on labor and other things consumers can sell in the factor market—were conveniently assumed to be given, and this assumption enabled us to isolate the study of consumer behavior from other parts of the economy.

Business firms as producers, who obtained various inputs in the factor market and combined them to produce goods and services in such a way as to minimize the cost of production subject to given prices of inputs and the known state of technology. Again we considered the production decision in isolation, and ignored the influences of such factors as the demand for the product and related goods, which are in turn influenced by employment, income, and taste of consumers.

Product markets, where buyers and sellers interacted with each other and among themselves to determine prices and outputs of various goods and services. Again the study of each market rested on the *ceteris paribus* assumptions, and relationships with other markets were ignored.

Factor markets, where business firms and households in their role as resource owners interacted with each other and among themselves to determine prices and quantities of various resources employed. Again, the employment of factors was considered with little attention paid to the fact that the demand for resources was influenced by the demand for the product, which in turn was affected by the prices received by the resource owners.

However, a *fundamental feature of any economic system is the interdependence among its parts;* everything depends on everything else. Each part of the economy we have been analyzing in isolation is really a different aspect of an interdependent simultaneously functioning system. For instance, consumers' demands for various goods and services (television sets, coffee, automobiles, meat, etc.) depend on their preferences and the incomes at their disposal. The incomes of the consumers, however, depend on the demand and supply for various factors (plumber's service, teacher's work, trucks, land, and so on). Producers' demand for factors, in turn, depends not only on the state of technology but also on the demand for their goods and services. But the demand for goods and services depends on consumers' incomes, which we have already observed to depend on the demand for the factors. Thus, we have run a complete circle.

There are innumerable possibilities for interconnections between the demand and supply for different goods and for different factors. The demand for a good depends not only on its own price but on the prices and availabilities of all other goods. Demand for a factor is similarly dependent upon the prices and availabilities of all other factors, as well as demand for products produced by using the factor. Relationships between different goods or factors may be complementary or competing. They may be closely related or imperceptibly related. In any case, the main feature of an economy is the *interdependence* of its numerous parts and the *simultaneous determination* of various prices and quantities. All prices are interrelated, and it is not possible to determine the price of a particular one without, in principle, knowing all other prices. Furthermore, such prices are not determined one by one in isolation; rather, they are all determined simultaneously.

19-2 GENERAL EQUILIBRIUM AND ITS EXISTENCE

We have seen that various parts of the economy function in close interrelationship with each other. A crucial question we must now ask is: "Do the various parts fit together to assure that equilibria in various markets are consistent with each other?" Is the behavior of each consumer consistent with that of every other consumer, with that of every producer, and with the equilibrium in every market? In other words, is there a set of prices that can equate demand and supply, and produce equilibriums in every product and factor market that are mutually consistent? If such a set of prices prevails in the economy, the economy is said to be in the state of *general equilibrium*. Note that the mere functioning of an economy does not guarantee that the economy is in general equilibrium. For example, an economy can be operating with a large amount of unemployed human and natural resources, indicating that quantities supplied exceed quantities demanded in these markets. Can a general equilibrium—mutually consistent simultaneous equilibrium in every market of the economy—exist? The idea of general equilibrium and the question of the existence of a general equilibrium price set was first rigorously introduced by French economist Léon Walras in the late nineteenth century.[1] Walras' work was rather formal and mathematical. The approach to the proof of the existence of general equilibrium accepted by modern economists has been developed only in recent years and depends on even more sophisticated mathematical techniques. Those who are interested in such mathematical treatment may start with an excellent summary of the literature given by James Quirk and Rubin Saposnik.[2] For our purpose, we shall merely note that recent inquiries have proved that the existence of a *general equilibrium is guaranteed for a perfectly competitive economy* in which there are no indivisibilities and no increasing returns to size.[3] The fact that a general equilibrium can be guaranteed for a perfectly competitive economy is important because a perfectly competitive economy has certain ideal properties in terms of social welfare and efficiency.

[1]*Elements of Pure Economics*, translated by William Jaffé (Homewood, Ill.: Irwin, 1954). The first edition was published in 1874–77.

[2]*Introduction to General Equilibrium Theory and Welfare Economics* (New York: McGraw-Hill, 1968), Ch. 3.

[3]K. Arrow and G. Debreu, "Existence of an Equilibrium for a Competitive Economy," *Econometrica*, July 1954, pp. 265–290, and J. Quirk and R. Saposnik, *op. cit.*, Section 3-5.

Note that a general equilibrium cannot be guaranteed if competition is imperfect or if there are increasing returns to size due to indivisibilities. Our current state of knowledge does not enable us to guarantee the existence of a general equilibrium in an imperfectly competitive economy; it may or may not exist in an imperfectly competitive market. The effect of indivisibilities will be discussed in section 19-6.

19-3 THE PARETO OPTIMALITY CRITERION OF SOCIAL WELFARE

The interrelationship among various parts of the economy implies that a specific change in the economy affects resource allocation in all other parts of the economy. Thus, a central question that must be answered is whether a particular change in resource allocation in the economy would increase or decrease its social welfare. *The subject matter of welfare economics is concerned with the evaluation of alternative economic states (configurations, situations) from the point of view of the society's well-being.*

Attempts to measure "social welfare" for groups of individuals, however, are most difficult because well-beings or welfares of different individuals defy objective measurement. In order to avoid making impossible interpersonal comparisons, it is traditional for the economist to use what is known as the Pareto optimality criterion for deciding whether the social welfare is higher in one economic situation than in another. *According to the Pareto optimality criterion, any change that makes at least one individual better off and no one worse off is an improvement in social welfare.* Conversely, a change that makes no one better off and at least one worse off is a decrease in social welfare. *A situation (state, or configuration) in which it is impossible to make anyone better off without making someone worse off is said to be Pareto optimal, or efficient.*

The concept of efficiency (also called Pareto efficiency) or Pareto optimality is rather basic in economics and has a great deal of applicability. Depending on the context in which efficiency is being evaluated, the economist talks of allocative efficiency, technical efficiency, etc. However, these are not different concepts of efficiency; rather, they are different applications of the same basic notion of efficiency. For instance, in discussing production, we said that production was efficient if it was not possible to use less of an input without using more of any other in producing a given output. This definition is entirely consistent with the concept of (Pareto) efficiency, because if it is possible for a producer to use less of an input without using more of any other, he can be made better off without making anyone else worse off.

We must observe a few important things regarding the Pareto criterion. First, the Pareto criterion *provides only a partial ranking* of possible changes. It renders no judgment on a change that makes someone better off and someone worse off. Since many social policies involve changes that benefit some and hurt others, the Pareto criterion, which has nothing to say about such changes, must be considered a very weak criterion. However, any change that is judged an improvement by the Pareto criterion will also be found an improvement by a more complete social welfare criterion that may be developed.

Second, a Pareto optimal state *does not guarantee a state in which the social welfare is maximized.* For instance, we have shown in section 5-5 that any point on the contract curve (of exchange between consumers) represents a Pareto optimal or efficient situation. Whether a particular point on the contract curve represents a social welfare–maximizing allocation of goods between two consumers cannot be known without making an interpersonal comparison of two consumers' utility or welfare. Thus, we may say that the Pareto optimal state is a necessary but not sufficient condition for maximizing social welfare.

19-4 MARGINAL CONDITIONS FOR A PARETO OPTIMAL RESOURCE ALLOCATION

In a Pareto optimal state of an economy, it is impossible to make anyone better off without making someone worse off by any of the following three means.

1. Reallocation of the already available goods among consumers
2. Reallocation of inputs among producers (in order to increase the output of some goods without reducing the output of any)
3. Changing the composition of output, that is, producing more of some and less of others

The rest of this section is devoted to developing three marginal conditions needed to satisfy the above requirements for the attainment of a Pareto optimal or efficient configuration of an economy.

ALLOCATION OF GOODS AMONG CONSUMERS: EFFICIENCY IN EXCHANGE

Let us assume that there are two individuals (Alice and Betty) and two goods (x and y), the available quantities of which are shown by the dimensions of the Edgeworth (Edgeworth-Bowley or Pareto) box diagram in Figure 19-1. Suppose that the initial allocation of x and y between Alice and Betty is shown by point J. Since point J

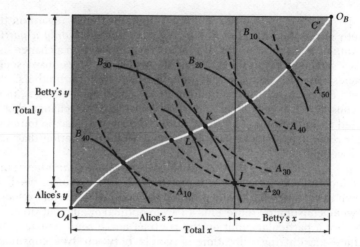

Figure 19-1 Pareto optimal allocation of two goods between two consumers

is not on the contract curve CC', any reallocation of x and y between Alice and Betty that will move them onto the contract curve will make one (or both) of them better off without making anyone worse off.[4] For instance, the movement to point K will make Alice better off without making Betty worse off, and the movement to L will make both Alice and Betty better off. Once Alice and Betty are on the contract curve, it is impossible to make either of them better off without making the other worse off. Thus, the contract curve CC', shows the locus of Pareto optimal or efficient allocation of goods between consumers. From our study of consumer behavior in Chapters Four and Five, we know that the contract curve is the locus of points at which the two consumers' indifference curves are tangent and the marginal rates of substitution, MRS, between two goods are the same for both consumers. Thus, the marginal condition for a Pareto optimal resource allocation requires that the MRS between two goods be equal for both consumers. It can be shown that the above argument can be extended for any number of goods and any number of consumers. *Therefore, we conclude that the marginal condition for a Pareto optimal or efficient allocation of goods among consumers requires the equality of MRS between any two goods for all consumers.*

[4]Those unfamiliar with the Edgeworth box diagram should consult section 5-5.

ALLOCATION OF INPUTS AMONG PRODUCERS: EFFICIENCY IN FACTOR SUBSTITUTION

In order to derive the marginal condition for a Pareto optimal allocation of inputs among producers, we follow an argument closely analogous to the one used to develop the marginal condition for allocation of goods among consumers. Assume two goods (food and clothing) to be produced and two inputs (labor and capital), the available quantities of which are shown by the dimensions of the production Edgeworth box in Figure 19-2. Suppose the initial allocation of labor and capital between the producers of food and clothing is given by point J where isoquants C_{400} and F_{300} intersect. Since J is not on the production contract curve, a reallocation of labor and capital in such a way as to move to a point on the contract curve will allow production of more of one or both goods without reducing the output of either. For instance, at point K, more clothing and the same amount of food are produced; while at point L the outputs of both food and clothing are higher. Once we are on the contract curve, it is impossible to increase the output of either good without reducing the output of the other; thus, the allocation of resources among the producers of food and clothing is Pareto optimal. The production contract curve is the locus of points at which the isoquants for food and clothing are tangent, and the marginal rates of technical substitution, MRTS, between labor and capital are equal for both food and clothing producers. Therefore, the Pareto optimal or efficient allocation of inputs between food and clothing producers requires that the

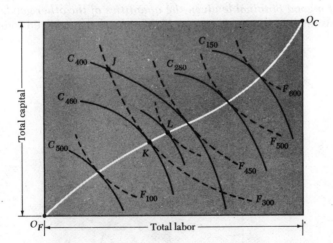

Figure 19-2   Pareto optimal allocation of inputs between two producers

MRTS between labor and capital be equal for both producers. Again, it can be shown that the same argument holds for any number of resources and any number of producers. *Therefore, we conclude that the marginal condition for a **Pareto** optimal allocation of inputs requires that the MRTS between any two inputs be equal for all producers.*

OPTIMAL COMPOSITION OF OUTPUT: EFFICIENCY IN PRODUCT SUBSTITUTION

The third possible way of increasing social welfare lies in the composition of output. Can we increase social welfare by changing the composition of output, that is, by producing more of some goods and less of others? In order to answer this question of what constitutes the optimal output mix, we must first introduce the concept of the transformation curve.

Let us refer to Figure 19-2 and recall that all efficient input combinations must lie on the production contract curve. Further, note that for each output of a good, there corresponds a given output of the other good. For example, if 100 units of food are produced, the amount of clothing obtainable is 500; if 450 units of food are produced the maximum units of clothing attainable are 400, and so on. Plotting such a relationship between various quantities of food and the corresponding maximum quantities of clothing available on a graph, we obtain the transformation curve shown in Figure 19-3. (When there are more than two goods, we talk of a transformation surface.) *Thus, a transformation curve shows the maximum quantities of a good obtainable given the quantities of the other good.* The curve is drawn assuming a given state of technology and fixed amounts

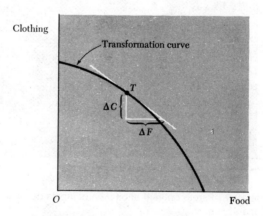

Figure 19-3 Transformation curve

of resources. The curve is called a transformation curve because it shows how a good is "transformed" into another by transferring some inputs from the production of one good to another.

Given a point on the transformation curve such as T, the slope of the curve at that point shows the amount of clothing that must be sacrificed in order to obtain an additional unit of food. We define the marginal rate of transformation (MRT) as follows:

$$\text{MRT} = -\Delta C / \Delta F$$

The negative sign is attached to obtain a positive expression from a transformation curve, which is negatively sloped. The economic meaning of the transformation curve is the ratio at which a good can be transformed into another. The changing slope of the curve shows that the rate at which a good can be converted into another is a function of the existing composition of output.

The marginal condition for a **Pareto** *optimal or efficient composition of output requires that the* MRT *between any two goods be equal to the* MRS *between the same two goods.* Since the MRT shows the rate at which a good can be transformed into another in production, and the MRS shows the rate at which the consumer is willing to exchange a good for another, the two ratios must be equal for Pareto optimality (or economic efficiency) to be attained. A simple numerical example may clarify the argument. Suppose the MRT is $2C/F$ while MRS is C/F. Thus,

$$\text{MRT} = 2C/F > \text{MRS} = C/F$$

According to the above inequality, the economy can produce 2 units of clothing by sacrificing a unit of food, while the consumer is willing to exchange a unit of food for a unit of clothing. Clearly, the economy can increase its social welfare by producing more clothing and less food.

In summary, **marginal conditions for a Pareto optimal** *resource allocation require that*:

1. The MRS between any two goods be equal for all consumers
2. The MRTS between any two inputs be equal for all producers
3. The MRS and the MRT be equal for any two goods

The economic welfare of a society cannot be at its maximum in the Paretian sense unless the above three marginal conditions—in exchange, factor substitution, and product substitution—are satisfied.

19-5 PERFECT COMPETITION AND PARETO OPTIMALITY

We noted in section 19-2 that it was important to prove the existence of a general equilibrium for a perfectly competitive economy because it has certain desirable properties. We will now see how all three marginal conditions for Pareto optimal resource allocation are satisfied in a perfectly competitive economy.

PERFECT COMPETITION AND EFFICIENCY IN EXCHANGE

The Pareto optimality condition for allocation of goods among consumers requires that the marginal rate of substitution, MRS, between any two goods be equal for all consumers.

In perfect competition, all consumers freely attempt to maximize their satisfaction subject to their budget constraints and to prices of goods that are uniform for everyone. Consumer equilibrium is attained where the consumer's indifference curve is tangent to his budget line. From section 3-7, we know that at the point of tangency between an indifference curve and the budget line, the MRS is equal to the ratio of two prices, p_f/p_c.

Now, all consumers face the identical price ratio (p_f/p_c), and adjust their purchases so as to equate their MRS to the common price ratio. It follows then that the MRS for all consumers (which are equal to the common p_f/p_c ratio) must equal. Clearly, the Pareto optimality condition in exchange is satisfied by perfect competition.

PERFECT COMPETITION AND EFFICIENCY IN PRODUCTION

The Pareto optimal allocation of inputs among producers requires that the marginal rate of technical substitution for any two inputs, MRTS, be the same for all producers.

From section 9-2, we know that the least-cost input combination is attained where an isoquant is tangent to an isocost line. Further, we know that the slope of an isoquant is the MRTS and that the slope of the isocost line shows the input price ratio, p_l/p_k.

In perfect competition, all producers can buy all inputs desired at the going input prices, which are the same for all input users. Every profit-maximizing producer adjusts his input combination in such a way as to equate his MRTS to the common p_l/p_k ratio. Thus, in perfect competition, the MRTS for all producers must be the same. Clearly, the efficiency condition in production, the equality of the MRTS for all producers, is satisfied in perfect competition.

PERFECT COMPETITION AND PARETO OPTIMAL COMPOSITION OF OUTPUT

In order for the composition of output to be Pareto optimal, the MRS must be equal to the MRT for all products. We have already shown that perfect competition allocates goods among consumers in such a way that the MRS $= p_f/p_c$. Now it can be shown that the MRT is equal to the ratio of the marginal costs of produc-

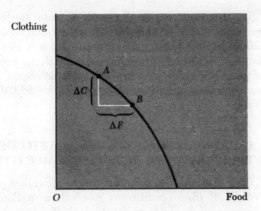

Figure 19-4 MRT equals the ratio of marginal costs

ing the two goods, MC_f/MC_c.[5] In perfect competition, each profit-maximizing producer produces that output at which his marginal cost equals his price. Thus, for every producer, $MC_f = p_f$ and $MC_c = p_c$, and

$$MRT = \frac{MC_f}{MC_c} = \frac{p_f}{p_c}$$

Combining this with the fact that $MRS = p_f/p_c$, we have

$$MRS = MRT$$

for any pair of goods. Again, perfect competition satisfies the marginal condition required for a Pareto optimal composition of output.

[5]Referring to Figure 19-4, consider reallocating some labor from the production of clothing to the production of food. As we move from point A to B along the transformation curve, the amount of labor released by the reduction in clothing is $-(dl/dc)dc$, which must be equal to the amount of labor added to the production of food, $(dl/df)df$. Therefore,

$$-\frac{dl}{dc} \cdot dc = \frac{dl}{df} \cdot df$$

and

$$MRT = -\frac{dc}{df} = \frac{dl}{df} \div \frac{dl}{dc}$$

Now dl/df is simply the marginal cost of food (MC_f) in terms of labor. Similarly, dl/dc is the marginal cost of clothing (MC_c). Thus, it follows that $MRT = MC_f/MC_c$.

In summary, we have seen that, under perfect competition, all three marginal conditions for Pareto optimal resource allocation are satisfied. In this sense, perfect competition is an ideal market structure. But before being unduly impressed with the Pareto optimal properties of perfectly competitive resource allocation, we must hasten to note some important qualifications that must be added to the preceding analysis.

19-6 QUALIFICATIONS ON THE PARETO OPTIMAL PROPERTIES OF PERFECT COMPETITION

Our argument in the preceding section that perfect competition satisfies all three conditions needed for a Pareto optimal allocation of resources depends on (1) the lack of externalities, (2) the lack of indivisibilities (which create increasing returns) and (3) the tacit acceptance of the existing distribution of wealth as ethically desirable. Thus, we must now examine how the optimal properties of perfect competition are affected by explicit recognition of externalities, indivisibilities, and the distribution of wealth. At the end of this section, we will also note that perfect competition is not the only system that is Pareto optimal.

EXTERNALITIES: EXTERNAL ECONOMIES AND DISECONOMIES

In examining the Pareto optimal properties of perfect competition, we have tacitly assumed that all benefits received and all costs incurred by consumers and producers are reflected in market prices, and that there is no divergence whatsoever between private and social benefits (or costs). But there are many cases in which the impact of an economic unit's action is not fully reflected in market prices, and the private and social benefits and costs diverge. *When an economic unit creates benefits for others for which he cannot collect payments, there occurs an external economy. Similarly, an external diseconomy exists when an economic unit imposes costs to others for which he is not required to pay. The term externalities includes both the external economies and diseconomies.* Externalities arise basically from the fact that not all the impacts of an economic activity on society — on employment, labor skills, technological capabilities, production costs, "quality of life," etc. — are reflected in market prices; market prices do not reflect costs or benefits external to a producer (or consumer), yet such costs or benefits are important to the overall social welfare.

A few examples of externalities that arise in production as well as in consumption should clarify the nature of external economies and diseconomies.

External economies in production. The opening of a new highway reduces transportation cost and increases land values for the surrounding areas. A manpower training program of a corporation provides a new source of skilled labor supply for other companies. Expansion of an industry may increase the demand for an input in such a way that the supplier can take advantage of the economies of large-scale production and can lower the input price to all users. If water is pumped from mine A, the cost of pumping water for an adjacent mine B is lowered. Honey producers' bees help pollinate oranges in the nearby orange groves, while the orange groves furnish the nectar for the honey bees.

External diseconomies in production. Smoke from factory chimneys pollutes the air, and wastes poured into streams and oceans create health hazards for human, animal, and plant lives. The introduction of a new industry in an area bids up wage levels and crowds the roads. Increased fishing in the present reduces the size of fish stocks available in the future. Increased drilling by an oil company increases the cost of pumping oil by an adjacent oil company.

External economies in consumption. Our neighbor's beautiful garden and manicured lawn make our neighborhood look better. When one keeps his car safe and well tuned, others' safety is improved, and the air they breathe remains cleaner. Money your parents spend in educating you tends to benefit not only you but those who come in contact with you directly or indirectly. Your violinist neighbor's music helps you enjoy your backyard patio more.

External diseconomies in consumption. Giving candy bars to your children makes your neighbor's children who cannot get them unhappy. Your teenagers' loud music disturbs you and your neighbors. Your neighbors' new car makes your own car look old. Your manicured lawn forces your neighbor to mow his lawn more frequently than he would otherwise.

When externalities exist and private and social benefits (or costs) diverge, a perfectly competitive economy guided by market prices alone fails to allocate resources optimally. *When there are external economies, equating price with private marginal cost results in an underproduction of a good or service.* For example, if there are external economies in production, the private cost tends to be larger than the real social cost because private cost fails to account for the external economy being generated. Thus, the output determined on the basis of private cost alone will be smaller than the socially optimal output. In Figure 19-5, let curve S represent the industry supply curve obtained by summing individual firms' marginal cost curves: it reflects private costs of production only. Let the curve S' represent the industry supply curve that accounts for the external economies in production generated by this industry: it is lower than S because the

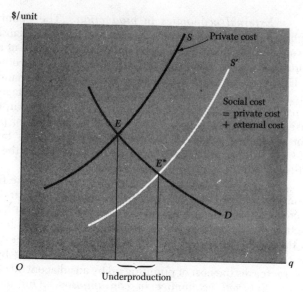

Figure 19-5   Private versus social cost

private cost must be reduced by the amount of external economies accruing to the society. Note that point E, which shows the equilibrium price and output established by private cost and benefit calculation alone, results in an underproduction of the good compared with point E^*, which takes into account the external economies created by the industry. When there are external economies in consumption, similarly, the demand curve will fail to reflect the external economies being created and the output desired by the private consumer tends to be smaller than the socially optimal amount.

A reasoning analogous to that of the preceding paragraph will show that *when there are external diseconomies, equating price with private marginal cost will result in an overproduction of a good.* A cigarette smoker who ignores the external diseconomy of the smoke he is producing tends to smoke too much. A factory that is not required to pay for the cost of keeping air or water around it clean tends to ignore the pollution cost and overproduces the product.

In summary, we have seen that the existence of externalities produces a misallocation of resources even if perfect competition were to exist. When there are external economies, the output produced tends to be too small; and when there are external diseconomies, the output too large.

INDIVISIBILITIES

The claim that perfect competition creates a Pareto optimal resource allocation does not necessarily hold true when indivisibilities are introduced. Suppose a large number of small firms are in competitive equilibrium and the marginal rate of transformation, MRT, in production and the marginal rate of substitution, MRS, in consumption are equal. Now assume that production processes are indivisible and that the small firms cannot take advantage of the economies of size that accrue to a larger production process. If so, a few larger firms employing the more efficient large-scale process can produce greater outputs using the same value amounts of inputs, although in different forms. This will mean that the transformation curve is pushed further outward from the origin and that the original situation in which the large number of small firms satisfied the marginal condition for efficient production was really inefficient—it produced less output using the same amounts of resources.

Furthermore, when indivisibilities and the economies of large-scale operation exist, a competitive solution may not be feasible at all. In the case of a *natural monopoly—in which the firm's LAC and LMC decline through the relevant range of output—* one or a few producers will eventually dominate the market, and a perfectly competitive solution will be neither feasible nor efficient.

DISTRIBUTION OF WEALTH

In discussing the Pareto optimal or efficient properties of perfect competition, we have said nothing about the ethical desirability of the existing state of income and wealth distribution. By default, the traditional claims for the efficiency of perfect competition accept the existing distribution of income and wealth. This implies that a rich man's dog is more deserving than a poor man's baby. It implies that a millionaire's yacht is far more desirable to society than a poor man's house. It accepts the ethical judgment that people born in poor families, or those with mental or physical impairments should have little claim over society's output. To the extent that the marginal decision rules for perfect competition tacitly accept the status quo income distribution, they fail to achieve a socially optimal resource allocation, and leave room for some forms of public intervention.[6]

[6]Tibor Scitovsky shows why an economist's policy recommendation cannot ignore matters of equity or value judgment. For detail, see his *Welfare and Competition*, rev. ed. (Homewood, Ill.: Irwin, 1971), pp. 64–73.

PERFECT COMPETITION IS BUT ONE OPTIMAL SOLUTION

We have shown that the marginal conditions for efficient resource allocation are satisfied in perfect competition if we assume away the problems associated with externalities, indivisibilities, and income distribution. However, it is important to note that perfect competition is a "sufficient" but not "necessary" condition for a Pareto optimal resource allocation. If perfect competition exists, the Pareto optimal resource allocation is attained, but there are other ways to attain the same Pareto optimal resource allocation, so perfect competition is not a necessary condition for a Pareto optimal allocation. A decentralized socialist economy, for instance, using "shadow" or accounting prices or some set of numerical points, and directing its individual economic units to maximize their gains can, in principle, achieve the same result as a perfectly competitive system.[7] Furthermore, when such shadow prices are used, the prices could, at least conceptually, be so adjusted as to reflect the externalities involved in the production and consumption of each good—a feature that cannot be accomplished by market prices in a competitive economy.[8]

In the preceding pages we have accomplished two major things. First, we noted the importance of interdependence among various parts of an economy and observed that general equilibrium can be assured for a perfectly competitive economy. Second, we have introduced the Pareto optimality criterion of welfare judgment, observed how perfect competition satisfies the marginal conditions required for welfare maximization in the Paretian sense, and noted the existence of some important gaps between Pareto optimal resource allocation, as in perfect competition, and the genuine maximization of social welfare. In the next chapter, we shall introduce some more simple criteria of welfare judgment and examine the input-output analysis and the cost-benefit analysis as examples of general equilibrium theory and welfare economics.

[7]See Abba P. Lerner, *The Economics of Control* (New York: MacMillan, 1944), and R. Dorfman, P. Samuelson, and R. Solow, *Linear Programming and Economic Analysis* (New York: McGraw-Hill, 1958).

[8]Of course, many difficulties face the socialist planners in trying to establish a system of shadow prices that will produce a Pareto optimal or efficient resource allocation. For instance, how does the state get its information, and how does it ascertain the benefits and costs associated with various externality-combating measures?

EXERCISES 19

General Equilibrium and Welfare Economics

19-1 Refer to the following Edgeworth exchange box diagram.

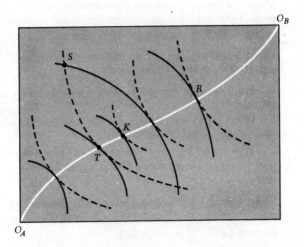

1. Explain what is the Pareto optimal condition for exchange between two consumers.

2. Is the marginal condition for a Pareto optimal allocation of goods between two consumers satisfied at:

   a. Point S? Why or why not?
   b. Point T? Why or why not?
   c. Point R? Why or why not?

3. From the society's (that is, both individuals) point of view, indicate whether the following combinations are preferable to combination S.

    a. Combination T. Why?
    b. Combination K. Why?
    c. Combination R. Why?

4. Does *any* point on the contract curve satisfy the Pareto optimal condition for exchange between consumers or is it defined by a *unique* point?

5. Many economists believe that the Pareto optimality criterion is a rather incomplete, limited criterion for social policy decisions. Explain why this is so.

19-2 "Externalities" are important considerations in our public policy decisions.

1. What are "externalities"?

2. Using the examples of basic research and air pollution, show how the usual marginal cost pricing fails to attain the socially optimal resource allocation when there is an external economy or diseconomy. Assume a competitive market.

19-3 Suppose the excise tax on gasoline is increased by ten cents a gallon from its current level:

1. How would the price and quantity consumed be affected?

2. What effect will it have on the distribution of income among the different income groups?

3. Will there be any "externalities" consideration that will increase or decrease the support for this increased tax?

19-4 Using the "energy shortage" created at least in part by the Arab oil embargo, illustrate the nature of interdependence among various parts of the U.S. economy.

19-5 The interdependence among its parts and simultaneous determination of prices and outputs are the essential features of any economic system. Does it then follow that the partial equilibrium analyses are of little value?

CHAPTER TWENTY

GENERAL EQUILIBRIUM
AND WELFARE
ECONOMICS – CONTINUED

This chapter continues the discussions of the previous chapter by introducing some additional criteria for welfare judgment and examining the input-output analysis and the cost-benefit analysis as applications of the general equilibrium theory and welfare economics.

20-1 MORE CRITERIA FOR WELFARE JUDGMENT

In section 19-4, we noted that the Pareto criterion cannot evaluate a change that makes some better off and others worse off. Since many policy changes tend to affect some people favorably and others unfavorably, the usefulness of the Pareto criterion is seriously limited. Let us, therefore, examine some other criteria that attempt to overcome the limitations of the Pareto criterion.

THE KALDOR (OR COMPENSATION) CRITERION

Nicholas Kaldor (and J. R. Hicks) proposed the following approach to establishing a welfare criterion.[1] Given a proposed change, ask the person who will gain from the change the maximum amount he would be willing to pay to have the change made, and call it $G (G for gain). Similarly, ask the person who would lose from the change the maximum amount he would be willing to pay to prevent the change, and call it $L (L for loss). If $G is greater than $L,

[1] Nicholas Kaldor, "Welfare Propositions of Economics and Interpersonal Comparisons of Utility," *Economic Journal*, Vol. 49 (1939), pp. 549–552. J. R. Hicks, "The Foundations of Welfare Economics," *Economic Journal*, Vol. 49 (1939), pp. 696–712.

then the gainer can "compensate" the loser and still be better off. The change, therefore, is an improvement. *Thus, the Kaldor or compensation criterion states that a change is an improvement in economic efficiency or social welfare if the gainers could compensate the losers, and would still be able to retain some net gains.*

The compensation criterion does not require that the compensation be made actually: it merely requires that the compensation *could be made*. (If the compensation is actually made, then someone will be better off without anyone being worse off; and the Pareto criterion would be satisfied.) Consider a numerical example. Suppose Alice is willing to pay $1,000 to have a change made and Betty is willing to pay $700 to prevent the change, then the change is, according to the Kaldor criterion, an improvement. The Kaldor criterion does not require that Alice actually pay Betty $700. If Alice did pay the sum to Betty, then the Pareto criterion would be satisfied.

In evaluating the economic efficiency of a change, the Kaldor criterion uses monetary valuations attached to a change by gainers and losers. However, there is a serious pitfall in evaluating the economic efficiency of a change on the basis of monetary valuations of different individuals. Consider our example in which the change affected Alice favorably and Betty adversely. The change is, according to the Kaldor criterion, a definite improvement in economic efficiency because Alice's gain ($1,000) exceeds Betty's loss ($700); Alice could compensate Betty and would still have $300 net gain. But if Alice is a rich millionairess, her gain of $1,000 may mean a trifle. On the other hand, if Betty is a poor girl, $700 may be a fortune to her. Thus, the damage suffered by poor Betty may far exceed the trifle gain enjoyed by rich Alice, and the proposed change is a deterioration rather than an improvement in economic efficiency or social welfare. Clearly, interpersonal comparisons like the one offered above have serious flaws.

If the marginal utility of money is equal to all persons and remains constant, then the Kaldor criterion would correctly evaluate the economic efficiency of a change. Otherwise, it falters. Thus, the Kaldor criterion of efficiency tacitly accepts the status quo of income distribution and makes hidden interpersonal comparisons in assuming that the same dollar values have the same importance to different individuals.[2]

[2]There are other important problems associated with this criterion. For instance, Scitovsky demonstrated that, having shown situation A to be more efficient than situation B on the basis of Kaldor-Hicks criterion, the same criterion might also reveal, following the society's adoption of situation A, that B was now more efficient than A. For an excellent explanation of such difficulties involved, see James Quirk and Rubin Saposnik's *Introduction to General Equilibrium Theory and Welfare Economics* (New York: McGraw-Hill, 1968), pp. 120–123.

THE SOCIAL WELFARE FUNCTION: THE BERGSON CRITERION

When a change makes some better off and others worse off, it is impossible to evaluate it without making some value judgment as to how much different individuals and groups deserve. When you refuse to make an explicit value judgment, it may creep into your analysis through a back door, as in the case of the Kaldor criterion. Since it is not possible to evaluate a change that hurts some and benefits others without making a value judgment, Bergson proposed the introduction of an explicit set of value judgments in the form of a *social welfare function.*[3] The value judgment may be that of a group of experts, of the elected government officials, of the dictator, of the religious leaders, or of any other individuals or groups in the society. In the simple case of a two-person economy, for instance, the social welfare function may be represented by a set of social indifference curves such as the one shown in Figure 20-1. A social indifference curve such as W_1 in Figure 20-1 shows the locus of combinations of A's and B's utilities that produce a given level of social welfare. Given a social indifference map such as the one given in Figure 20-1, the effect of a proposed change on social welfare can be evaluated unambiguously. For instance, the change from A to D is an improvement; the change from C to A is a deterioration; and the change from A to B does not affect social welfare.

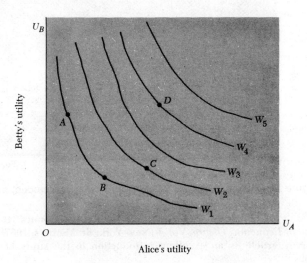

Figure 20-1 Social welfare function

[3]"A Reformulation of Certain Aspects of Welfare Economics," *Quarterly Journal of Economics*, Vol. 52 (February 1938), pp. 310–334.

The difficulty with the social welfare function is that there is no easy way in which we can construct a social welfare function. "Although the social welfare function had received continual mention since Bergson's 1938 formulation, no instruction in the drafting of this grandiose design had been hazarded."[4] Thus, the social welfare function remains an idealistic concept that we cannot translate into an earthly policy tool.

THE MAXIMIZATION OF SOCIAL WELFARE

Let us now combine the concept of the social welfare function with the Pareto optimal production, distribution, and composition of goods discussed in Chapter Nineteen. By this means, we can determine the social welfare-maximizing configuration of input allocation, output composition, and commodity distribution for the simple case of a two-input, two-output, and two-person situation.[5]

Grand utility possibility frontier. In section 19-5, we showed that a Pareto optimal composition of output requires the

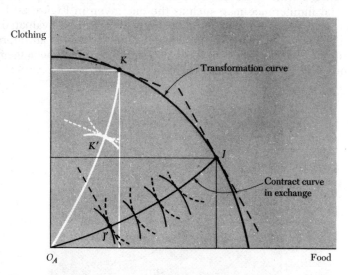

Figure 20-2 Pareto efficient distribution of a given product mix

[4]E. J. Mishan, "A Survey of Welfare Economics, 1939–59," in *Survey of Economic Theory*, Vol. I (New York: St. Martin's, 1967), p. 192. This survey article is an excellent introduction to the study of welfare economics.

[5]This section is based on F. M. Bator, "The Simple Analytics of Welfare Maximization," *American Economic Review*, March 1957, pp. 22–31.

equality of the marginal rate of transformation, MRT, and the marginal rate of substitution, MRS. Any point J on the production possibility or transformation curve in Figure 20-2 denotes a specific composition of food and clothing outputs. Given the food and clothing outputs, contract curve $O_A J$ shows the locus of Pareto optimal allocations of the available food and clothing to Alice and Betty. (The assumption of convex to the origin indifference curves produces this smooth contract curve.) All points along this contract curve satisfy the marginal condition for *exchange efficiency, that is, the equality of the MRS between two goods for Alice and Betty.* But only J' on the contract curve satisfies the marginal condition for the optimal composition of outputs as well. The slope of the dotted line at J' is equal to the slope of the transformation curve at J; thus, MRS = MRT. From the utilities associated with Alice and Betty's indifference curves through point J', we can get point J'' in the utility space of Figure 20-3: this point shows the utilities accruing to Alice and Betty when the product mix denoted by J is efficiently allocated between the two, as shown by point J'. It shows the maximum or *grand utility* attainable to the society from product mix J.

For each point on the transformation curve, we can follow through the same analytical procedure used for point J and obtain a point in the utility space. For instance, if the product mix is shown by point K in Figure 20-2, K' indicates the optimal allocation of this product mix between two individuals. The grand utility associated with this distribution is indicated by point K'' in the utility space of Figure 20-3. Repetition of this procedure for each point on the transformation curve yields the *grand utility possibility frontier* of Figure

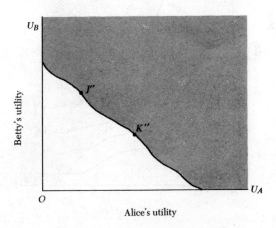

Figure 20-3   Grand utility possibility frontier

20-3. Each point on this frontier gives the maximum of Alice's utility for any given feasible level of Betty's utility and vice versa.

The constrained bliss point. In Figure 20-4, the grand utility possibility frontier is combined with the social welfare function shown by a family of indifference curves. *Social welfare is at maximum at point W° (the bliss point), where the utility possibility curve touches the highest social indifference curve.*

Note that all points on the grand utility possibility curve satisfy the Pareto efficiency conditions in production, distribution, and compostition of products. But some efficient points on the grand utility possibility frontier are inferior to inefficient points in the interior of the curve. For example, the efficient point Z in Figure 20-4 is definitely inferior to any inefficient point on or northeast of W_2. To claim that any efficient point on the grand utility possibility frontier is better than inefficient points that lie inside the frontier is indefensible. However, it is true that given an inefficient point, there will exist some point(s) on the grand utility frontier that represents an improvement.

From the bliss point to best inputs, outputs, and distribution. We can now retrace our steps and show that the welfare-maximizing configuration of output mix, output distribution, and input combination is determinate. The constrained bliss point, $W°$, is associated with a unique product mix on the transformation curve. To avoid drawing another graph, let us assume that point J in Figure 20-2

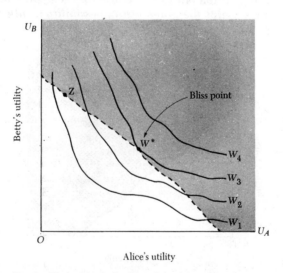

Figure 20-4   Maximization of social welfare

shows this product mix. Then, the food-clothing distribution between Alice and Betty implied by W^* is fixed by point J'. Further, we can now go back to the production Edgeworth box of the kind shown in Figure 19-2, and determine the efficient allocation of inputs needed to produce the output mix on the transformation curve of Figure 20-2. Observe that the maximum-welfare configuration is determinate. We have solved for the total outputs of food and clothing, for the distribution of these outputs between Alice and Betty, and for the labor and capital to be used in food and clothing production.

ECONOMISTS AND POLICY RECOMMENDATIONS

When a policy change involves redistribution of welfare between individuals and between social classes, there is really no satisfactory criterion by which the economist can unambiguously judge whether a policy change will or will not improve social welfare. However, this does not mean that economists cannot or should not make policy recommendations. There are a variety of policy recommendations the economist can make with a clear conscience. First, on many issues the efficiency consideration—which is in the expert domain of the economist—predominates. For instance, the economist needed little justification to uphold the reduction of unemployment as the primary goal during the Great Depression. Similarly, there is little doubt that a high priority can be assigned to the growth of per capita income in an impoverished underdeveloped country. Second, the economist can participate in policy matters by showing appropriate means of achieving some given ends. For example, in a country in which the government is seeking to control inflation, the economist is the person who must consider what are the best means available to achieve the end. Similarly, if a country is trying to build up its foreign exchange reserves, the economist is the person who must consider whether a foreign exchange control will make things better or worse.[6]

When a policy change affects significantly both efficiency and equity (that is, distribution of welfare), there is no scientific way of evaluating the net result. In such a situation, it is often argued that economists should concern themselves with efficiency considerations alone, and let others furnish their expert advice on matters of equity. However, there is no expert on equity in our society, and the economist is as good a judge of equity as anyone else. Besides, the economist is in a better position to appraise the relative importance of efficiency and equity involved in the proposed policy change. Furthermore, if the economist bases his recommendation on efficiency

[6]William Baumol, *Economic Theory and Operations Analysis*, 3d ed. (Englewood Cliffs, N.J.: Prentice-Hall, 1972), pp. 399–400.

alone, he may mislead the public to believe that efficiency alone is important or that efficiency is more important than equity. Thus, the economist must base his policy recommendations on careful evaluation of both efficiency and equity considerations.[7] There is no way the economist can completely avoid value judgment: he must judge that hurricane victims be assisted by the government at the expense of other taxpayers. He has to decide whether oil pipelines should go through an area even if it may damage the environment and inconvenience some property owners located in its path. Since most of the economist's recommendations affect the distribution of equity and welfare between individuals and social classes, he must possess not only a keen analytical mind but also a warm heart for his fellow citizen's welfare.

Since ethical conclusions cannot be derived scientifically, the economist must be careful not to be misled by his wishful thinking. Basically, he needs to distinguish, whenever feasible, his analysis *qua* economist from his value judgment *qua* citizen. He should make it clear that his policy recommendations are based on both efficiency and equity considerations, and that on the issue of equity he, like anyone else, is not an expert.

20-2 INPUT-OUTPUT ANALYSIS AND ECONOMIC INTERDEPENDENCE: An Application

THE NATURE OF INPUT-OUTPUT ANALYSIS

The *input-output analysis* pioneered by Harvard's Wassily Leontief[8] is an application of general equilibrium theory, and *is concerned with an empirical study of interdependence among various parts or sectors of an economy.* Various sectors (parts, or industries) are interdependent, for instance, because production in a sector must depend on inputs furnished by various sectors (frequently including itself). For example, the manufacture of motor vehicles uses as inputs products of such industries as primary metal, fabricated metal, machinery, rubber products, chemical products, textile mill products, and the motor vehicle industry itself. Thus, a change in the output of the motor vehicle industry requires changes in the output of all related industries, which in turn require many more changes in the output of still other industries.

[7]Tibor Scitovsky, *Welfare and Competition*, rev. ed. (Homewood, Ill.: Irwin, 1971), pp. 66–67.
[8]*The Structure of American Economy, 1919–1939,* (New York: Oxford University Press, 1941).

Input-output analysis has a wide range of applications. Given a certain final output target, it can show the production re- requirements of various sectors. It is used to obtain projections of demand, output, employment, and investment for a country or region. It is used in economic development planning, studies of interregional and international economic relationships, and of effects of wage, profit, and tax changes on prices, of military mobilization, and so on.

In order to keep the computational and statistical prob- lems manageable, input-output analysis makes an important assump- tion (known as the *linearity assumption*) regarding the technical relationships between inputs and outputs. It assumes that in any production process inputs are used in *fixed* proportions. Thus, in input-output analysis, a given change in the output of a sector requires proportionate changes in all inputs used by the sector.

THE INPUT-OUTPUT FRAMEWORK

In order to illustrate the nature of the input-output frame- work, consider a hypothetical three-sector economy composed of agriculture, manufacture, and service. The interrelationship among the three sectors is described by the annual flow of input and output in Table 20-1.

The columns show each sector as a purchaser or user. For instance, reading down the agriculture column, we see that agriculture purchased $72.7 million of agricultural inputs, $109.1 million of manufacture, and $72.7 million of service. Thus, the agri- culture sector purchased $254.5 million of intermediate inputs in producing $363.6 million of agricultural output, shown in the last column. Similarly, the manufacture (or service) column shows the dollar values of various inputs purchased by the manufacture (or service) sector in producing its output. The final demand column shows the purchases by the final demand sector (households).

Table 20-1 Input-Output Flow Table (in millions of dollars)

INDUSTRY PURCHASING

INDUSTRY PRODUCING	Agriculture	Manufacture	Service	Final Demand	Total Gross Output
Agriculture	72.7	109.1	81.8	100	363.6
Manufacture	109.1	436.3	245.5	300	1,090.9
Service	72.7	218.2	327.3	200	818.2
Total intermediate inputs	254.5	763.6	664.6	600	

The rows show each sector as a producer or supplier. For instance, the first row shows that agriculture supplied $72.7 million output to itself (for example, seeds and livestock), $109.1 million output to the manufacture sector, and $81.1 million worth to the service sector, and $100 million worth to the final demand sector.

The entries in the total gross output column show the sum of purchases by three intermediate sectors as well as the purchases by the final demand sector. In the input-output framework all outputs are imputed to some inputs. Thus, for each sector, the difference between its total gross output and its total intermediate purchases shows the sector's payment to households for their labor and capital. For instance, the agriculture sector's payments to households are $109.1 million, the difference between its gross output of $363.6 million and its total intermediate purchases, $254.5 million.

The input-output table reveals clearly the mutual interdependence of various sectors, as suppliers of inputs and users of outputs. Also, the relative importance of various sectors in the production process of a sector is readily seen from the table. For instance, in our hypothetical economy, the manufacture sector buys over half of its intermediate inputs from the manufacture sector itself.

TECHNICAL COEFFICIENTS

Table 20-2 shows *technical* (*production* or *input*) *coefficients* derived from the data in Table 20-1. Such listings of technical coefficients are referred to as a *structural matrix*. In order to see how these technical coefficients are derived, let us look at the manner in which the entries in the agriculture sector column are derived. The technical coefficients listed in the agriculture sector column are obtained by dividing all entries in the agriculture sector column of Table 20-1 by the value of the total gross agricultural output. That is,

$$\frac{72.7}{363.6} = .2, \quad \frac{109.1}{363.6} = .3, \quad \frac{72.7}{363.6} = .2$$

The economic interpretation of each column entry in Table 20-2, therefore, is the dollar value of input used in producing a dollar's worth of the sector output. For instance, the entries in the agriculture sector column show that, in order to produce a dollar's worth of agricultural output, 20 cents of agricultural inputs, 30 cents of manufacturing inputs, and 20 cents of services must be used.

The structural matrix shows even more clearly the relative importance of each sector input in the production of any sector output. Furthermore, using the information furnished by the structural matrix, we can calculate the total gross outputs of each sector

Table 20-2   Structural Matrix

INDUSTRY PRODUCING	INDUSTRY PURCHASING		
	Agriculture	*Manufacture*	*Service*
Agriculture	.2	.1	.1
Manufacture	.3	.4	.3
Service	.2	.2	.4

needed to accommodate any final demand requirements. Suppose we wish to have for final demand (consumption), $100 million of agricultural output, $300 million of manufacture, and $200 million of service. What are the total gross outputs needed to satisfy this composition of the final demand? This question is answered simply by solving a set of simultaneous equations. Let the total gross outputs of agriculture, manufacture, and service be represented by letters A, M, and S, respectively; and denote the final demand by letter F. Then, the gross agricultural output required is given by

$$A = .2A + .1M + .1S + F$$

That is, the total output of agriculture needed is the amount wanted for final consumption (in our case, $F = 100$), plus the amounts agriculture must furnish to various sectors as intermediate inputs: $.2A$ to agriculture, $.1M$ to manufacture, and $.1S$ to services. (Agriculture needs 20 cents' worth of agricultural inputs for each dollar of agricultural output it produces. Similarly, manufacture and services need, for each dollar of output produced, 10 cents of agricultural inputs.)

By similar reasoning, we can obtain the equations showing the total gross output requirements for the manufacture and service sectors. Thus, the three simultaneous equations showing the gross output requirements are:

$$A = .2A + .1M + .1S + 100$$
$$M = .3A + .4M + .3S + 300 \qquad \text{(20-1)}$$
$$S = .2A + .2M + .4S + 200$$

Solving these three simultaneous equations in three unknowns we obtain our solutions:[9] $A = 363.6$, $M = 1,090.9$, and $S = 818.2$.

[9]These solutions are the same as the total gross outputs of Table 20-1. Since the technical coefficients of Table 20-2 are derived from Table 20-1 and the final demand requirements are the same, the total gross outputs must also be the same.

THE EFFECTS OF A CHANGE IN FINAL DEMAND

Suppose our final demand for services increases from $200 million to $300 million (while the final demands for agricultural and manufacturing goods remain unchanged at $100 million and $300 million). How would this change affect the total gross outputs of the three sectors? To answer this question, we solve the following simultaneous equations.

$$A = .2A + .1M + .1S + 100$$
$$M = .3A + .4M + .3S + 300 \qquad (20\text{-}2)$$
$$S = .2A + .2M + .4S + \boxed{300}$$

The circled entry 300 is the only change from the set of equations in (20-1). The solutions to this set of simultaneous equations are $A = 409.1$, $M = 1,227.3$, and $S = 1,045.5$. Note that an increase in the final demand for services requires not only an increased total gross output of services but also increased outputs of the agriculture and manufacture sectors, which must furnish additional intermediate inputs to the service sector.[10]

EMPIRICAL INVESTIGATION OF
INPUT-OUTPUT STRUCTURE

Empirical investigations of input-output relationships are rather complicated and expensive, and therefore, appear rather infrequently. Studies of the input-output structure of the U.S. economy by the U.S. Department of Commerce are now available for years 1947, 1958, and 1963. The results of the 1963 study, in which estimates were prepared for about 370 separate industries, are reported in the November 1969 issue of *Survey of Current Business*.[11] The article presents the results of the 1963 study by aggregating the industry categories to 86 industries, the number of categories provided for the 1958 study. Even this summarized version of the input-output table should be sufficient to convey to the reader the complexity and enormity of the task involved in constructing a large-scale input-output table.

[10]If the complete input-output flow table (such as the one in Table 20-1) is desired, it can be readily constructed. For instance, to obtain the actual dollar value entries for the agricultural sector column, all that is needed is to multiply the technical coefficients in the agriculture sector column by the new total gross output of agriculture, $409.1 million.

[11]"Input-Output Structure of the U.S. Economy: 1963," pp. 16–47.

20-3   COST-BENEFIT ANALYSIS: An Application

Cost-benefit analysis provides an excellent example of an application of welfare economics.[12] In cost-benefit analysis, we are concerned with the welfare of the entire society, and not with the profit or utility calculus of individual producers or consumers.

In evaluating the merit of a proposed project, cost-benefit analysis uses the compensation (or the potential Pareto improvement) criterion. It compares the social benefit (rather than more readily identifiable private benefit) and the social opportunity cost (rather than the private cost), and evaluates whether the society would be better off by undertaking the project rather than not undertaking it, or undertaking some alternative project(s). A project is considered economically feasible if it is capable of producing an excess of benefit over cost such that everyone in society could, by a costless redistribution of the gains, be made better off. Thus, a project is economically feasible if the benefit-cost ratio, B/C, is greater than one. The extent of potential Pareto improvement is shown by the size of the difference between social benefit and social cost, $B - C$ or by the benefit-cost ratio, B/C. Thus, all calculations that enter a cost-benefit analysis must do so by affecting the estimated social benefit or social cost.

Suppose a cost-benefit analysis of a project shows the potential Pareto improvement or excess gain to be $100,000. What this shows is *not* that everyone will be made better off in varying degrees, but rather that it is *conceptually possible*, by costless redistributions, to make everyone better off *in total* by the sum equal to $100,000.

From our discussion of the compensation criterion in section 20-1, the reader may recall that we are completely ignoring the effect of the resulting change in distribution that follows from the implementation of a project. For instance, the excess gain of $100,000 can come from a project that benefits the rich by $250,000 and hurts the poor by $150,000. This suggests that a cost-benefit analysis needs to be accompanied by observations (and even recommendations) regarding the distributional effect whenever there is a substantial impact on distribution. Fortunately, according to E. J. Mishan, the distributional effects are usually rather small. Furthermore, the local effects of an irrigation, flood control, recreation, or electrification project tend to have an equalizing effect on distribution. However, in cases such as through-traffic and fly-overs going through (or over)

---

[12]This brief description of cost-benefit analysis is largely based on E. J. Mishan's *Cost-Benefit Analysis* (New York: Praeger, 1971), pp. 1–8, 316–321.

low-income neighborhoods, the external diseconomies suffered by the low-income groups may exceed the benefits derived from the projects, and the distributional impact may be substantial.

Cost-benefit analysis has been applied to a wide variety of projects: multiple-purpose river development, urban renewal programs, highway investments, preventing high school dropouts, government research and development programs, and so on.

20-4 COST-BENEFIT ANALYSIS OF ENGLISH CHANNEL TUNNEL

In order to obtain more insight into the nature of cost-benefit analysis, let us examine the cost-benefit study of the once proposed English Channel tunnel.[13]

In 1963 the result of a study jointly undertaken by British and French officials was published in the United Kingdom with the title, *Proposals for a Fixed Channel Link.* The study compared both a tunnel and a bridge with the existing means of cross-channel travel, predicted over a 50-year period, between 1969 and 2018. In selecting some features of this study, we can ignore estimates for the bridge project which, in any case, revealed a net loss.

In the *Proposals,* after much description of the physical details of the constructions possible, and the type, time and frequency of services, an upper and lower estimate of capital and operating costs were estimated. The difference between the upper and lower estimate for operating costs was not large, however, and was nonexistent for capital costs.

For the purpose of estimating benefits, the traffic expected over the future was broken down into three types: passengers, vehicles (including the private passenger cars), and goods. A division was then made between (1) traffic *diverted* from the existing means of travel, and (2) additional traffic that would be *generated* only due to the construction of the tunnel.

Following this distinction, the benefits over the 50-year period were calculated as follows:

For *diverted* traffic, which, as it happened, provided by far the greater part of the benefits, there would be a saving in both capital costs (of the existing means — ships and planes) and operating costs over time as a result of the tunnel construction. For instance, in the year 1963 it was expected that x_1 million passengers would make the channel crossing by the existing means, as would x_2 million vehicles and x_3 million tons of freight. In the *absence* of the tunnel

[13]This case is adapted from Mishan's *Cost-Benefit Analysis, op. cit.,* pp. 20–23.

project, each of these figures was expected to increase at a figure between some upper and lower percentage per annum over the future. If, on the other hand, the tunnel were to be built, at a cost of £141 million in 1969, the upper estimate of the diversion of traffic to it would release resources used by the existing means to an adjusted 1969 value of £308 million. Ships and planes might be scrapped sooner. But, more important, additional ships and planes that would have been built in the absence of the tunnel, would then no longer be built. The resources (men and materials) that would have been used in their operation, would also be released for other economic activities.

Against this saving of £308 million in capital expenditures, we have to place the costs of operating the tunnel transport, which were reckoned at an adjusted 1969 value of £68 million. The new saving in capital and other costs is, therefore, £308 million *less* £68 million, or £240 million.

For *generated* traffic, there would be a profit of £47 million from additional freight, which would not otherwise have been transported. To this figure was added an estimate of consumers' surplus of additional passengers, who would not otherwise have made the journey, of £7 million, a total of £54 million when adjusted to 1969.

The total benefits, on the upper estimates, were, therefore, £240 million from the diverted traffic *plus* £54 million for the generated traffic, a total of £294 million to be compared with the initial capital outlay of £141 million. If the criterion adopted was that of a benefit-cost ratio greater than unity, then certainly it would be met by the upper estimates of the project. The calculation based on the lower traffic estimates produced a benefit cost ratio of 215/141, which is also acceptable.

The costs and benefits were, as stated, spread over a long period. It was estimated that it would take six years, 1962–68 inclusive, to construct the tunnel, over which period the costs would fall most heavily in the last two years. The 1969 figure of £141 million, therefore, represented a *compounding* of the earlier capital outlays (at 7 percent per annum) to that date. Moreover, the figure represents the initial capital sum only. Beginning with the year 1973, and from then on, capital costs were expected to be incurred in almost every year down to 2018. These future capital costs, along with the annual operating costs, from 1969 to 2018, were *discounted* to 1969 to yield the upper estimate of £68 million already referred to. The saving of capital and the saving of operating expenses by the existing means were also expected to be distributed over a large number of years beginning from 1969. They were discounted at 7 percent to the year 1969 to yield the £308 million figure also referred to above.

The study mentioned other economic factors that were not quantified; for instance, (1) the fact that passengers are *not* indifferent to different modes of travel. If the tunnel-journey fare were the same as, or even lower than, that of the sea or air journey, passengers might still prefer to travel by sea or air. And (2) other repercussions on the economies of the Continental countries and Britain were mentioned, though without being specific. One can think of a number of unwanted effects in this connection, such as traffic congestion near the vicinity of the tunnel entrances, and what is now known as "tourist blight" resulting from the increased traffic.

EXERCISES 20

General Equilibrium and Welfare Economics— Continued

20-1 Suppose the government is proposing a new interstate highway that goes through a low-income neighborhood. The business and manufacturing interests in the city are for the program and are willing to spend $500,000 for the change to be made. The low-income neighborhood objects to the program and is willing to spend $50,000 to stop it.

    1. Does the proposed highway project satisfy the Kaldor criterion? Why?

    2. Is the proposed project an improvement for the society? (Consider the effects on the two groups only, and ignore any other externalities that may be associated with the project.)

20-2 Table A shows the input-output flow table and Table B shows the structural matrix (or input coefficients) derived from Table A.

Table A Input-Output Flow Table

INDUSTRY PRODUCING	INDUSTRY PURCHASING				
	A	M	S	F	G
A	9	6	5	10	30
M	5	10	10	15	40
S	3	4	8	15	30

Table B   Structural Matrix

INDUSTRY PRODUCING	INDUSTRY PURCHASING		
	A	M	S
A	.30	.15	.17
M	.17	( )	.33
S	( )	.10	.27

(Rounded to two decimal places.)

A, M, S, F, and G stand for agriculture, manufacturing, service, final demand, and gross output, respectively.

1. Explain what the agriculture row in Table A shows.
2. What does the manufacture column in Table A show?
3. Supply the missing entries in the structural matrix (Table B).
4. Explain the economic meaning of the entries in the above structural matrix. More specifically, what is the meaning of .33 in the above table?
5. Suppose the final demand for services increased from 15 to 20, what are the resulting changes in the outputs of agriculture, manufacture, and service sectors?

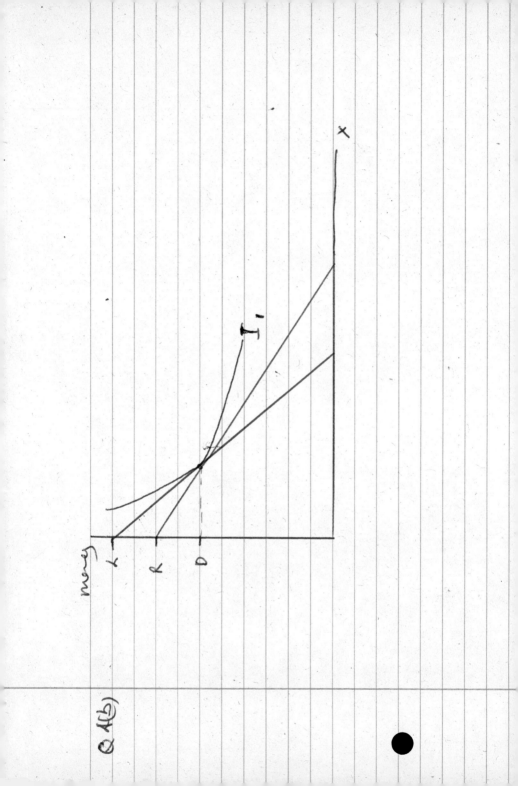

Q A(b)

INTERTEMPORAL
DECISIONS
BY CONSUMERS
AND PRODUCERS

In the preceding chapters we have not discussed the problem of making decisions involving time. However, *intertemporal decisions* —*decisions involving choice over time*—are choices from which consumers, producers, and governments cannot escape. Consumers must choose between current consumption and consumption after retirement, between a less expensive appliance with a shorter life and a more expensive appliance with a longer life, and between current consumption and current expenditures that increase future income, such as education and better health care. Producers must choose from among a variety of production processes that require different amounts of time, and between current dividend payments and retained earnings to be invested in more plants and equipment. A producer must also make such intertemporal decisions as selecting a desired pattern of profit distribution over time (a high profit today may mean a lower profit later) and choosing current prices and qualities of his products, which affect demand for his products in the future. Many governmental decisions involve choices over time. Should it spend more on welfare programs (current consumption) or on educational training (which increases future productivity and consumption)? Today's government policies on conservation and environment affect the qualities of resources and environment available in the future.

Decisions may involve time, but are not intertemporal unless they involve *choice* over time.[1] For example, the movement of the producer from the market period to short-run and long-run

[1]Kelvin Lancaster, *Introduction to Modern Microeconomics*, 2d ed. (Chicago: Rand McNally, 1974), p. 321.

equilibrium positions involves time but no choice on the part of the producer. The producer wishes to be in the long-run equilibrium position instantaneously if it were possible; he is in the market period or short run only because he has no choice but to do so.

In the following pages, the reader is introduced to an elementary presentation of intertemporal decision making by consumers and producers. Intertemporal decisions are shrouded with uncertainty in the sense that probabilities of various outcomes are not fully known.[2] When uncertainty exists some are anxious to avoid it, while others want to profit by assuming it. Speculation and hedging, discussed toward the end of this chapter, show the manner in which risk-avoiders and risk-seekers interact in their intertemporal decision-making processes, and secure, by and large, the results they seek.

21-1 CONSUMERS' INTERTEMPORAL DECISIONS

Consumers are interested in future consumption as well as present consumption. Thus, we may assume that the consumer attempts to maximize his utility function of the following form:

$$U = f(C_0, C_1, \ldots, C_n)$$

where subscripts identify consumptions in periods $0, 1, \ldots, n$. The equation says that the consumer's utility as of today is a function of consumption in the present and all future periods. Since a multiperiod analysis becomes rather complicated without adding much to the insight into the nature of choice over time, we shall mostly deal with simple *two-period* models. Thus, the consumer's utility function involving intertemporal decision is simplified as

$$U = f(C_0, C_1)$$

The pattern of a consumer's income stream over time and that of his desired consumption stream over time may not match. For instance, a young consumer's desired present consumption may exceed his present income, and he may want to increase his current consumption by borrowing (negative saving). On the other hand, a middle-aged consumer's present income may exceed his desired present consumption, and he may save part of his income. And a retired consumer may maintain his present consumption by drawing on his savings from his working days.

[2]The term *risk* is frequently used when the probability of an outcome is known. In this chapter, we shall use two terms interchangeably.

PREFERENCE BETWEEN PRESENT AND FUTURE GOODS

We can draw an indifference curve such as I_0 in Figure 21-1, which shows various combinations of present and future goods that are equally satisfactory to a consumer. The slope of this indifference curve, $\Delta C_1/\Delta C_0$, shows the *marginal rate of substitution between the future and the present goods*, MRS_{fp}. It is also referred to as the *marginal rate of time preference or the rate of discount of the future*. The absolute slope of an indifference curve between future and present goods is greater than 1; that is, the consumer prefers a given quantity of the present good over the same amount of the future good.

The consumer values an earlier availability for several reasons. A future availability is less certain than the present availability. An availability in a distant future has little value to a consumer, due to the certainty of death. A consumer also prefers a present dollar to a future dollar because he knows that by loaning a dollar today he can receive more than a dollar in the future. The more future good (relative to the present good) one has, the less he values it. Thus, it is reasonable to assume that the slope of an indifference curve will become steeper as it approaches the future good axis.

The indifference map shown in Figure 21-1 describes the utility function of a consumer as affected by various combinations of present and future goods. It is plausible that the MRS_{fp} will decrease as the amount of current income increases and the consumer is

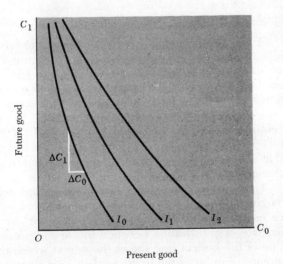

Figure 21-1   Indifference map showing intertemporal preference

able to reach a higher indifference curve. A consumer who has a sufficient amount of the present good is likely to have a less strong preference for the present good than a consumer who must have more to meet basic needs in the present. Thus, indifference curves with higher subscripts are drawn flatter than those with lower subscripts.

INTEREST RATE

Prices of goods in the commodity market show the rates at which they can be exchanged in the marketplace. *Similarly, the interest rate can be considered as showing the rate at which present and future goods can be exchanged in the market.* Thus, for our simplified two-period model, we define the interest rate as follows:

$$\text{Interest rate } (i) = \frac{\text{dollar sum of the future good}}{\text{dollar sum of the present good}} - 1$$

For instance, if one dollar of the present good can be exchanged for $1.10 of the future good in the market, the interest rate is

$$i = \frac{\$1.10}{\$1.00} - 1 = .10$$

Thus, the interest rate in the market is 10 percent. The difference between the dollar values of the future good and the present good, 10 cents in our example, is called *interest*. Since people prefer a present good to a future good, interest rate (and interest) must be positive.

INTERTEMPORAL UTILITY MAXIMIZATION

A consumer's choice between present and future goods in the simple two-period model is depicted in Figure 21-2. The indifference curves show the consumer's subjective taste between present and the future goods. The budget line cuts the present and future axes at $M and $M(1+i), respectively. This indicates that the consumer has currently $M at his disposal, and that if he chooses to spend the entire sum in the next period he can spend $M(1+i), that is , $M plus i percent interest on $M. The slope of the budget line is interpreted as showing the rate at which the present and future goods can be exchanged in the market.

The utility-maximizing intertemporal allocation by the consumer is given by point E, where his budget line is tangent to an indifference curve. Since the slope of an indifference curve shows the marginal rate of substitution between future and present goods and the slope of the budget line shows the rate at which the future and present goods can be traded in the market, $1+i$, the equilibrium condition is given by

$$\text{MRS}_{fp} = 1 + i$$

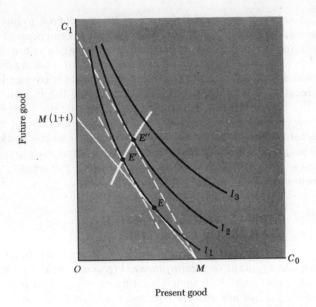

Figure 21-2 A consumer's intertemporal choice

How would an increase in the interest rate affect the consumer's intertemporal allocation? A higher interest rate makes the future good cheaper relative to the present good. Thus, the substitution effect of an increase in the interest rate is to make the consumer buy more future good. Since a higher interest rate will increase the amount of money at the disposal of the consumer, the income effect also tends to increase his demand for the future good. In Figure 21-2, an increase in the interest rate shifts the consumer's budget line from the original budget line to the steeper dotted budget line, through point M. The consumer's movement from E to E'' can be decomposed into the movement from E to E' (the substitution effect) and that from E' to E'' (the income effect). Both the substitution and income effects increase the quantity of the future good purchased.

The effect of an increase in the interest rate on the purchase of the present good cannot be known *a priori*. The substitution effect is to decrease the purchase of the present good, since the present good is now more expensive relative to the future good. The income effect of an increase in the interest rate, however, tends to increase his consumption of both the present and the future goods. Thus, depending on the relative magnitudes of the substitution and income effects, an increase in the interest rate may or may not decrease the purchase of the present good.

In the real world, the consumer can choose to buy more future goods (instead of spending all his income for the present good) by (1) holding various monetary assets such as savings account, bonds, stocks, life insurance, and demand deposit, (2) by purchasing durable goods, which can also be used in the future, and (3) by purchasing more education and better health, which increase the income available in the future. The reader should also note that the budget constraint relevant for the consumer's real world intertemporal choice is not determined simply by the present income and the market interest. The present income, expected future income stream, and the availability of credit and lending opportunities importantly affect the consumer's intertemporal decision as of today.

21-2 CAPITAL AND ALLOCATIVE EFFICIENCY OVER TIME

The capital or capital stock of an economy is given by the aggregate of plant and equipment, highways, bridges, port facilities, etc., that exist in a society at a given moment. It represents goods produced but not already consumed so that they may be used for further production; thus, capital goods are frequently referred to as the "produced means of production." Why do we bother producing capital (goods)? The answer is because we can produce more goods by using roundabout processes, which first transform labor and natural resources into capital. Since capital accumulation (addition to the capital stock) enables us to obtain more goods in the future than otherwise feasible, we talk of the *net productivity of capital.* A few simplified examples should clarify the nature of the net productivity of capital.

Example: Suppose that $1,000 worth of wine purchased today and aged can be sold for $2,000 in 9 years. Also assume that there are no other cost involved. From a compound interest table, we learn that this operation yields an annual rate of return of about 8 percent. The net productivity of capital in our example is 8 percent per annum. In our example all capital input occurs in one year and all output is produced in another year; thus, this model is referred to as a *point input–point output model.*

Example: Suppose $5 million are spent to build an office building. The building will produce $1 million per annum after allowing for all other expenses. Assume that the building can last forever with appropriate maintenance. Then the annual rate of return on the original investment, 20 percent, is the net productivity of capital. This case is an example of a *point input–continuous output model.*[3]

[3] The reader should be able to give examples of a *continuous input-point output* model and a *continuous input-continuous output* model.

In the simple case of point input-point output model, the technical relationship between present and future goods can be represented by the society's transformation (or production possibility) curve of Figure 21-3. The vertical intercept of the transformation curve is longer than its horizontal intercept, showing the productiveness of roundabout processes or capital accumulation. The absolute slope of the curve at any point on it shows the *marginal rate of transformation between future and present goods*. It also shows the net productivity of capital or the rate of return on capital. The flattening of the curve as more future good is chosen shows that the net productivity of capital decreases as capital accumulation increases.

In order to examine the efficiency condition for intertemporal allocation of resources, let us examine Figure 21-4, in which the transformation curve is combined with the social indifference map for present and future goods. Given the assumed social indifference map and the transformation curve, the socially efficient allocation over time is given by point E, where the transformation curve is tangent to an indifference curve. The rate at which the present good can be transformed into the future good is equal to the rate at which the society is willing to exchange the present good for the future good; and any movement away from the point will reduce social welfare. The white straight line, which is tangent to both the transformation and an indifference curve at point E, shows the market rate of interest. In equilibrium the market rate of interest must be equal (1) to the rate at which the present good can be transformed into the future good,

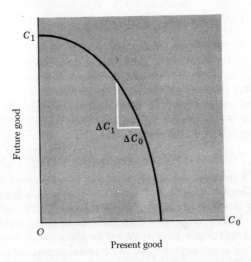

Figure 21-3 Marginal rate of transformation between present and future goods

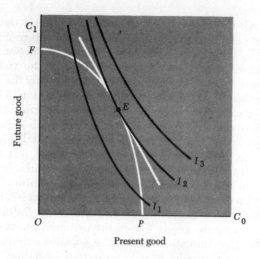

Figure 21-4 Efficiency condition for intertemporal resource allocation

and (2) to the rate at which the consumers are willing to exchange the present good for the future good. As already noted, the equilibrium market rate of interest must be positive, since consumers prefer the present good to the future good and since capital has a net productivity.

21-3 INVESTMENT CRITERIA

Roundabout processes, which depend on the use of capital, are more productive than direct processes, which take less time. In making their *investment decisions,* that is, decisions to add to the existing stock of capital, how do producers select from among many alternative projects? In other words, what are the criteria for selecting capital projects? In this section we will examine three frequently mentioned criteria.

THE MARGINAL REVENUE PRODUCTIVITY CRITERION

From our knowledge of the employment of productive resources (Chapter Seventeen), we know that it pays for the producer to add to the stock of his capital if the marginal revenue product of a capital good, MRP_k, is greater than the cost of using the capital good. *The cost of capital per year is equal to the annual interest cost on the price of the capital good and the annual depreciation cost on the capital good. Thus,*

$$\text{Annual cost of capital} = p(i + d)$$

where p, i, and d are the price of the capital good, the interest rate, and the rate of depreciation. *In equilibrium,* it should make no difference whether the capital good is purchased outright or rented annually. Thus,

$$\text{Rental rate of capital } (r) = p(i + d)$$

The marginal revenue productivity criterion of investment, therefore, says to add to the stock of any capital good as long as MRP_k *is equal to or greater than the rental rate or the annual cost of capital.* In Figure 21-5, given the MRP_k curve and the rental rate (or annual capital cost) line rr', the equilibrium amount of investment is at point E. A decrease in interest rate will lower the equilibrium rental rate and lead to an increase in investment. Investment will not keep on increasing forever, because MRP_k decreases as capital stock increases. A technological improvement will shift the MRP_k to the right and increase the volume of investment.

DISCOUNTED PRESENT VALUE CRITERION

If R dollars are loaned for a year at the interest rate of i percent per annum, it will grow into $R(1 + i)$ dollars—\$R of principal plus \$iR of interest. Using subscripts 0 and 1 to denote dollar sums in year 0 and year 1, we can write

$$R_1 = R_0(1 + i)$$

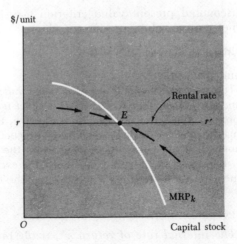

Figure 21-5 Marginal revenue productivity criterion

From this equation it follows immediately that

$$R_0 = R_1/(1 + i)$$

$\$R_0$ shows today's value of $\$R_1$ receivable in a year when the appropriate interest rate is i percent, and is called the *discounted present value*. Using the symbol PV to denote the discounted present value and R_1, R_2, . . . , R_n to show dollar sums receivable at the end of 1, 2, . . . , n years, we can generalize the previous result into n periods.

$$PV = \frac{R_1}{1 + i} + \frac{R_2}{(1 + i)^2} + \cdots + \frac{R_n}{(1 + i)^n}$$
$$= \sum_{j=1}^{n} \frac{R_j}{(1 + i)^j}$$

The *discounted present value criterion* of selecting capital projects says invest as long as the discounted present value is equal to or greater than the purchase price or cost of a capital project. That is,

$$\text{invest if PV} = \sum_{j=1}^{n} \frac{R_j}{(1 + i)^j} \geq \text{cost of capital, } C$$

The equilibrium level of investment, according to this criterion, is reached when $PV = C$.

The *net discounted present value*, NPV, *is defined as*

$$NPV = PV - C$$

Thus, the discounted present value criterion may be restated in terms of the net present value criterion as follows:

$$\text{invest as long as NPV} \geq 0$$

In equilibrium, $NPV = 0$.

Two projects A and B are said to be *mutually exclusive* if undertaking one project makes the other project useless. If there are *several* projects that are not mutually exclusive, the discounted present value criterion suggests to rank those projects according to their NPV and select successively starting from the one with the highest NPV. If projects, A, B, and C are *mutually exclusive*, simply choose the one with the highest NPV and discard the others.

INTERNAL RATE OF RETURN CRITERION

The *internal rate of return*, r^*, *is the rate of discount that will make the discounted present value of a capital project exactly equal to the cost of the project.* That is,

$$C = \sum_{j=1}^{n} \frac{R_j}{(1 + r^*)^j} = PV$$

In the above equation, r^* is the internal rate of return, which equates the discounted present value to the cost of capital good.[4] It shows the rate of return the producer can secure by tying up $C in a capital good.

According to the internal rate of return criterion, the producer must rank his capital projects according to r^*, and choose starting from the project with the highest r^* until he reaches the project for which $r^* = i$, the market rate of interest. A decrease in the interest rate will make projects with lower r^* acceptable to a producer, and accordingly, increase investment. A technological progress that tends to increase r^* will also increase the volume of investment.

EVALUATION OF MUTUALLY EXCLUSIVE PROJECTS

When two projects are mutually exclusive, the use of the internal rate of return criterion may lead to a wrong choice.[5] Let us see why. In Figure 21-6, two curves showing the relationship between NPV and the market rate of interest are shown. Project B has a longer life (produces a longer revenue stream), and is much more affected by the market rate of interest than project A. Thus, the NPV of project B is higher than that of project A at interest rates lower than k percent. On the other hand, a high interest rate reduces the NPV of project B substantially; at interest rates higher than k, project B has a lower NPV than project A.

Now, by definition, the internal rate of return is that rate which makes the net discounted present value equal to zero. Thus, the internal rate of returns for projects B and A are given by r^*_A and r^*_B on the horizontal axis. According to the internal rate of return criterion, a project should be selected if its r^* is equal to or greater than the market rate of interest. If two projects A and B both meet this criterion but are mutually exclusive, project A—which has a higher r^*—must be selected. This prescription, however, is wrong if the market rate of interest is lower than k percent; when the market rate of interest is lower than k percent, the NPV of project A is lower than that of project B. The correct choice is project B, not project A. Therefore, *we should not use the internal rate of return criterion in evaluating capital projects that are mutually exclusive.*

[4]This is also J. M. Keynes' *marginal efficiency of capital* and A. P. Lerner's *marginal efficiency of investment.*

[5]For more details, see A. A. Alchian, "The Rate of Interest, Fisher's Rate of Return over Costs and Keynes' Internal Rate of Return," *American Economic Review*, December 1955. For a simple exposition similar to our presentation, see N. S. Barrett, *The Theory of Microeconomic Policy,* (Lexington, Mass.: D. C. Heath, 1974), pp. 271–272.

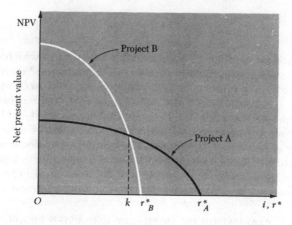

Interest rate and internal rate of return

Figure 21-6   Evaluation of mutually exclusive projects

21-4   COMPOUND INTEREST RATES AND THEIR DIVERSE APPLICATIONS

Table 21-1 shows the amounts to which $1.00 of today will grow by the end of 10, 20, and 30 years, at various interest rates compounded annually. This simple table can be used to solve many important real world problems.

Example: Suppose the annual rate of inflation is 7 percent, while the interest rate on your savings account (after allowing for income taxes) is 4 percent. If this is the case, it is clear from Table 21-1 that the real purchasing power of your savings is rapidly declining. Now you know why savings accounts or government savings bonds are not popular ways of holding wealth in an inflation-plagued economy. You will also understand why the real incomes of many workers go down in an inflationary period and why union negotiators are so anxious to include *an escalator clause, which provides for automatic wage increases as the consumer price index advances by a certain amount.*

Table 21-1   Compound Growth of $1

YEAR	4%	5%	7%	10%
10	1.48	1.63	1.97	2.59
20	2.19	2.65	3.87	6.72
30	3.24	4.32	7.61	17.4

Example: A finance professor is moving to a new university. His old university says he can leave his state retirement contributions of $10,000 ($5,000 of his own contribution matched by the equal sum contribution by the employer) and draw retirement benefits in 30 years when he reaches his retirement age or withdraw his $5,000 now and forfeit the employer's share of the contribution. If the funds in the state retirement system earn only 4 percent, while the professor can average 10 percent compound rate of growth in the stock market, what should he do? According to the table, $10,000 left in the state retirement system will grow in 30 years to $32,400; while $5,000 in the stock market will grow to $87,000. The discrepancy in the growth rates makes a tremendous difference in 30 years.

Example: Many people complain about high mortgage interest rates on their houses. Suppose you are paying 8.5 percent interest on your loan but the anticipated rate of inflation is 7 percent. Then, the *real rate of interest—the money rate minus the inflation rate—* is only 1.5 percent. By combining this rather low real interest cost with the special tax privilege accorded interest payments and with the fact that house prices have appreciated substantially in the recent past, we can see why many people are buying large houses, despite their complaints about high mortgage rates.

21-5 COST-BENEFIT ANALYSIS OF PUBLIC WORKS PROGRAM

Probably the most important real world application of the discounted present value criterion is found in the cost-benefit analysis of public works programs. The government taxes (or borrows from) the public, reducing their current consumption, and produces capital projects, which increase consumption levels in future periods. In order to decide whether a project is worth undertaking, usually the stream of benefits from the project in the future periods (B_1, B_2, . . . , B_n) and the stream of project costs incurred during the construction periods (C_1, C_2, . . . , C_m) are estimated, and the discounted present values of these two streams, PV_B and PV_C, are computed. That is,

$$PV_B = \frac{B_1}{(1+i)} + \frac{B_2}{(1+i)^2} + \ldots + \frac{B_n}{(1+i)^n}$$

$$PV_C = \frac{C_1}{(1+i)} + \frac{C_2}{(1+i)^2} + \ldots + \frac{C_m}{(1+i)^m}$$

If PV_B exceeds PV_C, the cost-benefit criterion says that the project is worth undertaking.

Since the government must also work under a budget constraint, it is necessary for the government to rank various projects according to their relative desirability. For this purpose, the *benefit-cost ratio*, PV_B/PV_C, is frequently used. If projects are not interrelated or mutually exclusive, a project with a higher benefit-cost ratio is preferred to the one with a lower ratio.

The widespread use of cost-benefit analysis permits many modern governments to evaluate and select their public works projects on the basis of careful studies of cost and benefits associated with various projects. However, there still remain many difficulties in computing the benefit-cost ratios of real world projects.[6] The values of three variables that enter the discounted present value formulas — the benefit stream, the cost stream, and the rate of discount — are hard to determine. Project benefits are particularly difficult to estimate because they occur in distant future periods and frequently involve intangible elements. Marketable benefits (such as electricity from a hydroelectric plant) are easiest to measure. But market prices cannot be used to measure benefits such as flood control and nuclear shelters, which are not capable of being marketed. A project may produce external benefits such as providing improved transportation facilities, which lead to greater profitability of stores and factories along the road, increased employment, and higher valuations of lands. The values of such external benefits are often not easy to estimate. Benefits such as the scenic effect of a dam and reservoir are intangible and cannot be quantified.

The estimation of a cost stream is somewhat easier than that of a benefit stream because costs are incurred in much nearer future periods. Still, the difficulty of estimating external costs and intangible costs associated with a project is as real as the difficulty of estimating external and intangible benefits referred to in the preceding paragraph. Furthermore, when a proposed change causes a major change in the area or region, or when there are market imperfections, the appropriateness of using market prices in estimating benefits and costs becomes questionable.

The choice of an appropriate interest rate with which to discount benefit and cost streams is a crucial issue in cost-benefit analysis. First, the selection of a lower interest rate will make many public projects worthwhile. Because benefit streams run further into the future, a lower discount rate tends to increase the present value of a benefit stream more than it does that of a cost stream.[7] Second,

[6]For an excellent introduction to the cost-benefit analysis and its applications, see A. R. Prest and R. Turvey, "Cost-Benefit Analysis: A Survey," *Economic Journal*, December 1965, pp. 683–735. This article is reprinted in *Surveys of Economic Theory*, Vol. III (New York: St. Martin's, 1967).

[7]For instance, consider a multipurpose river basin project such as the TVA system. Obviously, its benefit stream is much longer than its cost stream.

a relatively lower interest rate will tend to favor projects with longer life spans (or payoff periods) over those with shorter life spans. (Re-examine Figure 21-6.)

What should be the social discount rate in evaluating a public project? There is no simple answer to this question. But the choice must somehow be made, and the choice affects the types of projects selected as well as the number of public works projects undertaken.[8]

21-6 SPECULATION: ASSUMPTION OF RISK OVER TIME

Price movements of a commodity in a future period are uncertain. Prices of goods in a future period may be higher or lower than expected on the basis of today's information. Thus, time introduces uncertainty and gives birth to speculation. *Speculation is an act of buying or selling goods with the aim of making profit by correctly guessing uncertain future price movements.* Those speculators who guess the future price movements correctly will reap profit; and those with incorrect guesses will suffer losses.

There are well-organized commodity exchanges such as the Chicago Board of Trade[9] where well-standardized commodities (wheat, corn, cotton, copper, coffee, etc.) are traded for cash (or spot) prices as well as for future prices. *Cash or spot prices are prices for current transactions, while futures prices are prices determined today for future delivery.* For example, on March 1, the cash price of wheat may be quoted as $5.12 per bushel, while on the same day the July future price is quoted at $5.00.

Speculators who buy and sell futures contracts in organized commodity exchanges perform a rather useful function. Let us take the example of wheat futures contracts, and examine the impact of speculation on the price and supply of wheat as well as on who bears the uncertainty of changing market situations. The harvest of new crops increases the supply of wheat and tends to lower the current price of wheat. Speculators, taking advantage of the low current price, buy wheat to be delivered in a future month, say, May. Speculators are merely making profit-motivated responses to changing market situations. Yet, in their attempt to make profit, speculators who guess correctly perform quite useful functions. By buying wheat

---

[8]Those who would like to pursue this issue further may start with Prest and Turvey's article cited in footnote 6.

[9]Leading grain exchanges in the U.S. are in Chicago, Minneapolis, and Kansas City. Leading cotton and wool exchanges are in New York, where sugar, cocoa, rubber, hides, potatoes, and metals also have futures markets. Beef cattle, pork bellies, and egg futures markets are in Chicago.

when its price is low, they prevent price from becoming even lower. Speculators sell their wheat in May when the supply of wheat is lower and its price is higher. But the very act of supplying wheat when its price is higher tends to prevent wheat price from becoming even higher. Clearly an important function of speculators is to *stabilize* the price (and supply) of commodities. Speculators also help *allocate* a given stock of crop over the crop year more evenly. For example, assume that wheat crops in Russia and/or India fail due to bad weather. Speculators anticipating the acute shortage and much higher prices of wheat in future months start buying wheat. These purchases of wheat by speculators raise the current wheat price, and this higher price of wheat in turn leads to less current use of wheat and more availability in the future. Thus, speculators' actions contribute to the conservation of scarce wheat and make it last until the next crop harvest.

Note that incorrect guesses by speculators will tend to aggravate price fluctuations. A good example is found in the stock market. For example, during the great stock market boom of the 1920s speculators incorrectly visualized even higher prices and accelerated the price increases. When their expectation was finally betrayed and the boom collapsed, they again incorrectly guessed that prices would go down even further and sold their holdings and accelerated the stock market crash.

21-7 HEDGING: AVOIDANCE OF RISK OVER TIME

A grain elevator operator may wish to receive his normal operating profit by storing and delivering wheat and to avoid the risk that arises from a change in the price of wheat during the storage period. Similarly, a miller may wish to earn his income from his milling operation without having to worry about the loss he may suffer due to an unfavorable change in the price of wheat. Hedging is a method designed to minimize losses that may arise from adverse price movements. *In its simplest form, hedging involves the simultaneous purchase of a commodity for immediate delivery and the sale of the futures contract of the same commodity.*

Assume that on July 1 a grain elevator operator purchases 50,000 bushels of wheat from a farmer at $4.50 per bushel. This price is determined by subtracting the normal profit of grain elevator operation, freight, etc., from the spot price of $5.00 per bushel at the Chicago Board of Trade. The grain elevator operator wishes to dispose of his wheat in December, and in order to insulate himself from the risk of fluctuating price, sells 50,000 bushels of December futures at $5.00 per bushel. Now no matter what happens to the price of wheat between July and December, the grain operator is protected from loss due to wheat price changes.

Suppose on December 1 the grain operator sells 50,000 bushels of wheat at $5.50 per bushel. Since each bushel of wheat he had in his elevator actually costs him only $5.00 (including his normal profit), he gains $.50 per bushel. However, he must deliver at $5.00 per bushel (the futures contract price) wheat for which he must currently pay $5.50 per bushel. Hence, he loses $.50 per bushel. The gains and losses of the hedging exactly cancel, and the grain operator is left only with the income from the operation of the grain elevator.

Suppose the price of wheat declined $.50 per bushel during the July–December period. Then, the grain operator would have gained $.50 per bushel from his futures contract and lost $.50 per bushel from wheat stored in his elevator. Again, his hedging operation has shielded him from the hazard of wheat price fluctuations.

By hedging, the grain elevator operator has succeeded in *separating* his business of storing and handling wheat from the hazardous task of bearing the risk of changing prices. Hedging operations for many producers such as the above grain operator are made possible because there are speculators who are willing to deal in futures contracts. While hedgers seek the certainty of operating income and avoid uncertainty of fluctuating prices, speculators assume risks and uncertainty in order to make profit by correctly guessing future market movements.

In the grain elevator operator example, the current or spot price per bushel was identical to the futures price contracted, and the operator was able to shift all risks arising from fluctuating prices to speculators. *Hedging that eliminates the risk of a price change completely is called a perfect hedge.* In actual cases cash and futures prices are likely to diverge because changes in spot prices may exceed (or fall short of) changes in futures prices. Still a limited or *imperfect hedge* can be made to limit loss from fluctuating prices.

Suppose the grain elevator operator buys physical wheat at $5.00 per bushel and at the same time sells a futures contract for the same amount of wheat at $4.80. This hedging operation involves the loss of $.20 per bushel regardless of what happens to wheat prices during the period involved. If the price of wheat declines to $4.00 per bushel during the period, the operator loses $1.00 per bushel on wheat stored in his grain elevator, but gains $.80 from his futures contract (which allows him to collect $4.80 per bushel of wheat which he can now buy for $4.00). The net loss is limited to $.20. Suppose the price of wheat rose to $6.00 per bushel during the period. Then the grain operator would have gained $1.00 per bushel on his physical wheat, and lost $1.20 on his futures contract. Again the net loss is $.20 per bushel. (The reader should be able to show that if the futures price exceeded the current price by M, a hedging operation will involve the gain of M regardless of future price movements.)

In summary, hedging allows producers to limit their risks that arise from uncertain price movements and to transfer the burden of changing prices to speculators, who are more willing and able to bear them.

EXERCISES 21

Intertemporal Decisions by Consumers and Producers

21-1 The federal government advertises U.S. Savings Bonds as "your gateway to financial security." It says that a systematic payroll savings plan in U.S. Savings Bonds is one of the best ways to finance a child's education, to put extra comfort into retirement, or to protect against financial emergencies. Do you agree with the government's claims? Why or why not?

21-2 Suppose a parking lot in the downtown area of a large city can produce a permanent income stream of $20,000 per annum, after allowing for maintenance and operating expenses. How much would you be willing to pay for such a property? Why?

21-3 Show that, if the futures price of a commodity exceeds the spot (or current) price by $M, a hedging operation in the commodity can produce $M gain regardless of future price movements in the commodity.

21-4 Refer to Figure 21-6 in the text and show that the discounted (net) present value criterion offers the correct choice between the two mutually exclusive projects regardless of the market rate of interest.

21-5 The federal government requires a cost-benefit analysis for any newly proposed public works project. Discuss the advantages of such a requirement, as well as the dangers involved in selecting public works projects on the basis of their benefit-cost ratios.

INDEX

Index

Price stabilization:
  as business goal, 239
  speculation and, 477–478
Price support, **23–24**
  agricultural, 139–140
  minimum wage as, 399
Price-takers, 242–287
Price theory (*see* Microeconomics)
Pricing objectives in large corporations, 238–240
Primeaux, W., 344
Process ray, 181
Producer's surplus, 406*n*.
Product, average, marginal, and total
  (AP, MP, and TP), 156–160
  and cost curves, 216–219
  quantitative relationships among, 158–160
Product differentiation, 357–358
  in consumer goods vs. producer goods, 367–368
  as entry barrier, 330–331
  optimal, 358
  welfare effect of, 361–362
Production (physical), **151–199**
  economic region of, 162, 188–190
  with kinked isoquants, 181–183
  with single variable input, 156–163
  stages of, 161–163, 190
  symmetry of, 164–166
  with two inputs, 169–176
Production decisions:
  expansion path, 197
  input decisions vs., 393–394
  input price changes and, 196
  with kinked isoquants, 207–209
  Lagrange multiplier and, 206–207
  least-cost input combination, 194–198
  output-maximizing, 196
Production function, **152–153**
  CES, 188
  Cobb-Douglas, 178–179, 186–188
  empirical, 176–180
  linearly homogeneous, 184
Production processes, 181–183
Production surface and its slices, 153–155
Profit, **236**
  gross (residual), **389**
  and economic profit, 396–397
  necessary condition for maximum, 261
  necessary and sufficient conditions for maximum, 263–264, 292
  sufficient conditions for maximum, 261
  (*See also* Economic profit)
Profit-maximization hypothesis, 236–238

Profit tax, 312, 317
Progressive taxation, **62**
Public utilities, regulation of, 310–311
Pure competition, **243**
Pure economic rent, **407**
Pure monopoly (*see* Monopoly)
Pure oligopoly, **244**
Pure strategy (in games) (*see* Games)

Regulation of public utilities, 310–311
Reservation demand, **255–256**
Residual profit, **389**
  (*See also* Gross profit)
Resource price, 384–385
Returns to scale, **156**, 174–176
  classification of, 175
  constant, increasing, or decreasing, 174–175
  degree of homogeneity and, 184
  vs. economies of size, 227–228
    and increasing or decreasing cost industry, 279
  factors increasing, 175–176
  function coefficient and, 175
Returns to variable proportions, **156**–163
Revealed preference, **87**
  theory of, 87–90
Revealed preference analysis, 87–90
  assumptions of, 88
  of Slutsky theorem, 89–90
  of substitution and income effects, 88–89
Revenue curves:
  AR, MR, and TR, relationships among, 121–122
  curvilinear AR and MR, relationship between, 122–123
  of imperfectly competitive firm, 247–248
  of perfectly competitive firm, 246–247
Reynolds, L., 283*n*.
Ridge lines, 189

Saddle point, 373
Sales-maximization hypothesis, 344–**345**, 348
  and fixed cost, effect of, 347–348
  and profit constraint, effect of, 345–347
Samuelson, Paul, 7*n*., 87, 411*n*., 442*n*.
Saposnik, R., 429, 446*n*.
Savage, L., 63
Scale, returns to (*see* Returns to scale)
Scale line, **198**
Schumpeter, J., 421

Printed and Bound by KIN KEONG PRINTING CO. PTE. LTD. – Republic of Singapore.